Imagined Interiors:

REPRESENTING THE DOMESTIC INTERIOR SINCE THE RENAISSANCE

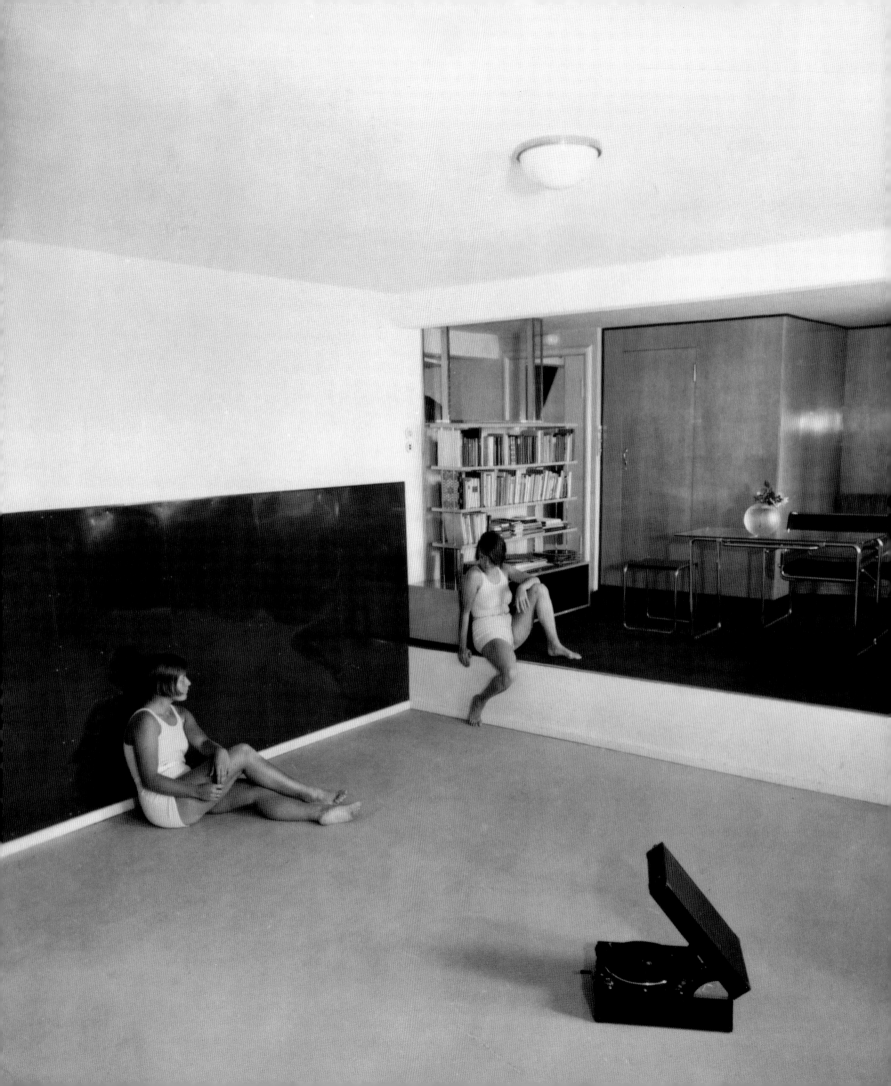

Imagined Interiors:

REPRESENTING THE DOMESTIC INTERIOR SINCE THE RENAISSANCE

Edited by Jeremy Aynsley and Charlotte Grant
with assistance from Harriet McKay

V&A PUBLICATIONS

First published by V&A Publications, 2006
V&A Publications
Victoria and Albert Museum
South Kensington
London SW7 2RL

Distributed in North America by Harry N. Abrams, Inc., New York
© The Board of Trustees of the Victoria and Albert Museum, 2006
The moral right of the authors has been asserted.

Hardback edition
ISBN-10 1851774920
ISBN-13 9781851774920
Library of Congress Control Number 2006928683

10 9 8 7 6 5 4 3 2 1
2010 2009 2008 2007 2006

Paperback edition
ISBN-10 1851774939
ISBN-13 978185774937

10 9 8 7 6 5 4 3 2 1
2010 2009 2008 2007 2006

Every effort has been made to seek permission to reproduce those images
whose copyright does not reside with the V&A, and we are grateful to the
individuals and institutions who have assisted in this task. Any omissions are
entirely unintentional, and the details should be addressed to V&A
Publications.

Designed by Nigel Soper
New V&A photography by Christine Smith, V&A Photographic Studio

Printed in Singapore by C.S. Graphics

FRONT JACKET/COVER ILLUSTRATION:
Pieter Janssens Elinga, *Interior with a
Gentleman, a Woman Reading and a
Housemaid* (detail, see pl.4.18)

BACK JACKET/COVER ILLUSTRATIONS
(clockwise from top left):
Workshop of Rogier van der
Weyden, *Annunciation* (see pl.2.23);
Gustave Caillebotte, *Portrait of a Man*
(see pl.7.15); Colour plate from *Ein
Wohnhaus* by Bruno Taut (see
pl.8.15); Alfred Hitchcock, *The
Thirty-Nine Steps* (see pl.10.1)

FRONTISPIECE:
Marcel Breuer and Gustav
Hassenpflug, *Gymnastics room in a
sports teacher's home* (see pl.9.9)

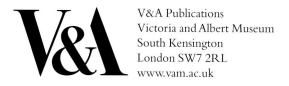

V&A Publications
Victoria and Albert Museum
South Kensington
London SW7 2RL
www.vam.ac.uk

Acknowledgements

This book derives from the work of the AHRC Centre for the Study of the Domestic Interior. The Centre was a five-year collaboration between three institutions in London – the Royal College of Art, the Victoria and Albert Museum, and the Bedford Centre for the History of Women at Royal Holloway, University of London, funded by the Arts and Humanities Research Council (AHRC). The AHRC funds postgraduate training and research in the arts and humanities, from archaeology and English literature to design and dance. AHRC Research Centres provide a focus for collaborative research in areas of strategic importance. We are grateful for the financial support of the AHRC, and the sustained intellectual and organizational support of the Centre's Management Committee and Academic Advisory Board. Members of the former included Tim Benton, Julius Bryant, Penelope Corfield, Nichola Johnson, Sandra Kemp, Nigel Llewellyn, Duncan Robinson, Carolyn Sargentson and Charles Saumarez Smith. Malcolm Baker, Christopher Breward, David Gaimster, Felix Driver, Matthew Johnson, Lesley Hoskins, Peter Mandler, Morag Shiach, Penny Sparke and Christine Stevenson served on the latter. While the RCA provided a physical home for the Centre, the V&A, above all the Research Department and the Publications Department, has played a vital role in producing this book. The editors would particularly like to thank Carolyn Sargentson and Mary Butler, whose enthusiasm and support has been crucial to *Imagined Interiors*.

Between 2001 and 2006, the Centre conducted a research programme bringing together scholars from many disciplines in an attempt to further the study of the domestic interior, both historical and contemporary, and we would like to acknowledge the contributions of many of our collaborators, particularly those who participated in the symposium held on Representing the Domestic Interior in 2002, some of whom are contributors to this book. Among the many colleagues whose interventions have helped shape this project the editors would particularly like to thank the associate directors of the Centre, John Styles, Amanda Vickery, Sandra Cavallo and especially Elizabeth Miller, whose support in the later stages of the book is much appreciated. Charles Saumarez Smith and Pat Kirkham gave us their time and we thank them for their careful reading and constructive criticism of the manuscript. We are, of course, grateful to our contributors, without whom there would be no *Imagined Interiors*, as well as to the many people who have helped bring the book together: our research assistant, Harriet McKay; Ann Matchette, Helen Baker and Wilhelmina Baldwin, Research Centre Co-ordinators; Beth Thomas for picture research; our copy-editor and proofreader Slaney Begley; the book's designer Nigel Soper; as well as Eleni Bide and Katherine Feo, who assisted with the compilation of the bibliography. Monica Woods, our managing editor, brought a sustained interest to the project and a welcome calm, patient efficiency.

We are grateful to those institutions and people who have given us access to and assisted with research materials and permission to reproduce material, especially V&A Images and the staff of the National Art Library. In a collaborative project many voices are heard beneath the surface. We owe a debt of thanks to those critics, historians, architects and designers whose imaginings of the domestic interior have shaped ours, and we hope that this volume will serve as a prompt to future research and consideration of the subject, a means of bringing together and juxtaposing disparate practices and methodologies. Finally, as this book suggests, the boundaries of domestic and work life are continually and fruitfully blurred, and we would like to thank the inhabitants of our own domestic interiors: Sarah, Agnes and Hugh Aynsley, and John, Samuel and Joe Reyntiens, for their support, tolerance and inspiration.

JEREMY AYNSLEY AND CHARLOTTE GRANT

Contents

List of Contributors

MARTA AJMAR-WOLLHEIM (PhD, Warburg Institute) is Exhibition Curator and Course Tutor in the Research Department at the V&A, specializing in the Italian Renaissance. Between September 2002 and March 2005 she was Lead Scholar of The Domestic Interior in Italy, 1400–1600, a collaborative research project funded by the Getty Grant Program. She is Lead Curator of the exhibition *At Home in Renaissance Italy* (V&A, 2006) and co-editor of the accompanying book.

JEREMY AYNSLEY is Professor of History of Design at the Royal College of Art where he is also Head of the V&A/RCA History of Design programme. He was Director of the AHRC Centre for the Study of the Domestic Interior between 2001 and 2006. Recent publications include essays in *Art Deco 1910–1939* (2003), *The Modern Period Room*, (2006) and, as a contributing co-editor with Francesca Berry, in 'Publishing the Modern Home: magazines and the domestic interior 1870–1965', *Journal of Design History* (2005).

TIM BENTON is Professor of Art History at the Open University. He has published widely on the history of modern architecture and design, and in particular on the work of Le Corbusier and Italian Fascist architecture. He has contributed to a number of exhibitions, including *Modernism: designing a new world 1914–1939* (V&A, 2006), *Art Deco 1910–1939* (V&A, 2003), *Le Corbusier: architect of the century* and *Art and Power* (both at the South Bank Centre). He has also contributed recently to the Charlotte Perriand exhibition catalogue at the Centre Georges Pompidou, France.

FRANCESCA BERRY is Lecturer in History of Art at the University of Birmingham. Her specialist interest is the representation of the domestic interior in France in the nineteenth and twentieth centuries. She recently co-edited, with Jeremy Aynsley, 'Publishing the Modern Home: magazines and the domestic interior 1870–1965', *Journal of Design History* (2005).

INGE MARIA DANIELS is an anthropologist working as a Lecturer at the University of Oxford. Her research interests are in material culture, consumption and design. Recent publications include 'The Material Culture of Luck' in *Anthropology Today* (2006) and *The Japanese House* (forthcoming, 2007).

FLORA DENNIS has been a Research Fellow at the AHRC Centre for the Study of the Domestic Interior since 2001, before which she studied and lectured at the University of Cambridge. Her research focuses on music, sound and domestic space. She is Co-Curator of the exhibition *At Home in the Italian Renaissance* (V&A, 2006) and co-editor of the accompanying book.

SIR CHRISTOPHER FRAYLING is Rector of the Royal College of Art, Chairman of Arts Council England, and author of 16 books on cultural history, including *Sergio Leone – something to do with death* (2000), *Ken Adam – the art of production design* (2005) and *Mad, Bad and Dangerous to Know? – the scientists and the cinema* (2005).

AMANDA GIRLING-BUDD is a design historian working at the London Metropolitan University. Her main interest is the history of furniture and she has recently completed a doctorate on Holland and Sons, nineteenth-century London cabinet-makers. Her publications include *Interior Design and Identity* (2004).

CHARLOTTE GRANT was a Senior Research Fellow at the AHRC Centre for the Study of the Domestic Interior from 2001 to 2006 and previously a Fellow and Director of Studies of English at Jesus College, Cambridge. Recent publications include articles on eighteenth-century women's poetry and the representation of women at the Society of Arts; she is guest editor of 'Literature and the Domestic Interior', *Home Cultures* (2005).

HANNAH GREIG was a Postdoctoral Research Fellow at the AHRC Centre for the Study of the Domestic Interior from 2003–6, and is currently a Junior Research Fellow at Balliol College, Oxford. A historian of eighteenth-century Britain, her research interests include fashion, display and material culture in Georgian London.

JANE HAMLETT is currently working as a Lecturer in Modern British History at the University of Manchester. Her specialist interest is gender and the middle-class domestic interior in Britain in the second half of the nineteenth century. She has recently published an article, '"Nicely feminine, yet learned": student rooms at Royal Holloway and the Oxford and Cambridge Colleges in late nineteenth-century Britain', in the journal *Women's History Review*.

KAREN HARVEY is Lecturer in Cultural History at the University of Sheffield. Her interest is in the gender history of eighteenth-century Britain, with a particular focus on masculinity. Her publications include *Reading Sex in the Eighteenth Century: bodies and gender in English erotic culture* (2005) and (ed.) *The Kiss in History* (2005).

MARK JONES is Director of the Victoria and Albert Museum. His work on medals has given rise to an interest in the nineteenth-century temperance movement and its development of a new ideology of domesticity.

TREVOR KEEBLE is Head of the School of Art & Design History at Kingston University. He researches nineteenth-century domestic design and has recently co-edited a collection of essays entitled *The Modern Period Room 1870–1950: the construction of the exhibited interior* (2006).

JOHN LOUGHMAN is a Lecturer in the School of Art History and Cultural Policy, University College Dublin. His specialist interest is the art and culture of the Netherlands in the sixteenth and seventeenth centuries. Among his recent publications is (with J.M. Montias) *Public and Private Spaces: works of art in seventeenth-century Dutch houses* (2000).

ANN MATCHETTE is a historian teaching at the V&A and Royal College of Art. Her specialist interest is in the visual and material culture of

Italy in the fifteenth and sixteenth centuries. Recent publications include articles in the collection *The Material Renaissance* (2006) and a special issue of *Renaissance Studies* (2006).

ALEXANDRA MCGLYNN is an artist and independent researcher currently working on a photographic project about the domestic spaces of modernity.

HARRIET MCKAY'S most recent work has focused on the home as gallery in Britain in the twentieth century. Until 2005 she was Curator of the National Trust property 2 Willow Road and has written on curatorial practice and the conservation of Modernism. Her most recent publication is 'Opening Willow Road to the Public' in *The Modern Period Room* (2006).

MICHAEL MCMILLAN is a writer, playwright, curator and Visiting Professor at the University of the Arts, London. He recently guest curated The 'West Indian' Front Room at the Geffrye Museum (2005–6) with an accompanying essay appearing in *Fashion Theory* (2004). Other recent publications include 'Black Theatre in Britain' in *Black Theatre* (2002) and *The Black Boy Pub & Other Stories* (1997).

ROD MENGHAM is Reader in Modern English Literature at the University of Cambridge, where he is also Curator of Works of Art at Jesus College. He is the author of books on Charles Dickens, Emily Brontë and Henry Green, as well as of *The Descent of Language* (1993). He has edited collections of essays on contemporary fiction, violence and avant-garde art, and the fiction of the 1940s, and was co-editor and co-translator of *Altered State: the new Polish poetry* (2003), and co-editor of *Vanishing Points: new Modernist poems* (2005).

ELIZABETH MILLER is a Prints Curator in the Word & Image department of the V&A and author of *16th-century Italian Ornament Prints in the Victoria and Albert Museum* (1999). Since November 2004 she has also been an Associate Director of the AHRC Centre for the Study of the Domestic Interior.

VIVIANA NAROTZKY is a design historian working at the Royal College of Art and Senior Research Fellow at the Centre for the Study of the Domestic Interior. Her research interests are Spanish design, consumption, urban identity and the construction of place, and non-hegemonic experiences of modernity. Her publications include 'Our Cars in Havana' in *Autopia* (2002) and 'Consuming Design in the Periphery: private and public' in *Design History Seen from Abroad* (2001).

HALINA PASIERBSKA worked for the V&A from 1969 until 2005. She transferred from the National Art Library to the Museum of Childhood in 1982 where she specialized in the design and history of educational toys and dolls' houses, eventually becoming the Curator of Dolls' Houses and Toys. She has written two books and several articles.

REBECCA PRESTON was formerly at the AHRC Centre for the Study of the Domestic Interior, and is currently a Research Fellow at the Centre for Suburban Studies, Kingston University, London. Her publications explore issues of landscape and identity, focusing particularly on suburbanization. She also works in the field of historic building and garden conservation, most recently for the Strawberry Hill Trust.

CATHERINE RICHARDSON is a Fellow of the Shakespeare Institute and Lecturer in English and History at the University of Birmingham. Her interdisciplinary research focuses on the material culture of early modern England, both on and off stage. Her recent publications include *Clothing Culture 1350–1650* (2004) and *Domestic Life and Domestic Tragedy: the material life of the household* (2006).

OLIVIER RICHON is Head of the Department of Photography at the Royal College of Art. A monograph of his photographic work, *Real Allegories*, is published by Steidl (2006).

GIORGIO RIELLO is Research Officer in Global History at the London School of Economics and is soon to take the position of

Lecturer in History at the University of Exeter. He has widely published on shoes and shoemaking, fashion and product innovation in the eighteenth and nineteenth centuries. He is the author of *A Foot in the Past: consumers, producers and footwear in the long eighteenth century* (2006) and the co-editor (with Peter McNeil) of *Shoes: a history from sandals to sneakers* (2006). He is currently writing a book entitled *A Global History of Cotton Textiles, 1200–1850*.

CAROLYN SARGENTSON is Head of Research at the V&A. She works on the decorative arts of seventeenth- and eighteenth-century France, specializing in furniture. She published *Merchants and Luxury Markets; the marchands merciers of eighteenth-century Paris* in 1996. Her current research includes a catalogue of 340 pieces of French furniture 1640–1800 in the V&A, and a book on the material culture of secrecy.

MICHAEL SNODIN is Senior Research Fellow in the V&A's Research Department. His specialist interest is in design and architectural history 1500–1800. His publications include *Design and the Decorative Arts: Britain 1500–1900* (co-authored with John Styles, 2001), *Exploring Architecture: buildings, meaning and making* (2004) and *The V&A Book of Western Ornament* (2006).

JOHN STYLES is Research Professor in History at the University of Hertfordshire. He has written on many aspects of British history in the eighteenth century, from crime and law enforcement to industrial design and decorative art. His most recent book (co-authored with Michael Snodin) is *Design and the Decorative Arts: Britain 1500–1900* (2001).

LUKE SYSON is Curator of Italian Painting, 1460–1500 at the National Gallery, London. He worked previously at the British Museum (as Curator of Medals) and the V&A. His publications include *Pisanello* (co-written with Dillian Gordon, 2001) and *Objects of Virtue: art in Renaissance Italy* (co-written with Dora Thornton, 2001).

1

Introduction

Jeremy Aynsley and Charlotte Grant

FROM THE VANTAGE POINT of the early twenty-first century, across all facets of the media, images, descriptions and discussions of the domestic interior surround us. From television to magazines, exhibitions, trade shows and the Internet, we constantly see and are sold images of real and ideal interiors. More than ever, our own interiors, and those of people in public life, are the subject of enquiry and curiosity. There is, in the West, an extraordinary fascination with the home, its appearance, function and identity. Given this public interest in the domestic interior, a book that seeks to understand the meanings of images and descriptions of the domestic interior across a broad historical span seems timely. *Imagined Interiors* surveys changing representations of the domestic interior and seeks to understand some of the meanings ascribed to them in Europe and North America from 1400 to the present. The interest in describing and portraying the interior of peoples' homes is clearly not a new phenomenon, and it is the history of those representations between 1400 and the present that this book engages with and investigates.

Rather than try to offer a complete or representative history, *Imagined Interiors* charts changes in domestic culture by working selectively across historical periods, representational mode, and kind of interior. It would be impossible to offer surveys of each form of representation, for example, to give an account of the entire history of painting, photography or poetry. Instead, moments of significance have been chosen, when a particular medium was at its height or appeared most influential. Each chapter places those representations in an historical and geographical context, asking when such representations came to prominence, how they relate to contemporary developments both in the home and in the media that supported them. Chapters follow a broadly chronological organization, and the book falls into three sections: Developing a Domestic Culture, 1400–1750; The Interior Defined, 1650–1900 and Displaying the Modern Home, 1850 to the present. This structure allows us to

focus on the key technological developments in the field of representation in each period, and to highlight issues pursued in the chapters in each section. Within each section, between chapters, are a series of feature spreads that provide punctuation and different kinds of focus, while adding to our understanding of the diversity of forms that representations of the interior take. To take one example, in the eighteenth-century in Britain, schematic representations of interior designs for rooms were codified to show room plan and arrangement of furniture (see pl. 1.1).

There has long been a fascination with the domestic arrangements and artefacts of the past. From the exploration of Domus Aurea around 1500 and the ruins of Roman villas and the discovery of Pompeii and Herculaneum in the 1740s, to the public fascination with the architectural remains of kitchens and bathhouses of Cistercian monasteries, and glimpses of crowded, squalid interiors of London represented by the artist William Hogarth and the investigative journalist Henry Mayhew, we have been intrigued by the evidence of previous lives.

In 2001, as part of the Research Centres Scheme introduced by the then Arts and Humanities Research Board (since 2005 the Arts and Humanities Research Council), the Centre for the Study of the Domestic Interior was established. It formed a collaboration between three London institutions: the Royal College of Art, the Victoria and Albert Museum and the Bedford Centre for the History of Women at Royal Holloway University of London. At its inception, the aim of the Centre was to develop what had been up to then a discrete set of academic interests into a more defined field of research. The complementary approaches to material culture represented by the Research Department of the greatest museum of art and design and the academic departments of, respectively, design history and gender history in a world-leading art and design institution and university, have been joined at the Centre by researchers trained in anthropology, art history, literature, and the history of music, as well as cultural, social, economic and

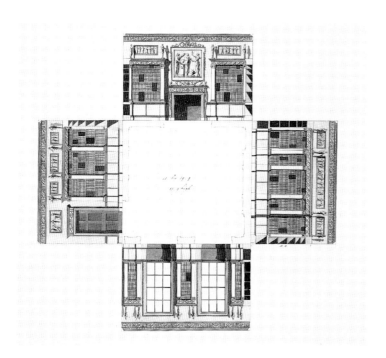

1.1

Robert Adam, *Presentation Design for the Library at Mamhead House, Devon.* Pen, ink and wash. 1766. V&A: D.2174–1896 (see pl.5.26)

design history. The Centre was designed to be greater than the sum of its parts and to set the agenda for future studies of the domestic interior. All essays and spreads in *Imagined Interiors* either result directly from the Centre's research programme and its series of symposia and international conferences, or reflect its interests. The focus on representation of the domestic interior mirrors another important aspect of the Centre's work, which is the compilation of a database of sources for understanding and interpreting the historical domestic interior that serves as an extended resource for those interested in the subject, available from October 2006.[1] The book and database are at the forefront of a move to work across disciplinary boundaries, and to make available to as broad an audience as possible the most current research from a wide variety of academic areas, some of which have been traditionally more visible than others.

A conservative list of those disciplines in which the idea of the domestic interior has gained currency might include archaeology, anthropology, art history, design history, architecture, cultural, economic and social history, cultural geography, material culture studies, literature and media studies, the history of music, fashion, psychology, psychoanalysis, politics, sociology, women's studies and gender history. Representing work from and influenced by as many of those areas as possible has been one motivation in selecting chapters for this volume.

Any study of the representation of the domestic interior in the West in this period is indebted to the work of Mario Praz, a professor of English Literature at the University of Rome,

whose publication of 1964 – *An Illustrated History of Interior Decoration, from Pompeii to Art Nouveau* – established the ground for many subsequent works.[2] Praz's book is a broad cultural study of 400 images that draws its examples from Europe. Its emphasis is on the aesthetic interior, and the method Praz employed was to combine visual analysis with reference to literature and wider cultural history. On his own admission, Praz was most particularly drawn to watercolour depictions of interiors, which showed aesthetic values he admired. As Hugh Honour observed, Praz's 'true subject' is not interior decoration but the ruminations and memories, the visions and the fancies prompted by paintings of interiors.'[3]

The next stage in histories of the interior concentrating on their visual representation came 20 years later with the publication in 1984 of Peter Thornton's *Authentic Décor*. Subtitled 'The Domestic Interior 1620–1920' the compilation of images of the interiors featured was in part directed towards establishing what the author called 'a period eye' – an historical period's own way of seeing things. Peter Thornton, Keeper of the Department of Furniture and Woodwork at the Victoria and Albert Museum, later succeeded John Summerson as the Curator of the John Soane Museum, a museum that combines the qualities of a domestic house with an architectural masterpiece. A characteristic of Thornton's approach is that the images themselves are not his subject, rather it is what they tell us about 'the decoration and arrangement of the domestic interior in the Western world between 1620 and 1920'.[4] Writing in 1984, Thornton suggested that his topic no longer needed justifying, but that the seriousness of his approach might require apology. Many scholars followed in the Thornton mould, making available an extended set of sources across the centuries for what were often designs of significance. Notable among these were Charles Saumarez Smith's *Eighteenth-Century Decoration: design and the domestic interior* (1993), Charlotte Gere's *Nineteenth-Century Decoration: the art of the interior* (1989) and Stephen Calloway's *Twentieth Century Decoration: the domestic interior from 1900 to the present day* (1998). To these were added Thornton's own more recent work, *The Italian Renaissance Interior, 1400–1600* (1991).[5]

Working across a range of sources, from paintings and watercolours, to archival photographs, architectural plans, trade

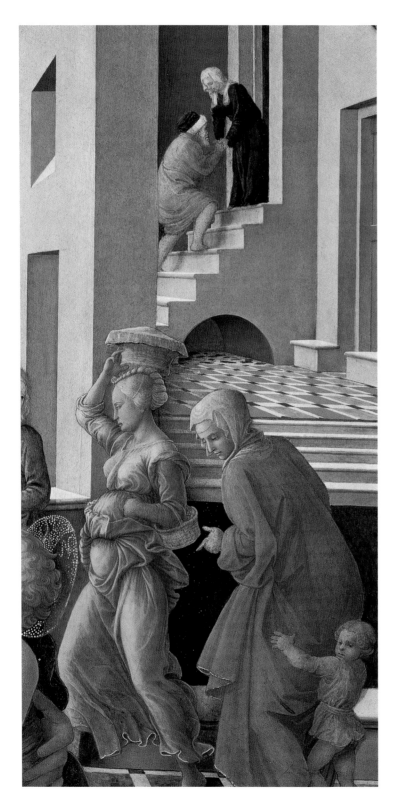

literature and advertisements, *The Scottish Home* (1996), a project for the National Museums of Scotland, identified changes in the domestic interior in a study of Scotland between 1650 and 1950, taking room types and their uses as a principle for its organization.[6] In 2003, London's Geffrye Museum organized the exhibition and published an accompanying catalogue on the theme of the English middle-class home, *Home and Garden: paintings and drawings of English, middle-class, urban domestic spaces, 1675–1914.*[7] Using paintings and drawings as evidence, the project questioned the extent to which they can be taken as 'literal records of actual spaces'.[8] *Imagined Interiors*, in turn, shares the concerns of the Geffrye Museum and extends the range to a diverse set of sources. The book seeks to explore the images and texts it discusses, not so much for what they tell us about the interior they represent, but for what that representation is designed to convey. The emphasis is on how conventions of representation can tell us about attitudes to the interior at a given moment. For example, during the Italian Renaissance, domestic detail provided a context for religious scenes, which were more symbolic than actual (see pl. 1.2).

Descriptions of and allusions to domestic surroundings occur in literary texts throughout the period of this book. The depiction of the interior in novels, in particular, has received a fair amount of critical attention, and looks likely to continue to do so.[9] Philippa Tristram's *Living Space in Fact and Fiction* (1989) was one of the first to look in detail at representations of interiors in British fiction.[10] Inga Bryden and Janet Floyd concentrated on the nineteenth century in *Domestic Space: reading the nineteenth-century interior* (1999), as did Sharon Marcus in *Apartment Stories: city and home in nineteenth-century Paris and London* (1999).[11] Whereas Marcus looks at one type of building, Thad Logan's *The Victorian Parlour: a cultural study* (2001) focuses on a single room and uses literary and other sources to investigate how the parlour could function as a practical and aesthetic space, while its very making could be informed by prevailing customs and beliefs.[12] Other critics have used ways of thinking about architecture and space to examine the literary in various innovative ways that clearly link to or help to situate the domestic. For example, John Bender in *Imagining the Penitentiary: fiction and architecture of mind in eighteenth-century England* (1987) links narrative style and architecture, Simon Varey considers distinctions between private and public in *Space and the Eighteenth-Century Novel* (1990) and Franco Moretti maps the geographical locations of novels and their readership in his *Atlas of the European Novel, 1800–1900* (1999).[13]

The Centre for the Study of the Domestic Interior: 'Approaching the Domestic Interior'

One of the first events organized by the Centre in 2001 was a cross-disciplinary conference that aimed at taking stock of the current positions and methods informing a range of academic interpretations of the domestic interior, called 'Approaching the Domestic Interior'. Out of this, and from internal discussions, we developed a set of questions that have informed all subsequent work. We needed to assess the limitations and possibilities of the available sources for studying the history of the domestic interior. As so many representations of the domestic interior over the centuries concern ideals rather than lived realities, from sources such as architectural treatises of the Renaissance, the pattern books of Gillow and Co. in eighteenth-century London, Victorian advice manuals, Ideal Home exhibitions and recent TV makeover programmes, the first question was to ask, what is the relationship between precept and practice at any one time?

We needed to keep reminding ourselves that all representations are constructed from a particular point of view and none should be read unproblematically as an accurate record of how things actually were. Codes and conventions inform even the most apparently straightforward representation. Nonetheless, their undoubted value as evidence is as imaginative responses to particular places and times, and as Mario Praz suggested above, they are invaluable records of the changing meanings of the domestic interior over time. It is also clear that a search for authenticity haunts our response to representations of the interior. For instance, visitors are intrigued by viewing historic houses and period rooms in museums to see things 'as they really were'. The curator Christopher Wilk has shown how the specialized conventions that inform much curatorial activity frequently dissociate museum displays from many lived experiences.[14] We become

used to seeing exhibited rooms arranged with minimal objects and without inhabitants, often with the fourth wall removed. A frequent aim is to display a particular style of decoration and period. The apparatus employed to present rooms to the public often excludes many of the attributes we associate with everyday life. Real rooms, by contrast, rarely represent a single historical moment, being accretions over time.

A second, large question surrounding the work of the Centre has been that of judgment. As historian Leora Auslander has suggested, throughout their history domestic interiors, and in particular their furnishings, have been controversial in matters of taste.[15] What criteria – aesthetic, functional, experiential or ideological – are employed when domestic interiors are judged? *Imagined Interiors* offers commentaries on examples of prescription, from fifteenth-century Italian advice manuals, eighteenth-century etiquette books, 'how-to-do-it' decorating books and official design discourse stemming from both educational and government institutions.

Throughout history, the boundaries between exterior and interior space in the domestic interior have been in flux, as, too, has the idea of home as a place for work or domicile. It is therefore appropriate that a study of the domestic interior concerns itself with the boundaries of the domestic. One of the ongoing questions across all periods is the relationship between the domestic and that which lies beyond. One way of describing this is the public/private divide, which has interested historians, especially in response to the work of the German philosopher Jürgen Habermas.[16] Since its publication in English in 1989, *The Structural Transformation of the Public Sphere* has had a profound effect on history and cultural studies for its investigation into bourgeois society. In the course of this engagement, the rigidity of Habermas's initial categories has been questioned, as has his portrayal of women in connection with the public sphere. The debate about the divide between public and private, and its relation to the notion of separate spheres for male and female activity, has been well rehearsed elsewhere.[17] It is interesting to note here that current research into the domestic interior consistently emphasizes the permeability of the public/private dichotomy, and stresses how the private sphere can be often also public. Accordingly, the domestic interior is clearly never merely private – it is a place of hospitality and business, production and

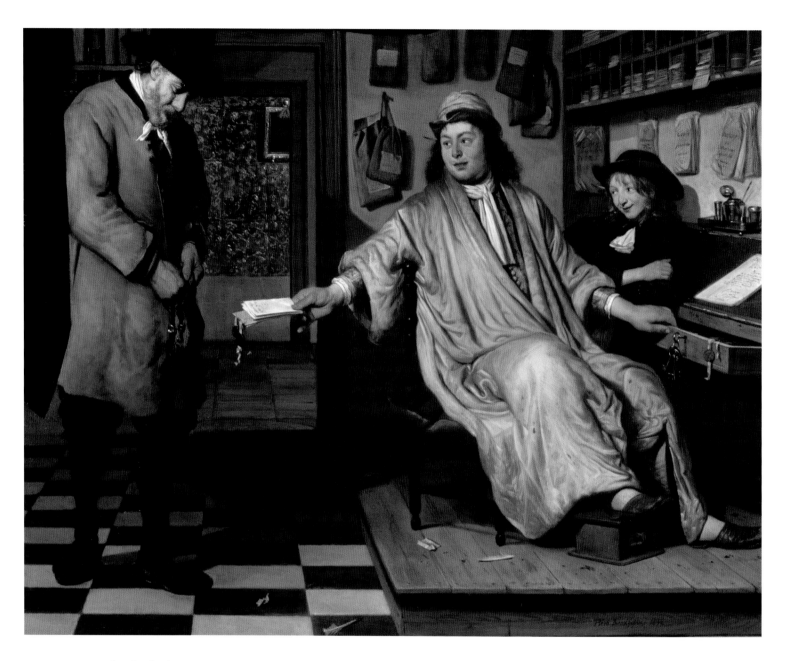

consumption, all of which activities inevitably challenge any notion of an impermeable boundary, as John Loughman demonstrates in his consideration of the *voorhuis* or front hall, in seventeenth-century Dutch houses (see pl. 1.3).

Our title *Imagined Interiors* suggests both an inside and an outside. 'Interior' can refer to the interior of a country, or to the interior of a person's mind. The domestic interior is neither of these, and yet related to both. The inside of a house, apartment or other dwelling defines itself in relation to or even, on occasions, in opposition to the outside, to the surrounding environment whether urban or rural, and to a social, political and economic context. It is also, frequently, a projection of its inhabitants' interiority in that the environment we create around ourselves tells us and others a great deal about our

selves, our thoughts, dreams, aspirations, successes and failures as well as our taste, priorities and economic status.

Contributors to this book pay special attention to the representation of boundaries, both physical thresholds and divisions between inside and outside – the loggia, terrace or hallway, as well as the conceptual boundary between domestic and other space. Room names tell us about changing attitudes to behaviour in different places at different times – as, for instance, the terms drawing-room, parlour, sitting-room, lounge and living-room. Rooms can be more or less specialized, boundaries between activities established or blurred. So, too, with boundaries between the domestic and other more institutional living spaces – the hospital, prison, school, monastery, nunnery, brothel, boarding house, hotel or commune.

1.3
Job Berckheyde,
Notary in his Office.
Oil on canvas. 1672.
Private collection/Sotheby's
(detail, see pl.4.13)

To what extent do these different locations constitute a challenge to representations of the domestic interior?

A final spatial boundary that has considerable impact on the following essays is that defined by changing notions of economic power as represented through different geographies. The domestic interior under consideration is that of the 'Western' world. However, contributors to the book are aware that ideas of the European interior travelled to other parts of the globe and that, in turn, the Western interior was susceptible to a myriad of influences, often understood within the concept of Orientalism.[18] How has the domestic interior travelled between Europe and the United States, and beyond to the Caribbean and other continents? In the process, what was rejected, and what adopted or adapted? The contribution of Michael McMillan to this volume indicates what was brought to Europe through processes of migration and diaspora in the case of West Indian families arriving in Britain in the 1950s and '60s.

Histories of the home have, of course, existed for a while in the area of analysis of style, often related to the upper classes or élites. Style was central to both fine and decorative arts history for most of the twentieth century. Mark Girouard's study of *Life in the English Country House* (1978) was groundbreaking in its combination of social and architectural history.[19] Girouard, an architectural historian, set out to think about how houses were used, how families lived in them, and how the architecture they commissioned or inherited was expected to work. He acknowledges that 'the range of sources for an approach of this kind is almost infinite', and that in sampling such sources he is straying outside his discipline. His analysis depends on representations of the interiors of the houses he studies, but his aim was to build up a picture of life in those houses rather than offer an analysis of the representations enlisted in his argument. British architectural history motivated by Mark Girouard has combined with social and economic historians' work in recent years to give us an increasingly full and nuanced view of domestic life and its locations. Girouard's approach combined with museum curatorship has broadened the public's interest and understanding of historical domestic interiors through the work of such bodies as English Heritage and the National Trust, the Attingham Trust Summer School programme aimed at specialists in the field, and television's *Time Team*.[20]

Archaeology is another academic discipline that can offer an understanding of the domestic interior as a site of active material culture. Through excavations of dwelling places, for instance, of the labouring poor, otherwise often absent from history, a sense of the behaviour, movement and distribution of different social groups, genders or classes can be gathered, as detected from the survival of object remnants and traces of shelter.[21]

While archaeologists and historians have made available many more sources for understanding what the domestic interior might actually have been like, as our title *Imagined Interiors* suggests, we aim to examine how people have imagined their interiors as much as how they have been accounted for or described. In this respect, our work develops a line of enquiry pursued by the Canadian architect and writer Witold Rybczynski in *Home: A Short History of an Idea* (1986). He acknowledged that there is no single concept 'home' or 'interior'. Instead, ideas and ideals of home have changed over time, and such apparently universal concepts as 'comfort' are historically specific.[22] Likewise, the term 'domestic' itself might be more precisely located. As many commentators have shown, in many respects, the domestic is a construct of nineteenth-century bourgeois ideology, and the term should only be employed in relation to earlier periods with extreme caution and qualification.[23] It might even be questioned whether, by the early twenty-first century, we have reached a period of the 'post-domestic' when, in the guise of much post-modern self-fashioning, interiors are used to fulfil other requirements than simply the replication of familial values that were once so strongly associated with the domestic ideal.[24]

Historical studies of the domestic interior have taken more account of gender and attended to a wider variety of social classes over the last 20 years. As Inge Daniels sets out in her contribution, anthropologists in recent years have given the home and domestic interior considerable attention. The use of ethnography, gathering data through observation, has led to a shift of emphasis from product to process in the domestic sphere. Judgments are not only guided by aesthetic choice but also by life patterns and rituals. With the emphasis on practice, or the narrative of people's lives and their relations with objects and spaces, attention turns towards understanding the home as part of a life process. Recent anthropological attention has

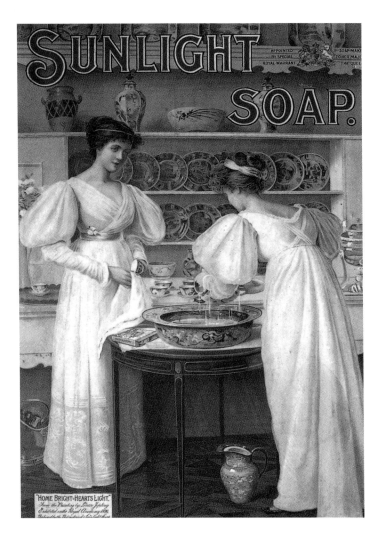

focused on setting up home, for example, as well as its divestment. How this approach can inform history, in the case of sixteenth-century Florentine households, is discussed in this volume by Ann Matchette.

One of the first works to bring together anthropology and economic history was by Mary Douglas, who reflected on the interface between the two disciplines in her 1979 study *The World of Goods: towards an anthropology of consumption*, co-authored with Baron Isherwood.[25] Drawing on earlier anthropological work by Marcel Mauss and others, Douglas reminds us of the importance of context in the construction of meaning and, by extension, in acts of interpretation: 'Goods are neutral, their uses are social; they can be used as fences or bridges.'[26]

This dynamism of objects is key to the work represented in social anthropologist Daniel Miller's collection *Home Possessions* (2001), in which contemporary attitudes to the home in different cultures are fruitfully analyzed, using ethnographic techniques to reveal the contemporary complexity of meanings associated with goods and their relation to individuals' changing lives.[27] One timely example of the anthropological

1.4
Louise Jopling, *Home Bright Hearts Light*. Sunlight Soap poster. 1896. Unilever Archive, Port Sunlight (see pl.7.27)

and design historical working together was in the exhibition and publication *Household Choices* (1990), organized by Middlesex University and the Victoria and Albert Museum.[28] This was a further indication of the apparent benefits of interpreting the domestic interior as a space for social practices as well as design ideals. Like the work of the Centre, the project was cross-disciplinary, embracing anthropology, photography, design history and decorative arts curation. The exhibition's premise was that 'home is both a space we inhabit and a place we imagine'.[29] In terms of the range of representational sources used to understand the home, *Household Choices* signalled the shift away from the professional example of the interior designer or authority of the design critic, to alternatives such as amateur and professional photography, interviews, ethnographic fieldwork and various forms of graphic ephemera, trade literature, advertising and leaflets.

Gender relations and the home

The turn to focus on everyday life, including the home, can be linked to an interest from Marxist and post-Marxist historians in the lives of those previously ignored – the poorer sectors of society and those for whom few records exist.[30] Feminist history similarly makes visible and renders the subject of analysis the breadth of women's experience.

The domestic interior is, above all, home to the family, and the work of historians of the family – predominantly Philippe Ariès and Lawrence Stone – has been very important in this area.[31] The domestic interior has also traditionally been the province of women, as a site paradoxically of both oppression and power. Feminist theory and practice, from Mary Astell, who in the 1690s proposed communal living for women, to the feminist experiments in collective living of the twentieth century, have consistently challenged the dominance of familial structures.[32] One of our initial questions was whether women's cultural association with the domestic sphere translates into control of the appearance and use of the domestic interior (see pl.1.4). Renaissance familial life has, for example, recently been examined by Raffaella Sarti in her *Europe at Home: family and material culture, 1500–1800* (2002).[33] Amanda Vickery in *The Gentleman's Daughter* (1998) looked at the consumption patterns of eighteenth-century Lancashire gentry women in relation to their domestic and social lives, and paid particular attention to lifecycle events.[34] The drive to reconstruct the household has thus been furthered by cultural historians' attention to the specifics of everyday life, what is sometimes termed a micro-history, an interest in aspects of life that have frequently been dismissed as insignificant. In her contribution to this volume Hannah Greig reveals the benefits of combining empirical evidence from archival study with a variety of other sources in more formal or established representations. In so doing, her reading of women's unpublished letters and diaries locates particular female experiences of the home in the wider cultural discourse of taste, manners and domesticity. Feminist historians have also uncovered the work of female designers in creating the interiors of the past, and collections such as Judy Attfield and Pat Kirkham's *A View from the Interior: feminism, women and design history* (1989) have done much to disperse the myth of women's passivity.[35] In a related vein, American architectural historian Alice Friedman has examined the negotiation of Modernist twentieth-century interiors by women in *Women and the Making of the Modern House* (1998).[36] The field had already been extended to embrace gender and the uneasy place of the domestic in Modernism and its critiques, for both men and women, is analyzed in Christopher Reed's anthology *Not at Home: the suppression of domesticity in modern art and architecture* (1996).[37]

Representing the domestic interior

All representation is complex and coded, which means that its subsequent interpretation depends on understanding the original context of production, its limits and possibilities. If we look at a brief list of some of the types of texts examined and analyzed in this book, ranging from account books and inventories to manuscripts, letters, essays, fiction, poetry and drama – from surveys and advertisements, to conduct and design manuals – we can clearly expect to find very different attitudes and codes of representation. So, too, with visual and material representations, from frescoes to miniatures, oil paintings and prints to illustrations of all kinds, furniture, dolls' houses, portraits, architectural designs and plans, exhibitions, photographs, film and television, advertisements, trade cards and catalogues, there is an overwhelmingly rich collection of

sources. To call them 'sources' is already to enlist them in an argument. For many historians of different periods, as well as for much public interest in the domestic interior, representations of the interior have tended to figure as evidence. Paintings, photographs, wills and inventories have all been examined for testimony of what the homes of our ancestors actually looked like, how they were lit, how decorated, how they smelt: in short, how people lived in the domestic interior.

As is abundantly clear, representation is a highly selective process. We need to acknowledge that an artist or novelist, designer or journalist, represents the interior within specific conventions not necessarily defined by the actual subject, so much as a set of wider cultural attitudes and responses that may fall outside the immediate concern of the domestic interior. After all, similar strategies of representation are employed in other subject matter; for instance, the novelist preoccupied with a domestic scene can also deal with all manner of other settings and scenes with the same literary skills and devices.

To start at the most minimal stage, an interior can be suggested by something as simple as a chair or curtain as a prop, as Catherine Richardson explains in relation to Elizabethan and Jacobean drama. Furthermore, as Flora Dennis and John Loughman reveal in their essays, artists are free to combine aspects of interiors from different sources to make them appear as one space – in so doing, they can also idealize, elevate or simplify. It would be misleading to distinguish between visual and textual representations and three-dimensional objects in terms of their capabilities to represent ideas about the home. As Carolyn Sargentson and Halina Pasierbska suggest, items of furniture from cabinets to dolls' houses may at first appear to be static. Yet, in many respects, they argue, items of furniture are constructed to respond to their owners' needs and they offer varied performative possibilities, whether these are playful or functional. In so being, objects enter discursive spaces, they engage in representation and should not be taken as straightforwardly 'real' or as evidence.

Charlotte Grant reveals how poets, novelists and philosophers in the eighteenth and nineteenth centuries engaged with ideas of subjectivity and interiority through writing. Francesca Berry analyzes the particular ability of paintings in late nineteenth-century France to resist easy categorization. At the time of increasing interest in psychology, modes of representation developed to suggest that they were not dependant on the effective transcription of outward physical reality, which had been such a major defining aspect of the previous artistic movement of Realism.

Since the Renaissance there have been attempts to find a more straightforward language of representation for interiors. This was particularly so for the transmission of design ideas, which increased with the emergence of architectural and design academies and schools, and the need to teach principles of composition. Conventions for drawn plans, elevations and cross-sections of buildings, and more recently some photographs, attempt to avoid emotional effect to concentrate on the transmission of ideas; the contributions of Michael Snodin, Jeremy Aynsley and Tim Benton explore different stages of this history. The idea of design communication as apparently transparent or neutral needs to be treated with some caution. For, as Giorgio Riello suggests in the case of the inventory, even the apparently objective act of compiling a list of household goods can be defined by interests and decisions made according to what to omit and what to include. Nevertheless, wills, legal papers and insurance documentation, which sometimes provide the only record of actual households, while they may not offer much by way of detail of room arrangement or spatial configuration, are valuable documents for historical reconstruction (see pl.1.5).

To look at representations of the domestic interior from the Renaissance to the present is to examine an extraordinarily diverse body of material. The depiction or description we focus on can be tangential to the original functions of the text, image or object. In approaching such representations in the chapters and spreads that follow, authors have questioned how does a particular representation function? Where does it fit in a history of similar and dissimilar representations? Is it typical or atypical? Certain stages of historical development are marked by technical innovations; these include the development of printmaking techniques and mechanization of the printing press, the inventions of the camera obscura and later photography, film, television and computers.

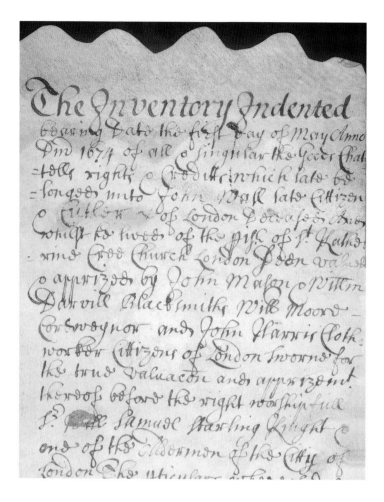

Imagined Interiors differs from other literature on the domestic interior in its equal consideration of textual and visual sources. Alison Light has suggested that fiction offers a useful counter to the architectural diagram, for instance, as it enacts time and can relate movement through time and space.[38] She has argued that the act of representing is active, and that through major cultural forms such as the novel, film and television, new versions of experience of the interior become widely available. In this sense, representation structures thinking and shapes attitudes, rather than merely reflecting pre-established meanings. Rod Mengham explores how British films of the 1930s and 1940s depicted homes metaphorically to convey issues of national and international significance.

In studying representations of the domestic interior we are constantly searching for indications of practice. In the early periods people's lives came into focus at moments of change. The lifecycle is punctuated by key events, which, as rites of passage, frequently include changes of location as well as changes of role. Thus women's lives, in particular, come into focus at betrothal, marriage, the birth of a child, when widowed, remarried or at death. The birth of a child brings about specific rituals and associated domestic objects. So, too,

1.5

Inventory of John Wall. 1674.
Corporation of London Record
Office, Orphans' Court
Inventories, Box 3. Inv.916,
John Wall (detail, see pl.4.23)

do the significant moments of a child's life. Baptism and the sending of a child to a wet-nurse prompt a new collection and arrangement of objects.

As Flora Dennis, Elizabeth Miller and Luke Syson reveal, suggestions of contemporary everyday life can occur almost accidentally in religious depictions in the Renaissance.[39] In such paintings and prints, domestic detail does not detract from the implicit praise of the Virgin, it honours Her through representing Her as surrounded by the best the world can offer, and, of course, in so doing, in the case of paintings often simultaneously records the power, wealth, good taste and piety of the donor. This is a very public display of the private and serves to remind us that representations of the domestic frequently fulfil social and political functions, as indeed interiors themselves do. By contrast, in the era of the Dutch Golden Age in the seventeenth century, considered here by John Loughman, painted domestic scenes depict details of household practices in their own right, filled with symbolism and nuanced meaning, aimed to instruct, correct or admonish.

At the turn of the twentieth century, the possibility for new forms of interaction became available on a mass scale with the introduction of the home computer. As Viviana Narotzky explores, the increasing association of interiors with lifestyle has meant that personal selection or choice features as a central means by which to navigate representations of alternative dream worlds.

───────◆───────

Domesticity confirmed

Historians of various persuasions are not alone in their use of representations of the domestic interior to say something about their culture or the culture of the past – writers of all types have regularly turned to the domestic. In *Orlando*, first published in 1928, Virginia Woolf used her gender-changing, time-travelling hero/heroine to survey social and domestic life through three centuries. At many points in the novel Woolf describes the domestic scene in detail, but one is particularly pertinent to the concerns of *Imagined Interiors*. Woolf figures the dawn of the nineteenth century, often seen as the epitome of a culture that privileges the domestic, as a 'great cloud', producing 'damp', with a number of effects on domestic life:

Thus, stealthily and imperceptibly, none marking the exact hour of the change, the constitution of England was altered and nobody knew it. Everywhere the effects were felt. The hardy country gentleman, who had sat down gladly to a meal of ale and beef in a room designed, perhaps by the brothers Adam, with classic dignity, now felt chilly. Rugs appeared; beards were grown; trousers were fastened tight under the instep. The chill which he felt in his lungs the country gentleman soon transferred to his house; furniture was muffled; walls and tables were covered; nothing was left bare. Then a change of diet became essential. The muffin was invented, and the crumpet. Coffee supplanted the after-dinner port, and as coffee led to a drawing-room in which to drink it, and a drawing-room to glass cases, and glass cases to artificial flowers, and artificial flowers to mantelpieces, and mantelpieces to pianofortes, and pianofortes to drawing-room ballads, and drawing-room ballads (skipping a stage or two) to innumerable little dogs, mats, and china ornaments, the home – which had become extremely important – was completely altered.'[40]

Here Woolf allows us to feel at second hand, and through the medium of a catalogue of domestic objects, the type of changes in the allocation of objects in the home which Thornton refers to as 'a matter of density'.[41] The accuracy of Woolf's representation is not the point here. Her comic depiction of cause and effect, which, as she acknowledges in her aside, skips 'a stage or two', which takes us from the highly dubious assertion of a climate change to 'innumerable little dogs, mats, and china ornaments', is salutary and revealing. When Orlando wakes up in 'the present' it is with the shock of the prevalence of electric light, speed and crowds. Woolf writes: 'It was the eleventh of October. It was 1928. It was the present moment.'

Imagined Interiors, through an analysis of acts of representation of domestic interiors in different media at different periods seeks to illuminate some of the ways in which people recorded and imagined the interior. We are striving to recover meanings and to locate changes over time in those acts of representation, because, as Virginia Woolf suggested in 1928, 'the home … had become extremely important'.

1 DEVELOPING A DOMESTIC CULTURE, 1400–1750

IN EUROPE the period 1400 to 1750 witnessed an explosion of techniques for creating pictures and text. Frescoes on walls date back to antiquity, but the techniques of oil painting on panel and subsequently on canvas, developed in the late medieval and Renaissance periods, revolutionized both the depiction of the domestic interior and the capacity of paintings to feature in the interior. While furnishing textiles, particularly tapestries, had dominated the decoration of élite interiors, and wood had been used as a support for egg tempera, it was the introduction of oil, and especially oil on canvas, that changed the walls of the Western domestic interior for the economically privileged. The implications of the development of panel painting for the domestic interior were huge. Unlike frescoes, panel paintings were transportable, and they brought devotional images into the home in a quite different way from those found, for example, in earlier domestic devotional illuminated manuscripts. Paintings could be treated like an item of furniture and incorporated in the decorative scheme of rooms for which they were often individually commissioned.

First printmaking around 1400, then the printing of texts with movable type, invented by Johann Gutenberg in Germany around 1450, created a double revolution in pictorial and written communication. Broadsheets typically combined the text with images, frequently woodcuts. With the full publication of Alberti's *De re aedificatoria* in 1485, architectural drawings of both ideal and realized buildings began to be widely disseminated and discussed.

In literature, the interior was made visible, if frequently only fleetingly or through tangential reference. Social situations, including domestic ones, were played out on the stage and were recorded in poetry and prose, while household accounts allow us a glimpse of how particular buildings were used. Among other kinds of written representations we have manuscripts in the form of diaries, letters and inventories, as well as court records, surveys and texts about sales of goods and estates. All of these, in seeking to document the interior, provide essential evidence as to how the domestic interior was imagined in the early-modern period.

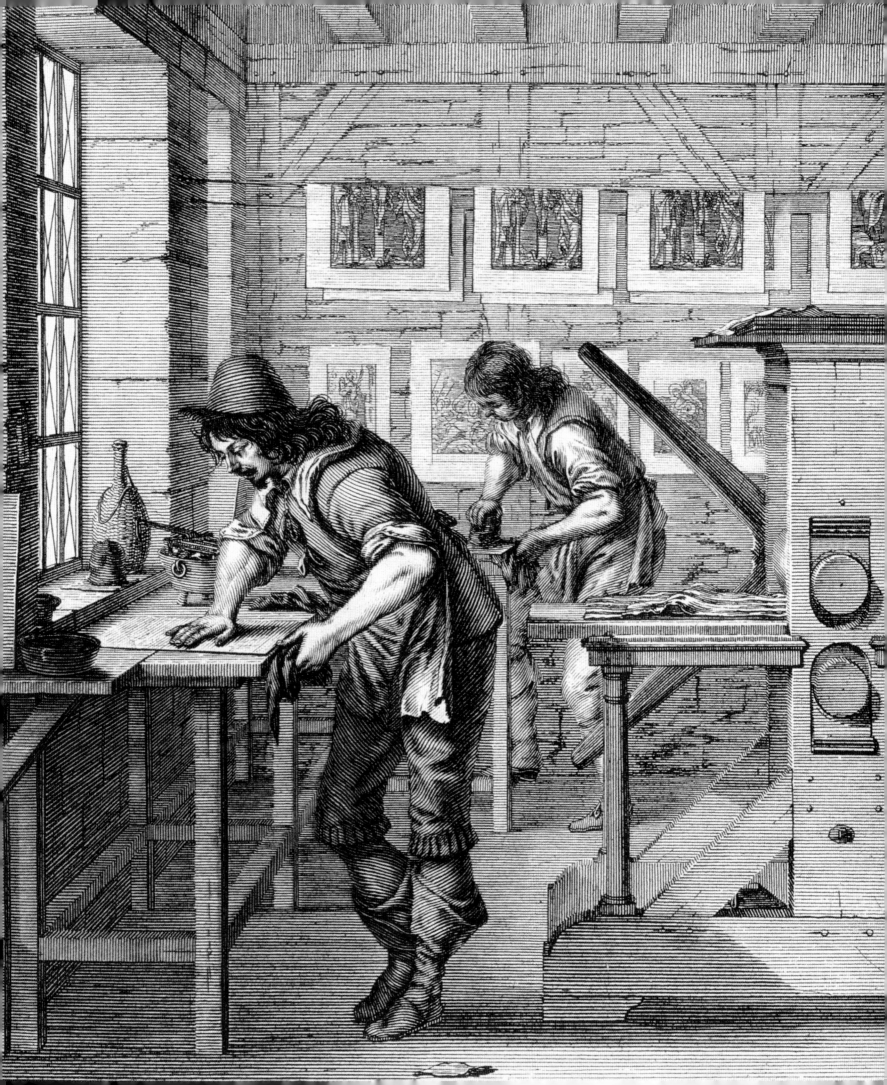

2

Representing the Domestic Interior in Fifteenth- and Sixteenth-Century Italy: from the birth of the Virgin to palaces of cheese

Flora Dennis

THE ELEGANT AND sumptuously furnished scene of the *Birth of the Virgin* by the Osservanza Master is typical of early Renaissance representations of the domestic interior (see pl. 2.1). Depicted in rich detail, the textiles, ceramics and inlaid wooden bed furnishing the room reflect those found in contemporary homes. The mother is attended by women who wash her hands, bring her nourishing food and swaddle the new-born baby. Only the haloes of Sts Anne and Joachim, the Virgin's parents, and the small angel swooping down to place a crown on the baby's head, allude to the biblical subject. The image's calm serenity is supported by a strong visual sense of order – in the activities carried out by St Anne's attendants, the regularity of the architecture and in the subdivision of the painting into two discrete spaces: the bedroom occupied exclusively by women and the area outside in which Joachim and his companion await news of the birth.

In contrast, the following text of *c*.1349-51 represents the interior as disordered and indecorous, a dynamic place of lust, transgression and punishment. Zeppa, discovering that he has been cuckolded by Spinelloccio, his friend, decides to exact his revenge. He tricks Spinelloccio into hiding in a chest in Zeppa's bedchamber and then

> … led Spinelloccio's wife into the bedroom and locked the door. 'Alas!' said the lady, hearing the key turn in the lock, 'what does this mean, Zeppa?'… By the time she had finished speaking, Zeppa, still keeping fast hold of her, was beside the chest, in which her husband was locked. 'Madam', he said, 'spare me your reproaches, until you have heard what I have to say to you. I have loved, I still love Spinelloccio as a brother; and yesterday, though he does not know it, I discovered that … he lies with my wife, as with you. Now, because I love him, I intend to have no revenge on him except in the manner in which he offended. He has had my wife, and I intend to have you.' … Which said, he took her in his arms and fell kissing her, and having laid her on the chest, in which her husband was safe under lock and key, disported himself with her there to his heart's content, as she with him.[1]

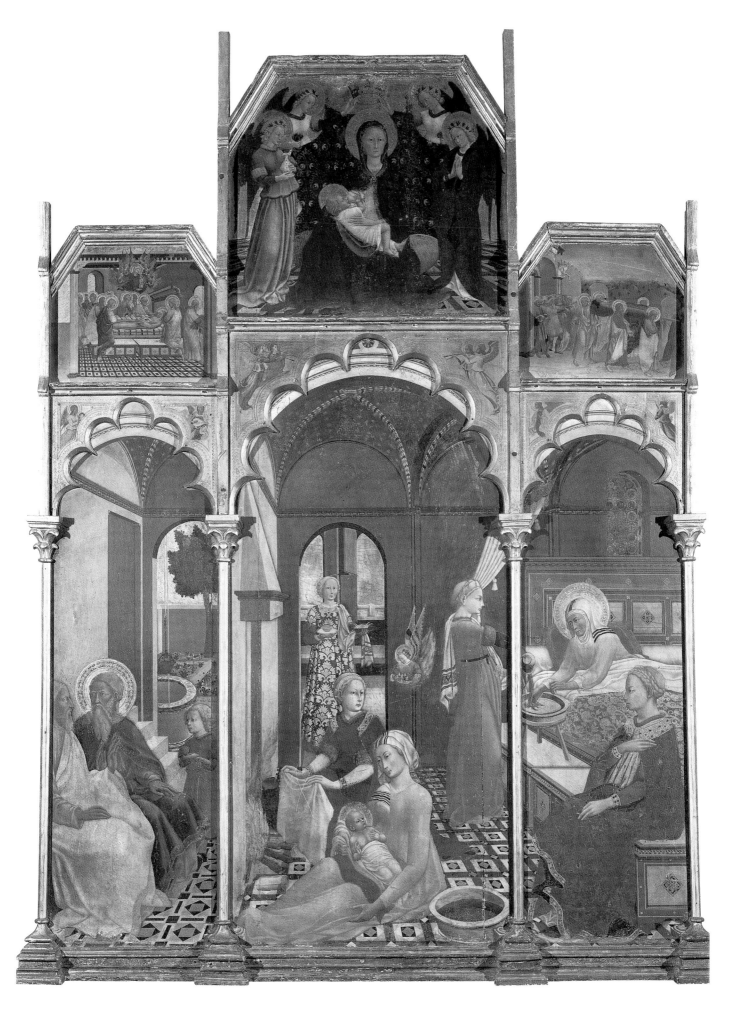

This profoundly influential tale or novella from the eighth day of Boccaccio's *Decameron* remained popular throughout the fifteenth and sixteenth centuries. Here, objects (the door, the key, the chest) and spaces (the bedchamber) are invoked only when they impinge directly on the action of the narrative, and are not described in any detail. This approach differs from that of the *Birth of the Virgin*'s tranquil interior, in which carefully depicted objects make the biblical event more intimate, striking chords of familiarity with the viewer.

These examples illustrate two significant strands of representation of the domestic interior throughout fifteenth- and sixteenth-century Italy: as an idealized, ordered space with sacred resonances and as a secular, contested setting where order is disrupted and illegitimate desires satisfied. But the painting and the novella exist within a much wider range of visual and textual representational types. The extent and development of these representations was affected by the cultural and technological changes for which this period is celebrated – from the renewed interest in the classical past to the introduction of printing and the development of perspective. The direct impact of these forces on the depiction of the domestic interior is the subject of this chapter.

In the late-fourteenth and early-fifteenth centuries most visual representations of the interior were painted as settings for religious subjects, and were created for a sacred context. Ranging from large frescoes on church walls to miniatures in liturgical manuscripts, they drew on a limited number of biblical events that typically took place around a bed, a scholar's desk or a dining table. These items of furniture clearly defined the otherwise non-specific spaces as domestic bedrooms, studies or dining rooms. Beds appear with most frequency, forming the focal point of birth scenes, usually that of the Virgin, and also, particularly in Florence where he was patron saint, St John the Baptist. Less often, the bed depicted was a death-bed, in images showing the Virgin (see the top left-hand corner of pl.2.1) or other holy figures departing this life. Beds also featured in episodes

from saints' lives where their intercession impinged on the domestic world of others, such as Sts Cosimus and Damianus who transplanted the leg of a Moor onto a white amputee, or St Nicholas of Bari, who threw three golden balls through the bedroom window of a poor man with three daughters without dowries, enabling them to marry. Less prominent, but ever present, beds are found in the plethora of Annunciation scenes that started to appear in Italy during this period (see pl.2.15). The study was a common setting for Sts Jerome and Augustine, who, as learned Doctors of the Church, were commonly represented seated at a desk surrounded by the accoutrements of the scholar. Dining tables feature in many biblical scenes: the Marriage at Cana, where Jesus turned water into wine; the Supper at Emmaus, where the resurrected Christ revealed himself to two of his disciples; the story of Salome, who danced for Herod at a banquet before requesting the beheading of St John the Baptist; and the Last Supper.

Images of the domestic interior played a central role in bridging the gap between Renaissance audiences and the biblical events of a historically and culturally remote, even imagined, past. Long considered a vital means of transmitting both knowledge and understanding of the Bible to the non- and semi-literate, religious paintings were described as the 'books of the simple' by the Dominican preacher Fra Giovanni Dominici in the early fifteenth century.[2] The messages of sacred texts were given additional visual power and resonance by setting the episodes they describe in a contemporary context – thus the beds in birth scenes or the vessels on dining tables bore a familiar relationship to objects that the viewer might have experienced in everyday life. This process of making sacred narratives familiar by relating them to a recognizable domestic realm was also recommended in texts prescribing devotional practices:

> The better to impress the story of the
> Passion on your mind … it is helpful
> and necessary to fix the places and

2.2
Giacomo Rufinelli, under the supervision of Isaac ben Solomon, Mantua, illustration from *Haggadah*. Woodcut. 1550. Civica Raccolta della Stampe Achille Bertarelli, Milan

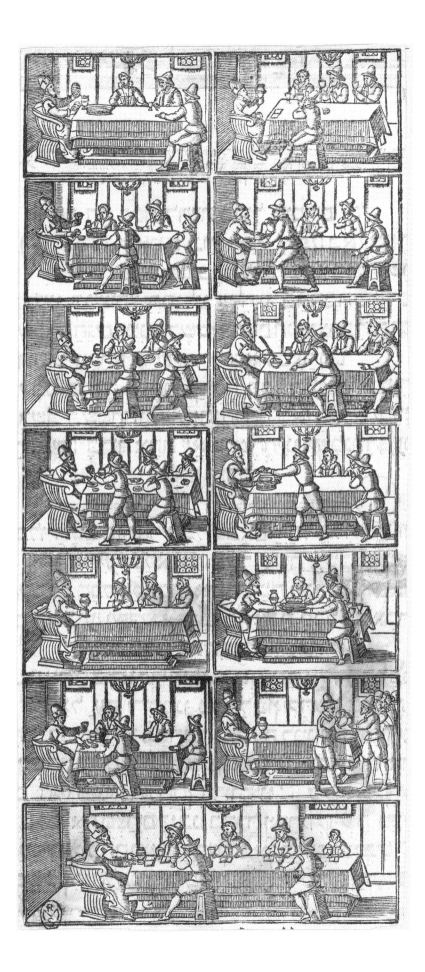

people in your mind: a city … which will be the city of Jerusalem – take for this purpose a city that is well known to you. In this city find the principal places in which all the episodes of the Passion would have taken place – for instance, a palace with the supper room where Christ had the Last Supper with the Disciples.[3]

However, not all religious imagery in this period was Christian. The woodcut in plate 2.2 illustrates the subsequent stages of the Jewish Passover feast.

The period 1400–1600 witnessed fundamental changes in the quantities, forms and functions of representations of domestic space. With the remarkable increase in the number of household goods came the development of new types of furniture and furnishings.[4] These items in turn often featured images of interiors: from paintings containing narrative scenes inserted into the panelling of rooms (*spalliere*), beds and chests (*cassoni*)[5] to painted objects such as wooden birth trays (*deschi da parto*, used to bring nourishing food to new mothers) or the ceramic tableware that Italy started manufacturing in this period.[6] The spectrum of formats was further expanded during the sixteenth century as canvas painting, as opposed to fresco or painting on panel, became a more common feature of domestic decoration.

Sacred images continued to be produced for the church, although these too underwent significant changes in format. Until the late fifteenth century, religious paintings were often composed of a number of smaller, individual scenes built up into a whole, described by Leonardo da Vinci as like shop displays in which wares were on show in little rectangular cubbyholes.[7] The sixteenth century witnessed a shift towards single scenes painted in oils on huge canvases that permitted the depiction of large-scale architectural structures and a more detailed rendering of objects. In addition to painting, representations of interiors inspired by biblical events were also found in relief sculpture in stone, terracotta or bronze (see pl.2.9). Placed

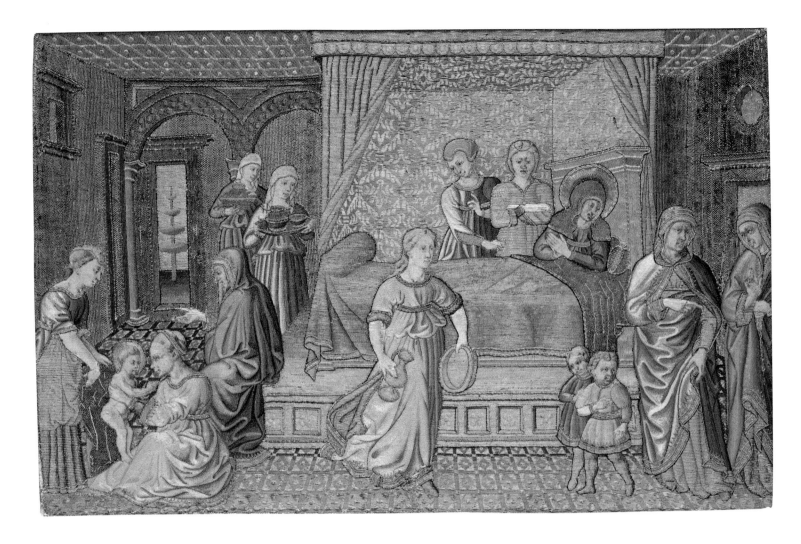

on the façades and in the interiors of churches, these sculpted interiors were visible to a wide audience. Textiles, in the form of ecclesiastical embroideries (see pl.2.3), also used the same repertoire of Christian events as paintings.[8]

The emergence of portrait painting provided an important new secular type of image that reflected the domestic sphere. The earliest Italian portraits, from the mid-fifteenth century, showed figures against a dark, anonymous background, but from the latter part of the fifteenth century sitters were increasingly set in a vividly depicted domestic context. Initially, the sitter's head and shoulders were shown close-up against a corner of a non-specific room, or small portion of wall or window, an arrangement taken directly from fifteenth-century Flemish models.[9] These tended to be portraits of individuals or married or betrothed couples in paired panels. Davide Ghirlandaio's *Portrait*

of a Woman (see pl.2.4) shows the sitter against a niche containing objects associated with marriage, including a large brooch or pendant, a ring, a needle, coral beads and a small devotional book.[10] Gradually, a wider and more detailed sense of the specific domestic location emerged. In Bronzino's *Portrait of a Young Man* (see pl.2.5), partially visible architectural elements (a carved hanging pediment and stone door frames) and furniture (a highly ornamented table and chair) imply an impressively grand Florentine *palazzo* that continues beyond the picture's frame.[11] Carefully chosen objects that cast light on the individual's character, status or interests continued to be included, such as the book in this young man's hand. Later in the sixteenth century, sitters appeared in half- and full-length, and clusters of figures – fathers and sons, mothers and daughters, or the whole family together – were united in one room.[12]

2.3
Anon., *Birth of the Virgin*.
Embroidery. *c.*1475–1500.
The Metropolitan Museum of
Art, New York

2.4
Davide Ghirlandaio (attr.),
Portrait of a Woman.
Tempera on panel. *c.*1500.
Gemäldegalerie, Berlin

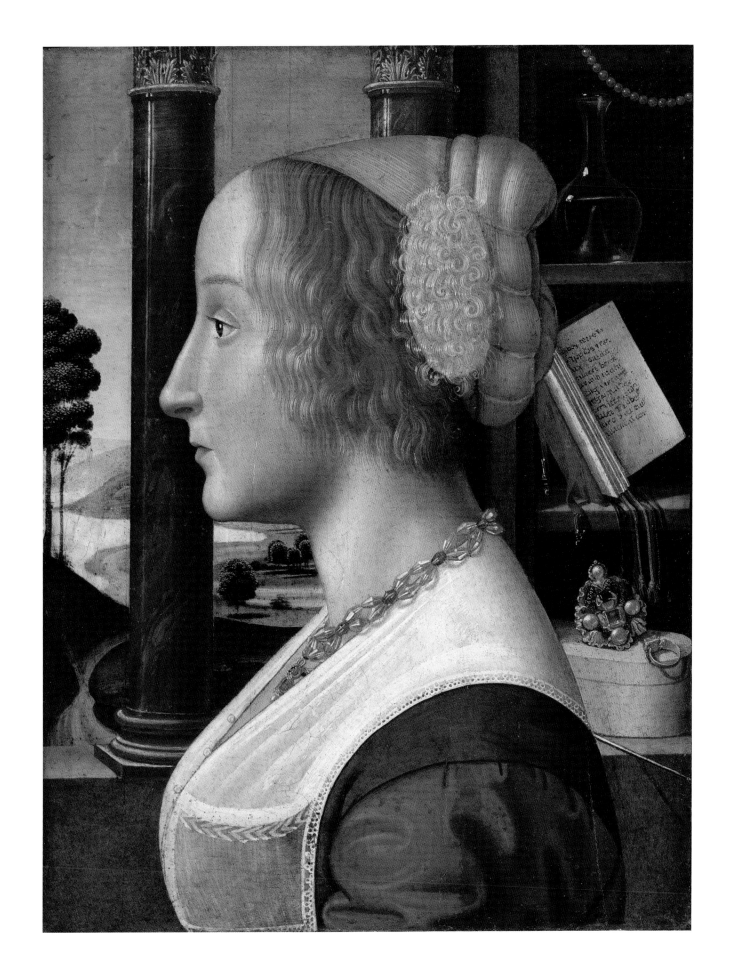

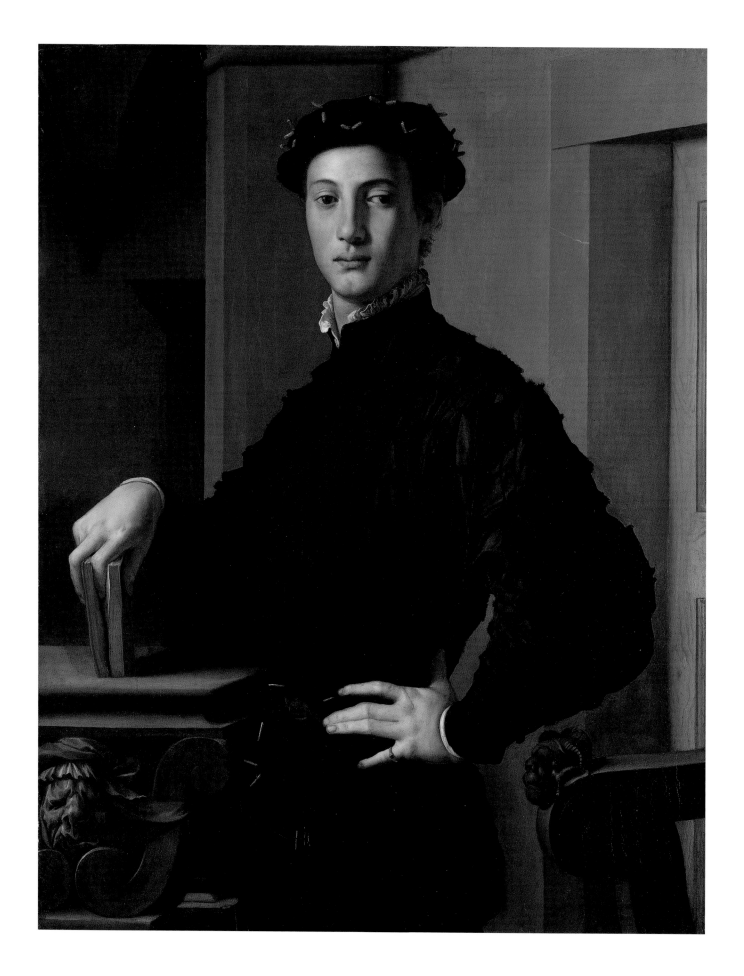

2.5
Bronzino, *Portrait of a Young Man*. Oil on wood. 1530s. The Metropolitan Museum of Art, New York

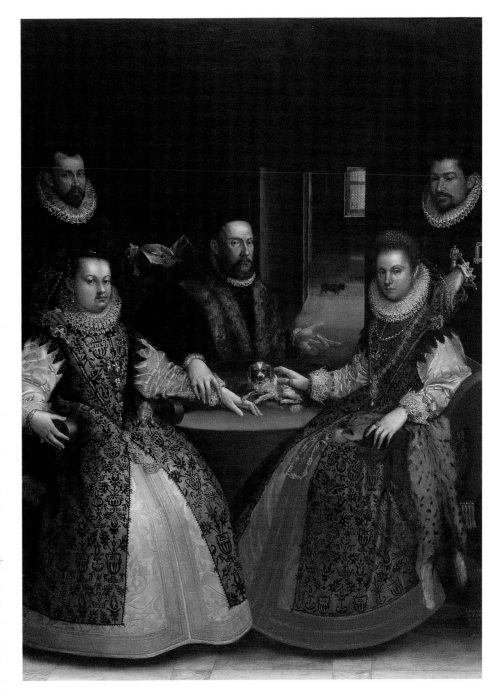

2.6
Lavinia Fontana, *The Gozzadini Family*. Oil on canvas. 1584. Pinacoteca Nazionale, Bologna

Lavinia Fontana's painting of the Bolognese Gozzadini family (1584) is a potent dynastic statement, grouping living and deceased relatives around a table in what appears to be the family *palazzo* to create a fictional image of a family that no longer existed (see pl.2.6).[13]

Printing

The introduction into Italy of the new technology of printing – of images in around 1400 and of texts in the last decades of the fifteenth century – had a fundamental impact on the range of representations that described interiors and significantly affected the extent of their dissemination.[14] Texts representing the interior that were previously circulated in manuscript, such as fictional prose, were now available to a wider audience in printed form. The genre of prescriptive literature, ranging from architectural treatises, literary dialogues discussing the roles of men and women within the home, to practical advice on household matters, expanded dramatically. Previously ephemeral forms commenting on or describing interiors, such as sung poetry or comic plays performed in public spaces by street players, were now printed and sold to their audiences. Letters passed between educated élites, originally intended for a restricted audience, assumed literary status and circulated publicly in print. However, most non-literary letters and legal documents that could also represent the domestic interior (including court records, inventories and wills) remained in manuscript.

Printed books provided a new context in which textual and visual representations of interiors could be experienced simultaneously. Fifteenth- and sixteenth-century books were typically illustrated with woodcuts that appeared on title pages and within the book itself. Unlike the intricately detailed, highly coloured and often sacred illuminations appearing in manuscripts,[15] illustrative woodcuts tended to depict scenes from everyday life, accompanying texts such as the lively tales of Boccaccio's *Decameron*, narrative poetry describing tragic love stories (see the intimate scene depicted in plate 2.7) or

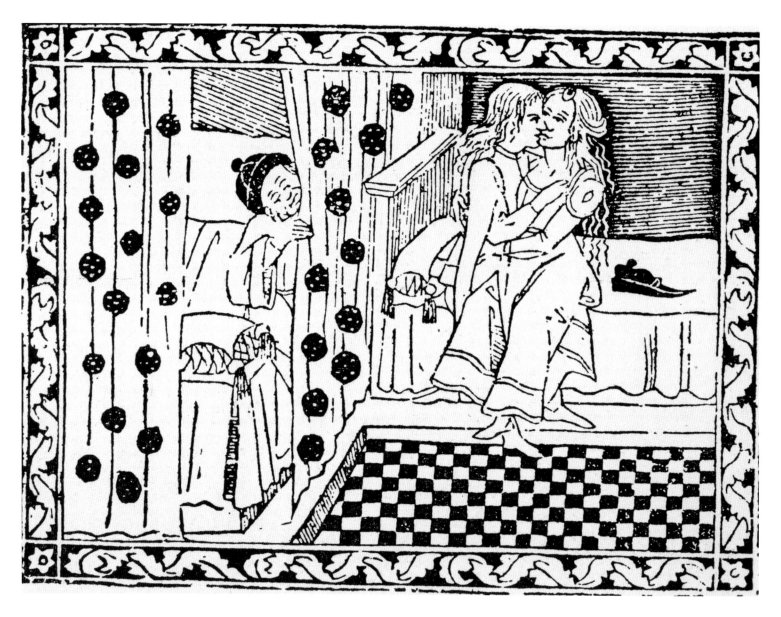

Savonarola's more sombre *Predica dell'arte del ben morire* (*The Art of Dying Well*).

During the sixteenth century, engraved book illustrations permitted more meticulously detailed representations of the interior. However, engravings became more important as art objects in their own right, particularly as a means of circulating the content of paintings.[16] By multiplying and disseminating images, engravings contributed to the development of a visual culture related to the interior and played an important role within artistic cross-currents between northern Europe and Italy. This led to interesting hybrid representations of interiors, as northern artists working in Italy engraved scenes that melded elements of the

visual traditions and typical rooms and furnishings of both cultures. Northern European images were also reproduced wholesale by Italian print-makers, bringing northern visual culture (and its moralizing messages) to a wider audience within Italy.

The influence of classical culture

Depictions of the domestic interior were also radically affected by the enthusiasm for Greek and Roman culture that intensified during this period. Particularly influential on theoretical discussions of domestic architecture, rediscovered classical texts also provided new sources for visual imagery and inspired lively debates regarding both the décor and decorum of

2.7
Illustration from the title page of *Historia de Guiscardo e Gismonda*. Woodcut. Florence, 1553

the household. Built architecture, architectural theory and painted depictions of domestic buildings were transformed by the study of surviving Roman structures combined with the close attention paid to the treatise of the ancient Roman architect Vitruvius.[17] This resulted in a new schematic presentation of the structure of domestic buildings, manifested in plans, elevations and cross-sections (see pl.2.8). Theoretical discussions in Renaissance architectural treatises focused on the functional aspects of the interior: the provision of water; adequate heat and light; the circulation of air and the appropriate disposition of rooms. With these issues in mind, Leon Battista Alberti's *De re aedificatoria* (*On the Art of Building*, 1450), discusses the relationship of domestic buildings to their surroundings, the relationship of interior spaces to each other and the best placement of doors and windows.

The modern concept of the architect, someone whose energies are focused solely on the design and construction of buildings, emerged during the sixteenth century and was typified by prominent figures such as Andrea Palladio or Vincenzo Scamozzi.[18] Prior to this, there was a strong reciprocal influence between the professions of artist (whether painter or sculptor) and architect, with authors of influential architectural treatises, such as Alberti, Filarete and Francesco di Giorgio, also enjoying active careers as artists.[19] The contribution of fictive painted architecture to the formation of new classical styles should not be underestimated, as Alberti's comment demonstrates: 'unless I am mistaken, the architect took from the painter his architraves, capitals, bases, columns, pediments and all other similar things'.[20]

Classical texts, from episodes in Roman history to classical mythology, also provided inspiration for images that appeared in domestic paintings, tapestries and on decorative ceramics. These texts dramatically expanded the repertory of secular narratives in which the interior played a prominent role, but, like the biblical scenes described above, they were often set in familiar, contemporary contexts. The stories of exemplary Roman men and women such as

Scipio or Lucretia (see pl.2.11) could also have an instructive or moralizing function, providing models of good citizenship or female virtue. But tales of the loves of the gods (such as Venus and Mars) also created opportunities for the depiction of erotic scenes in a bedroom setting.

Prescriptive literature

Classical models also had a profound effect on the genre of prescriptive literature, ranging from practical household advice to literature on the education of children and architectural treatises, that expanded rapidly during these centuries

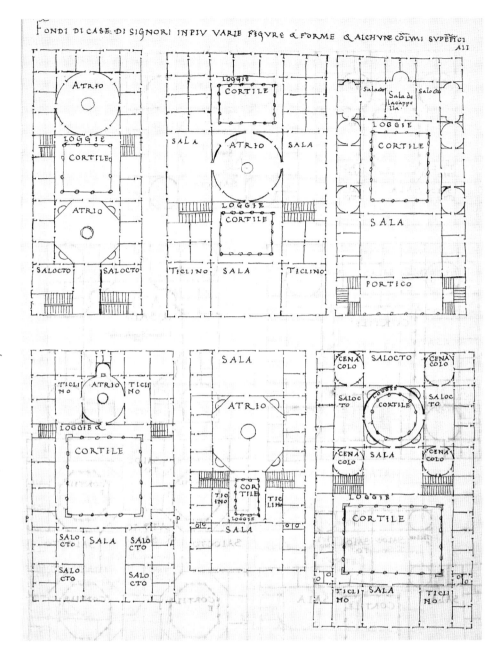

2.8

Francesco di Giorgio, *Trattato di Architettura*. Pen on paper. *c*.1480. Biblioteca Nazionale Centrale, Florence

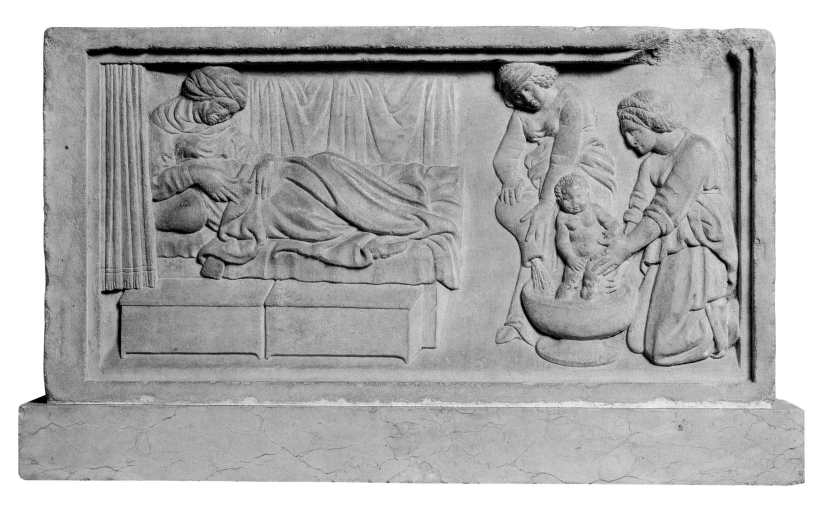

(see pp.68–9).[21] Two texts concerned with the art of managing the household were particularly influential, inspiring many Renaissance imitations: the *Oeconomia*, a tract thought to be by Aristotle, and the *Oeconomicus*, a literary dialogue by Xenophon. As well as provoking discussions about practical aspects of managing the domestic sphere, this literature contributed to debates about splendour and magnificence in domestic architecture and furnishings.[22] These representations present a forceful picture of the interior as an ordered and regulated space, and stress the political role of the household as a unit of society.

Many of these prescriptive texts express a concern with the decorum of the architectural structure and content of houses, depending on social level. Giovanni Pontano's Latin treatise *De splendore* (1498) demonstrates how important an awareness of maintaining an appropriate relationship between status and surroundings was:

The base man and the splendid man both use a knife at table. The difference between them is this. The knife of the first is sweaty and has a horn handle; the knife of the other man is polished and has a handle made of some noble material that has been worked with an artist's mastery.[23]

Civic anxieties over the appropriate decoration of the interior also appear in sumptuary legislation. This prohibited or limited the use of particularly luxurious domestic furnishings during celebrations such as marriages, or in particular types of interiors, such as those belonging to prostitutes. Forbidden to dress in gold, silver or silk and jewels, Venetian prostitutes in 1542 were also told that they could not have in their houses 'any furnishings of silk, or tapestries, or upholstery, or bench-covers, or leathers of any kind, but only cloths of Bergamo or Brescia, and these must be plain and have no patterns cut upon them.'[24]

2.9
Follower of Jacopo della Quercia, *Birth of St John the Baptist*. Marble. Early 15th century. Museo Civico Medievale, Bologna

Prescriptive texts convey the importance of ordering possessions in appropriate places within the interior according to their appearance and function. One book on the Christian education of children considers what should be on view, and what, conversely, should be hidden away. Religious images, statues and books should be displayed in particular rooms within the house in certain ways: 'it is very expedient to have images of saints in your own house … and to arrange them well according to the size of the house, not in a confused manner, but in certain important places…',[25] but 'the good father, raising his children in a Christian manner, must take great care not to have in his house vain and dishonest pictures, which can ferment and stimulate the greatest vices'.[26]

During the sixteenth century, behaviour within the home – including the different roles of men and women, their relationship with the interior's contents, and the ordering and upkeep of the house – became the focus of this more practical type of prescriptive literature and of literary dialogues. Stefano Guazzo's *Dell'onor delle donne* lists the tasks that he believed women should be responsible for, including

> hangings, and other textiles for the use and ornament of the house, keeping the furniture clean, doing needlework, spinning, winding wool, raising silk-worms, visiting the cellars, the granary, the pantry, garden, poultry shed…, and keeping track of the laundry, crockery, cooking ordinary food, and the preserving for the year.[27]

The everyday processes of ordering and maintaining the interior and its contents are reflected in practice in domestic account books. For example, the Florentine widow Maria Ridolfi Strozzi's household accounts for 1551–4 include regular payments to a woodworker to replace the waxed paper that covered her windows and to a mattress-maker for restuffing mattresses.[28]

Perspective

The development of perspective – the depiction of people and objects proportionally within a unified three-dimensional space – radically transformed visual representations of the interior in this period. Here the desire to express the key events of unfolding narratives within a single image produced more spatially complex representations of the domestic sphere, as depth, width and height were exploited as a means of separating different temporal episodes of the story.

Before the development of perspective, the domestic interior was mostly depicted as a single, claustrophobic room, something Alberti commented on vividly in *De pictura*: 'Another thing I often see deserves to be censured, and that is men painted in a building as if they were shut up in a box in which they can hardly fit sitting down and rolled up in a ball' (see pl.2.9).[29] In the late fourteenth or early fifteenth-century painting shown in plate 2.10, the room fills the entire architectural shell of the house, despite the fact that the exterior shows windows at different storeys. It is as if this one room constitutes the entire interior. The spatial relationships between the kneeling figure and the structure and furnishings of the room are out of proportion, whilst the bed recedes in uneasy opposition to the room's sloping walls.[30]

Although interior spaces continued to be shown as 'boxes', they were increasingly contextualized during the fifteenth century, with a greater emphasis placed on the relationship between adjacent rooms. Perpendicular walls that had previously functioned as boundaries between the inside and the outside now divided the interior to articulate a series of related spaces. This type of separation was used in early fifteenth-century large-scale paintings built up of smaller panels, to provide architectural structure (as in the triptych in plate 2.1) or to separate scenes within a narrative sequence. In the late fifteenth century this use of perpendicular walls was particularly suited to the wide oblong formats of *cassone* fronts and *spalliera* panels (see pl.2.11), which often

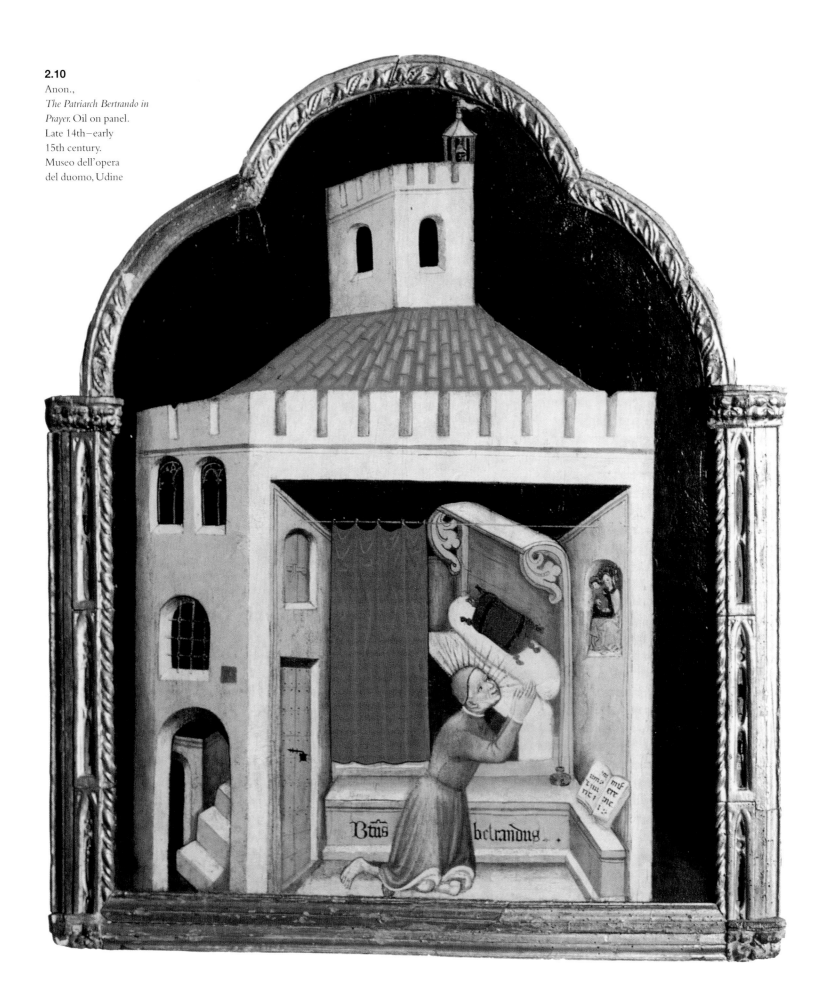

2.10
Anon.,
The Patriarch Bertrando in
Prayer. Oil on panel.
Late 14th–early
15th century.
Museo dell'opera
del duomo, Udine

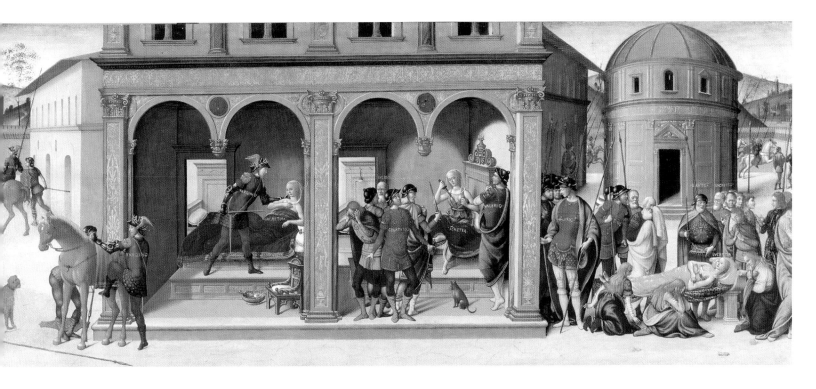

2.11
Biagio d'Antonio Tucci,
Stories from the Life of Lucretia.
Tempera on board.
Early 1480s. Ca' d'Oro, Venice

depicted instructive tales of exemplary figures. Although this permitted different adjacent room-types to be included within the same representation (such as a bedroom next to a dining scene), the clarity of narrative progression could take precedence over the realistic depiction of interior space. For example, plate 2.11 situates the story of Lucretia in two bedrooms that are actually the same room at different moments in the narrative: the first contains a depiction of her rape and the second her suicide.

The development of linear perspective also led to an exploration of the depth of interior spaces. Early examples dramatically foreshortened the walls of 'the box', exaggerating this effect with chequerboard floors or employing layers of arches and columns to emphasize receding domestic space. However, the most commonly adopted technique for suggesting other rooms beyond that depicted was the inclusion of an open door, window or corridor in the background of the image.

Boundaries

Puncturing or dissolving walls between rooms also highlighted connections between interior spaces. These were not always straightforward architectural relationships, but could indicate a functional interplay between different spaces in a house. For example, Antonio Tempesta's engraving 'January', part of a series of the months, depicts a busy kitchen in the foreground, with some form of entertainment in the *sala* beyond (see pl.2.12).[31] The two rooms are juxtaposed without a dividing wall and a clear connection is made between the preparations in the kitchen and the eating and drinking that will take place in the social space of the *sala* beyond. However, it would be wrong to read this as a depiction of a real interior: kitchen and *sala* were not usually next to each other in buildings of the period. Tempesta highlights a symbolic, functional link between these two spaces, stressing the important, long-established role of the house as a site of entertainment and feasting at the start of the year.

The boundaries between the interior and the exterior also form a focus of images of domestic space and are treated with similar techniques to interior divisions. Walls (and ceilings) are 'reduced', pierced or removed to reveal relationships between the inside of the house and its immediate, external surroundings. In Fra Carnevale's *The Birth of the Virgin* (see pl.2.13), elegant open arches are substituted for interior and exterior walls, demarcating a series of austere, receding spaces with exaggeratedly high ceilings.[32] The stark severity of the unfurnished interior forms a continuum with the ambiance outside; decoration is focused entirely on the façade of the building and in the niche just visible on the furthest internal wall, filled with an assortment of carefully described objects. The arches, the niche and the three clusters of women – one outside, one in the nearest room and one in the furthest – draw the eye into this majestic interior. A more complex relationship between interior and exterior is at play in Jacopo and Francesco Bassano's *Supper at Emmaus* (see pl.2.14).[33] Here the deliberate blurring of the boundaries between the two spheres creates confusion: is the outside natural world encroaching on the kitchen's domestic order or vice versa?

Domestic boundaries were also a key element of the iconography of the Annunciation. Most Italian examples depict the Virgin inside or on the threshold of the house on the right-hand side of the image, with the Archangel Gabriel appearing in a garden or courtyard-like space on the left. An architectural feature, such as the column in plate 2.15, usually separates the two figures, denoting the division between the spiritual and temporal worlds. Pesellino's small painting includes all the common symbolic elements found in the fifteenth-century *Annunciation*: the garden and the lily (representing the Virgin's chastity), and the lectern and the bed (suggesting her thalamus or bridal chamber).[34] Later fifteenth- and sixteenth-

2.12
Antonio Tempesta, 'January' from a series of the months. Engraving. 1599. NAL: 93.E.149

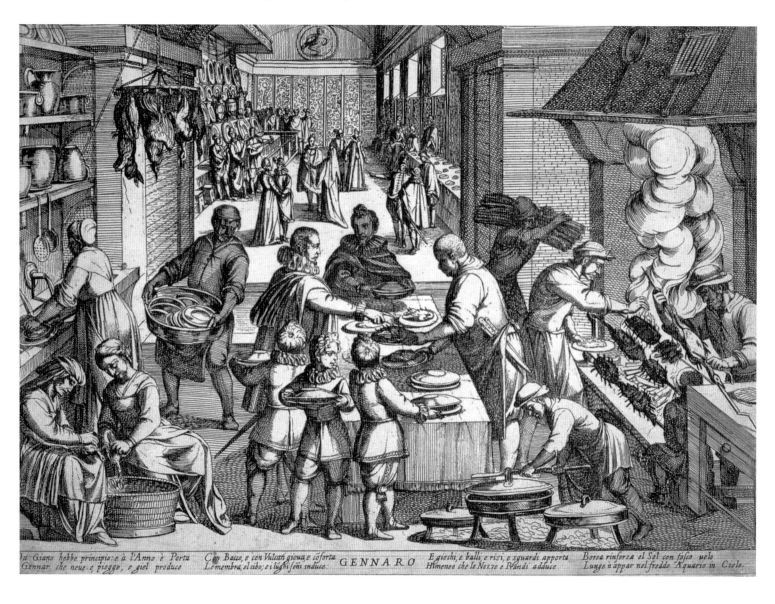

Da Giano hebbe principio: e à l'Anno è Porta   Con Bacco, e con Vulcan gioua, e conforta   GENNARO   E giochi, e balli, e risi, e sguardi apporta   Borea rinforza el Sol con fosco velo
Gennar che neue, e piaggie, e giel produce   Le membra, el cibo; e i lieti suoni induce   Himeneo che le Nozze e Pandi adduce   Lunge n'appar nel freddo Aquario in Cielo.

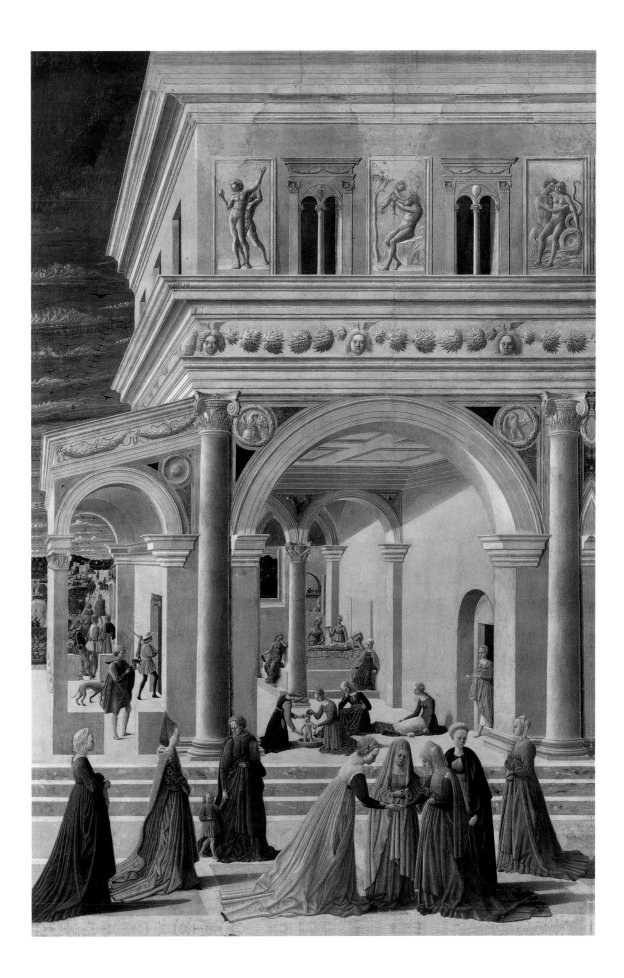

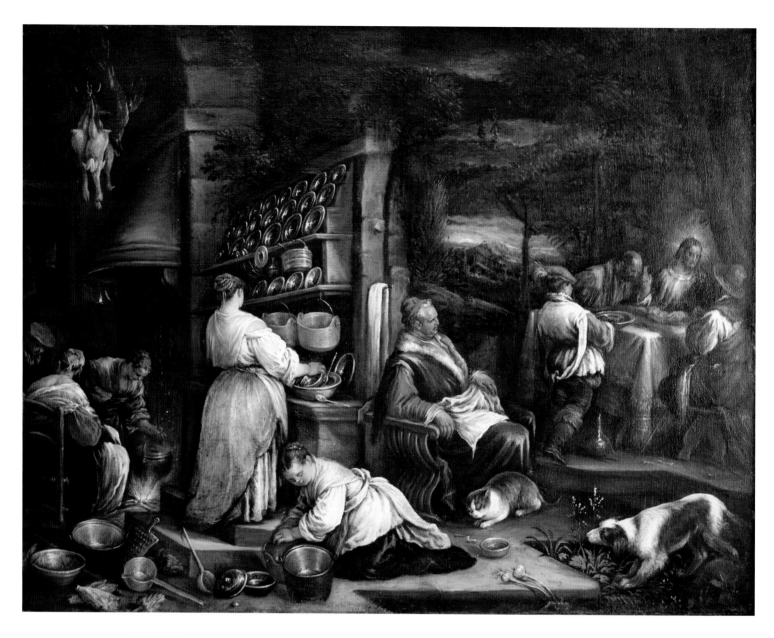

century scenes moved both figures into an interior setting, but continued to use structural elements of the interior to separate them.

Architectural plans form the clearest visual expression of the relationship between inside and outside. During the sixteenth century, plans were juxtaposed with elevations, either of façades or of cross-sections of buildings, providing highly schematic representations of interior space in three dimensions. In the plan and elevation of the Poggio Reale at Naples, published by Serlio in 1537 (see pl. 2.16), the façade of the palace is cut away to reveal two slices through the building at different depths. A strikingly unusual drawing of a row of houses

and workshops from Bergamo (see pl. 2.17) provides a rare glimpse into non-élite housing of the period. Flaps of the buildings' exteriors can be lifted to reveal the cross-sections beneath.[35]

Texts of this period are also preoccupied with the boundaries of the interior, expressing concern over the physical demarcation of the domestic sphere in an era that saw buildings occupied by several households even at élite social levels. In his *ricordanze* or diary, the Florentine Bartolomeo di Tommaso Sassetti records that when he and his brother Francesco inherited and subdivided the family house, they discovered that a room that should have been

2.14

Jacopo and Francesco Bassano,
Supper at Emmaus.
Oil on canvas. *c*.1576–77.
Private collection

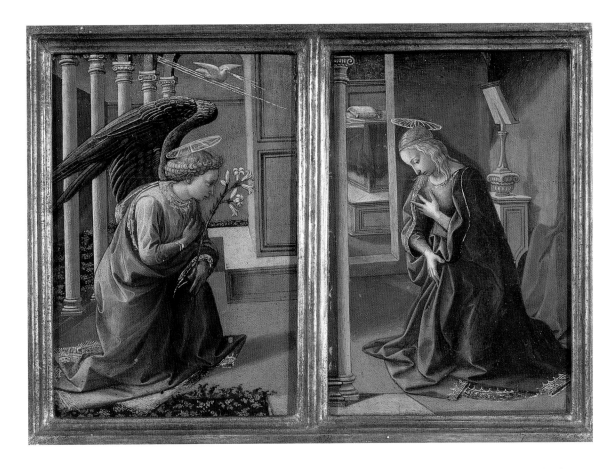

2.15
Francesco Pesellino,
Annunciation.
Tempera on panel.
Early 15th century.
Courtauld Institute of Art
Gallery, London

2.16
Sebastiano Serlio,
Quarto libro d'architettura.
First published Venice, 1537.
NAL: 87.A.27

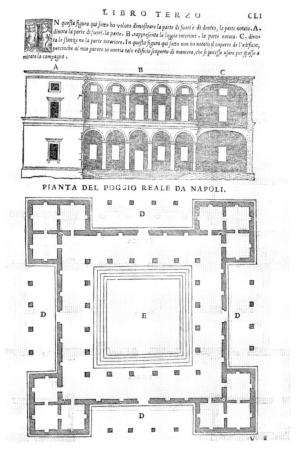

theirs had somehow been given to the house next door.[36] The potential permeability of these boundaries causes both anxiety and annoyance. Vasari's account of the life of the Florentine painter Buonamico Buffalmacco describes how the artist took revenge on a neighbour who started her noisy weaving early every morning, disturbing his rest. Discovering a hole in the wall next to the kitchen fire on which she cooked, he surreptitiously used a long, hollow reed to over-salt her dishes, making them inedible.[37] Diaries and court records show how larger holes in walls could be exploited by amorous men and women to move furtively between adjacent houses.[38] The boundaries between interior and exterior were accorded great symbolic potency, something recorded in the transcripts of legal trials. Weak points – doors and windows – became the focus of both rowdy attacks on the house's honour, in which ink, blood or excrement was smeared on doors and windows,[39] and of practices that offered supernatural protection of the house, such as annointing doorsteps with specially prepared oils or holy water.[40]

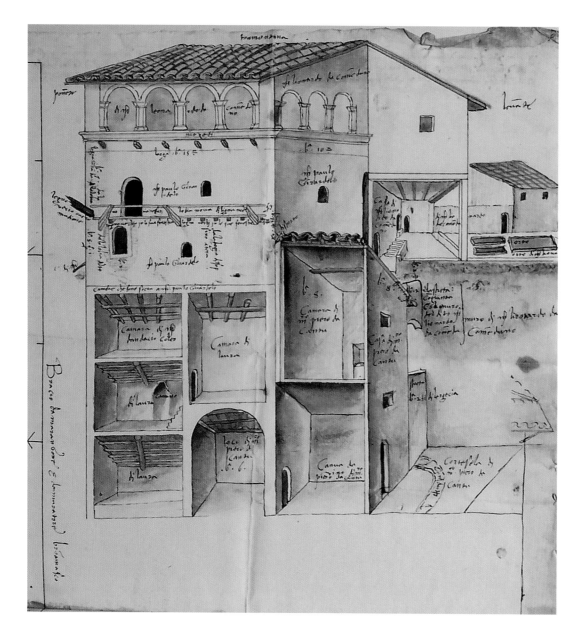

2.17
Lucano da Rimini,
*Houses on the Via Porta Dipinta,
Bergamo.* 1533. Biblioteca Civica
A. Mai di Bergamo

Protecting and instructing

Representations of the interior also played a vital role in the protection of the domestic sphere, something highlighted in an exceptional painting by Filippo Lippi known as *The Bartolini Tondo* (see pl.2.18).[41] A sophisticated, complex and virtuosic rendering of domestic space, this image combines the dividing walls and receding spaces described above with elaborately juxtaposed levels of flooring and staircases. In addition, however, it is an extraordinary amalgamation of domestic artefacts new to this period which bear images of the interior and that had a potent protective function. The Madonna and Child in the foreground are typical of the painted and sculpted images that were ubiquitous in households of all social levels, whose figures came to be shown increasingly in a non-specific but nevertheless intricately depicted domestic setting. These images, which were often directly addressed during prayer (see pl.2.10), had an iconic efficacy and protected the domestic sphere.[42] The inclusion of contemporary decorative details resonated with the rooms in which they were placed, enabling contemporary viewers to empathize more easily with the mother of Christ and even imagine her presence in the room with them. The circular tondo was itself a specifically domestic type of devotional painting that emerged during the fourteenth century.

The *Bartolini Tondo*'s depiction of two moments from the Virgin's life – the meeting of her parents at Jerusalem's Golden Gate, regarded by some as the moment of her Immaculate Conception, and the scene of her birth – initially appears surprising on an object we know was intended for the interior of a private palace, since images of the life of the Virgin were most usually found in churches. But this prominent birth imagery, combined with the painting's circular form and the (albeit later) coat of arms on its reverse, suggests that we view the tondo in

2.18
Filippo Lippi, *Virgin and Child with Episodes from the Life of the Virgin (The Bartolini Tondo)*. Oil on panel. *c.*1452. Galleria Palatina, Palazzo Pitti, Florence

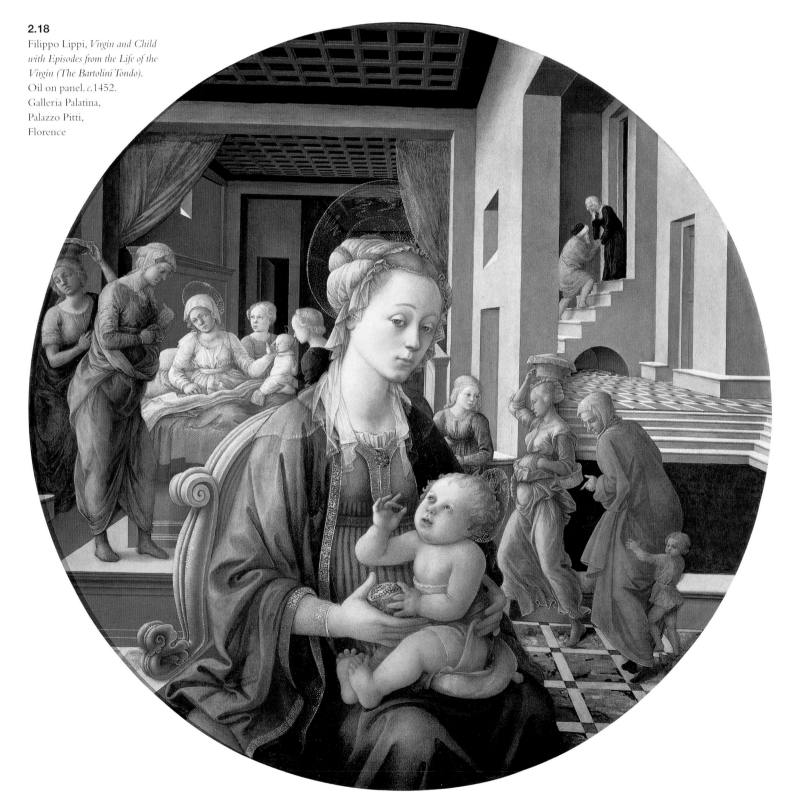

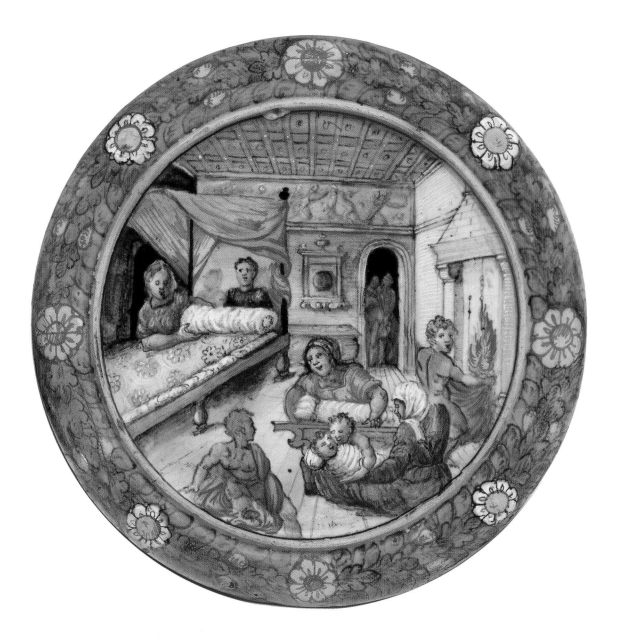

2.19
Francesco Durantino,
lid of a footed bowl from a
childbirth set. Mid-1540s.
Philadelphia Museum of Art

the context of the wooden birth trays that were commonly painted in the fifteenth and early sixteenth centuries to commemorate the arrival of a new child. A relationship to these objects lends Lippi's image another layer of talismanic potency: as well as their practical use, birth trays had a symbolic function, forming part of a spectrum of objects that were produced to reassure, protect and instruct the expecting mother during the perilous processes of pregnancy and childbirth. Birth trays, and the sets of ceramic bowls and dishes that in the sixteenth century took on their didactic function (see pl.2.19), were characterized by their intimate depictions of the domestic calm following a successful birth.[43] The coalescing of these elements in *The*

Bartolini Tondo, together with its overwhelming size (135 cm in diameter), renders it a powerful object that used a vivid representation of the interior to influence the behaviour and attitudes of the inhabitants of the house where it hung.

The poor and the disrupted interior

The representations considered so far, from biblical and classical narratives to prescriptive literature and objects that protected the house or helped guide a mother through childbirth, were intended to have an actively instructive effect on readers and viewers. Providing models of good mothers, chaste women, or authoritative heads of households, their purpose was to influence behaviour, using a particular view of the interior as an increasingly regularized, internalized and ordered place. However, a number of literary and visual representations that fall into a different category, characterized by the quotation from Boccaccio at the start of the chapter, have been less widely recognized. They show interiors that are disrupted, in disarray – disordered, even uncomfortable places that do not respect conventional norms or are removed from the splendour described in prescriptive literature because of poverty.

Literary descriptions of the uncomfortable interior can be highly evocative. In a letter of 1550, Anton Francesco Doni provides a vivid account of living in Venetian squalor:

> I have the most wretched room (if you can call it that) in the whole town, and the worst company, and I suffer the worst discomfort in the world. For the consolation of sleep, I have a solid mattress, a good, soundly made hard bed, an empty pillow, coarse sheets and a blue counterpane of the type used in hospitals; at night, in the manner of a cruel doctor, an army of huge bedbugs, as large as Mocenigos [sizeable silver Venetian coins], and a mob of fat fleas, test my pulse and bleed me; above my head, in an old loft, I think there is a college of mice and a consistory of cobwebs; below, there is a street where all night long wretches who waste the daytime pass up and down singing lewd songs noisily and certain erotic little madrigals … On the other side of me I have an old woman and a tailor who, what with the noise of the scissors and the coughing of the toothless crone, pass away two thirds of the night for me with pleasures of the most wretched sort to be found in all the world.[44]

However, a poem published in 1607 reveals a contrasting romantic sensibility of happiness in noble poverty, evoking the harmony of the disparate household (consisting of the aged, the

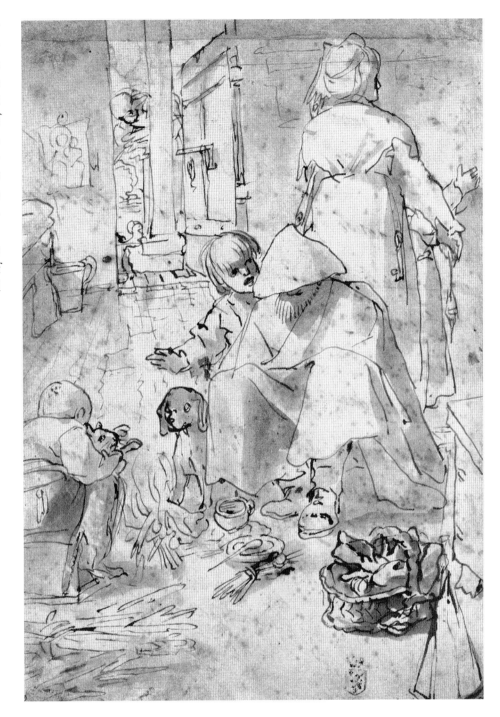

2.20
Annibale Carracci (attr.),
Interior of a Poor Household.
Pen and ink wash.
Late 16th century.
Private collection

young and domestic animals) caused by their communal want, and seeing 'infinite beauty in a thousand rags': 'gentle company … under a single roof / that is broken in a hundred places / through which the moon and the sun / make the house so much happier and lighter…'.[45] The drawing in plate 2.20 shows a poor family, and their cat and dog, huddled around a small fire in an interior that seems deprived of physical comfort. This image reflects the culmination of an interest in depicting the domestic sphere more realistically, explored particularly by north Italian artists in the latter half of the sixteenth century, and typified by the closely studied, often grotesque drawings of the Bolognese artist Annibale Carracci.[46]

The fantasy interior

Alongside a fascination with the everyday interior, fifteenth- and sixteenth-century writers and artists also enjoyed representing the domestic in extraordinary, exaggerated ways. These imagined interiors verge at times on the surreal. When fantastical interiors are represented in images and texts, the overall structure of the interior usually remains the same, but its scale, the density of its contents and its materiality are transformed. Giovanni Filoteo Achillini's *Epistole* (c.1510), a satirical text purporting to describe the 'admirable and stupendous' collection of the minor artist Ombrone, concentrates on the vast quantities of objects he owned, listing them obsessively in extraordinary detail, in what becomes a parody of an inventory.[47] Room by room, they are either named individually, in the case of the hundred-odd precious gems, or in a series of comprehensive categories, as with the sculpture collection: 'famous statues: equestrian, pedestrian, standing, seated, prostrate … made of stones, irons … silvers, golds'.[48] Combined with a vivid evocation of the immense architectural spaces in which these objects are housed, this description provides an exaggerated sense of an encyclopaedically complete collection. This type of spatially inflated representation, filled with an overabundance of objects, finds a visual parallel in early seventeenth-century Italian paintings, such as the *Kitchen Scene* by Joseph Heintz the Younger illustrated on page 69. A similar subversion of a legal document – this time a will – can be seen in a sixteenth-century poem. Here, the parody goes to the other extreme. Instead of an overabundance of riches, the deprived interior of 'Messer Faustin Terdotio' is conjured up by listing the disparate, shabby objects it contains. He leaves his heirs

all the spiders' webs / that you find in the house / with household goods and vessels / of various types / three spindles and two baskets / a winding distaff / a jug without spout … / a handful of sticks / and three matches / with two pestles / and half a bowl / *item* one slipper / with three broken shoes.[49]

Fantastic representations also transformed the very materials of the interior. In a late sixteenth-century poem, a spurned lover views 'The house where my beautiful treasure [his beloved] rests' and describes it as 'more gracious and lovely than any other / The walls of alabaster, the roof of gold / Of Zephyr the window where she stands / Of beautifully-worked ivory the door':[50] his emotional attachment mentally transforms the fabric of the house into precious materials. Excluded from the beloved's interior, he focuses on its furnishings, imbuing them with emotional responses: 'Happy seats and chests / Where she often sits / … to rest',[51] and even imploring domestic objects to argue his case with her: 'Oh little bed where she rests / Fine little sheets that cover her body / Oh pillow … Oh kind and precious bedcover … / Oh soft feathers where she turns over / You speak on my behalf, since she doesn't listen to me.'[52]

The material transformation of interiors also occurs in escapist descriptions of the land of *Cuccagna* (Cockaigne in English), where 'he who sleeps most, earns most', and anyone speaking of work faces a year in prison. Late sixteenth-century accounts in poems and large engravings of this carnevalesque topsy-turvy world promise such delights as roast chickens that rain down from the sky and a sea of Greek wine.[53] Their rich accounts of fantasy interiors sometimes focused on costly, luxurious textiles: 'You sleep in beds of cotton, with fine linen sheets, and stupefying bed-curtains, covers and canopies, all the quilts made of damask',[54] but could at times be mouth-watering: 'I want to tell you about the beautiful houses there / The walls are of pecorino cheese / And are white-washed with ricotta'.[55] The interior becomes a focus for expressing the extravagant comfort

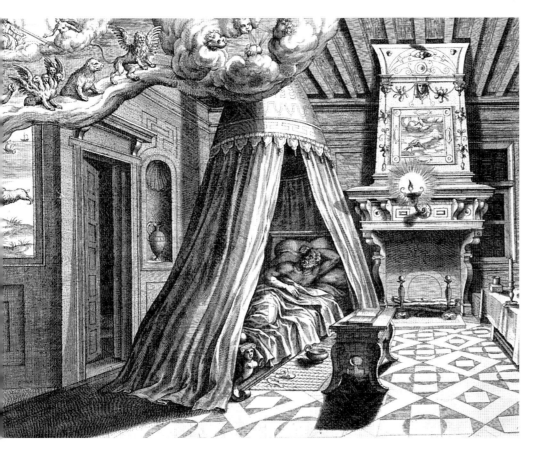

2.21
Anon. (Italian),
Man in Bed Dreaming.
Late 16th century.
Gabinetto disegni e stampe
degli Uffizi, Florence

the rest is made of dirty wool, combed little by little by a wax baboon next to the fire'.[57]

Imagination and the interior

In plate 2.21 a man lies in bed dreaming, the fantastic animals that are entering his unconscious imagination depicted invading the room in which he sleeps. This highly unusual print represents one intersection of mental and physical space. Another intersection was fundamental to a Renaissance technique for developing the memory, derived from classical sources. People were instructed to create mentally a 'house of memory' in which to situate the words, ideas or images they wished to recall.[58] In one exceptional text from 1435, the Florentine Michele del Giogante's home is constructed as a house of memory, with the actual objects of the physical interior and fantastical imagined symbols intertwined into a bewildering mnemonic concoction:

3. The large chest beside the door …
   the keys of the door

4. The closed-off window above the large
   chest … hanging from it the arms for
   defence …

19. The water dipper beside the door to
    the cellar … flames of fire upon it…

22. The staircase up from the ground
    floor to the sala … the wheel of
    fortune upon it.

23. The door at the half-landing of the
    stair below the sala … Hope dressed in
    green upon it …

39. The flour supply on the shelf on the
    right-hand side of the bread …
    Abundance in the figure of a woman.[59]

and abundance of this fictional country.

Giulio Cesare Croce's poem *The Fantastic and Bizarre Palace* employs a similarly inventive play on the materials from which the domestic sphere was composed in order to satirize the building aspirations of the wealthy and their interactions with architects. Here he undermines the very materiality of the palace itself by imagining a structure composed of acts and emotions:

> I want all the paving / to be made of
> the wrong-doings of villains / The
> Loggia, of the lies of charlatans / The
> rooms and the landings / Made of the
> sighs of passionate lovers… / the doors
> will be made / of the fury of soldiers /
> all the doors and balconies of the
> impudence of clowns.[56]

His architect's response, given at the end of the poem, provides an equally outlandish, but rather more down to earth, picture of the interior's eventual make-up: 'The *sala* will be made of pomade, and the kitchen of black soap … all

Conflating the actual house of an individual with the realm of the symbolic produces an uncanny combination of the 'real' and the 'unreal'. However, this extraordinary text is composed to be remembered rather than read or recited aloud. Existing primarily in the mind, it is a truly imagined interior.

Fifteenth-Century Interiors in the Netherlands

Luke Syson

Two figures, a bed, an oriental carpet laid down in front of it, a candelabrum with a single lit candle, a convex mirror surrounded by miniature roundels of the Passion of Christ, a carved figure of St Margaret of Antioch (patroness of childbirth), fruit, a dog, a hiked-up green dress with elaborate dagging, and an inscription: '*Johannes de eyck fuit hic. / .1434.*' or 'Jan van Eyck has been here' (see pl.2.22). In this 'here', it might be supposed, are the Lucchese Giovanni di Nicolao (?) Arnolfini and his (undocumented, second) wife, standing in the very chamber that Van Eyck visited to paint their portraits. Historians of all persuasions have therefore felt justified in treating this painting as a document of real life, perhaps the witnessed record of the moment of their marriage, and hence compelling evidence of the appearance of a room and its furnishings in the mercantile Bruges of the 1430s. At the same time, art historian Erwin Panofsky and his followers treated the objects depicted in the room as 'concealed' or 'disguised' symbols, which, once decoded, would reveal this great painting's single message. Even those who question these two approaches have not satisfactorily resolved the issue of why such realistically rendered details, seemingly carefully selected, were included in an image that is primarily a portrait of a man and his wife. While the individual objects that surround the Arnolfinis are of a kind that could be found in mercantile and aristocratic palaces (and their inventories), it seems likely that they were selected, placed and combined, not because they had been seen together in real life, but to act as visual prompts to think through St Augustine's concept of the three ends of marriage: offspring (*proles*), fidelity (*fides*) and the sacrament (*sacramentum*) deriving from the Passion of Christ (hence the scenes around the mirror).

It is helpful to compare the *Arnolfini Double Portrait* with one of several fifteenth-century Netherlandish scenes of the Annunciation and the Virgin and Child that have provoked similar contradictory responses. The *Annunciation* painted by a skilled member of

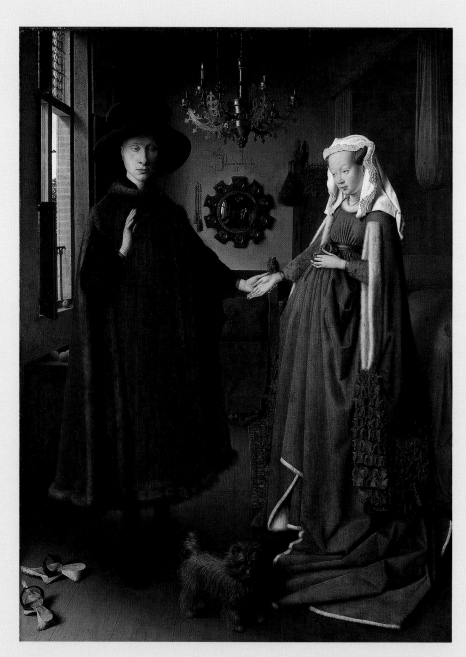

2.22
Jan van Eyck, *Arnolfini Double Portrait*. Oil on wood. 1434. National Gallery, London

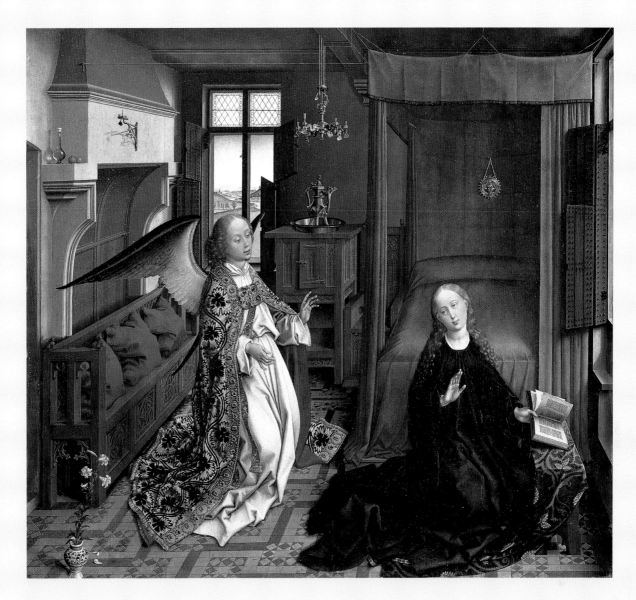

2.23
Workshop of Rogier van der Weyden, *Annunciation*. Oil on wood. Mid-1430s. Musée du Louvre, Paris

Rogier van der Weyden's workshop in the mid-1430s (see pl.2.23) is likewise set within a domestic interior and contains many of the same objects, depicted in such a way as to convince the viewer of their reality, and thus of the physical and spiritual 'truth' of the event. Closer examination reveals some deliberate incongruities intended, at the same time, to alert the viewer of the scene's unreality and therefore its broader religious significance. That the Virgin is seated close to the ground, indecorous were she of the status her costume implies, suggests her humility, and the vase and lily placed prominently on the floor prompts consideration of the Virgin as the pure vessel of God. The picture was intended, in a manner advocated by the current *devotio moderna*, to assist the private devotions of laity, here to support a member of the moneyed classes (for whom possessions were all-

important) in his or her contemplation of the mystery of the Incarnation of Christ the Word made Flesh. Indeed, by these increased levels of attention, the objects depicted, when encountered in real life, might themselves become devotional prompts rather than merely luxury items, and the spiritual could be connected with the real in the manner advocated by the painting. The bedchamber setting would have been connected with the Virgin's thalamus, the bridal chamber in the Song of Songs, the place where Mary became the Bride of Christ and also which the devout were sometimes urged to imagine as the location for their 'memories' of the sacred event. Thus its furnishings all pertain to this main theme, not symbols with single meanings – if an image could be 'solved', the process of looking would be less potent – but as multivalent prompts to contemplation.

Dismembering the Home in Renaissance Italy

Ann Matchette

The sixteenth century in Italy witnessed an unprecedented growth in the public sale of household furnishings. While auctions had existed in urban centres since ancient Rome to sell all manner of commodities, sales of house wares in open spaces became increasingly important in an expanding world of material goods. Common throughout Europe, auctions were an efficient way to liquidate assets. Traditionally, they were held to settle debts and raise income for the support of widows and orphans after the death of a head of household. This familiar scenario is evoked by a Florentine fresco of the late fifteenth century where the spartan interior and dispersal of furnishings signals the family's poverty

(see pl.2.24). Despite this negative image, by the mid-sixteenth century, the public sale of household goods was popular. Civic auctions were opened up to elective sales and became a central venue for the display, acquisition and disposal of domestic objects.

Apparently unlikely forms of representation of the domestic interior, auctions and auction records reveal widespread attitudes and practices. Since they were meant to document the sale of property, the records are essentially inventories of household goods along with an estimate and price paid for each item. At first glance, they are economic representations of the interior (see pl.2.25). But because they also indicate objects that did not sell or were to remain at home,

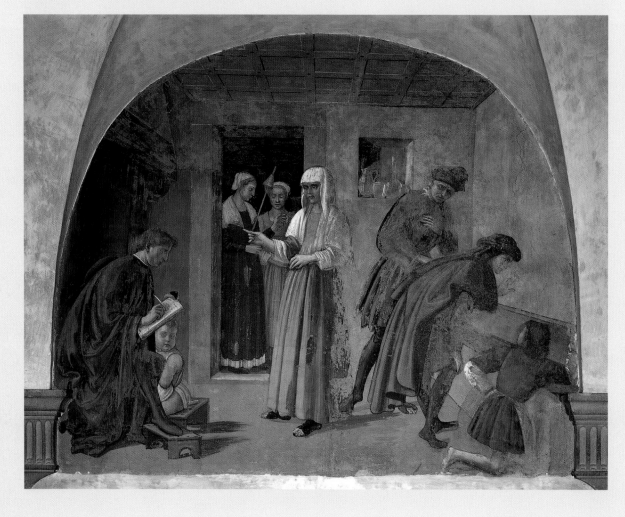

2.24
Workshop of Domenico Ghirlandaio, *A Widow Directs the Recording of Household Goods in an Interior*. Fresco. Late 15th century. Oratory of San Martino del Vescovado, Florence

2.25
Auction record of furnishings belonging to a woman named Madonna Francesca. 1551. Archivio di Stato, Florence

2.26
Scene from the *Life of St Carlo Borromeo*, Fol. 29. Late 16th century. Civica Raccolta delle Stampe Achille Bertarelli, Milan

2.27
Woven silk damask. 16th century. V&A: T.913–1899

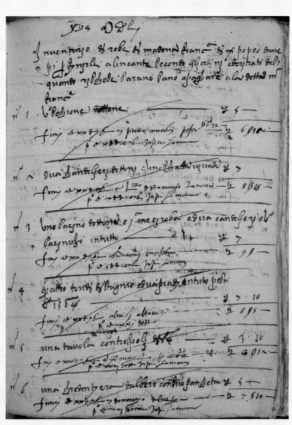

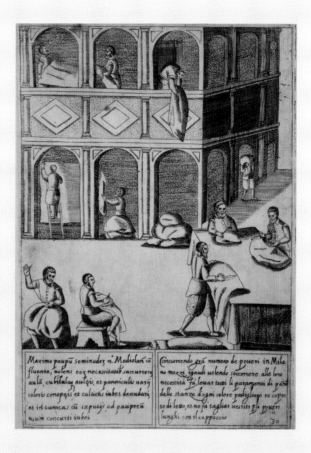

they also shed light on hierarchies of value. Successive sales from the same estate over time further reveal people's strategies for the disposal of furnishings and animate what might otherwise seem like a static picture of the home. Ultimately, the records point to a vibrant market for used furnishings before industrialization made an array of new goods available in greater quantities and at cheaper prices.

That many people's homes were affected by these sales suggests that the Italian interior was perceived as something that could be fragmented. Interiors were fluid spaces constructed not only by the walls that defined them, but also through the objects that moved into and out of the home during various points in the lifecycle of inhabitants. Furnishings too were flexible. The multi-functional rooms typical of the Renaissance were transformed by a number of mobile furnishings, such as trestle tables, benches and pillows. However, large-scale furnishings such as built-in bedsteads were also dismantled and reconfigured, either complete or recycled from constituent parts. Even aspects of the interior that might be considered integral to the architectural

fabric, such as windows, doors and mouldings, were moveable.

All of this suggests how Renaissance interiors were both transferable and transformable. Textiles, such as tapestries, curtains and bed coverings, were particularly costly, and their portability and adaptability made them well suited to new environments (see pl.2.27). But because distinctions between furnishing and garment textiles were not made until the seventeenth century, these fabrics could also be redeployed to functions outside the home. A scene from the *Life of St Carlo Borromeo* depicts a flurry of activity where the wall hangings and bed coverings furnishing Borromeo's house are dismantled and made into clothing for Milan's poor (see pl.2.26). The removal of the textiles from their domestic context is emphasized by setting the cutting and sewing of clothes outside, with men carrying bundles and dropping fabric from the loggia upstairs. While here the dissolution of the interior resulted from an act of charity, the adaptability and marketability of domestic objects ensured that no interior remained completely intact for long.

Home, Household and Domesticity in Drama in Early Modern London

Catherine Richardson

MY FOCUS HERE IS the comparatively short period from the establishment of commercial theatre in London towards the end of the sixteenth century until its closure as the Civil War takes hold in 1642. These few decades were arguably the most fertile and influential in English theatre history, and the plays they produced display their authors' passionate excitement about the possibilities of the English language. English cultural identity has to an extent been built upon the achievements of Shakespeare and, partly as a result of colonial expansion, literatures across the globe have been influenced by his plays. Just as their original dissemination was made possible by the explosion of print technology, so they remain at the centre of contemporary developing media. Television adaptations are regularly screened, and Laurence Olivier, Kenneth Branagh and Baz Luhrmann, amongst many others, have made them into commercially successful films.

In both amateur and professional contexts, 'playing Shakespeare' has been consistently popular since shortly after his death. His plays are currently performed at a reconstructed Globe Theatre on London's South Bank, as well as in one in Tokyo, and around the world from Alaska to Zimbabwe. The authors and readers, designers and clients of the following chapters of this book are likely to have been actors in, producers of, or audiences for those plays.

Stage plays offer a unique context for the representation of the domestic interior, because drama as a medium is fundamentally different to any other discussed in this volume. Reading a novel, looking at a picture, or even the television, is primarily an interior individual experience. Watching a play, like a film, involves engaging with the representation as part of a group, sensitive to the responses of those with whom one shares the experience. Furthermore, it means being a part of the story, contributing an immediate response that shapes the way the play's energies develop on that particular occasion – a subtly different experience every time it is staged. When a play represents a domestic interior, the dynamic between the public and the private, the domestic and the communal, is altered as private scenes are performed in public.

This shared view opens up all sorts of possibilities for interpretation. Everything represented on a stage is potentially called into question, because public attention is drawn to its operations and its meanings. 'Seeing' on the stage means seeing critically, looking objectively at the experiences of others and comparing them to one's own and those of other audience members. And the audiences for plays at the theatres of early modern London were by and large socially inclusive. Within this highly stratified society, high and low mixed as theatre audiences: the Venetian ambassador may have seen the same performance as a sailor from Stepney.[1]

Early modern plays often engaged in an intense form of ideological debate, and the issues they treated were frequently ones that were being hotly discussed off the stage. Their narratives focused upon issues that were of relevance to all, crucial questions of social life such as the nature of authority, the rights of the individual within the community, and the conflict between the priorities of different generations.

Because drama does not have the guiding voice of a narrator, the issues it treats become atomized into the distinct views of different characters, and the audience has a role to play in assessing their competing claims. The function of domestic settings in these debates is the subject of this essay.

The plays were staged in two main types of venue. Amphitheatre playhouses such as the Globe, the Rose, or the Swan as pictured in Johannes de Witt's sketch (see pl.3.1), had a stage projecting out into a yard in which the

3.1
Johannes de Witt.
Sketch of the Swan Theatre.
Copied by Aernout van Buchel.
*c.*1596. Rijksuniversiteit
University Library, Utrecht

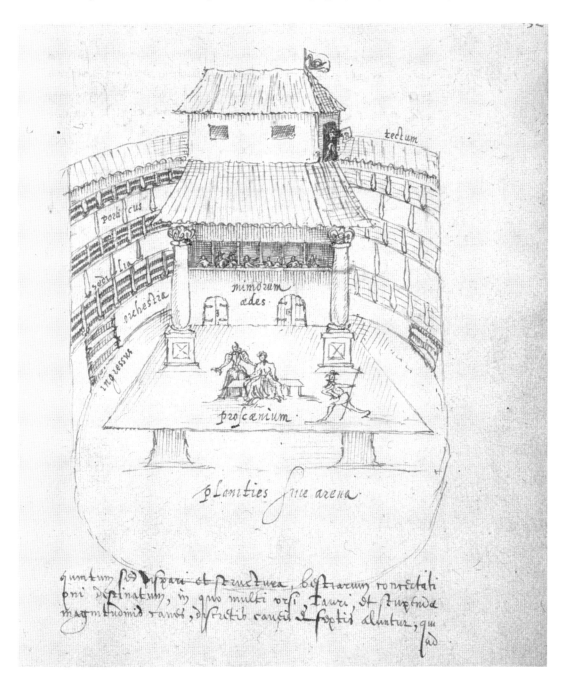

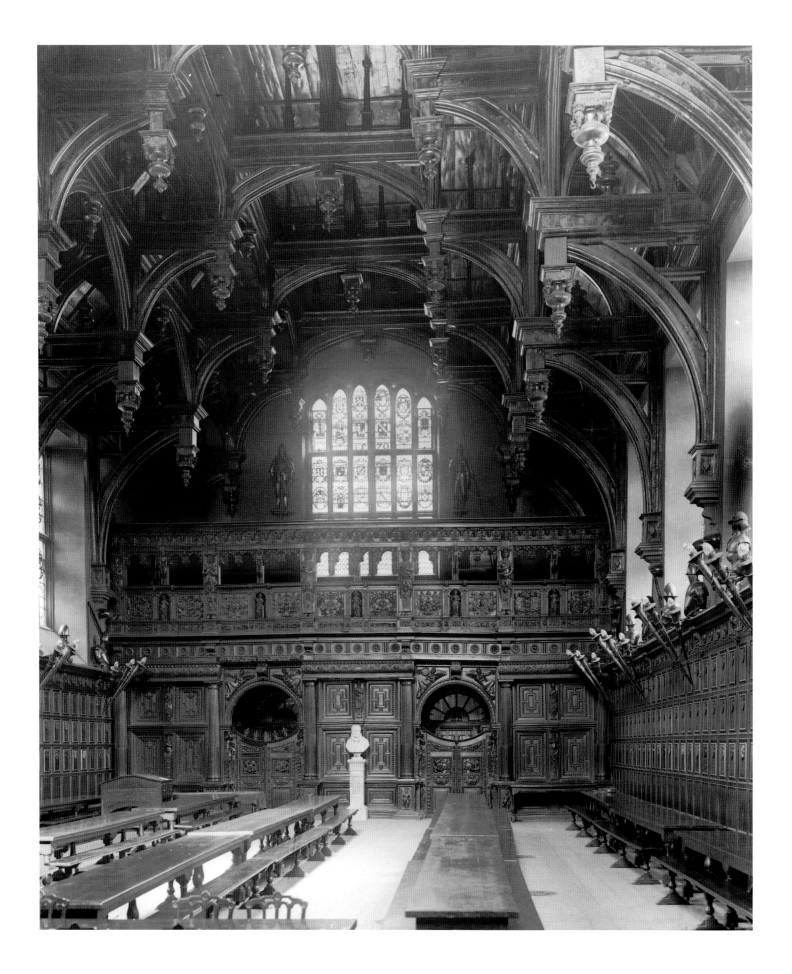

audience stood, their more prosperous peers seated behind them in several galleries. The sketch suggests doors at the rear of the stage, and pillars on it, holding up a canopy which protected the actors from the rain and amplified their voices within the crowded and noisy space.[2] The indoor playhouses, in the old monastic buildings of Blackfriars, the Middle Temple Hall in the Inns of Court (see pl.3.2) or the Banqueting House at Whitehall, are closer to the theatres with which we are familiar: an enclosed space insulated from the distractions of the weather.

These very different types of playing space seem to have encouraged particular developments in acting styles. The ambient audience noise in the amphitheatre playhouses, combined with the fact that the majority of spectators paying higher admission prices were further from the stage, seems likely to have necessitated a more vigorous style of performance. In the hall houses the situation was different. Prosperous patrons were nearest to the stage, sometimes even sitting on it, and the roof and fully seated audience made a quieter delivery possible. In both cases, in comparison to our experience of the theatre, the physical conditions of performance – with their noise, and the thrust stage which encouraged a close relationship with the audience – mitigated strongly against the illusion of 'simulated reality'.[3] But the fact that plays had to be capable of being staged in both types of arena demanded supreme flexibility in the way they represented different kinds of spaces. The representation of the domestic interior could not be solely dependent upon the enclosed spaces of the indoor playhouses, for instance, nor could it be indicated with elaborate static scenery.

Although it is the function of theatre in every age to suggest to its audience things that it cannot show them, things that are not physically present, the early modern stage was an especially 'bare' stage. Surviving inventories of properties offer invaluable evidence for the ways in which the stage of the Rose theatre was filled.[4] They include objects that suggest specific types of physical location, such as a rock, several tombs and a hell mouth, a little altar and two moss banks. There are more general indications of setting, for instance a rainbow and the cloth of the sun and moon, and there are objects that are tied to specific plays, like the 'sign for mother Redcap' and the 'cauldron for the Jew'.[5]

This is a fairly limited range of scenic properties. Only one object, a backcloth described simply as 'the city of Rome', comes close to what we would think of as scenery. But it presumably offered a vista representing the city as a whole, as a concept of 'foreign location', rather than a specific place within it. Location, then, was not tied to the physical representation that scenery offers; staging a bedchamber, for instance, certainly did not involve recreating the walls of such a room. The inventories contain a bedstead, suggesting that stage properties worked as physical indicators of interior space.

To anyone familiar with the opening Chorus to Shakespeare's *Henry V* (1598–9) this paucity of scenery will not be surprising. He initially calls for,

> a muse of fire, that would ascend
> The brightest heaven of invention:
> A kingdom for a stage, princes to
> act … (1–4)[6]

This would be a representation that transcends representation, where the gap between appearance and reality disappears. But he goes on to acknowledge that such a show would explode theatre's role as an indicator of absent possibilities:

> But pardon, gentles all,
> The flat unraiséd spirits that hath dared
> On this unworthy scaffold to bring forth
> So great an object. Can this cock-pit hold
> The vasty fields of France? (8–12)

The answer is, of course, no. This is a problem of scale, he suggests. It is simply not possible to cram France onto the stage; it can never be sufficiently represented theatrically. And it is for this reason that the actors must 'On your imaginary forces work', encouraging the audience

3.2
Hall of Middle Temple, London, where *Twelfth Night* was staged in 1602. Country Life, Picture Library

to 'suppose', to 'piece out', and to 'think' because, ''tis your thoughts that now must deck our kings' (28).

As such a bold and witty opening speech makes clear, this was a theatre that derived amusement and great power from its 'limitations'; within its disingenuous apology for physical limitation is a delight in the incredibly potent force of imagination. The comparative bareness of this stage, then, was celebrated as a fruitful conjunction of language and imagination which was never restricted by the kind of visualizations of Agincourt which have since become familiar through the medium of film.

Visualizing battlefields is a very different enterprise to staging a domestic interior, however. In *A Midsummer Night's Dream* (1595), as the citizen actors plan their play of the death-marked love of Pyramus and Thisbe in the wood outside Athens, they discuss a series of difficulties with their impending royal performance. A central one is how to overcome the fact that they 'must have a wall in the great chamber [where they are to play]; for Pyramus and Thisbe, says the story, did talk through the chink of a wall.' 'You can never bring in a wall', Snout points out somewhat obviously, but Bottom has the solution 'Some man or other must present Wall; and let him have some plaster, or some loam, or some rough-cast about him, to signify "wall"; and let him hold his fingers thus, and through that cranny shall Pyramus and Thisbe whisper' (3i, 57–66).

The humour of this absurdly cumbersome solution to the disparity between representation and reality reveals, to an audience that the play constructs as intellectually superior, a very sophisticated metatheatrical assessment of how spaces come into being on the early modern stage. If we find this funny, then we understand that, as in *Henry V*'s Prologue, 'total representation' is neither possible nor desirable. But we also see that space is in fact produced as actors describe it; setting is constructed primarily through the language that the characters speak and the gestures they make. As the literary critic Alan Dessen states, 'For the original spectator, the penthouse, bulk or hedge corner came into

existence when the actor gestured towards something (a pillar, a railing) or some place, thus giving a local habitation and a name to an otherwise neutral area (a technique used many many times in this period to "create" a city, a cave, a cell, walls, a tree, and more).'[7] Bottom and Flute should *act* the concreteness of intimacy and separation around an area of the stage which they identify as the wall. In an earlier kind of less realistic theatre, they might indeed have used symbolic props to indicate the unstageable; in this new theatre, interested in realistic representation of all human life, visual statements of fact were replaced by cues to the audience's imagination. The crucial quality of space in these plays, then, is that it is created by dramatic action. Action and setting are therefore inseparable, reciprocally shaping one another's meanings.

When the theatres opened again in 1660, after the Civil War and with Charles II on the throne, the joke about Bottom's wall had lost some of the metatheatrical complexities of its humour. This new theatre, with its aristocratic impresarios, imported several significant features of the masques that had formed such an important aspect of royal entertainment up to the Civil War. In addition to the greater levels of realism brought by having female parts played by women, action from the Restoration theatre through to the nineteenth century was framed by a proscenium arch, and surrounded by 'scenes' or flats.[8] The depth of the stage in which the narrative was played out was now encased within the border of an arch, rather than projecting out into the audience, and the use of perspective on the 'scenes' increased this impression of a depth of field in which realistic portrayal of an interior was possible. The illustration of *Romeo and Juliet* in plate 3.3 shows a world set apart. Such elaborate sets aimed to recreate exact locations, perfect illusions of a stage reality separate from the audience's experience. In the exciting world of the toy theatre, children could imagine the prostrate Desdemona speaking her final words, picturing the space in which she did so, as they cut it out and pasted it onto card (see pl.3.4, 3.5a–b).

3.3
Edwin Booth's Theatre, New York, set for *Romeo and Juliet* from the opening night, 1869. Shakespeare Birthplace Trust, Stratford-Upon-Avon

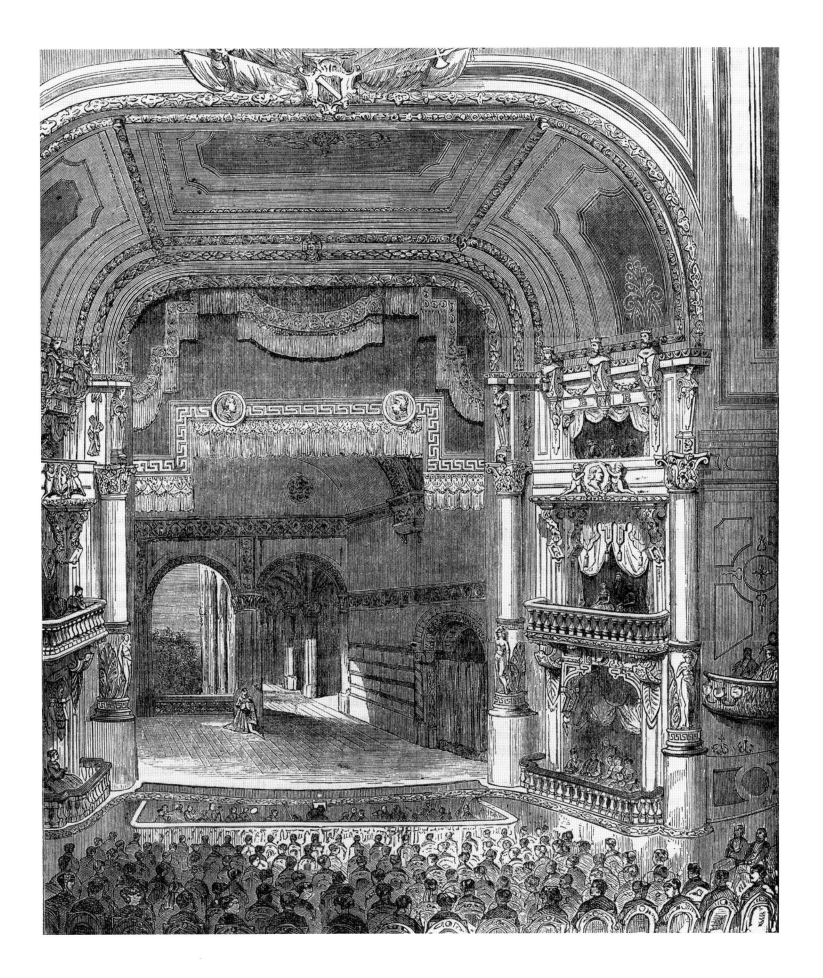

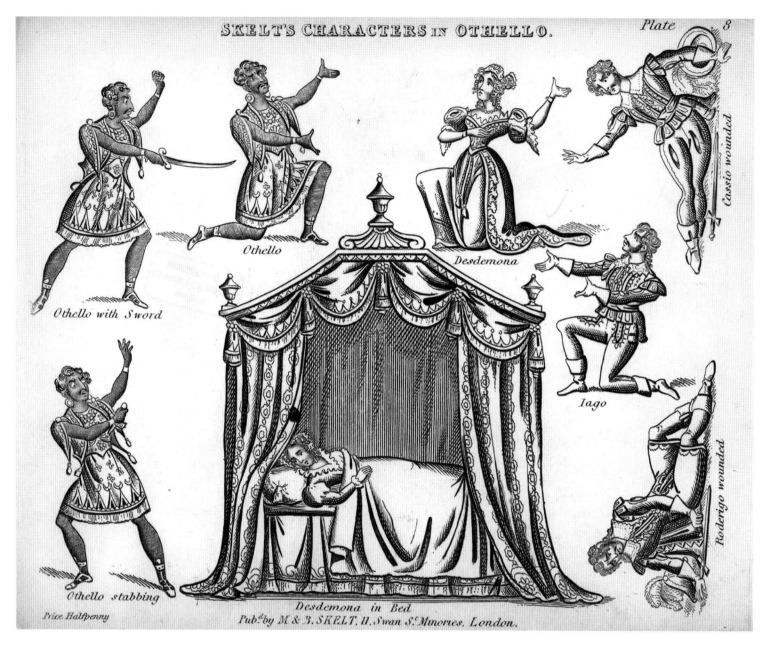

3.4

Skelt's characters in *Othello*.
Shakespeare Birthplace Trust,
Stratford-Upon-Avon

Spatial imagination became less significant in this theatre as designers limited the play of potential settings to the one that they painted on their scenery; the balance had shifted decisively from verbal to visual construction of space. By 1839 this was so well accepted that the programme for William Macready's production of *Henry V* included the telling note that, 'The narrative and descriptive poetry spoken by the Chorus is accompanied with Pictorial Illustrations from the pencil of Mr. Stanfield.'[9] These examples help to clarify the difference that realism makes to domestic representation. It allows actors and their words to inhabit, rather than help the viewer create, a sense of inside space, and it separates setting from action. It is not that the visual aspects of performance were unimportant in the early modern theatre, rather that they did not do the work of illusion, of situating action; whilst props and the bodies of the actors themselves characterized space, they did not contain or envelop it.

The meanings generated by domestic interiors on stage are partly determined by genre because the subject matter of comedies, histories and tragedies call for different types of household scene. In the majority of cases, the

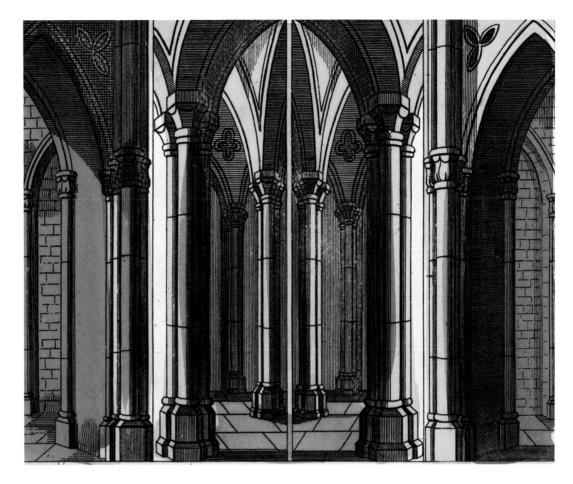

3.5a
Hall wings, Skelt's sets for
Othello. Shakespeare Birthplace
Trust, Stratford-Upon-Avon

3.5b
Curtain wings, Skelt's sets for
Othello. Shakespeare Birthplace
Trust, Stratford-Upon-Avon

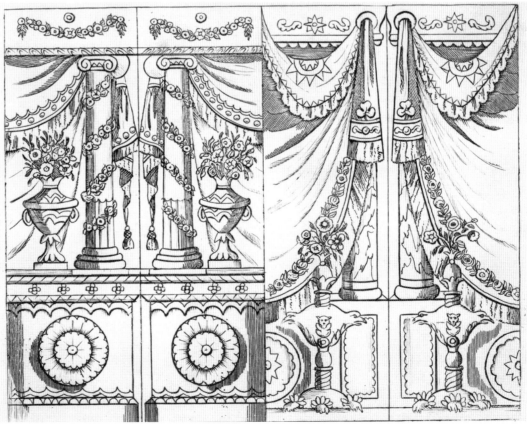

domestic setting was subordinate to other locations, interactions staged there providing a contrast to those taking place outside. Shakespeare's early comedy *The Two Gentlemen of Verona* (1590–1), for instance, begins with a conversation between two young men, one interested in love and one in travel:

> VALENTINE Cease to persuade,
>   my loving Proteus.
> Home-keeping youth have
>   ever homely wits.
> Were't not affection chains thy tender days
> To the sweet glances of thy honoured love,
> I rather would entreat thy company
> To see the wonders of the world abroad
> Than, living dully sluggardized at home,
> Wear out thy youth with
>   shapeless idleness.

Proteus is 'home-keeping' in the sense that he will relinquish the enticing delights of Milan to remain in Verona, not in the sense that he will remain within his house. It is a home comprised of ties of affection and the necessity of staying within eye-shot of the beloved, and characterized, by a Valentine eager to leave the town for 'wonders', as idle, dull and sluggardly. The location is domestic, in other words, to the extent that the subject is, but we have little sense of a domestic interior. Home is family, clarifying the significance of parting which is played out in comic terms in another scene between the servant Lance and his 'sour-natured' dog Crab who, 'My mother weeping, my father wailing, my sister crying, our maid howling, our cat wringing her hands, and all our house in a great perplexity', did not 'shed one tear' (2iii, 5–9). Only the 'pebble-stone' pitiless dog can restrain his emotions as Valentine's household leaves his father's behind, and the *idea* of the house acts as a foil for the energies of youth and the breadth of masculine opportunity.

But home also positively signifies intimacy, such as the confidences between Julia, Proteus's beloved, and her maid Lucetta. At their entry in Act 1, Scene ii the former states 'But say,

Lucetta, now we are alone – / Wouldst thou then counsel me to fall in love?'. The intensity of this scene, its emotions understood but not fully articulated between mistress and servant, is economically set up in this opening line, their seclusion necessary for and conducive to the discussion of love between two women. These conventional associations between love and privacy develop through the scenes of suggested and actual spatial distinction between lover and beloved, in which Valentine plans to ascend to Sylvia's window on a rope ladder and Proteus and Thurio serenade her at that same window. Separating the qualities of the interior from some of the meanings of domesticity, the upper stage is used to represent the inaccessibility of the house as it symbolizes the unattainable heart and body of the lover.

Part of comedy's ideological project is to insure that the energies of youthful rebellion and unacceptable passion are subsumed within the crucial institution of marriage. The symbolic significance of the interior and the more stable and conservative meanings of the domestic need, in other words, to be brought together.

Domestic scenes are far less numerous in history plays because the genre focuses upon affairs of state and shifting royal fortunes on the battlefield. But the household enables exploration of national issues through the contrast of a smaller scale of action, and an investigation of the personal implications of national politics. In an odd little scene in *1 Henry VI* (1592), the Countess of Auvergne tries to trick the English champion Lord Talbot by inviting him to 'visit her poor castle' (2ii, 41). The first act has been taken up with a variety of skirmishes in which the town of Orleans changes hands several times, and Burgundy makes the point that such a meeting would offer a distinct change of tone: 'I see our wars / Will turn unto a peaceful comic sport, / When ladies crave to be encountered with' (44–6). In a sentiment famously encapsulated in Richard Gloucester's distinction in *Richard III* (1592–3) between 'mounting barbed steeds / To fright the souls of fearful adversaries' and capering 'nimbly in a lady's chamber / To the lascivious pleasing of a lute' (1i, 10–3), the lords joke about this intrusion of a possible seduction, in the wake of the sounding of retreat and with the Earl of Salisbury's body still onstage awaiting burial. As these lords exit through the doors at the back of the stage, the Countess simultaneously enters with her Porter, naming him as such and admonishing him to 'remember what I gave in charge,/ And when you have done so, bring the keys to me.' (2iii). The interior of her castle is established through the presence of these two characters, and the prominence of the keys which symbolize the most important quality of domestic space, its capacity to be controlled and contained.

This juxtaposition of public and private scenes is used here to question the distinction between war and peace, masculinity and femininity. When the Countess meets Talbot she feigns surprise at his physical presence: 'report is fabulous and false./ I thought I should have seen some Hercules,/ A second Hector'. 'It cannot be', she continues, 'this weak and writhled shrimpt/ Should strike such terror into his enemies.' (17–23) Her insults draw attention to the gap between military reputations and physical substance, and between the field of war and the household as offering different scales of action. The Countess lies about recognizing him, and Talbot too has been dishonest and has not, as he promised, come alone. Describing himself as 'Talbot's shadow' rather than his substance, he tells a riddle of the relationship between a commander and his army: 'what you see is but the smallest part/ And least proportion of humanity./ I tell you, madam, were the whole frame here,/ It is of such a spacious lofty pitch/ Your roof were not sufficient to contain't.' (52–6) The soldiers who enter when he blows his horn 'are his substance, sinews, arms, and strength'. Like *Henry V*'s Prologue, he points out the uncontainableness of the army, but here in relation to the Countess's domestic space and as a comment upon her attempt to bring the household into play as an arena for a kind of 'feminine war'. Talbot's riddle, coupled with the Countess's joke about the diminishment of proportions involved in comparing great men to their reputations, is given meaning by their location within a domestic space as opposed to a public one. They vividly suggest the idea of a space that is fitted to the human body, designed around and given meaning by its needs and its proportions. It is the juxtaposition of these different contexts for different types of conflict and stability that gives domestic space its particular significance in plays about national events.

The tragedy of *Romeo and Juliet* (1595), we are told, springs from the 'new mutiny' between '[t]wo households', and its patterning of different kinds of space is instructive in just those terms. The play rotates its action between the open street, the public areas of the Capulet house with their stately routines of festivity, the balcony which is positioned between the house and the world outside, Friar Lawrence's cell and the Capulet tomb. The distinction between public and domestic spaces mediates the play's progression from comedic courtship to the tragic forms of mischance. Juliet is introduced by her mother's and nurse's discussion of her childhood, in a domestic scene defined by its subject matter and by the striking presence of three women alone on the stage together after the opening frictions and negotiations between men. As the young couple's fresh love begins to develop in 2i, Juliet's attention is divided between Romeo in the garden below her, and her nurse in the bedroom behind her. The tension of their illicit liaison is expressed spatially through the relationship between the house and the world outside it, and Romeo's night in Juliet's chamber represents a heavily symbolic penetration into the heart of the Capulet mansion.

But in the eighteenth century it was the play's final space, the tomb, which provided the environment for a particular kind of emotional climax. David Garrick, actor, playwright and great promoter of Shakespeare's work, had written extra material for this scene. He gave the lovers a brief reunion before death, an emotional crescendo that demanded a fitting setting: 'It was not only the elaborate design of the tomb and the suggestions of landscape and moonlight that engineered the effect. The closed space, claustrophobic and confined, distant from the audience, emphasized the intensity of the scene, allowing Garrick's largest addition to the play its full emotional scope.' (see pl.3.6).[10] The interpolated reunion offered eighteenth-century sensibilities a negative counterpart to the couples' joyful union in Juliet's chamber.

Although Garrick created this moment, the deeply painful emotions of tragedy recall a particular kind of focused intimacy found in other Shakespearean scenes. For instance Hamlet, thinking he is alone with his mother in her closet, tells her to 'Come, come, and sit you down' so that he can 'set you up a glass/ Where you may see the inmost part of you' (III, iv, 18–20). The chair that this invitation presupposes serves to anchor the scene to a particular spot. The 'glass' he shows her is 'The counterfeit presentment of two brothers' (53), the pictures of her current and erstwhile husbands, and the intensity of mother and son's focus upon these images then develops the illusion of a 'closet', a bounded space. The other aspect of the boundedness of this scene is the shattering of privacy, first by the presence of Polonius and then by the entrance of the ghost. In *Ham-*

3.6
Benjamin Wilson, *David Garrick as Romeo, George Anne Bellamy as Juliet and Charles Blakes as Tybalt in* Romeo and Juliet.
Oil on canvas. *c.*1753. V&A/ Theatre Museum, London.
V&A: S.1452-1986

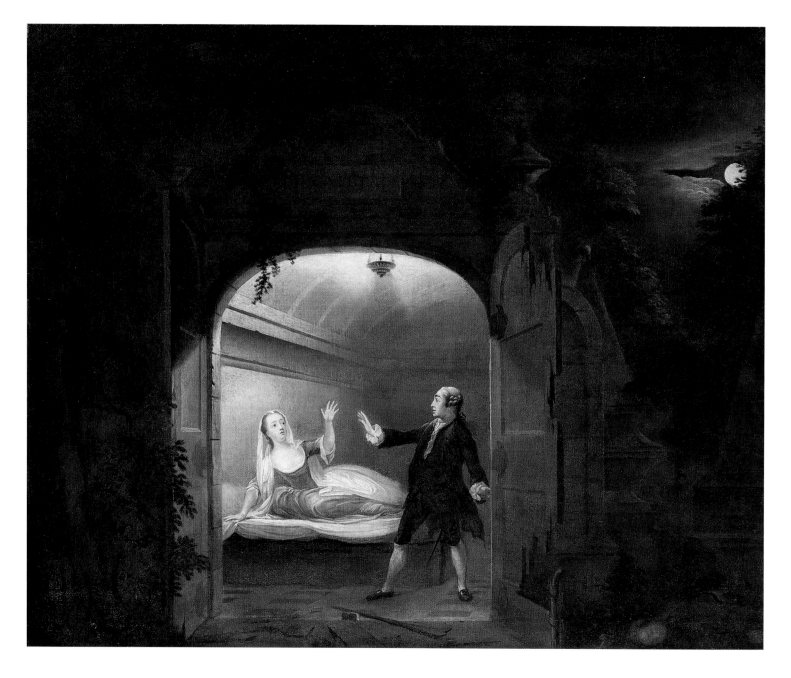

let (1600–1), kindred and a brutal honesty are the dynamics around which domestic space takes shape, as the competing intimacies of the prince's passionate quest for justice and the 'rank sweat' of Claudius's 'enseamed bed' are opened out to particularly fierce emotional competition in Gertrude's closet.

In *Othello* (1603–4), the marriage that has been the play's subject is revealed as an intimacy only in the last scene, as we finally see husband and wife alone together in their chamber. The darkness that is indicated by Othello's entry '*with a light*' and his discovery of Desdemona '*asleep in her bed*' (Vii) insists upon a rapt attention to the dynamic between them. And again it is a domestic prop, the bed, which structures and directs the intimacy of the scene, focusing the audience's attention. It signals her isolation, the exclusion of the other characters and the elimination of external reason which Othello's mental state has caused.

The intimacy of these intense interiors is perversely crystalized by the threat of physical entry posed by characters from outside. But it is also threatened emotionally by those inside, and the signalling of such a restricted domestic space for the scenes serves to point up the characters' complicated and destructive attitudes towards 'home' as a location for family.

◆

Unlike many of his contemporary playwrights, Shakespeare generally holds his examination of politically significant issues at one remove. He sets his plays in past times or foreign locations, and peoples them with characters of noble or gentle birth. For the majority of audiences for these plays, constructing the mansions of men like Capulet or the palaces of Cyprus or Elsinor, with their halls, closets, great chambers and balconies in their minds involved recourse to the imagination, rather than the memory. Their experience was of smaller houses embedded within local communities, around which communal as well as familial issues were negotiated. In the houses depicted in plates 3.7–3.9 inhabitants could hear their neighbours through flimsy partitions, they could look out of the windows and see them going about their business in their yards and in the street. The reality of early modern houses was that aural and even visual privacy was extremely hard to find, and in any case morally suspect in a life led in communal view.

One of Shakespeare's plays stands out in this context because it does stage a recognizable contemporary household of middling status, one which mediates the values and concerns of the local community. *The Merry Wives of Windsor* (1597–8) is a play about women's sexual honesty, and it concerns itself with very contemporary issues about women's work and their role within the household. As a result, the domestic interior is a considerably more prominent feature of its staging and its narrative. In one plotline, Sir John Falstaff arranges meetings with the two Windsor wives, Mistress Page and Mistress Ford, in order to lay hands on their husbands' money. Of the three trysts which the wives arrange to teach him a lesson, two take place within the Fords' house. In the first, Falstaff is forced to jump into a buck-basket in which dirty laundry is being taken to be washed as Mr Ford is approaching the house and likely to discover him. The domestic location of the scene is set up through the wives' instructions to the servants:

> MISTRESS FORD What, John!
>   What, Robert!
> MISTRESS PAGE Quickly, quickly!
>   Is the buck-basket –
> MISTRESS FORD I warrant, –
>   What, Robert, I say!
> *Enter John and Robert, with a buck-basket*
> MISTRESS PAGE Come, come, come!
> (3iii,1–4)

The comedy of this scene in particular is generated by the wives' ability to hide their famously over-weight would-be lover within the house. Just as John and Robert are leaving with their heavy load of washing, Master Page, the Doctor and Sir Hugh the parson enter, led by Master Ford, who invites them to search his house for his wife's lover:

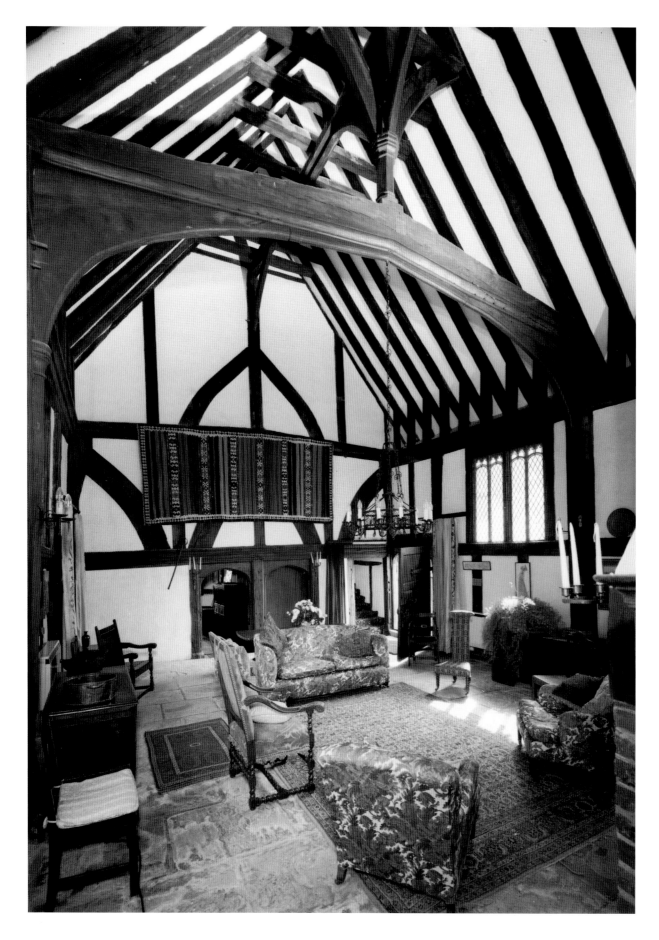

3.7
The open hall, Dukes
Place, West Peckham,
Kent. English Heritage

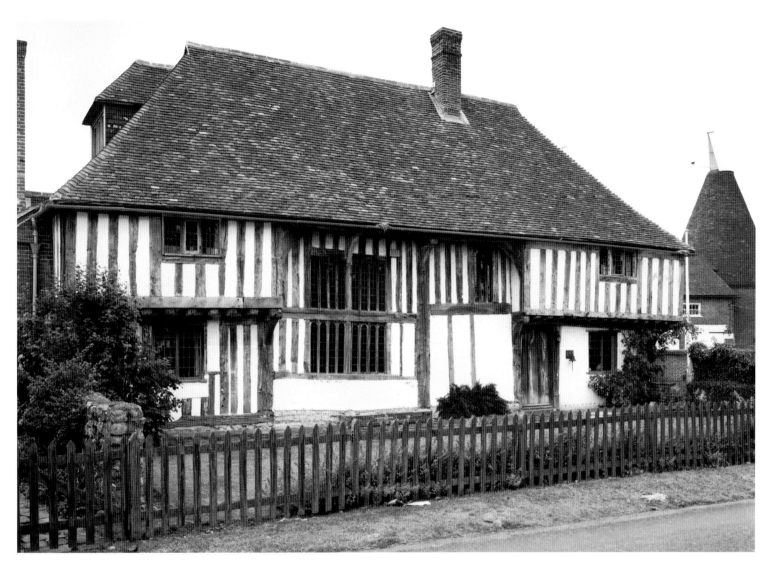

3.8

Exterior showing the recessed hall in the centre of the building, Shieling Hall, Langley, Kent. English Heritage

Here, here, here be my keys. Ascend
my chambers, search, seek, find out.
I'll warrant we'll unkennel the fox.
Let me stop this way first.
He locks the door
So, now, uncoop. (154–7)

Ford locks one of the doors at the back of the stage at this point, ironically stressing the importance of being able to control the domestic space as he tries to lock his wife's 'lover' inside. With the rallying cry of 'Up, gentlemen!' he leads his friends and neighbours offstage, on a tour of the rest of his property. For the next 20 lines, the wives are left on stage discussing their jest, and the audience are left to imagine the men searching the upper chambers for the knight. The metonymic representation which

the stage space offers, of a part of a house against which the whole is measured, makes the whole domestic interior present without the need for scenery. It employs the audience's imagination to consider what might be happening offstage, where the men might be searching, and therefore what this house is like.

The significance of this scene is infinitely greater, however, when it is seen in relation to the moral and political meanings of the household outside the theatre in this period. Plays such as *Merry Wives*, which staged recognizably contemporary households familiar to their audiences, invited spectators to compare staged representation to extra-theatrical practice. And the household was central to the ways in which social order was achieved in early modern England. Men and women lived in constant fear of

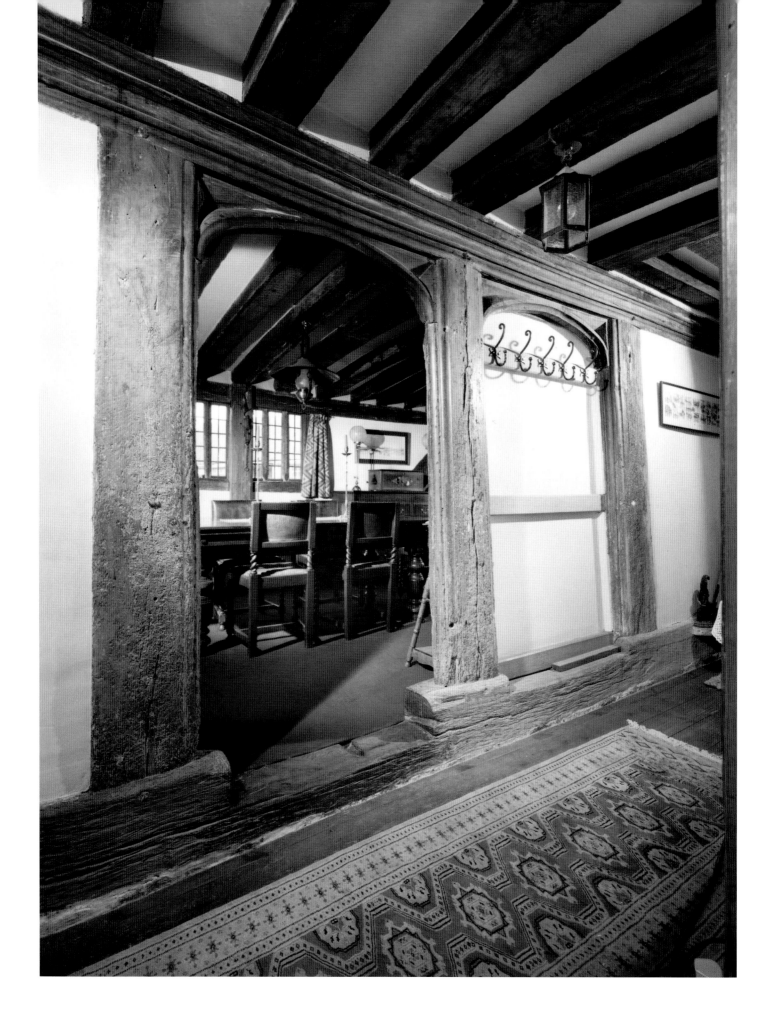

communal disorder; patriarchy was the dominant mode of social organization because it was thought to be the most effective way of ensuring that someone was responsible for the behaviour of each individual, with a vested interest in guaranteeing their peaceful conduct. This need for responsibility generated a focus on the dynamics of power – the relationship between those who were in authority and those who owed them obedience. In exploring these dynamics, early modern writers saw society as a series of related spheres, in which a man's control over his household was directly analogous to the magistrate's government of his community, and the king's command over the subjects of his realm. In the same way that living in England made individuals subject to her rules and her monarch, so living within the household made all its members subject to the supposedly wise rulership of its head. The *Homilie Agaynst Disobedience and Wylful Rebellion* (1570), one of the ready-made sermons appointed to be read in all churches, stated that in order to avoid a universal anarchy God had 'ordayned that in families and housholdes, the wyfe shoulde be obedient unto her husbande, the children unto their parentes, the servantes unto their maisters.'[11]

'Private life' begins to disappear as 'a conscionable performance of houshold duties, in regard of the end and fruit thereof, may be accounted a publike worke';[12] there can be no works that are not public in their implications, if not in their location, and therefore all human activity must be performed well, it must tend towards order. The binary between public and private, open and closed, house and community, was therefore of the utmost political significance.

In his conduct manual about household roles the preacher Robert Cleaver stressed that 'For the houshold, when their maister and their mistresse, or dame, are at debate, can no otherwise bee in quiet, and at rest, then a cittie, whose Rulers agree not'.[13] His insistence makes clear the wider significance of the disagreement and distrust between the Fords in *Merry Wives*. Every representation of domestic disorder offered audiences a taste of the uni-

versal anarchy that might occur if husbands lost control of the house. Realistic portrayal of contemporary houses of the non-élite in some plays of this period therefore offered a representation of the domestic interior that was simultaneously strikingly realistic and shockingly symbolic of the political.

Within the comic form there need be little engagement with the strong emotions that occasion and are generated by domestic anarchy, however, and situations are capable of being resolved in theatrical ways. *Merry Wives* eliminates the bitterness of jealousy through the transformative power of Falstaff's penance, dressed in antlers and pinched by fairies in Windsor forest. But the significance of domestic order also gave rise to a subgenre of tragedy, a handful of plays referred to as domestic tragedies because of their intense focus upon the significance of the household as a location for adultery and murder. It is these plays, above all others in the period, which treat the house both as location for, and subject of, their narratives.

Domestic tragedies were often based on true stories, for instance, *The lamentable and true tragedie of M. Arden of Feversham in Kent, who was most wickedlye murdred, by the meanes of his disloyall and wanton wife …* (1590).[14] They were stories that had captured the public imagination because of the shocking nature of the crimes involved, crimes in which those crucial power relations of the household were undermined when women murdered their husbands in their own parlours at the bidding of their lust, husbands killed their children in their bed-chambers whilst in the grip of madness, or neighbour murdered neighbour in the garret at the prompting of greed.

Rather than exploiting the kind of contrasts between domestic and non-domestic settings examined above, these plays are based firmly within the household. They offer instead contrasts between different rooms, or between the domestic and the street outside the door. They often focus on the doors at the rear of the stage as a way of drawing attention to the extent to which it is possible to maintain the barrier between inside and outside. In his friend

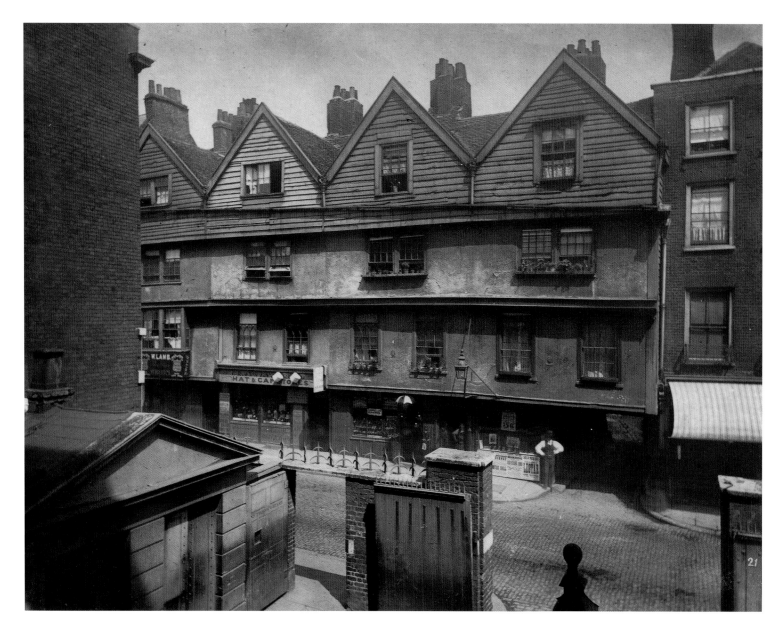

Franklin's house, the soon-to-be-murdered Arden of Faversham's servant agrees to leave the doors unlocked for the assassins. The audience see Arden giving himself an unwitting reprieve by trying these doors from the inside, and then, when they have been re-locked, the assassins try the same doors in the next scene – now representing the outside of the house. Characters publicly assess their motives for such actions. Loyalty, which should tie those within the house to one another and keep others on the outside, is a subject of intense interest.

Props are particularly significant in these plays; in addition to key individual objects such as beds, they are used in some numbers to build up a sense of domestic space. Arden's death is made all the more shocking by its location in his parlour, amongst the table, stools and chair that have been provided for the guests whom he has invited for dinner. The woodcut from the 1633 quarto of the play (see pl.3.11) conveys a sense of a crowded scene which an audience might reconstruct from repeated mentions of spatial relations and proximity in the dialogue.

The properties associated with dining are also prevalent. Scene 8 of *A Woman Killed With Kindness* (1603), for instance, begins with the stage direction, '*Enter 3 or 4 Servingmen, one with a voider and a wooden knife to take away all, another the salt and bread, another the tablecloth and napkins, another the carpet. Jenkin with two lights after them.'* The insistence which such a display of domestic plenty puts upon the provision of hospitality is ironically undercut by the less-than-hospitable murders and sexual encounters with which guests and subordinates reward their hosts. It is a characteristic of these plays that the scenes in which domestic life is particularly insistently presented are those in which its meanings are threatened, and the fullness of representation comments ironically on the way action undercuts the careful hierarchies of the household.

Dialogue ties those objects into the webs of interpersonal conflict, making the connection between objects, spaces and the intensity of emotion: When John Frankford banishes his wife for adultery in *A Woman Killed With Kindness*, he articulates their separation through the material qualities of their household: 'Choose thee a bed and hangings for a chamber; Take with thee everything that hath thy mark.' (xiii, 163–4). The domestic interior has meaning within the action as ground for the tragedy and as a way of exploring its implications.

Domesticity is a powerful force in early modern drama then, offering playwrights a way of contrasting the small and the large, the national and the personal, the public and the private across a range of genres; and the idea of the interior offers a forceful intensity in which relationships can be fully explored. But their combination in full, contemporary representations of the domestic interior is comparatively rare. When such representations do occur those connections between action and setting which make this theatre so powerful are at their most compelling.

Seeing the domestic interior critically, ruptured as it is in tragedy, or with its meanings brought into focus around marriage as is the case in comedy, means thinking explicitly about its significance. In such a theatre the call to imagine is also, implicitly, a call to compare, and the process of comparison mediates the ideologies of household: staged representation, ideologies of appropriate behaviour and personal practice are brought together by the imagination. In a period in which the public nature of domestic conduct underpinned social order, audience interaction with and judgement of such representations in the public theatre was of considerable political importance.

3.11

Arden of Faversham.
Woodcut. 1633. Huntington Library, San Marino, California

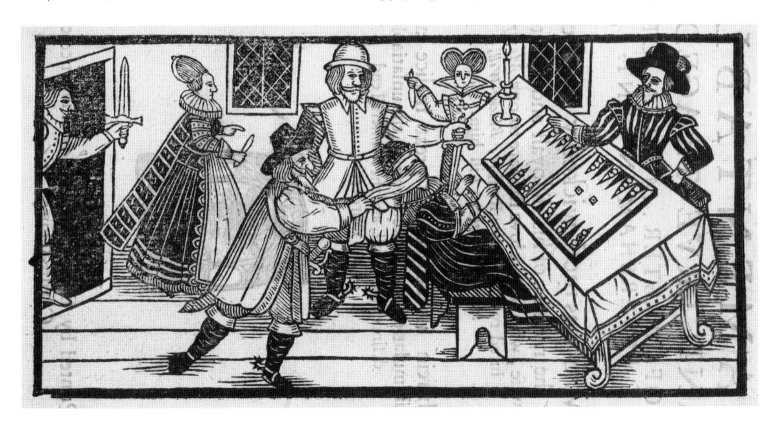

Domestic Life: instructing on the art of living well

Marta Ajmar-Wollheim

During the early modern period in Italy domestic advice underwent an extensive conceptualization both in writing and visually. Ideas and concerns at the heart of domesticity – regarding financial matters, gender relations and roles, the upbringing of children and the management of servants and personal health – gained unprecedented importance within literature and the visual arts.

Domestic advice writings – covering subjects as diverse as building and household management, devotion, needlework and even medical recipes – changed substantially between the fifteenth and sixteenth centuries. They generally evolved from being rhetorically-charged texts, heavily indebted to classical precedents, or manuals inspired by Christian ideals, to being more hands-on practical guides to everyday living. Thanks to the invention and developments in printing, many of these prescriptive books – often carefully indexed for easy consultation and generally produced in formats for all budgets – became more subject-specific and more widely available.

Prosperous domesticity was seen to depend on the relationship between husband and wife, presented as clear cut and naturally instituted. In his treatise on household management, *Della Economica* (see pl.3.14), Giacomo Lanteri prescribes the duties of the husband and of the wife in two separate books. A good housewife must know how to obey her husband and to execute his orders, and her domestic authority is defined as complementary to his. She is expected to perform her duties indoors, while he looks after the external activities. She is assigned a conservative role, that is, taking care of the existing possessions and running the household,

3.12
Giuseppe Maria Mitelli, *Gioco delle donne e sue facende* (Game of Women and their Chores). Engraving. *c.*1690. Civica Raccolta delle Stampe Achille Bertarelli, Milan

3.13
(detail of 3.12)

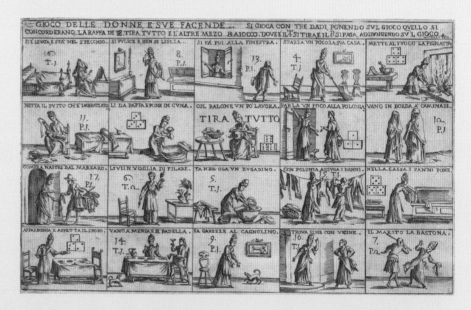

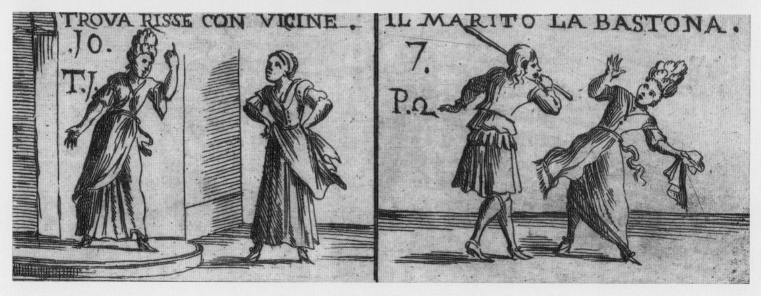

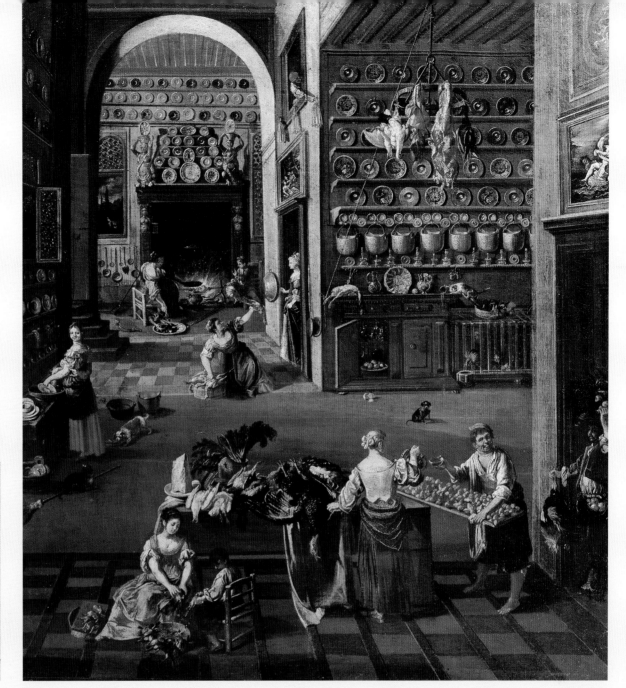

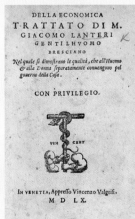

while he is endowed with acquisitive skills. Order is the principle ruling this belief system.

Visual sources often subvert this scheme, thus arguably providing insights into domestic practice. The precarious position of the lady of the house is illustrated in this fantastic representation of a kitchen by the Venice-based painter Joseph Heintz (see pl.3.15). While she appears at the threshold to impart directions, her authority is playfully undermined by the conventional motifs of the cat spilling wine and the *garzone* getting drunk on the house wine. A more complex scenario is represented in the allegedly moralizing print *Gioco delle donne e sue facende* (see pl.3.12–13) by the prolific printmaker Giuseppe Maria Mitelli of Bologna. The protagonist is a married

woman of adequate means, as can be gathered from her furnishings and from the presence of a servant. The woman's day is paced according to a tight schedule of chores, including sweeping, cooking, nursing her baby, sewing and laundering. However, she is diverted from her duties – engaging in conversation at the window with a male passer-by and arguing with her neighbour – and this leads her husband to beat her soundly. In fact, this misogynistic print is a sheet designed to play raffle with dice and money, an activity in which both men and women engaged passionately. Seen in this light, this print's agency as a table game comes to the fore and with it the ironic undermining of its supposedly exemplary role about domestic living.

Renaissance Prints and the Home

Elizabeth Miller

Printmaking consists of the creation of multiple examples of the same image usually on sheets of paper. The earliest European prints date from just before 1400, and until 1600 most European prints were woodcuts, engravings or etchings. Prints are mass-produced objects and with careful handling it is possible to produce over 1,000 prints from an engraved plate and even more from a woodcut block. It is this multiplication of images that made the new technique of printmaking such an extraordinarily powerful and transforming medium of communication in the Renaissance. Many Renaissance prints drew on the same repertoire of Christian imagery as medieval painting and manuscript illumination.

Even a simple German woodcut dating from 1460–80 of the Madonna and Child (see pl.3.16),

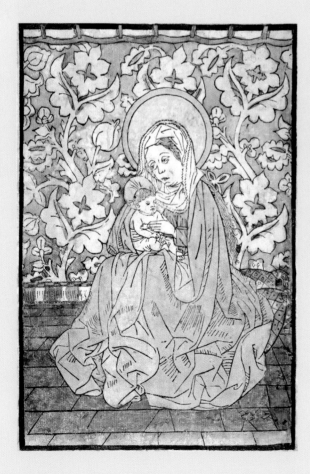

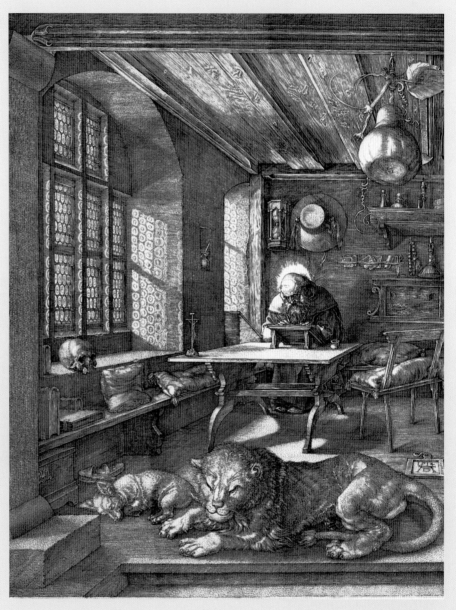

3.16
Anon., *The Virgin and Child Seated before a Curtain*. Woodcut coloured by hand. 1460–80. The British Museum, London

3.17
Albrecht Dürer, *St Jerome in his Study*. Engraving. 1514. V&A: E.4624-1910

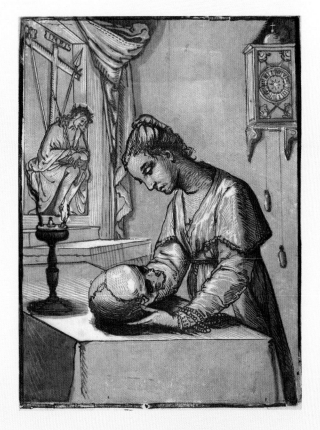

The sculpted altarpiece of Christ as a Man of Sorrows, the rosary looped twice around the woman's wrist, again a skull, and the clock on the wall topped by a crucifix all convey ideas of piety and awareness of the transience of human existence.

The fourth, an etching (see pl.3.19), incorporates lettering in Latin, specifying that the section of arched wall with grotesque decoration depicted is in the Vatican Palace in Rome, residence of the Pope. That the composition does not precisely correspond to what was actually painted on one part of the wall in the barrel-vaulted balcony for taking the air, known as the Logetta of Bibbiena, should not detract from the significance of this print as an attempt to record and disseminate the appearance of an aspect of a real interior.

contains a surprising amount of domestic detail. The Madonna is of a type known as the Madonna of Humility because she sits on the floor rather than a chair (albeit on two tasselled cushions). The floor is covered with tiles, some of which are cracked. Behind the Madonna hangs a fringed floral furnishing textile suspended by loops from a wooden pole.

Generally engravings enjoyed a higher status than woodcuts. *St Jerome in his Study* (see pl.3.17) is an outstanding example of the art by Albrecht Dürer. It demonstrates Dürer's interest in perspective and includes objects that are symbolic (the skull, the cardinal's hat) with the practical (the writing slope, the ink pot) and the homely (the cast-off shoes). The effect of bright sunlight casting a shadow of the glazing arrangement on the window recesses hints at the world beyond this scholarly space.

Printmaking liberated artists to explore new sorts of imagery. The other four images in the set from which the third print comes (see pl.3.18) are of conventional saints or scenes from the Life of Christ. In contrast, this print shows an unidentified woman in contemporary dress standing near a domestic altar.

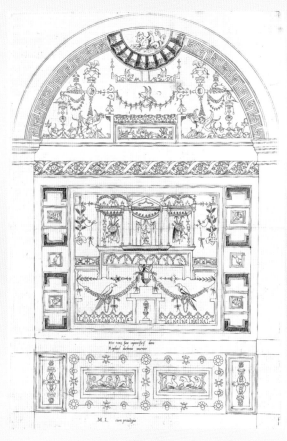

4

Between Reality and Artful Fiction: the representation of the domestic interior in seventeenth-century Dutch art

John Loughman

A KEEN AWARENESS of domesticity is often believed to be a defining attribute of the Dutch during the seventeenth century. For many observers, various modern concepts of the home and family life first took root in the Northern Netherlands: a desire for privacy and retreat from the outside world, the development of relationships between parents and children based on careful nurturing and mutual respect, and a sense of pride in the appearance and cleanliness of one's dwelling.[1]

Newly independent from the Habsburg Empire, this tiny country (variously referred to as the Dutch Republic, the Northern Netherlands, the United Provinces and increasingly as Holland in deference to its most powerful province) was a seedbed of artistic creation with hundreds of painters producing in excess of five million paintings during the course of the century.[2] Among their most recognizable productions are painted representations of the domestic interior, which have disproportionately shaped our notion of how contemporary households appeared and functioned.[3] These depictions reveal a light-filled, secluded and neatly organized domestic world peopled by a relatively limited range of types such as virtuous and hard-

working housewives and their maids, playful contented children and gallant suitors.[4]

For most of Western Europe in the early modern period the typical household model was nuclear in that it consisted of a single couple, who generally married in their mid- to late-twenties, and what few children were fortunate to survive infancy.[5] Alternatively, because of the high mortality rates, the family unit could comprise a widow or widower with or without children. In the Dutch Republic, however, the insularity of the family was more pronounced than in neighbouring countries. The household was considerably smaller, particularly in the western and northern provinces, averaging 3.5 to 4.0 persons. Homes with a live-in servant or an apprentice were the exception rather than the norm. The economic historians Jan de Vries and Ad van der Woude also point to other, more difficult to quantify, aspects of seventeenth-century Dutch family life that they consider characteristic of the modern nuclear family, such as growing affectionate relationships between family members, a more equal companionable relationship between husband and wife, and the declining power of the extended family and neighbours to impact on the individual family unit.[6]

Dutch domestic life

Various explanations have been offered for the peculiarly inward-looking nature of domestic life in seventeenth-century Holland. Certainly advanced urbanization and commercial capitalism created new economic opportunities for men and women and eroded the traditional alliance between the immediate family and more distant kin. Although the official Calvinist church never dominated religious life, and other creeds were allowed to flourish, Protestantism had a major impact on marriage and the family.[7] Marriage was no longer regarded as morally inferior to a celibate existence and became a civil contract legislated, regulated and occasionally dissolved by the state. By insisting that parental consent was essential for marriage, Protestants restored the authority of the paterfamilias. Patriarchy was also encouraged in other ways and the respective roles of the husband and wife were repeatedly outlined; the most widely read moralist writer, Jacob Cats, addressed his remarks specifically to women in successive stages of life, listing their duties in the service of husband, family and home.[8] The male head provided for the family and represented it in the outside world; his wife raised the children, administered the household budget and undertook all the domestic duties, including the supervision of maids. Although married women had strong legal rights and were sometimes involved in independent trading activity, especially in continuing the business of a husband who was deceased or overseas, their position was always a subordinate one.[9] The family was to become a microcosm of the Dutch state, a 'little church' where children received their basic religious education and were inculcated with values and good manners.

The seventeenth century saw dramatic advancements in the material circumstances of the Dutch. Until the latter part of the eighteenth century, the Dutch Republic enjoyed the highest standard of living in Europe; wages were higher and inflation practically non-existent. While this wealth did not filter down to all sectors of society, it did mean that the purchasing power of most Dutch people, particularly in the Holland and Zeeland towns, was unparalleled at this time.[10] Not surprisingly their houses filled up with a vast range of fashionable and often luxurious commodities. Gradually during the course of the century, massive linen cupboards, often with intricate carvings, bulbous feet, and inlaid or veneered with varieties of exotic wood, began to replace the chest as the principal repository of textiles, clothing and family valuables. In a painting of 1663, Pieter de Hooch gives great prominence to an impressive cupboard inlaid with ebony and to the housewife who carefully takes the freshly washed and pressed linen from a maid (see pl.4.1). While the mistress is distinguished from her subordinate through the expensive fur-trimmed jacket that she wears and by her authoritative posture, the two work in silent and harmonious partnership. Linen, often kept under lock and key as testified by the De Hooch painting, was among the most prized possessions of a household and formed a substantial part of a bride's dowry; in upper-class homes individual pieces were embroidered with the owner's initials and rigorously detailed in inventories. Increasingly sculptural and lavish in their decoration, linen cupboards were indicators of wealth and status.[11] Also during the seventeenth century, a variety of chairs designed for comfort and decoration rather than utility superseded the heavy oak benches and stools of the medieval period. In Emanuel de Witte's family portrait (see pl.4.2), dated 1678, the couple sit on so-called Spanish chairs, upholstered with leather or fabric. They rest their arms on a table covered with a vibrant 'Transylvanian' carpet.[12] The table, with its carved and curving legs (only two of which are visible), is typical of the small to medium-sized items of occasional furniture that gained in popularity at this time.

Further colour and allure was brought to the domestic interior by the success of Dutch overseas trade, and the respective activities of the Dutch East and West India Companies. Tropical woods were used for furniture; an ebony picture frame with gilt inlay surrounds

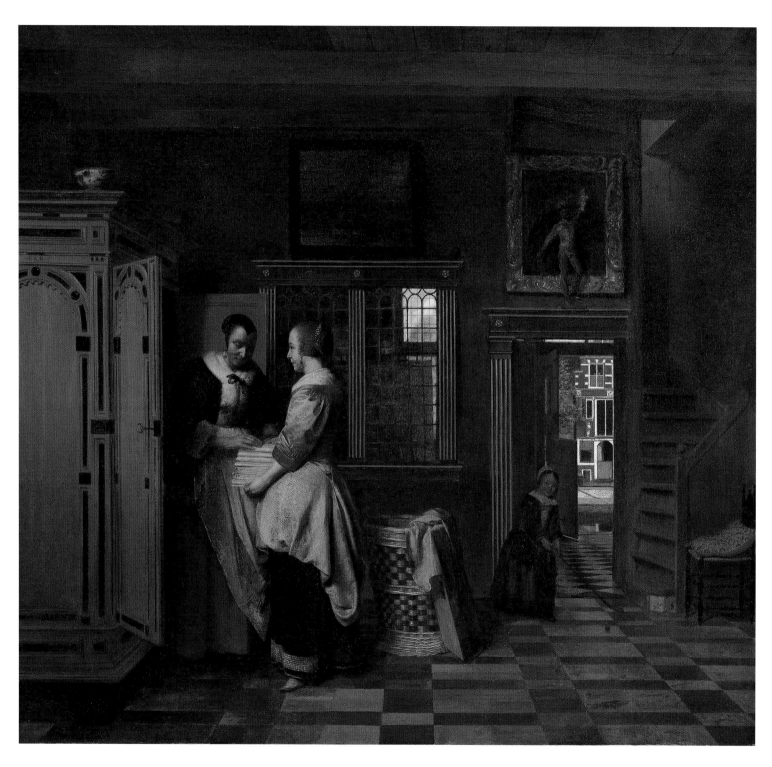

the church interior painting on the rear wall of plate 4.2. Chinese porcelain became a fashionable form of decoration. In De Witte's portrait two large porcelain jars stand like sentries on either end of the high mantelpiece. Of local manufacture and covering the lower part of the wall is lustrous gilt leather, embossed with a foliated motif against a blue background. More

affordable and modish than tapestry, panels of gilt leather often enveloped the entire walls of rooms in élite houses.

For nineteenth-century writers such as Théophile Thoré-Bürger and Eugène Fromentin, who 'rediscovered' seventeenth-century Dutch painters like Johannes Vermeer, the two most significant characteristics of this

4.1
Pieter de Hooch,
*Interior with Women
beside a Linen Chest.*
Oil on canvas. 1663.
Rijksmuseum, Amsterdam

art was its realism and encyclopaedic scope.[13] They believed that Dutch artists of this period had represented the world around them with such exact transcription and inclusiveness that it would be a relatively easy task to reconstruct their environment and social practices simply by recourse to the images that they produced in such prodigious numbers. Since at least the 1930s, however, scholars have questioned the validity of such assumptions and have suggested instead that while Dutch artists were centrally concerned with verisimilitude in their work, the transmission of various ideas and associations was equally of relevance. The unravelling of these layers of meaning and the methods applied to convey them continues to be a matter of debate among art historians. There is agreement, however, that the art of the period is highly selective and restrictive both in the range of its subject matter and in its modes of representation. Stock characters and situations are endlessly repeated, while artists regurgitated favoured motifs and pictorial elements.

4.2
Emanuel de Witte,
A Couple in an Interior.
Oil on canvas. 1678. Alte
Pinakothek, Munich / Artothek

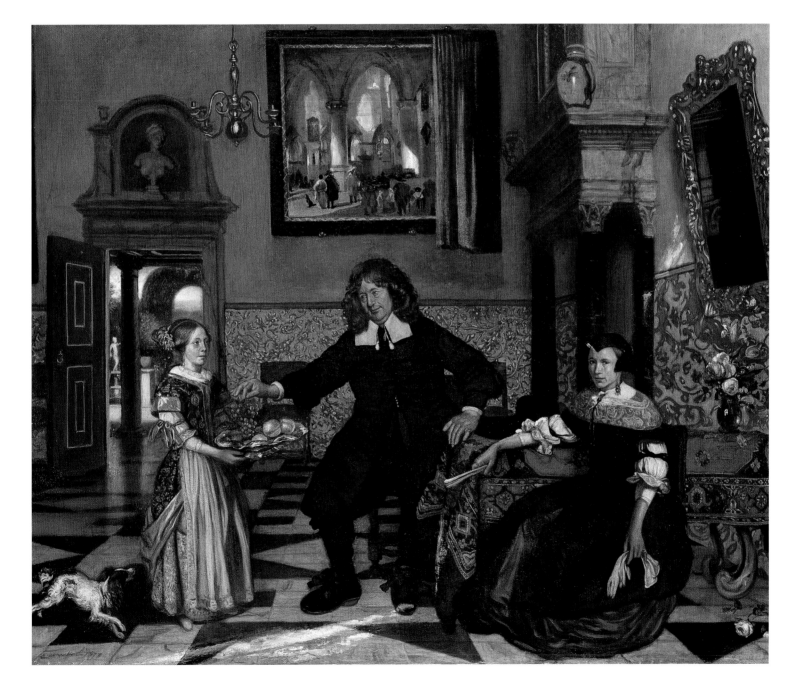

Pictorial representational schema

The way in which Dutch artists depicted the domestic interior was governed by various factors such as established pictorial traditions, personal aesthetic taste and market forces. Among the first to set their scenes in interiors was a group of pioneering Haarlem and Amsterdam artists who in the opening decades of the seventeenth century began to paint so-called 'merry company' scenes.[14] These depictions showed gatherings of elegant young men and women indulging in the leisurely pursuits of dining, drinking, making music, dancing or amorous dalliance. This sub-category of genre painting has its roots in the medieval garden of love theme and also in sixteenth-century Flemish representations of religious and mythological subjects involving feasting or merry-making figures. Initially represented out-of-doors in parkland environments, Dutch artists later moved these depictions of revellers to the interior, albeit one where there is frequently insufficient visual information to allow identification as a home, an inn or a brothel. The indoor location for these subjects essentially consisted of two spatial types: shallow stage-like settings, which are sparsely furnished and ill-defined (see pl.4.3), and much more elaborate box-like rooms with Renaissance decorative elements (see pl.4.4). In the collaborative painting by Dirck van Delen and Dirck Hals of 1629 features such as the elaborate doorcase, the richly carved overmantel with its niched sculpture, and the cassette ceiling have been adapted from architectural pattern books, especially those of Hans Vredeman de Vries, such as this example from 1560 (see pl.4.5). The artificiality of the setting is an appropriate context for the extravagantly attired figures and their mannered postures. Whether this work should be interpreted as an allegory of the five senses or as a moralizing condemnation of the idleness and vanity of Holland's newly enriched élite is a matter of conjecture.[15]

4.3
Willem Duyster,
Musical Company.
Oil on canvas. 1632–5.
V&A:WM.1524-1948

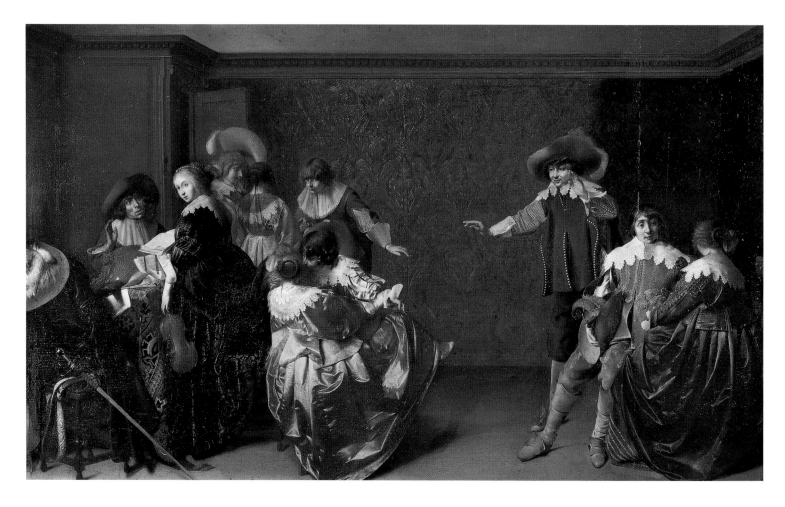

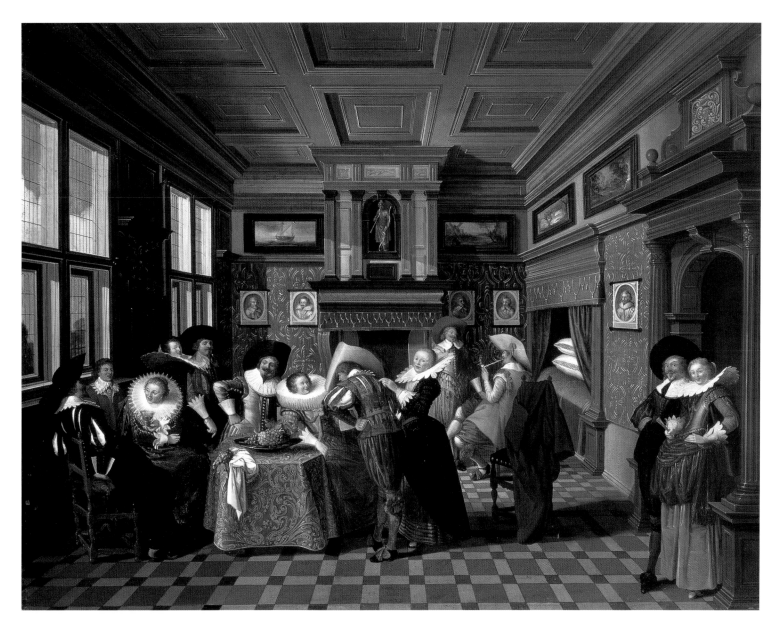

4.4
Dirck van Delen and Dirck
Hals, *An Interior with Ladies and
Cavaliers*. Oil on panel. 1629.
National Gallery of Ireland
Collection

Jan Steen's scene of domestic mayhem (see
pl.4.6), probably painted in the mid–1660s, also
carries references to the work of his predecessors and contemporaries.[16] His practice of
inscribing the title of the painting directly onto
the canvas – in the lower left is a slate, more
commonly found in taverns for recording
drink orders, which is marked 'bedurfve
huishow' (dissolute household) – and of illustrating popular proverbs harkens back to the
sixteenth century and specifically to the work
of Pieter Bruegel the Younger. The clearly
defined structure of the room and the reliev-
ing view into a secondary space through a door
on the right also recalls the domestic interiors

of Pieter de Hooch (see pl.4.1, 4.15 and 4.16).
Steen purposely invokes the tranquil, ordered
and virtuous depictions of De Hooch as part
of a strategy to create an inversion of appropriate familial behaviour. His painting catalogues
the effects of intemperance as they reverberate
through a household. While the mother has
keeled over in a drunken stupor at the table, her
young son steals from her money purse, her
leering husband cavorts with a woman of dubious morals, her maid plunders the family
cupboard, a dog eats the unguarded meal, and a
fire rages uncontrolled in the adjoining chamber. The clear narrative and didactic nature
of the scene is completed by the suspended

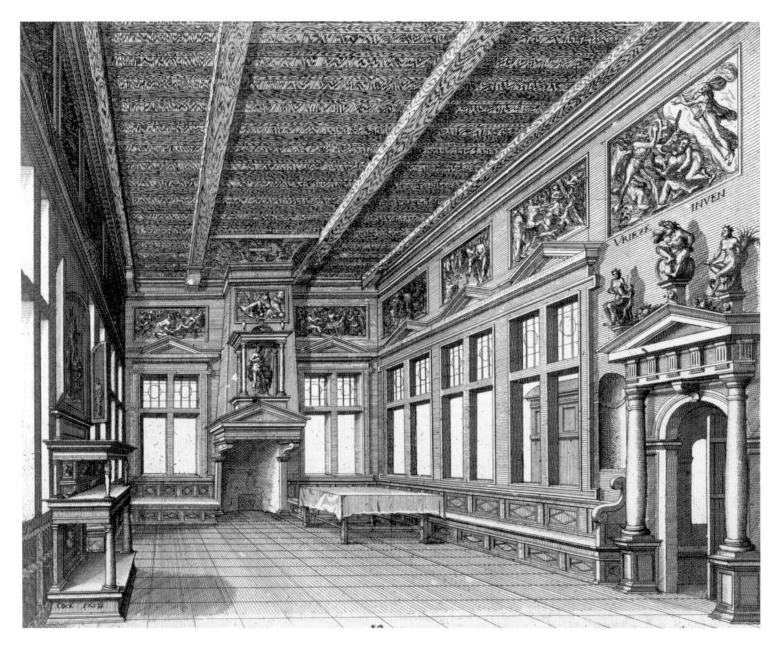

basket above which reminds the motley assembly that they must curb their excesses or face the consequences. It contains objects associated with punishment, poverty and disease, such as a switch, a sword, rags, a beggar's crutch and a leper's clapper.

After 1650 Dutch genre painting became progressively more refined in its style and themes, perhaps reflecting the growing prosperity and sophistication of the picture-buying public. Gerard ter Borch, for example, developed a new type of interior scene featuring a few brightly illuminated figures who are concentrated in their expressions or lost in reverie

(see pl.4.7). Contemplative subjects such as letter-writers or lace-makers abound in his work and also ambiguous scenes of ritualized courtship. Although the world that Ter Borch describes is essentially a secluded feminine environment where males appear almost as intruders and behave in a deferential way, his interest is more in the figures, their shimmering fabrics and their intriguing actions, rather than in the interior setting which is often cast in semi-shadow and vaguely defined. While Pieter de Hooch shared Ter Borch's interest in female activities, his imagery is more direct and largely concerned with domestic virtue.[17] His indus-

4.5

Hans Vredeman de Vries, *Scenographiae, sive perspective* (Plate no. 10). Engraving. 1560. V&A: E.O. 103

4.6

Jan Steen, *The Dissolute Household*. Oil on canvas. *c*.1663–5. V&A: WM.1541–1948

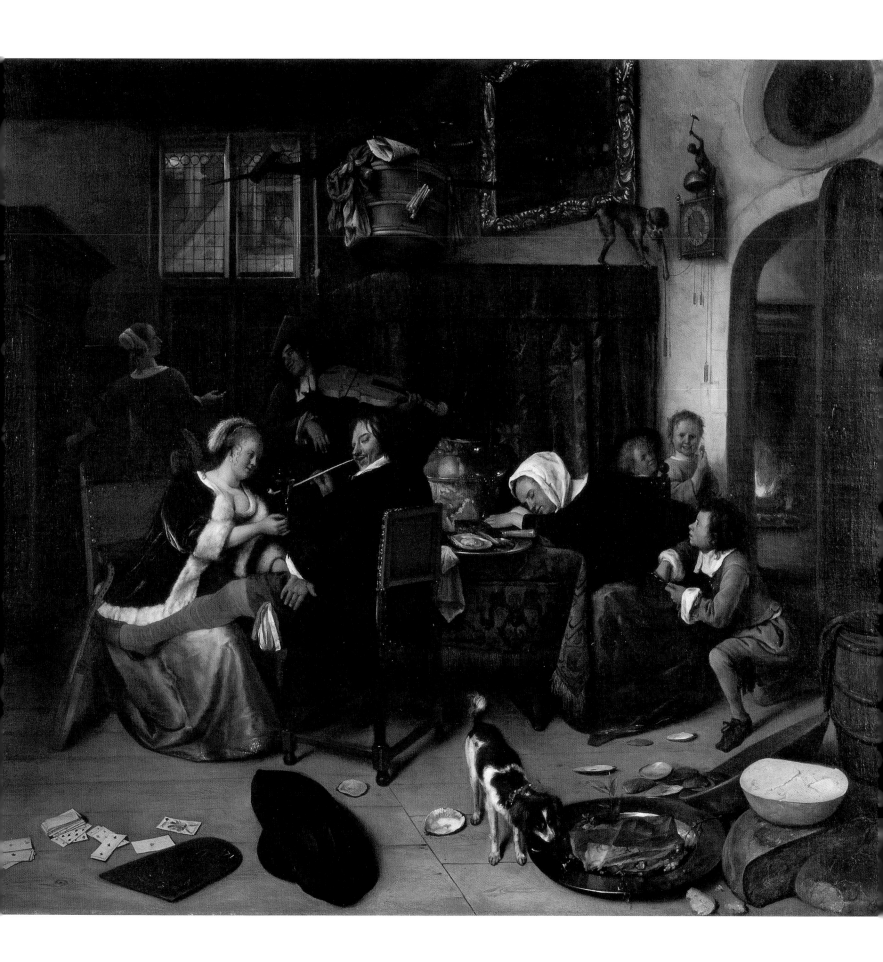

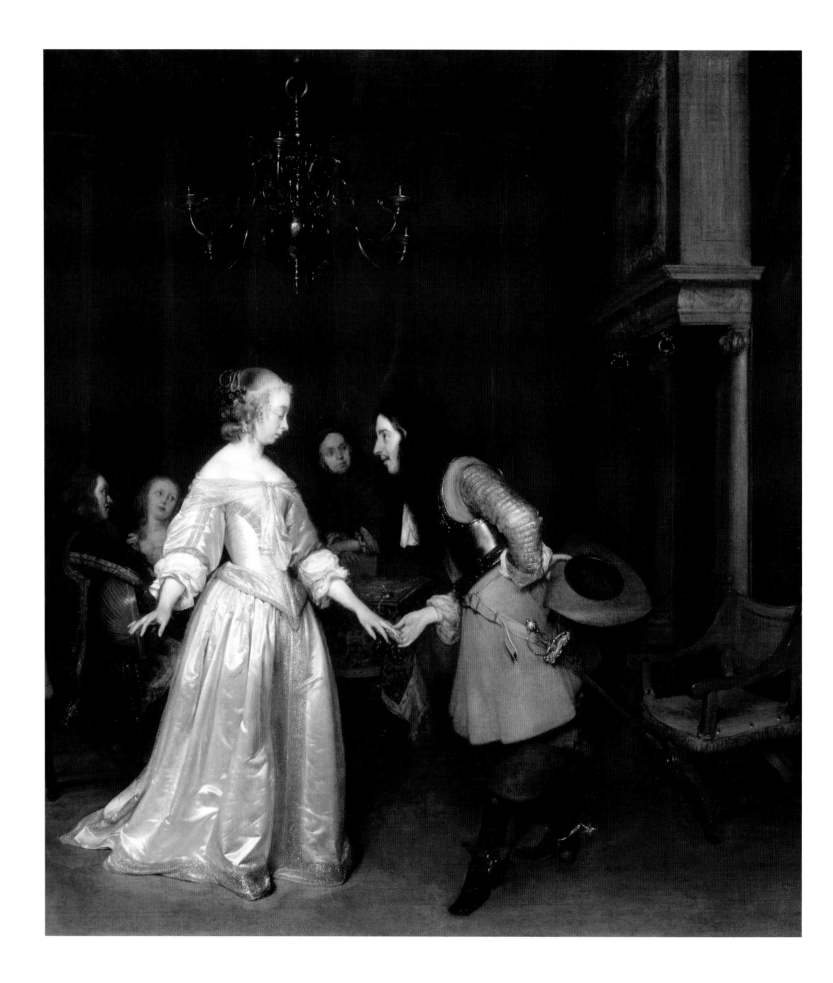

trious and maternal housewives and their maids often inhabit complex spatial settings achieved through a meticulous handling of perspective and an acute awareness of light. Expensive genre paintings by De Hooch, Ter Borch and their contemporaries reflect the lifestyle and living arrangements of the upper burgher and regent or ruling class who presumably also formed the main market for them.[18]

Room arrangement

It is difficult to reconstruct the actual appearance of seventeenth-century Dutch houses with complete accuracy. No interiors from this period survive entirely intact and unchanged. Inventories can offer some indication as to the composition, distribution and use of household items but these legal documents are usually sparse in their descriptive language and the rooms they enumerate are not easily visualized. A unique glimpse into the interior of a typical middle-class Amsterdam home is offered by Jan van der Heyden's dramatic engraving from 1690 of a house consumed by fire (see pl.4.8). An entrepreneurial inventor as well as an artist, Van der Heyden had recently patented a new type of pump and hose that drew water directly from the canals. The illustration appeared in a book published by him that celebrated and extolled the fire-fighting virtues of his invention, which would explain the care taken in documenting the scene. Van der Heyden has removed the side wall from this house and allows us to look inside and see the room layout

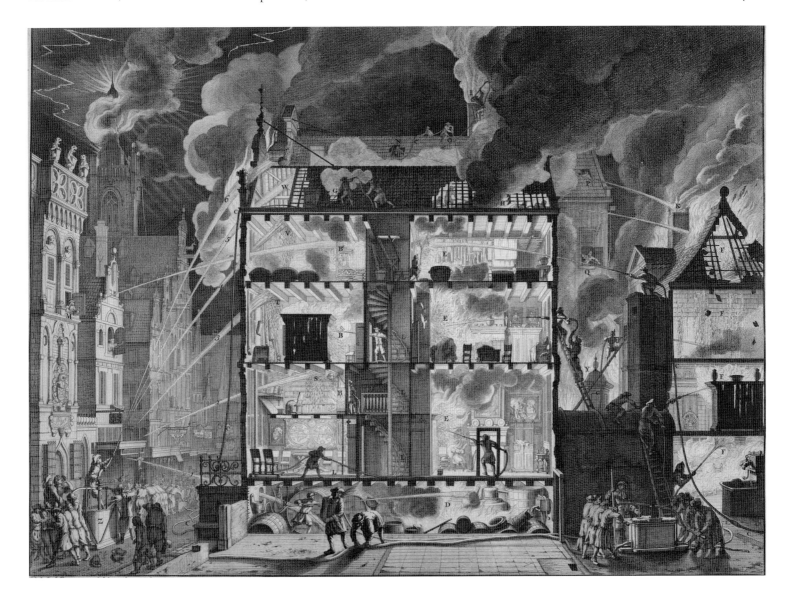

and furnishings. It is a large multi-storey dwelling consisting of two parts: the main house fronting the street and an annex at the rear separated by an inner courtyard that provided much needed daylight and ventilation. Land in Amsterdam was in short supply and its expense was exacerbated by the need to drive pile foundations into the boggy soil. Consequently houses tended to be built on narrow and deep sites, which forced builders to construct tall, slender brick dwellings that extended quite a distance from the street.

In Van der Heyden's engraving, a narrow spiral staircase connects the various levels of the main house. The basement was used primarily for storage, particularly for large barrels of wine. Directly above was the main floor, known as the *bel étage*, which was reached from street level by a small flight of steps. A visitor to the house would have first entered the *voorhuis* or front hall. This space is furnished in characteristic fashion: six chairs and a small carved table are neatly aligned on two sides, while decorating one wall is a large map of the world suspended between wooden rods. The *voorhuis* has been divided vertically through the construction of a mezzanine floor and this secondary space has been made into an office or library for the man of the house – books line the walls and globes are visible on top of the bookcases. Also on the primary floor is the main reception room, generally known as the *zaal*. Among its contents is a prominent linen press, a functional but expensive piece of furniture, which is rarely depicted in Dutch paintings. On the first floor are two family rooms used for living, sleeping and storage purposes. Indeed, until well into the seventeenth century most rooms had a multifunctional purpose and specifically designated bedrooms and dining rooms were slow to emerge. While the beds are obscured by plumes of heavy smoke, we can see large linen cupboards, chairs, a low table with toiletries, family portraits and porcelain on the mantelpiece and elsewhere. The attic rooms were used as storage areas for provisions and turf, the staple fuel of the day, and for the drying of linen and clothes. The rear annex building (the *achterhuis*),

accessible from the main house by a covered corridor that ran alongside the courtyard, also consisted of various storeys, including a basement kitchen and directly above a living space where the family probably dined.

Among the most distinctive spaces of the house was the *voorhuis*. In larger houses built after 1650 this space became a small entrance vestibule, but in older dwellings it was a substantial hallway sometimes spanning the entire width of the house. In the homes of artisans the *voorhuis* doubled as a place of work; the Leiden painter Quiringh van Brekelenkam specialized in depictions of tailors and shoemakers busily toiling with their apprentices in this space on elevated makeshift benches (see pl.4.9). In this example from around 1660, an open hearth provides warmth for a nursing mother, and further underlines that rooms in Dutch houses rarely had a restricted use at this time. Indeed merchants also conducted business in the *voorhuis* or in an adjoining office directly above or next to it. In Nicolaes Maes' light-hearted admonition of domestic neglect (see pl.4.10), probably painted in the mid-1650s, the mistress of the house descends into the *voorhuis* from an upstairs office to engage directly with the viewer. She raises a finger to silence us and also to direct our attention to her maid in the room to the right, cavorting with a young man who brazenly leans in through an open window and distracts her attention from the child in the cradle. Female servants, found in only 10 to 20 per cent of all households, are represented as either trusted companions, who were barely distinguishable in their dress from their mistresses, or as lazy, insolent and dissipated wreckers of the domestic equilibrium. The same ambivalent attitudes are found in contemporary documentary and printed sources.[19] The *voorhuis* in Maes' painting is furnished in characteristic fashion with a coarse circular mat and, as in plate 4.8, with a map of the world. Because of the superior quality of light in the *voorhuis*, it was also a place where concentrated activities took place such as sewing, lace-making or reading. In the left foreground of Maes' painting a chair is placed behind a counter on a *zoldertje*, a wooden platform that

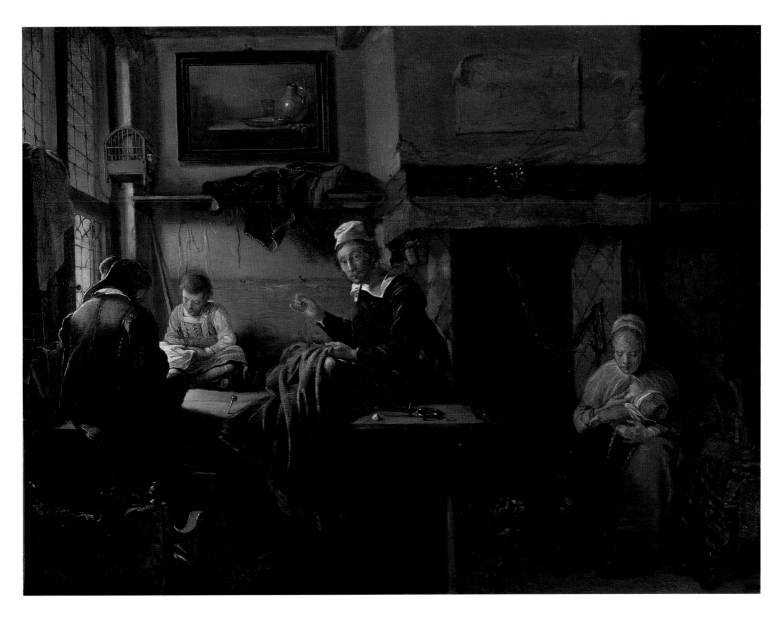

4.9
Quiringh van Brekelenkam,
Interior of a Tailor's Shop.
Oil on wood. *c.*1655-61.
The National Gallery, London

raised the women who sat here above the cold stone floor and away from draughts, bringing her closer to the source of light. Gabriel Metsu depicted a particularly absorbed letter-reader using this device in a painting from *c.*1665–7 (see pl.4.11). Some moralists criticised this custom of sitting close to the street window because it encouraged passers-by to stop and chat, interrupting household activities, and also, more seriously, because it could lead to flirtation between the sexes. Other aspects of Metsu's *voorhuis* strike us as true to contemporary practices: the natural stone polychrome tiles, the row of ceramic tiles placed along the lower edge of the wall to prevent rising damp, the mirror that is propped forward for greater ease of use, and the

expensive seascape picture protected from light, dirt and grime by the addition of a rail and curtain to the frame. As the line of demarcation between the public world of the city and the private life of the home, the *voorhuis* became a central theme during the 1660s in the work of Ludolf de Jongh, Pieter de Hooch and especially Jacob Ochtervelt (see pl.4.12). Ochtervelt's so-called 'threshold' paintings juxtapose elegant upper-class women, children and their maids with shabbily dressed street musicians and vendors who remain firmly on the street side of the open doorway.

Another room that had a unique identity from at least the early seventeenth century in both visual and documentary sources was the

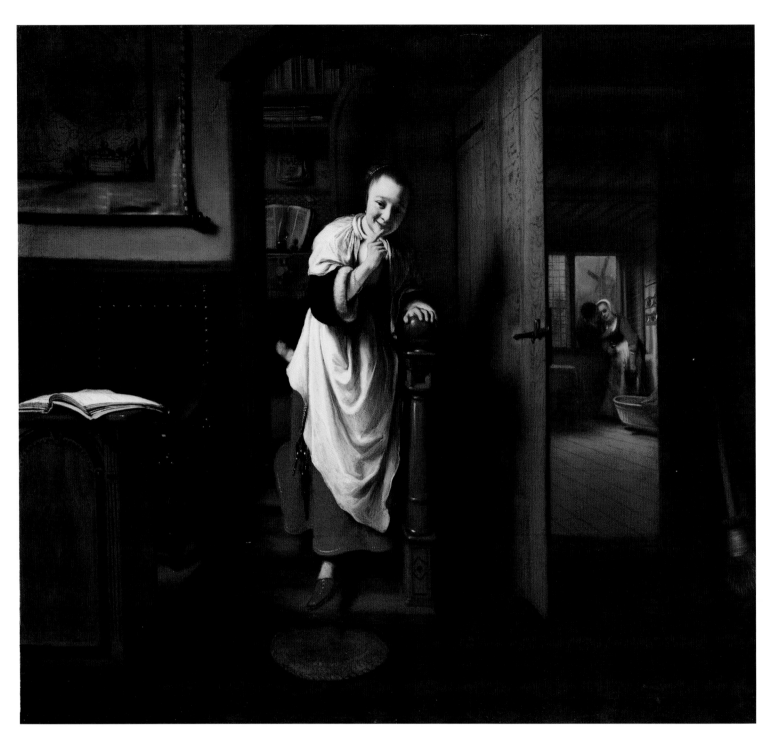

office (*comptoir*). An exclusively male domain, this space was located close to the *voorhuis*, either immediately above or in an adjoining room. It was here that business was transacted with clients; in the houses of scholars, advocates and Reformed ministers this type of room could take the form of a more privately oriented library or study, or for others a cabinet of curiosities.[20] Dressed in a comfortable

and informal Japanese gown, the notary, in a rare genre scene of 1672 by Job Berckheyde (see pl.4.13), hands a customer a deed.[21] This transaction takes place in an office next to the main entrance of his home. The position and posture of the notary curiously forms a counterpoint to the many representations of industrious women in seventeenth-century Dutch art. Seated on a more substantial *zoldertje*

4.10
Nicolaes Maes,
The Eavesdropper.
Oil on canvas. *c.*1655–6.
V&A:WM.1503–1948

4.11
Gabriel Metsu,
Woman Reading a Letter with a Servant. Oil on panel. *c.*1665–7.
National Gallery of Ireland
Collection

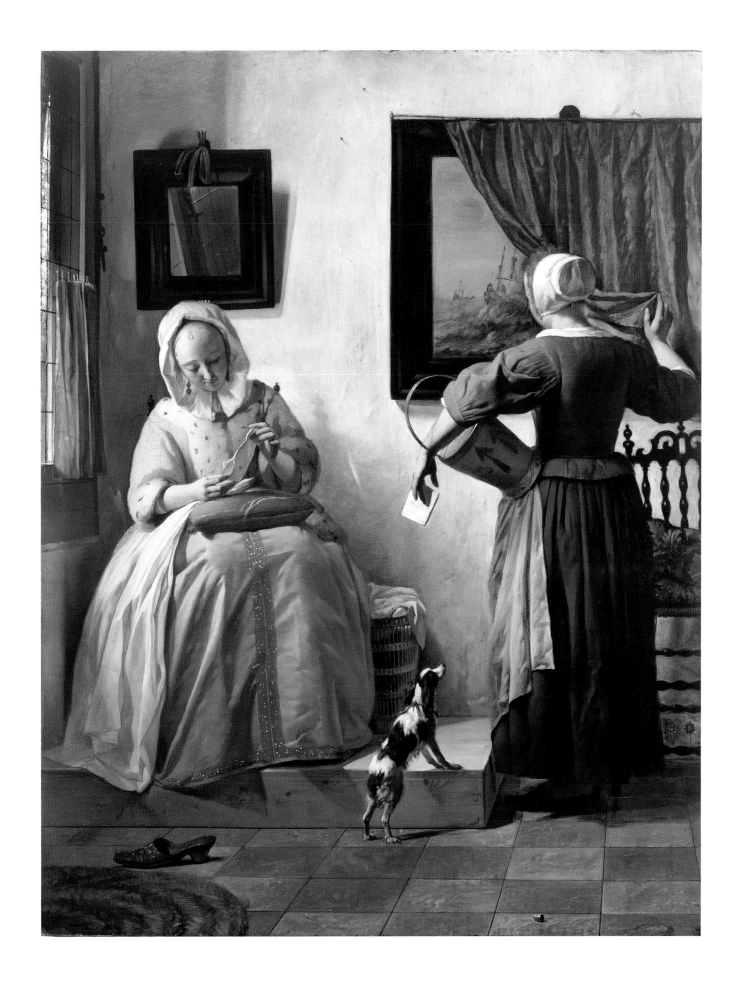

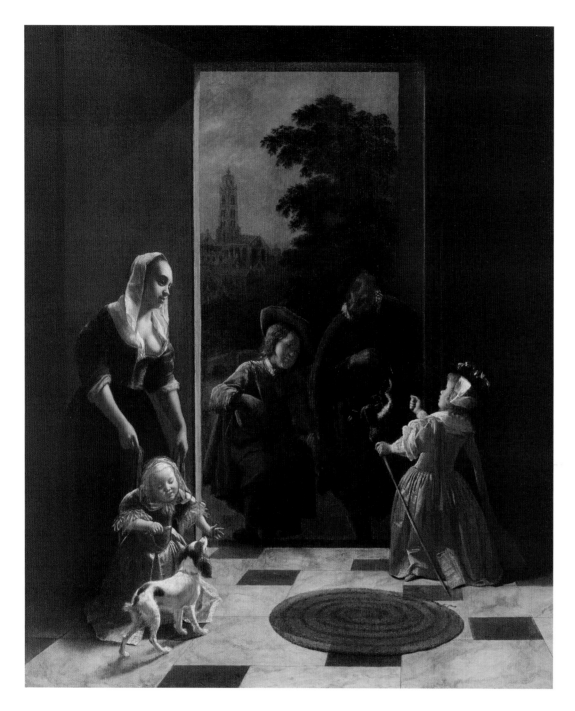

4.12
Jacob Ochtervelt,
Street Musicians.
Oil on canvas. *c.*1667–8.
Gemäldegalerie, Berlin

4.13
Job Berckheyde,
Notary in his Office.
Oil on canvas. 1672.
Private collection/Sotheby's

than the one used by females in the *voorhuis*, he also makes use of a foot warmer, a heating device normally associated with women. This office is furnished in a relatively simple way with a lectern and drawer, and vast quantities of documents arranged in specially constructed shelving or hanging in loose bundles and canvas bags. In an etched portrait of 1647 (see pl.4.14), Rembrandt sites the wealthy Amsterdam regent and man of letters Jan Six in a room referred to by a contemporary as a 'book room' (*boekkamer*),

a term that could refer to a library or place of study where curiosities and antiquities may also have been found.[22] Nonchalantly leaning on a widow ledge and absorbed in study, the room contents (the books piled on a chair, the ornamental sword, the curtained painting) identify Six as a cultivated gentleman of leisure.

There is evidence of an increasing desire for privacy in the second half of the seventeenth century, especially in wealthier homes, and a compulsion to draw a clear distinction between

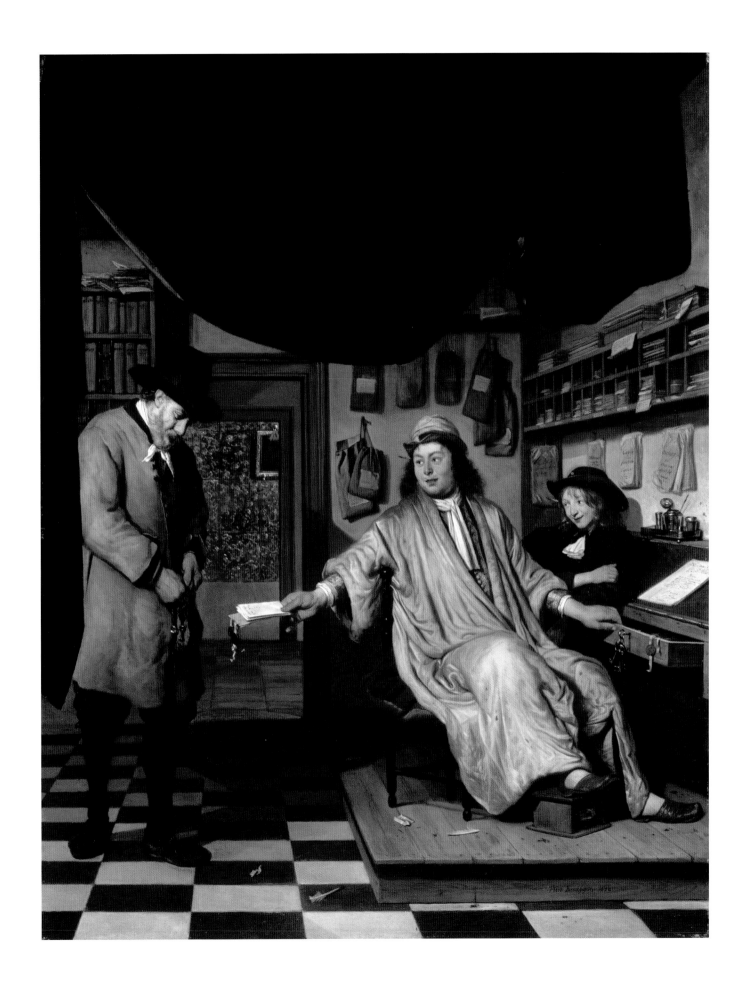

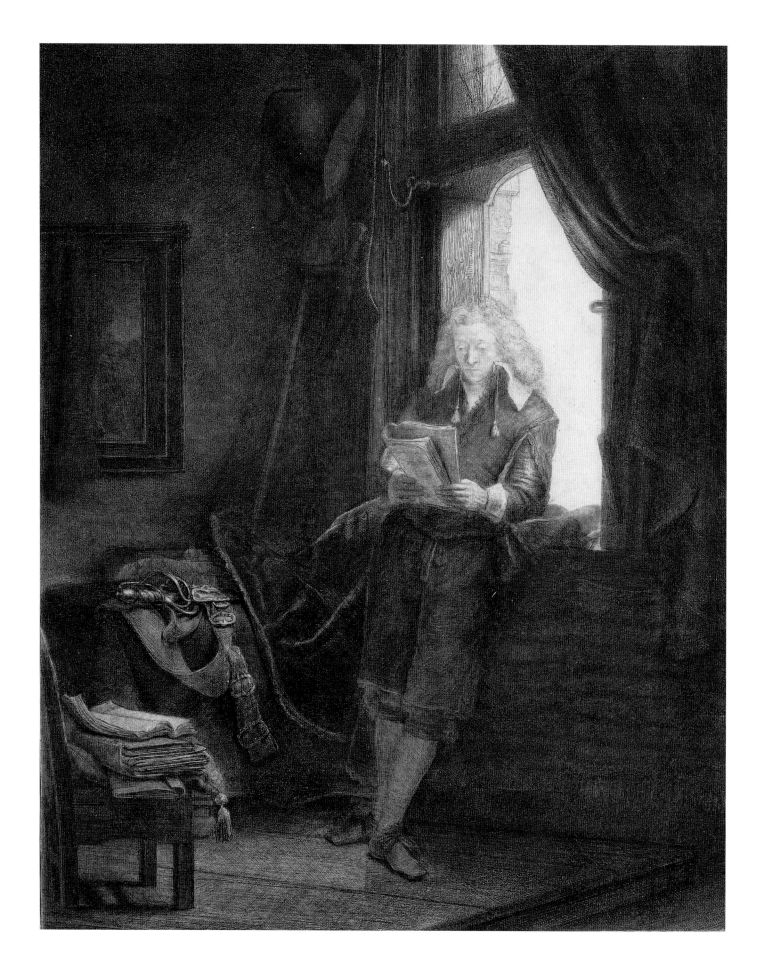

those areas of the house that were accessible to visitors and those that were off-limits to all but the family. In newly built houses and renovated larger dwellings, the function of rooms was more precisely defined. Reception rooms, for instance, were no longer used as living spaces by the family; separate bedrooms were increasingly identified as such in the upper stories. An inner chamber (sometimes referred to as the *binnen-haard* or *binnenhuis*), where formerly food had been prepared and consumed, now became the main family living area, and more specialist kitchens, as we saw in plate 4.8, were located in a rear or basement area. Corridors and staircases gave each room its own distinct entrance. These structural developments coincided with an expanding recognition among the ruling oligarchy and other wealthy classes of the importance of civility or correct public conduct in order to demonstrate breeding and refinement. Such notions were partially motivated by the spate of manners books that appeared after mid century, outlining appropriate modes of behaviour for dining etiquette and personal deportment, and relegating activities such as personal hygiene and the exercise of unedifying bodily functions to the private sphere.[23] There was an increasing awareness of dividing the house along gender lines. The Middelburg-born bookseller Willem Goeree wrote an architectural treatise in 1681 where he set out his plans for the ideal house and differentiated between front stage activities (to use the sociologist Erving Goffman's terminology), which were the locale of the male, and backstage pursuits where the female dominated:

> In almost all cases the foremost part of a house must be reserved for the man or house father, in order to have there his shop, his office, his *salet* or consultation room, and his storage cellar etc. The woman or house mother has her quarters in and around the rear rooms where also are situated the cooking and living kitchens, wash-house, and the rest of the things necessary for the housekeeping.[24]

Everyday practices

These expanding concerns with privacy, civility, and gender demarcation are reflected in the art of the period. Genre painters after 1650 introduced more domestic imagery into their work. Pieter de Hooch, for instance, painted an almost exclusively female world, inhabited by housewives, maids and children, and secluded from the male parts of the house and the wider world which can only be glimpsed though open doors and windows. In *The Intruder* (see pl.4.15), painted in around 1665, an unexpected and intrepid male visitor steals into this domain of women and surprises a lady at her toilet. Families also chose to have themselves portrayed in more consciously domestic settings and with attributes and emblematic references to family unity and interdependence. A mother singing to the accompaniment of her husband and two children in a portrait of 1663 by De Hooch (see pl.4.16) acts as a metaphor for familial concord. In a second room to the right is a maid and two further children, one of whom carries a basket of oranges and grapes to symbolize the abundant fruit that her mother has borne. This family also ostentatiously displays its wealth. Among the signifiers of social status are the richly carved fireplace, the free-standing bed, the tapestries, the brass chandelier, the marble floor and the extraordinarily ornate linen cupboard, its door panels carved in such high relief that this piece of furniture was often called a *kussenkast* or pillow chest. More unconventional was Hendrick Sorgh's portrait of the Bierens family, which was painted in the same year (see pl.4.17). This Mennonite family had themselves portrayed in a modestly decorated kitchen and, for the most part, in the postures of everyday life. Jacob Bierens is represented in his role of provider, entering from the left with his youngest son and holding a fish, an appropriately frugal foodstuff. His apple-peeling wife and his daughter who plucks a bird are indistinguishable in their dress from the maid filling a vessel with water in the background. Only the eldest son, Abraham, playing a viola da gamba, and thus alluding to the harmonious togetherness of these family members, adds an

4.14
Rembrandt Harmenszoon van Rijn, *Portrait of Jan Six*. Etching. 1647.
V&A: CAI.720

incongruous note to this scene of domestic virtue and relative frugality. The emphasis on sobriety and hard work in this portrait clearly extends from the Bierens' religious beliefs, which privileged moral plain living.

Elements in the interior are rendered with remarkable fidelity in seventeenth-century Dutch painting and can even assist with dating the work of art, particularly as some artists liked to include the most up-to-date fashionable object that had just come onto the market.[25] However, the overall composition is invariably an imaginative construction that deviates from the physical reality of the home. The domestic scene by Pieter Janssens Elinga from around 1670 is typical of the process of enhancement and modification that took place (see pl.4.18). The home that Janssens Elinga describes is pristine in its cleanliness and its pure geometry created by the interlocking cubic forms of

4.15
Pieter de Hooch,
The Intruder: A Lady at Her Toilet,
Surprised by Her Lover.
Oil on canvas. *c.*1665.
V&A:WM.1571–1948

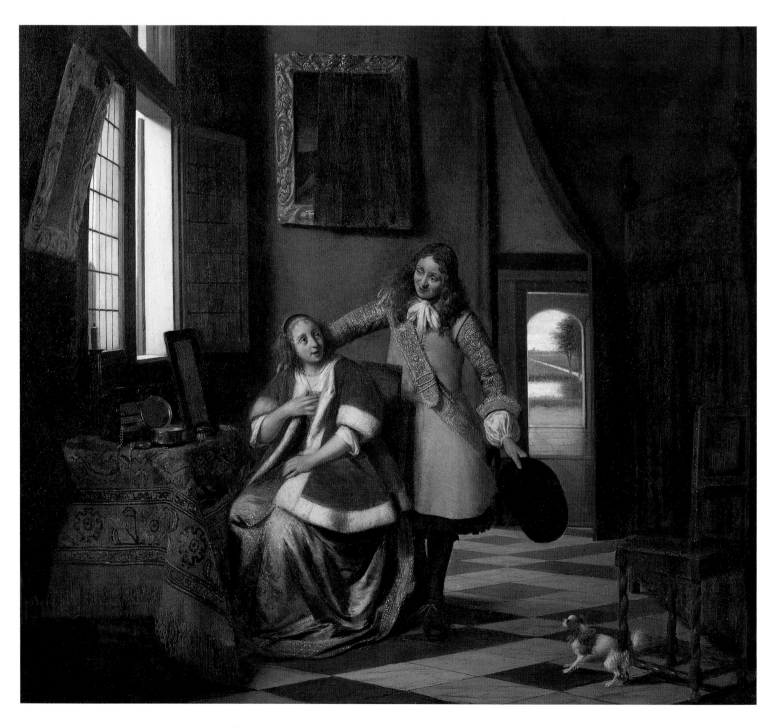

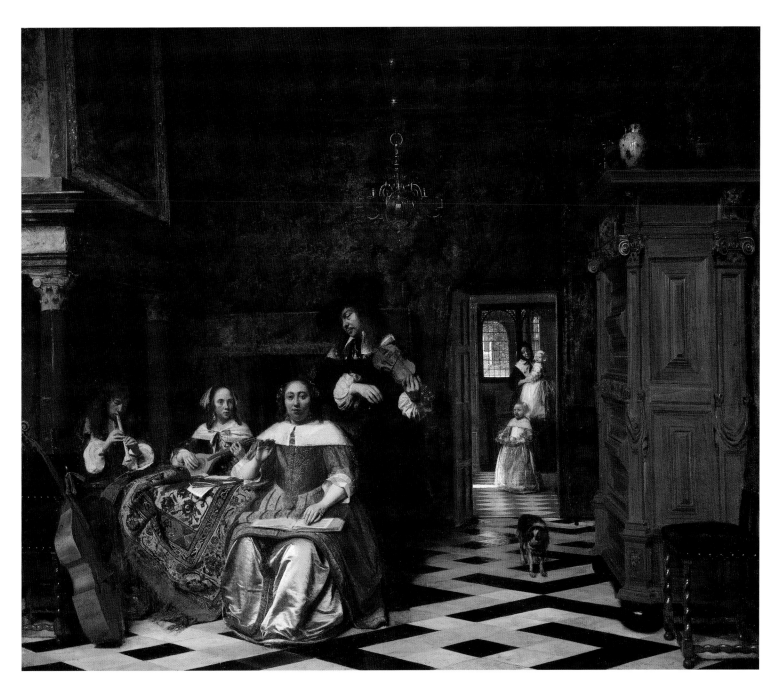

4.16
Pieter de Hooch,
Portrait of a Family Playing Music.
Oil on canvas. 1663.
The Cleveland Museum of Art

rooms and the rectangular shapes of the windows, the hanging pictures and mirror, the chair backs, the door frame, and the patterned marble tiles. Self-absorbed and industrious, his figures do not distract from this carefully elaborated environment. In addition, the light that enters the room is so strong that it forms impastoed highlights on the floor and wall, and the lower windows need to be shuttered against its intensity. Janssens Elinga's painting contributes to the myth that Dutch homes were tranquil, light-filled and excessively clean spaces. Despite

the unusual density of pictures on the walls, these rooms are relatively uncluttered. Where are the cupboards, the major storage unit that was found in almost every room of a house, or the fireplaces or beds? Perhaps they are in those corners of the rooms not visible to us. However, the general sparseness of furniture and the strong sense of order and symmetry present in seventeenth-century Dutch domestic interior paintings is at variance with the volume and variety of household goods described in inventories. The natural light that could penetrate

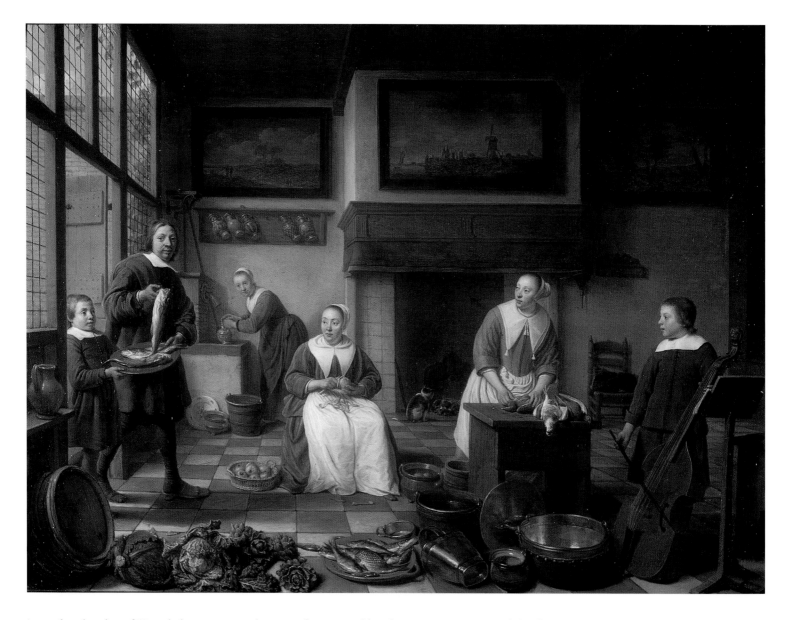

into the depths of Dutch homes must have been extremely limited in the seventeenth century, particularly during the long severe winters.[26] Windows were tall and narrow and found only at the front and rear since most Dutch houses were built as part of a terrace. Intense direct sunshine was a relative rarity, and householders had to depend on a meagre supply of diffuse light from the sky, supplemented even during daylight hours by artificial illumination from fireplaces and from candles and oil lamps for those who could afford it.

The other exaggerated aspect of Janssens Elinga's painted interior is the prevailing sense of sanitation: everything is spotless and gleaming. This painting, with the maid in the foreground busily sweeping, is one of the few examples that actually show cleaning chores. Images of women scouring pans and, more rarely, sweeping floors have also been interpreted as references to spiritual and moral purity.[27] In the seventeenth century, the fastidiousness of the Dutch housewife and her employees was legendary, largely as a result of travellers' reports which demonstrate an occupational interest in standards of hygiene and tidiness.[28] Famous anecdotes, such as the one recounted by Sir William Temple of the muscular and quick-thinking maid who carried a visiting magistrate across a floor rather than risk mudding it, are part of a literary tradition celebrating the proverbial cleanliness of the Dutch

4.17
Hendrick Sorgh,
Portrait of the Bierens Family.
Oil on canvas. 1663.
Instituut Collectie Nederland

which extends from Erasmus.[29] These apocryphal tales gained in credence through their rehashing in the publications of foreign tourists, most of whom never actually entered an indigenous home, but perhaps spotted the occasional housewife or maid scouring the front steps. Despite their best efforts and the entreaties of domestic conduct books, Dutch women must have been fighting a losing battle against candle soot, dust from burning turf and general grime in an age before detergents and vacuum cleaners. The prevalence of infectious diseases and the recurrence of plague throughout the century are stark reminders of the grim reality of urban life.

Just as foreign visitors extrapolated many of their ideas about Dutch homes from visits to public buildings, native artists also introduced elements from the same structures into their fictionalized depictions of the domestic interior. At first glance Gabriel Metsu's formal assemblage of figures (see pl.4.19), which dates from 1661, appears to be a convincing representation of a visit by a female guest to the lying-in room of a young mother, an almost ritualized event that was generally the preserve of women. The

4.18
Pieter Janssens Elinga, *Interior with a Gentleman, a Woman Reading and a Housemaid*. Oil on canvas. *c*.1670. Städelsches Kunstinstitut, Frankfurt am Main/ Artothek

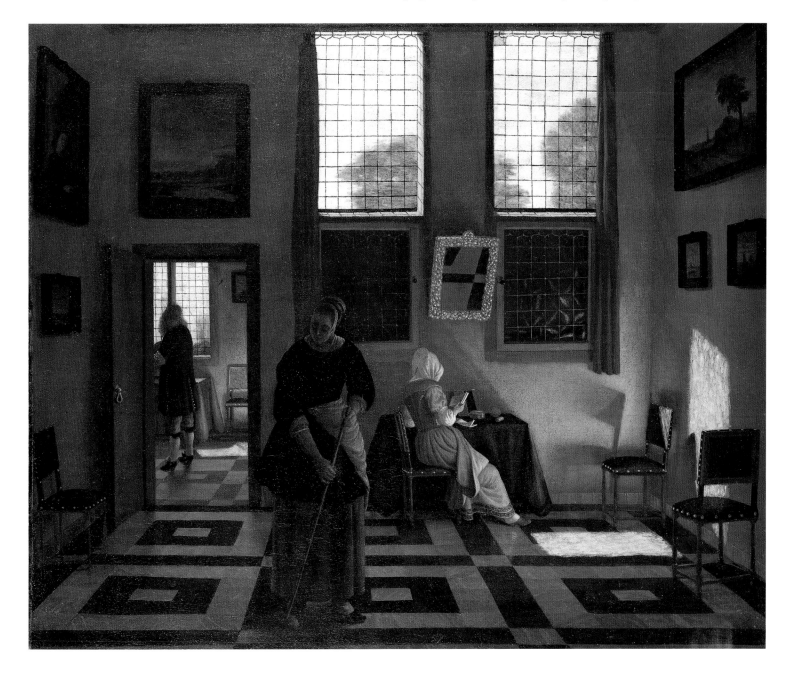

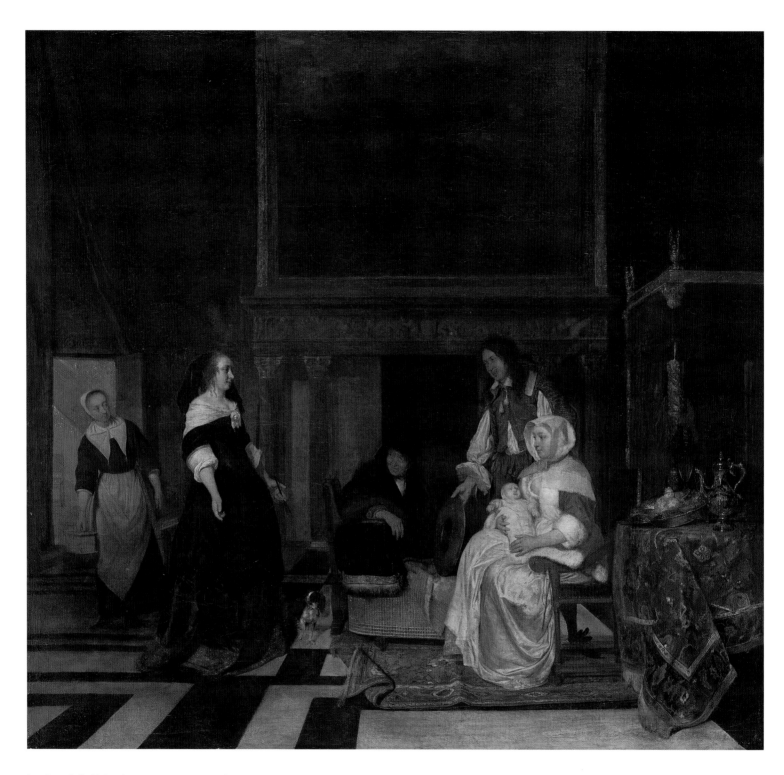

husband doffs his hat in response to the visitor's well wishes, while a servant scurries into the room with a chair and foot warmer for her comfort. Indeed, scholars identify this painting with the one seen by the poet Jan Vos in the *zaal* of the Amsterdam alderman Jan Jakobsen Hinloopen and celebrated in the former's laudatory poem for its lifelike qualities, the dignified ges-

tures and expressions, and the rare glimpse offered to male viewers of an essentially female ceremony. There is even speculation that this is a genre-like portrait of Hinloopen and his wife, whom he married in 1657, together with other family members.[30] However, on closer inspection we realize that this room with its lofty proportions, monumental fireplace and enor-

4.19

Gabriel Metsu,
The Visit to the Nursery.
Oil on canvas. 1661.
The Metropolitan Museum of
Art, New York

mous overmantel picture, and the geometric patterns of the marble floor belongs not to a wealthy regent's residence but to either the Burgomasters' Cabinet or the Council Chamber of the town hall of Amsterdam. Since Hinloopen belonged to one of the city's ruling oligarchies, it is entirely appropriate that this interior should reflect the location of his political power base.[31] Other aspects of the room also deviate from contemporary domestic practice in order to create an image of exclusivity and luxury. Outside of court circles, oriental carpets were hardly ever placed on floors during this period.[32] Similarly, the four-poster bed with its elaborate carving and unusual finials bears little resemblance to surviving examples. Finally, recent research by C. Willemijn Fock has concluded that black-and-white marble floors were almost never found in the main reception rooms of seventeenth-century houses.[33] Even the very wealthy preferred pine deal floors, which could be just as expensive as marble, because they were more homely and warmer underfoot. When patterned marble floors were encountered in élite Amsterdam homes, they were invariably confined to a small narrow area such as an entrance hallway or a corridor.

Certain aspects of the domestic interior and the conduct of family life were clearly over-represented by artists. For example, when confronted with these paintings we would be forgiven for believing that there was a craze among the merchant élite and regent class for oriental carpets. In fact, these carpets, largely imported from Turkey, Persia, India and Egypt, were very expensive objects and were usually placed on tables to prevent their wear rather than on floors.[34] Despite the care that was bestowed on them, only three oriental carpets have survived in continuous Dutch ownership since the seventeenth century. Surveying a sample of upper-class inventories compiled in three towns in around 1660, Thera Wijsenbeek-Olthuis found limited possession of oriental carpets. Only one-quarter of those sampled who lived in The Hague had an oriental carpet, one-third in Delft, and one-half in Leiden.[35] Artists seem to have repeatedly used the same patterns for the carpets that appear in their works, suggesting that they re-used drawings of actual examples or copied the carpets that appear in the work of others. The type of carpet in Vermeer's *The Music Lesson* of *c.*1662–5 (see pl.4.20) has been identified as a Turkish example from the town of Ushak, characterized by a star-shaped medallion in the centre.[36] Vermeer recycled the same carpet for three other paintings in his small oeuvre. Similarly, musical instruments are a constant presence in Dutch genre scenes. The virginal that appears in Vermeer's painting was an expensive instrument that was beyond the reach of most. Wijsenbeek-Olthuis's analysis of inventories unearthed only one household in Delft, where Vermeer was working, that owned a virginal or a harpsichord and one in The Hague.[37] Ownership of these keyboard instruments was a lot more prevalent in Leiden because of the influx of immigrants from Antwerp, a centre of production for harpsichords in the Netherlands. Finally, the brass chandeliers that add lustre to so many Dutch genre scenes (see pl.4.2, 4.7 and 4.16) were a far from ubiquitous feature in Dutch houses. In inventories of Leiden's most fashionable and luxurious houses that lined the Rapenburg canal, Fock found only five chandeliers of this sort listed for the entire seventeenth century.[38] Like marble floors, these costly items were more common in public buildings and churches than in private homes.

The human subject matter of most domestic interiors is also restricted and stereotypical. The housewife is portrayed as a type of secular Virgin Mary, primarily concerned with tending to the needs of her children, but also busily involved in spinning, sewing and other needlework, purchasing and preparing food and, most popular of all, supervising her maids. These are exactly the ideal types of housewifery and motherhood that are propounded in marriage and household manuals of the period.[39] Men are generally absent from these scenes of domestic virtue, pushed to peripheral secondary spaces as if they wanted to avoid emasculation through contact with

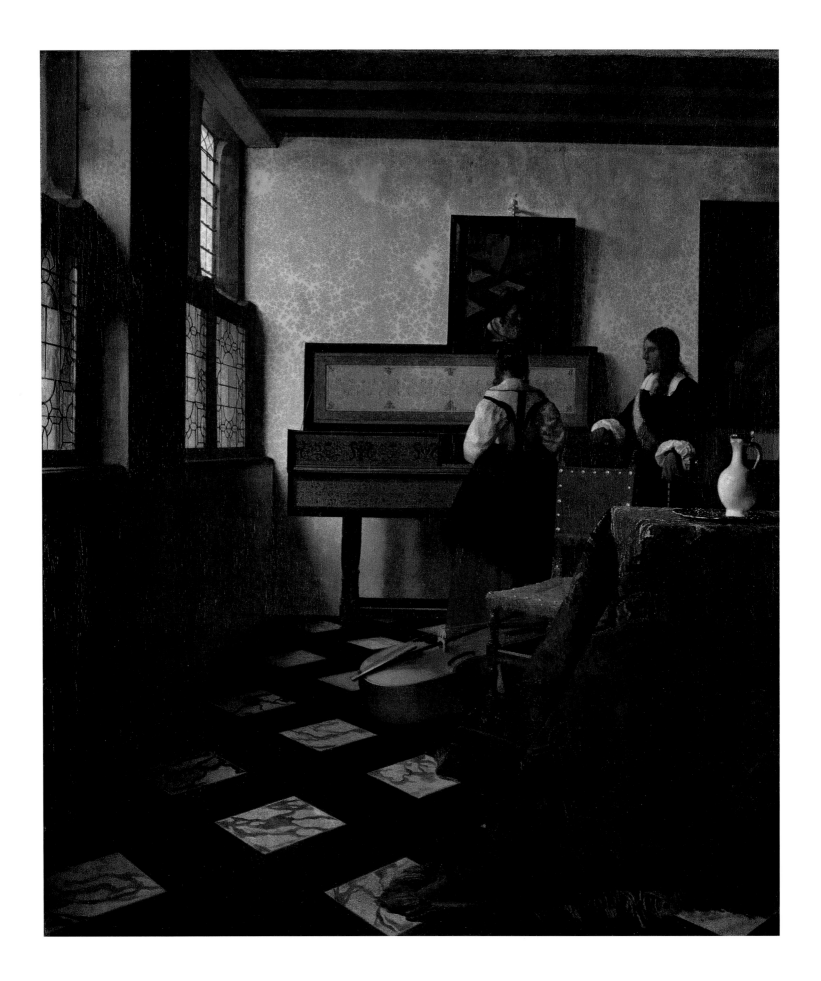

household chores and feminine spaces, or depicted alone and introspective in an office or library. Even in the 'high life' genre scenes popularized by Ter Borch, De Hooch, Metsu and others during the 1660s and 1670s, and which usually revolved around the theme of romantic love, the number of social situations is limited: reading and writing letters, playing cards and various parlour games, and making music or singing. While suitors may occasionally be too forthright in their amorous intentions, particularly young officers who had a questionable reputation, the female object of their desire is always demure and restrained. This limited repertoire of imagery conveyed and underpinned basic societal and religious values.

Genre painters neglected other elements of interior decoration and domestic activities. Given the scarcity of natural light in the interior, it is surprising how seldom sources of artificial light such as simple candles, wall sconces or oil lamps are represented. Striped wall hangings, which became popular in the third quarter of the century, and were often en suite with curtains and valences, are also a relative rarity in domestic interior paintings.[40] Artists preferred to keep walls clear of coverings or to depict more artistically challenging and expensive tapestries and gilt leather. While we know from inventories that paintings must have been tiered on walls and substantial numbers of porcelain and Delftware vases and jars decorated cupboards and mantelpieces, large displays of pictures and vessels of this sort are infrequently found in genre paintings. The general orientation towards order and spaciousness that we find in representations of the domestic interior, which acted as an appropriate setting for scenes of tranquillity and familial harmony, perhaps precluded artists from including these facets of room decoration. Exclusively female gatherings are seldom represented as taking place in these genre paintings. The visit to the lying-in room or nursery, and the tea party that became fashionable towards the end of the century, are rarely depicted.

Why did artists exaggerate the popularity of patterned marble floors, oriental carpets, musical instruments, tapestries, gilt-leather and brass chandeliers in their work? One plausible suggestion is that these items allowed artists to demonstrate their artistic facility. The complicated and colourful pattern of Eastern carpets, the sheen of brass and the intricate arrangement of receding tiles, gave the artist an opportunity to demonstrate his ability at imitating texture and constructing perspective.[41] Such mimetic skills were highly valued in art-theoretical textbooks of the period. A lot of these objects and furnishings possessed a degree of opulence and extravagance to which many upper-middle-class consumers could only aspire. They represented an ideal of the interior – brighter, cleaner, neater, tended to by servants, and more richly decorated – and of social activities such as refined courtship and musical interludes. For such viewers these depictions stimulated desire in much the same way as lifestyle magazines do today.[42] Others, who were fortunate to own some of these privileged objects, would have had their social distinctions endorsed through looking at or possessing these paintings. Indeed, images of the domestic interior by progressive artists such as De Hooch, Vermeer, Metsu and Ter Borch were expensive commodities in themselves and their ownership would have bolstered cultural pretensions. Finally, it must be emphasized that the artists who painted the domestic interior and the purchasers who coveted them, as far as we can determine, were predominantly male. They were less interested in accurately depicting furniture and interior decoration because most parts of the home, to judge from contemporary texts, were regarded as chiefly the domain of women. Domestic activities such as the tea party or the visit to the nursery were also largely excluded because these rituals generally involved only women. As those who were primarily active in the commercial and public sphere, men valued status symbols more, and as guardians of the family's honour in the outside world, they hankered after images that reinforced prevailing notions of domesticity and nurturing.

4.20
Johannes Vermeer, *The Music Lesson*. Oil on canvas. *c.*1662–5. The Royal Collection

Cataloguing the Domestic: inventories

Giorgio Riello

Inventories are lists of household or stock goods and have been a common feature of legal practices across Europe and the Middle East from the later Middle Ages to the end of the eighteenth century. Inventories were drawn up for a variety of legal and administrative purposes. In countries such as eighteenth-century Finland, for example, inventories were taken for all people dying over the age of 18. Elsewhere they were often produced in cases of bankruptcy, loss from fire, admittance to a hospital or orphanage, and in cases of wardship or the sale of a property (see pl.4.21). The most common event in which an inventory was produced was the death of a property owner. In this case, a probate inventory was created to protect the deceased's patrimony and eventually tax it.

An inventory can range from a few lines to several hundred pages long. While most sixteenth- and seventeenth-century Florentine inventories are one or two pages long, the 1531 inventory of Alessandro de Medici's palace in via Larga in Florence lists 80 pages of goods. Most inventories record goods by item (single objects or a group of objects), with or without an associated value. If rooms are distinguished, each of them can comprise one or more items. Inventories such as the one in plate 4.22 (1552) have a precise layout and the neat calligraphy conveys notions of order and worth. Inventories provide a wide range of information about furniture, taste, religious values, habitat, the cause of death, the family, business, credit and debit relationships, wardrobe, social standing and occupation.

Inventories have been widely used by historians to study consumption patterns, the level of material culture, the layout of buildings and the economic activities of pre-industrial households. This is possible because millions of inventories survive in archives throughout Europe, North America and the Middle East. It is important to remember, however, that inventories are very particular representations of the domestic. They are produced as a result of a legal

procedure and they capture the life of a household at one particular point in time. In this sense, inventories are 'snapshots of reality' and they tell little about family stories, lifecycles or what happened after they were taken. Historians use wills, probate accounts (accounts of expenditure after the death of a property owner), as well as diaries, letters and other personal documents to enhance their interpretation.

Inventories are not exhaustive records of the contents of a domestic space. By simply listing the possessions of individuals, they can only partially

4.21
'A list of what I lost at the unhappy fire in Charles Street, Westminster, April 9th 1707'. Corporation of London, London Metropolitan Archives WJ/SPD 78

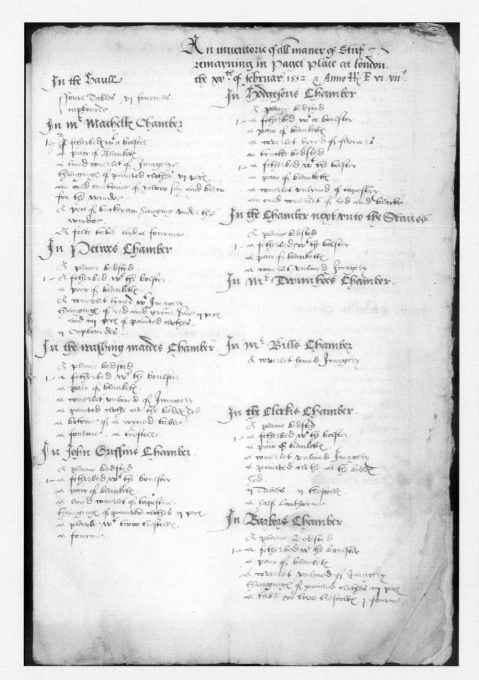

4.22
'An inventorie of all maney &
stuff remayning in Paget
Place at London'. 1552.
Corporation of London,
London Metropolitan
Archives ACC/466/H001

4.23
Inventory of John Wall. 1674.
Corporation of London
Record Office, Orphan's
Court Inventories, Box 3,
inv.916, John Wall

capture the domestic sphere. Often inventories
include the non-domestic: the shop, the stock,
business money, credits, crops and livestock (see
pl.4.23). Notably they exclude debts, land and, very
importantly, buildings and fixtures. Thus inventories do
not mention windows and doors, corridors and empty
rooms. Even in recording objects they are very
selective. They tend to exclude objects of little or no
value. Historians interested in analyzing the role of
newspapers or children's toys in family life would find
little help from inventories. Similarly, inventories

exclude non-durable goods. A chunk of cheese could
be considered valuable enough to be included in an
inventory, but other foodstuff for daily consumption
would not have been recorded. Inventories
sometimes exclude even valuable objects such as
jewellery, silver or glass. It could be claimed that these
were 'personal' objects that could not only be
excluded from an inventory, but also disposed of
before the inventory was taken. By contrast, wills are
rich in legacies and gifts which were only rarely
included in inventories.

2   THE INTERIOR DEFINED, 1650–1900

THIS PERIOD WITNESSED a phenomenal growth in the number of consumer goods available, and their increasing trade in Europe and North America. Improved communications and transport in the form of turnpikes and canals furthered both the movement of goods and developing markets. In Britain, élite houses became the subject of public interest through the spread of domestic tourism. Further afield, reports of European customs became widespread through the phenomenon of the Grand Tour across Europe to Italy and Greece, while other travel accounts brought back descriptions and depictions of interiors from across the globe. New printmaking techniques in the form of stipple engraving, mezzotint and aquatint allowed for increasingly refined reproduction of artistic images and designs for the interior.

The development of the novel, as well as newspapers and magazines, prompted an increase in written and published descriptions of the interior. The interior began sometimes to figure as the subject of these writings as it had in works prescribing particular behaviour known collectively as conduct literature. The private consumption of prints further helped to develop a domestic space as one in which representations of different kinds played an increasingly important role. Interest in the historically distant past, as well as the geographically distant present, was fuelled by the recovery of remains of past civilizations in, for example, Pompeii and Herculaneum in Italy, and elsewhere in Egypt, North Africa and the Middle East. This outward vision was balanced by a growing interest in the interior as a focus for female pursuits and, above all, a place of psychological interiority.

Mary Ellen Best,
Painting Room in our House at York. Watercolour and body colour over pencil. *c.*1838.
York Museums Trust
(York Art Gallery)

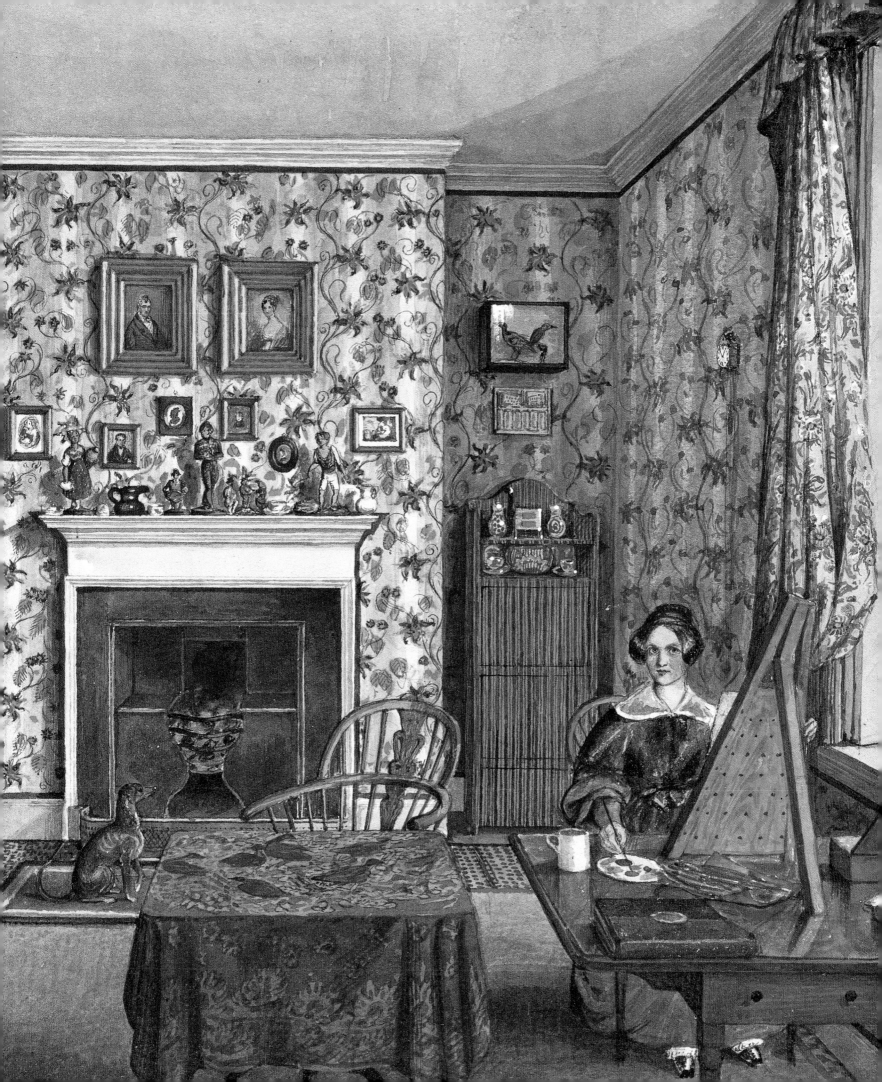

Eighteenth-Century English Interiors in Image and Text

Hannah Greig

THE EIGHTEENTH CENTURY was the first period in which English domestic interiors were represented extensively in both image and text. From personal correspondence to newspapers, individual portraits to multiple prints, private diaries to published periodicals, not to mention bills and receipts, pattern books, magazines, novels, poems, plays and more, portrayals of the domestic interior were both copious and varied. The diversity of representations is arresting, but their abundance prohibits an exhaustive survey. Instead, by examining a selection of typical material, extending from well-known paintings by Arthur Devis to lesser-known letters by eighteenth-century women, this chapter explores the relationship between visual and textual representations, identifying which concerns and themes were common, and which were unique, to different media. Rather than charting the development and significance of one particular type of representation, it is the emergence and co-existence of a range of representations that is the focus here.

Fundamental social and cultural changes occurred in the late seventeenth and early eighteenth centuries. Dramatically improved communications were a prominent feature of the age. Turnpikes and, later, new road building techniques cushioned and accelerated travel. By 1750 major routes connected London to expanding provincial centres, including Manchester, Bristol, Birmingham and York. In 1700 the journey from London to Bath was a 50-hour expedition. By 1800 it had been slashed to a 16-hour trip. Faster travel revolutionized the relationship between the metropolis and the provinces, propelling goods, people and information around the country.[1] A more sophisticated postal system, which included the first cheap London service as well as a regular national network, also smoothed the channels of communication.[2]

Thanks to crucial improvements in the printing industry, eighteenth-century England also had the most fully developed press in Europe.[3] The lapsing of the Licensing Act of 1695 freed the press from the legal constraints that had previously thwarted its advance, and innovations in printing techniques transformed production. In the 1730s, the larger provincial areas of England, Wales and Scotland had a regular local newspaper and by 1760 some 35 provincial papers were in circulation.[4] By 1783, London alone had 9 different daily papers (rising to 14 by 1790) in addition to numerous weekly editions.[5] The growth of the printing and printmaking industry also stimulated new forms of publication, both text (such as periodicals) and images (such as caricatures). Facsimiles of exhibited paintings and old masters, or reproductions of popular satires, were

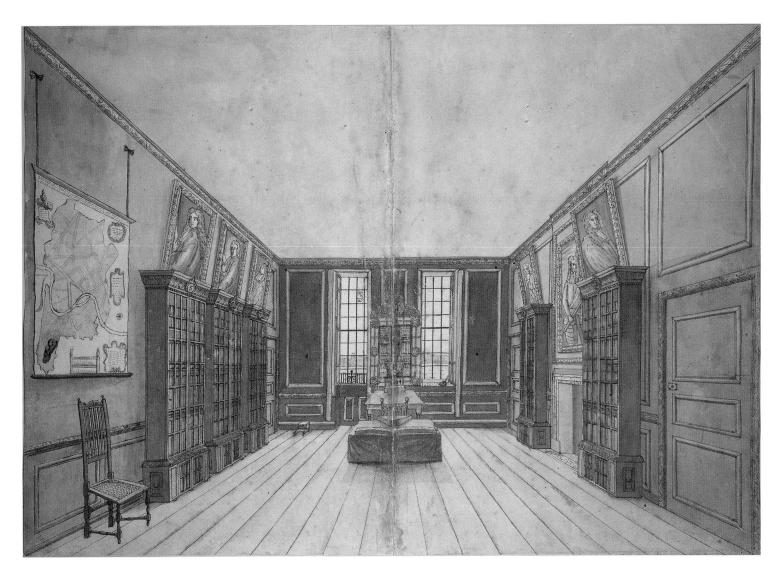

available for purchase, costing from a few pence to a few shillings apiece. The cultural transformation was spectacular. In the late seventeenth century London was host to just two significant print-sellers. By the end of the eighteenth century it was well established as the centre of the European print trade.[6]

Such data, though impressive, may seem tangential to the history of interior representations, yet these changes are crucial to understanding the character of the age. It was only during the 1700s that representations of interiors featured in English visual culture in any significant way. Whereas Renaissance Italy was rich in interior scenes, and seventeenth-century Netherlandish artists perfected the art of genre painting with carefully realized images of interiors, pre-eighteenth-century English images of the interior were remarkable for their extreme rarity.[7]

Two late seventeenth-century views of Samuel Pepys's library are acknowledged as the earliest surviving English visual portrayals of a whole and identifiable room (see pl.5.1).[8] Early architectural drawings paid little heed to interiors *per se*. In contrast, late seventeenth-century and early eighteenth-century architects such as William Talman (1650–1719), Sir John Vanbrugh (1664–1726), William Kent (1685–1748) and later Robert Adam (1728–92) designed both interior and exterior schemes.[9] More broadly, from the 1730s onwards, a glut of images can be identified in impressively varied forms. Indeed, the metamorphosis of England's visual culture, from an impoverished starting point to an embarrassment of riches, is

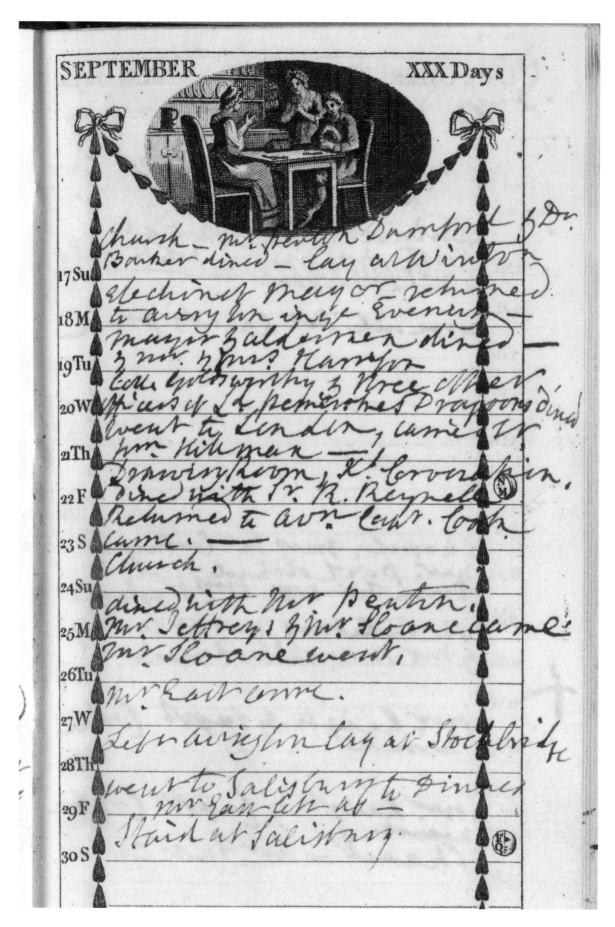

September XXX Days

17 Su
18 M
19 Tu
20 W
21 Th
22 F
23 S
24 Su
25 M
26 Tu
27 W
28 Th
29 F
30 S

5.2
Page from pocket book, *The Royal Engagement Pocket Atlas of the Year 1786*. The Huntington Library, San Marino, California

5.3
'Mr Morden taking leave of Miss Bowyer', plate VI from *The Town and Country Magazine*. 1769. The British Library, London

startling. Even modest and compact pocket books, used as diaries or memorandum books, had miniature illustrations, including depictions of interior scenes (see pl.5.2). Similarly from the 1750s, new weekly and monthly periodicals, such as *The Town and Country Magazine*, illustrated moral tales or educational essays with appropriate imagery, some of which referenced the domestic interior in a manner that echoed the popular illustrations of Samuel Richardson's novels (see pl.5.3 and 6.5–6.8).

The eruption of England's visual arts also had a wider impact, and images of interiors can be found beyond the printed page. The diary of Gertrude Savile, written in the 1720s and 1730s, records her selection of commercial prints of interior scenes as designs for seat covers in her own home.[10] She worked on six seat covers based on contemporary prints over a nine-year period. For two of her seats, Savile chose William Hogarth's colourful harlot, Moll, as her inspiration and copied plates two (see pl.5.4) and three (see pl.5.5) from the series of six devised by Hogarth for *A Harlot's Progress*. These pictures chronicled the fate of a country girl duped into urban prostitution and succumbing to disease and death. The speed of Moll's demise is told in these two plates, which move from the luxurious interior of plate two, to a scene of decline in plate three.

Savile's use of Hogarth's prints in this way exemplifies the proliferation of reproduced images in the eighteenth century. Painted in 1731, and engraved for prints in 1732, Hogarth's cautionary tale inspired verses, plays and ballads as well as selling widely in prints.[11] This success was not a one-off. Other series by Hogarth, including *A Rake's Progress* (1735) and *Marriage à la Mode* (1745), were also widely dispersed with new reproductions still appearing in the early nineteenth century. The interiors conjured by Hogarth for *A Harlot's Progress* featured the vicious and the dissipated, with disorderly rooms and criminal occupants, yet the pious and matronly Savile obtained these prints and worked fictional representations of the interiors into the fabric of her own domestic environment.

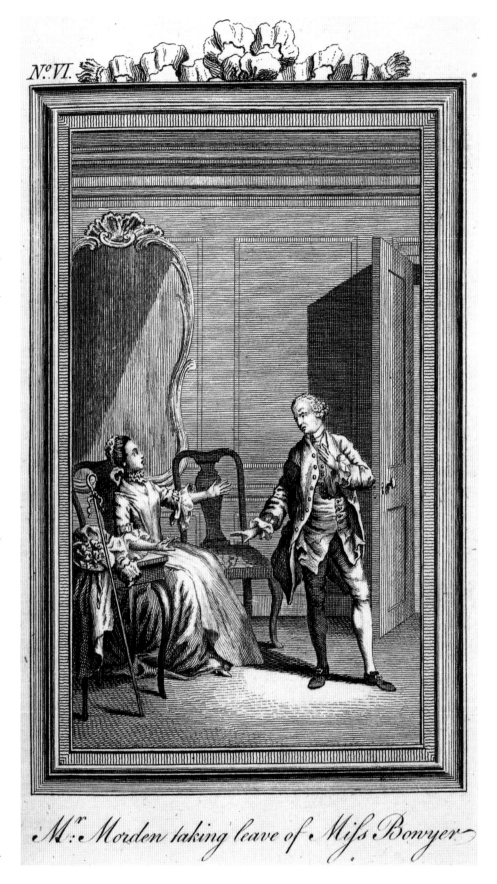

N.°VI.

M.ʳ Morden taking leave of Miſs Bonyer

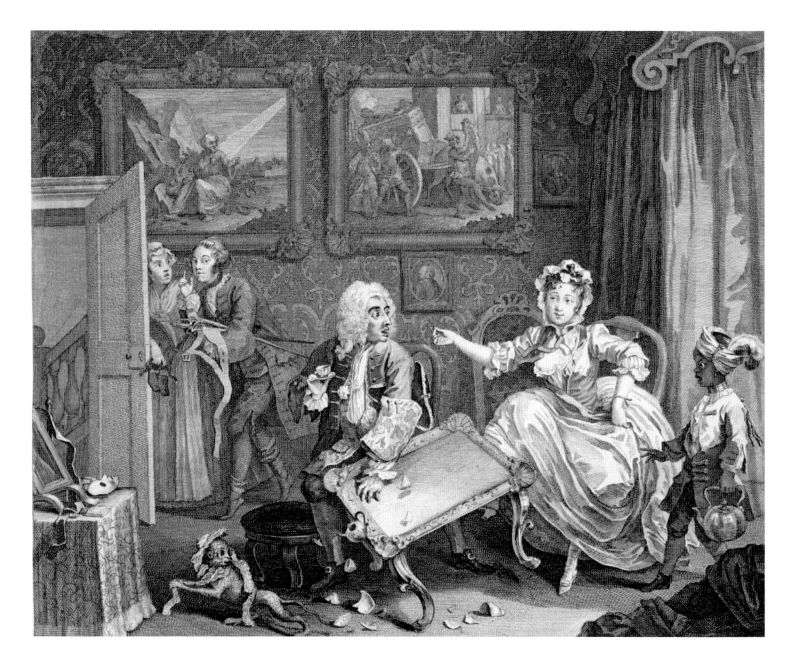

Additional examples reveal that domestic scenes, transferred from graphic images, decorated homes in a range of ways. Not all were bleak Hogarthian interiors. The embroidered seat cover (1728–40) in plate 5.6 has a densely realized interior scene. Again, the subject was inspired by a famous contemporary narrative, this time taken from Gay's *Fables*. The interior is refined and orderly, distinct from the varied accommodation of Hogarth's unruly Moll.[12] Other well-ordered interiors can be found illustrated on different types of domestic goods. For example, an interior scene of a group drinking tea is shown on the tea tray in plate

5.7. The interior on the tea tray is conspicuous for its simplicity. A few unadorned lines delineate the walls and windows, yet its very bareness conveys a spacious and elegant interior. Made in England in 1743, the domestic scene depicted on the tray reflected the function of the object itself (and indeed a tea tray of the same shape is shown in use within the illustrated scene). This echoing of use within the image is reminiscent of the decorative schemes seen on certain domestic objects of the Italian Renaissance. However, the subjects depicted on eighteenth-century English objects were not the birth rites of the Renaissance bedchamber

5.4

William Hogarth,
A Harlot's Progress, plate two.
Engraving and etching. 1732.
V&A: F.118:37

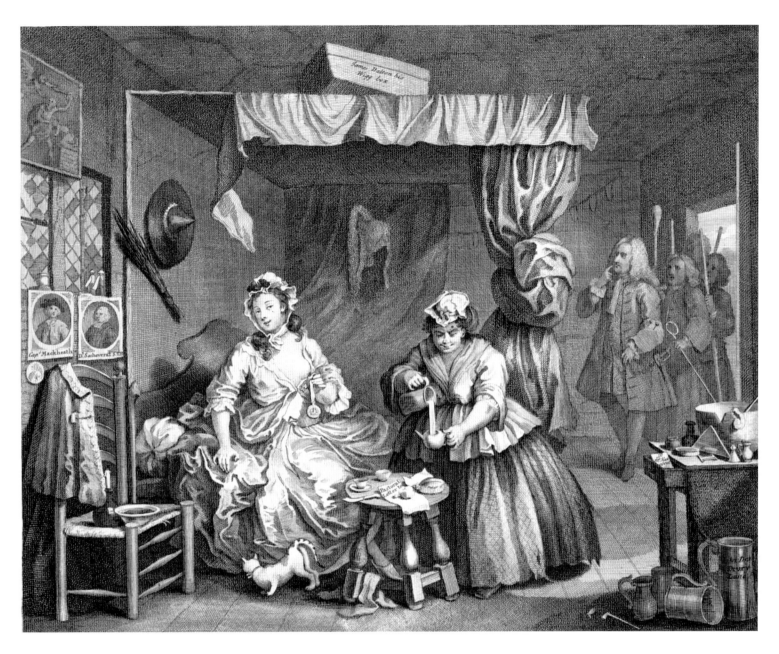

5.5
William Hogarth,
A Harlot's Progress, plate three.
Engraving and etching. 1732.
V&A: E.118:38

but the ritualized ceremonies of the Georgian tea table. Their concern was less with the drama of new life and religious ritual, and more with the everyday display of gentility and status.

It was not only the emergence of new prints, whether circulated on paper or as products, which pointed to a new stage in the history of interior representations. Other areas of English visual culture were also transformed in the eighteenth century. In particular, the preponderance of the painted 'conversation piece', a specific mode of eighteenth-century portraiture with two or more people posed in a social setting, is conspicuous. Seventeenth-century

portraiture typically glorified the individual, with the subject standing against a backdrop of luscious drapery or beside an imposing column. At most only a bare hint of interior detail was drawn in the shadows, just the corner of a desk or the back of a chair. In contrast, the eighteenth-century conversation piece presented the sitters as a social group amid familiar scenery, typically within an interior or in the grounds of an impressive estate.

With varying degrees of success, artists endeavoured to show the sitters in a comparatively relaxed guise, demonstrating a 'natural', easy gentility through everyday acts such as card-

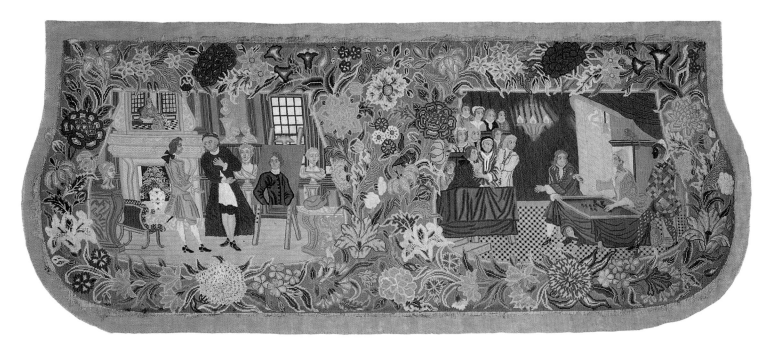

playing, tea-drinking or playing a musical instrument.[13] Fashionable from the late 1720s until the early 1770s, this style of portraiture appealed to a broad section of the Georgian well-to-do, from the titled to the self-made. Although the distinguishing traits of the conversation piece can be reduced to a short list of common features, within its strictures the domestic interior was represented in a range of ways, indicating diverse imaginings of domestic space.

A preoccupation with domestic activity is apparent in examples of this genre from the second quarter of the eighteenth century. As seen in early English compositions by Marcellus Laroon (the younger) and Samuel Wale (see pl.5.8–5.9), informal domestic groups dominate the canvas. Apparently beguiled by the novelty of tea-drinking, artists strove to capture its complex rituals and associated domestic scenes.[14] Both drawings study this ceremony and each makes strong reference to interior space, emphasizing the room's depth and scale. In Wale's, this is achieved by the inclusion of a doorway opening to a second interior. In Laroon's, size is suggested by the perspective view of a corner of a room. Both are concerned to show certain interior features, such as panelling and decoration. Yet, noticeably, the finer details are reserved for the figures, their clothing and utensils.

As the century progressed, fuller expression was given to the interior setting. With rich furnishings, elaborate lighting and imposing gilt framed pictures, the minutiae of the interior shown in Charles Philips's *Tea Party at Lord Harrington's House, St James's* (see pl.5.10) are delineated in far greater detail than Wale and Laroon's tea parties. By showing three walls Philips suggests the interior in full and the fixtures and furnishings are as sensitively traced as the activities and attitudes of the sitters. With the group pose restricted to the lower half of the canvas the interior looms large. Such a relationship between figures and the space they occupy is common to many English conversation pieces from the 1730s onwards. In Devis's *The Duet* (see pl.5.11) the proportions suggest an expansive interior in which the sitters are anchored by a single piece of furniture, a harpsichord.

Later in the century, music emerged as a common theme of group portraits, as tea-drinking had been previously.[15] John Greenwood's portrait of Richard Comyns and his daughters (see pl.5.12) and Johann Zoffany's image of the Gore Family (see pl.5.13) centre on music-making and offer remarkably similar representations of domestic space. Both depict a family group brought together around a keyboard; the main female character sits and plays,

5.6
After illustrations by William Kent, settee seat cover. Embroidered on canvas in wool and silk. 1728–40. V&A:T.473–1970

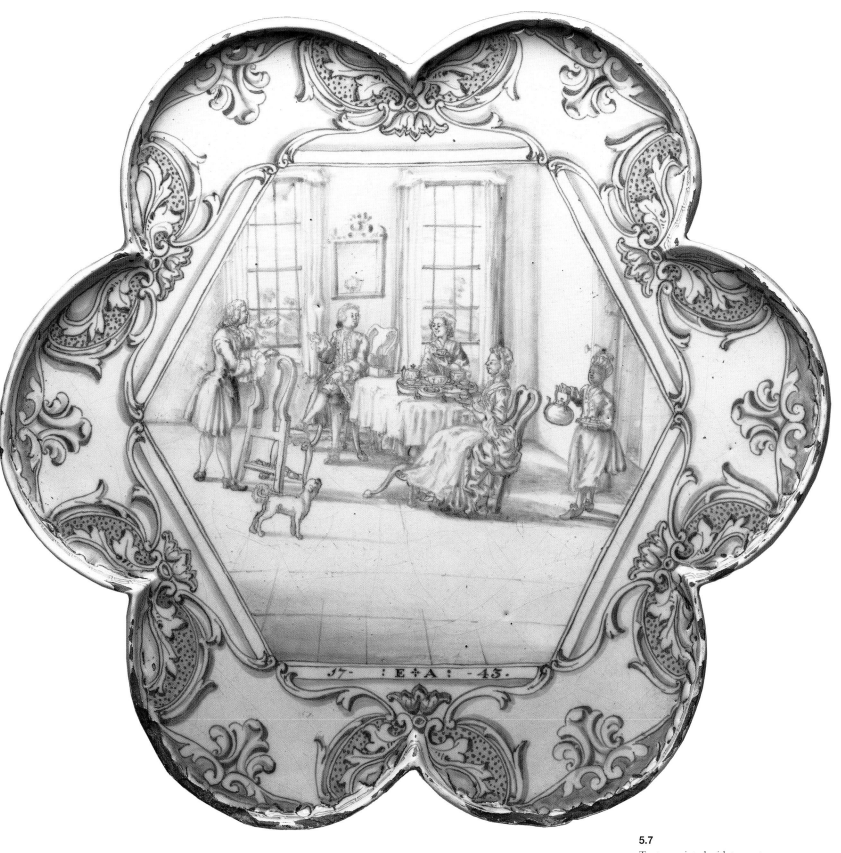

5.7
Tea tray painted with tea party
scene. Tin-glazed earthenware.
1743. V&A: 3864.1901

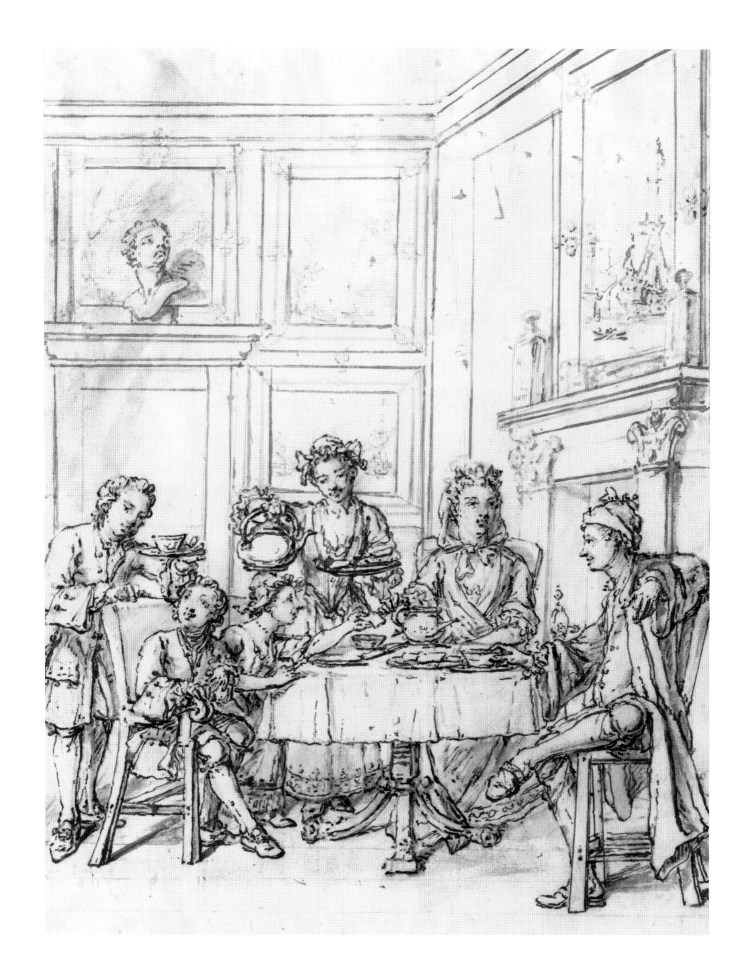

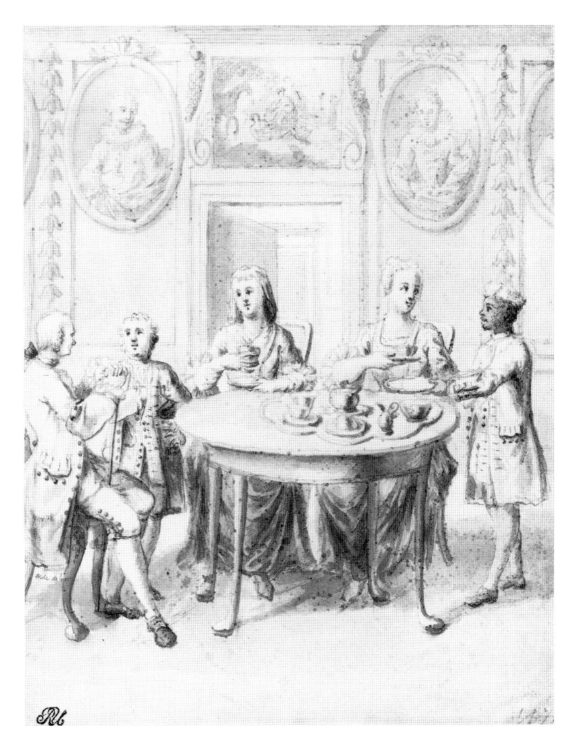

while the central male figure watches in a pose of relaxed but studied gentility. As in Devis's *The Duet* (1749), a window view highlights the relationship between outside and inside; although in Zoffany's portrayal this is significantly exaggerated with one wall dissolved, blurring these boundaries and giving enhanced expression to the exterior scene.

There are also striking contrasts between the Greenwood and Zoffany paintings. In the former, the simplicity of the interior mirrors the modest and unfussy dress of the figures. In Zoffany's, the aesthetic qualities of the interior space correspond to the riches of the Gore family's attire. Opinions differ as to whether 'real' interiors or fictitious backdrops were portrayed in such portraits. Hogarth's *Assembly at Wanstead House* (see pl.6.1) shows Sir Richard

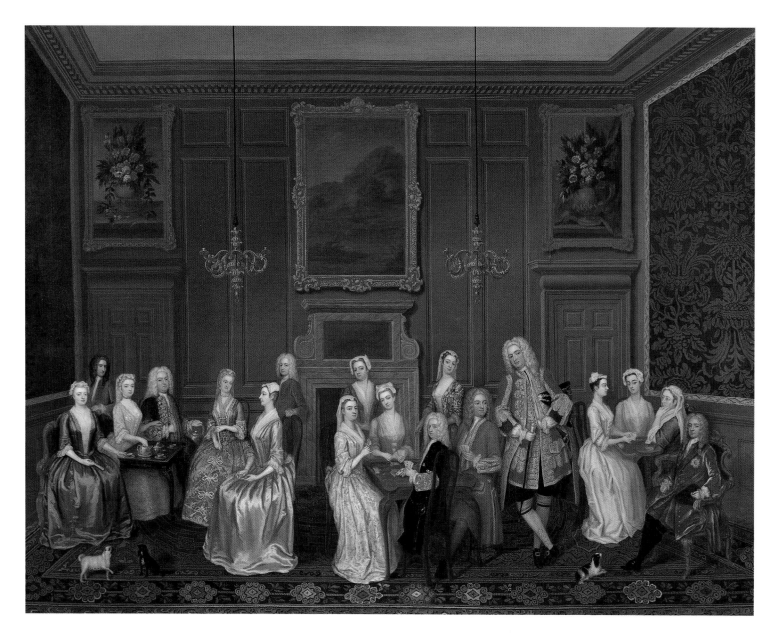

Child, his family and friends in the ballroom of his new home, it incorporates aspects from other parts of the house (such as the ceiling from the great hall) bringing them together within a single imagined interior. Arthur Devis, it has been suggested, drew almost entirely from a set repertoire of interior features, creating in some cases near identical interiors in portraits for different patrons.[16] We may never know for certain the ratios of 'real' to 'imagined' within these paintings. However, even interiors that are clearly fictitious (such as those painted by Devis) were significant responses to contemporary perceptions of domestic interiors, and therefore important to our understanding of

the development of such representations and of how people imagined interiors.

Why did domestic space emerge as a dominant visual strategy from the 1730s? The precedents set by European artists are well documented. Huguenot and Dutch artists, such as Philippe Mercier, Marcellus Laroon (the elder) and Van Hemmskerk, are widely credited with introducing the style to England.[17] Yet, to argue that the English trend was no more than a predictable emulation of European examples fails to account for the specific periodization. Why was it *eighteenth*-century England that experienced this new visual concern?

The opening decades of the century

5.10
Charles Philips,
Tea Party at Lord Harrington's House, St James's.
Oil on canvas. 1730.
Yale Center for British Art,
Paul Mellon Collection

5.11
Arthur Devis, *The Duet.*
Oil on canvas. 1749.
V&A: P.31–1955

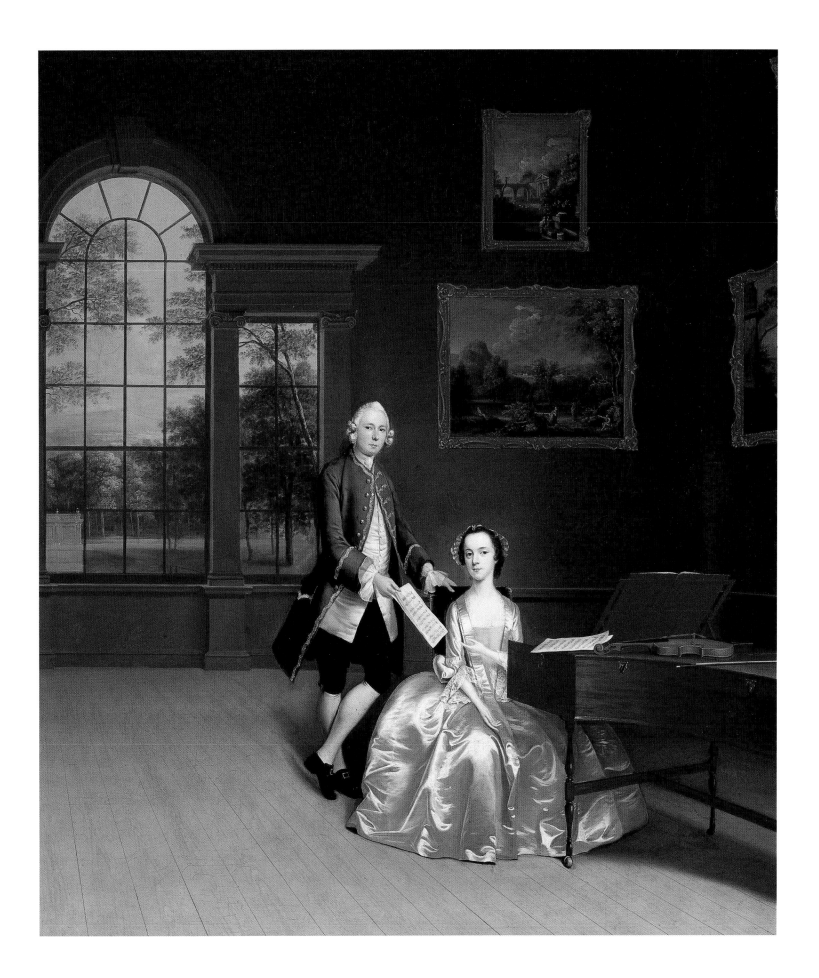

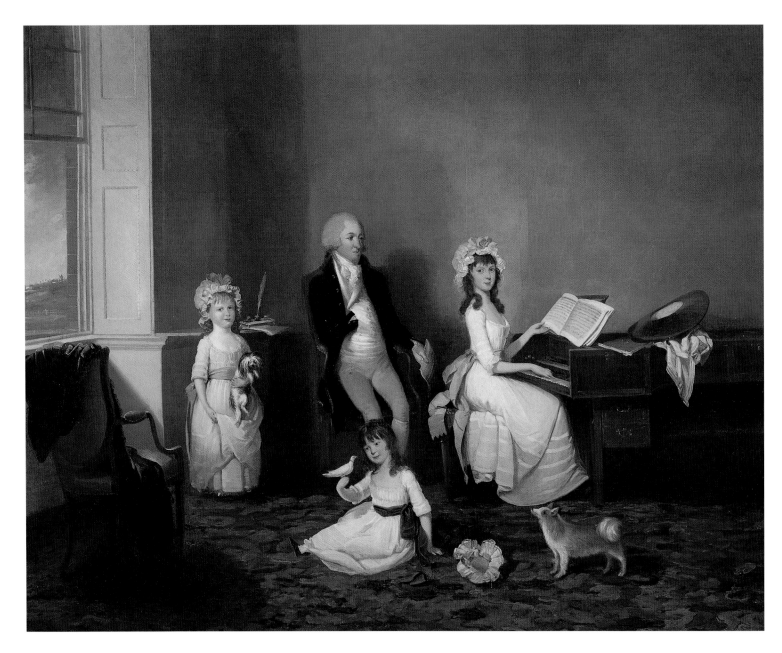

witnessed a remarkable building boom that permanently altered the appearance of the metropolis and the provinces.[18] The opportunity to build new housing specifically to the requirements of a developing urban environment, rather than patching-up old and inherited properties, had a lasting impact on interior planning. Whereas the country house occupied its own parkland, with ample space for expansion, the slender town house demanded a tidy vertical arrangement that made efficient use of the available space. With these changes in accommodation came new concepts of property. Urban housing offered

an alternative to the country estate and to the prioritization of land ownership, which had previously been the main determinant of status. The town house, grand though it might be, lacked the open acreage of the country seat, and its riches were tightly contained within its walls.

In this context, it is perhaps unsurprising that painted celebrations of property also incorporated a different, interior view. Of course, alongside conversation pieces that documented an interior were a comparable number that were set outside, either on terraces or over-looking an estate. Moreover, as has already been

5.12
John Greenwood,
John Richard Comyns of Hylands,
Essex with his Daughters.
Oil on canvas. 1775.
Yale Center for British Art,
Paul Mellon Collection

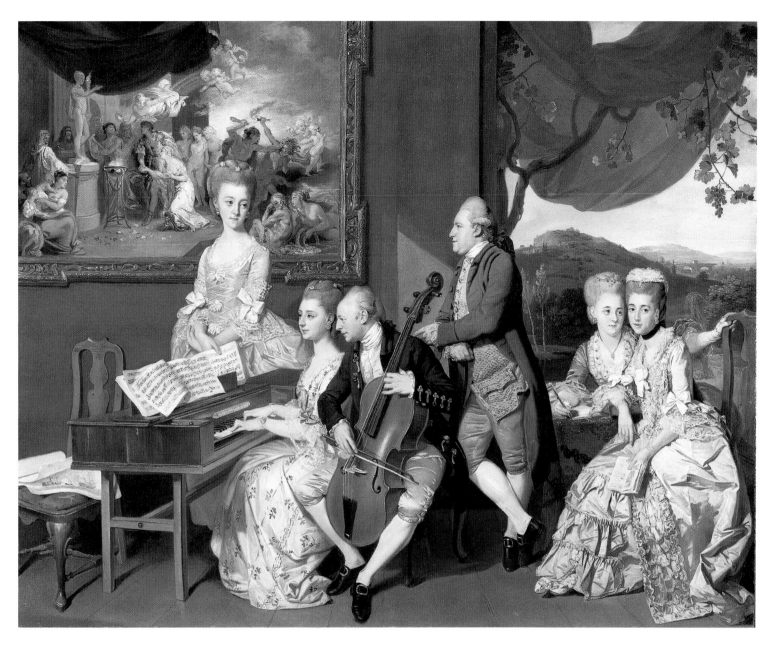

5.13
Johann Joseph Zoffany,
George, 3rd Earl Cowper, with the
Family of Charles Gore.
Oil on canvas. 1775.
Yale Center for British Art,
Paul Mellon Collection

seen, where interiors were used to stage group portraits it was often the case that a window was included in the scheme to offer an idealized view of rolling hills. Living space and property values may have changed, but the continued celebration of rural views is a reminder that new codes and values may well have co-existed with the old.

It was not only the built environment that altered in eighteenth-century England. The world of goods too was dramatically restyled, with new types of furniture, furnishings and domestic objects available for purchase. Indeed, the nation witnessed an increasing diversifica-

tion, number and circulation of consumer goods throughout the century.[19] The lengthy list of new and improved goods included teapots, cutlery (from soup spoons, teaspoons, and sugar tongs to cheese knives, fish knives and fish forks), large and varied dinner services (with dinner plates, side plates, dessert bowls, fruit bowls, punch bowls, gravy boats and fish dishes), carriage clocks, pocket watches, wall clocks, grandfather clocks, printed wallpaper, pianos, upholstered chairs, Chinese ceramics, French porcelain, Turkish carpets, Spitalfields silk, Indian muslin, Brussels lace and much more. Some of these items had been available to the most privileged in previous decades, but new trade routes, new financial systems and a widespread acceptance of commercial culture stimulated the supply of new and better products, and endowed those goods with a new significance. Lorna Weatherhill's comprehensive survey of probate inventories in the late seventeenth and early eighteenth centuries brings into sharp focus the extent of the change. Between 1675 and 1725, the percentage of households in her sample that owned pictures increased from 9 per cent to a more substantial 21 per cent, and ownership of utensils for hot drinks increased from 0 per cent to 15 per cent. These figures do not reach to the very poorest households. Nonetheless the expansion of consumer goods was extensive.[20]

Many items associated with this burgeoning commercial culture were depicted and privileged within the representations of the interior considered here. Although only part of the paraphernalia specific to the ceremony of tea drinking, the tea tray was reflective of this new consumerism and was an item designed with a particular purpose specific to the age. Furthermore, when families chose to be painted in the midst of this ceremony they displayed not only their ownership of a fashionable tea service, but also their skill at handling it. Equally, when refined ladies and gentleman were painted nonchalantly seated at a musical instrument, it was their education, accomplishment and enjoyment of expensive leisure time that was shown along with their impressive purchases.

Another major change was the prioritization of domestic sociability within the new code of conduct and manners articulated in the eighteenth century: the code of politeness.[21] Politeness was designed in part to ease social interaction in the confined quarters of urban space. Extending beyond simple prescriptions of etiquette (such as bowing, handshaking and appropriately acknowledging acquaintances) to be 'polite' in the eighteenth century involved understanding and enacting a whole philosophy and code of behaviour, from dress and decorum to speech and letter-writing. Together

these skills were believed to comprise the 'art of pleasing', smoothing interpersonal interaction. Polite conduct was presumed to apply to all forms of social behaviour, indoors and outside, and in both familial and professional life. However, its regulations had particular implications for the use and design of domestic space.

For those wealthy enough to participate, new forms of sociability were popularized, such as the assembly and later the ball, both of which were hosted in specially designed interior spaces, and often within a domestic interior. Circuits of interconnecting rooms became essential features of a large town house if crowds of guests were to be comfortably accommodated. As Lady Hertford complained to Lady Pomfret in 1741, 'every creature fancies themselves obliged to invite their acquaintances three or four times to their houses, not by small parties for that would be supportable, but they must all come at once'.[22]

Indeed, a common concern of eighteenth-century letter-writers was that family homes doubled as crowded assembly rooms. Consequently, within surviving contemporary correspondence, the domestic interior was typically represented as a significant social space. In January 1748, for instance, Mrs Boscawen described her first social encounter in a recently refurbished room. 'This afternoon I saw company in my dressing-room for the first time since its being furnished', she reported to her husband, 'and had Mrs Evelyn, Mrs Boone, her sister, two Mr Evelyns … Mrs Porter, Miss Cotterell and Lady Sandwich, and everyone admired my apartment, which is indeed a very pretty one'.[23]

In this instance, the precise details given regarding the appearance of the interior are few, but the room was nevertheless powerfully conveyed through the reported approbation of her visitors. For Lavinia, Countess Spencer, her house was at its most glorious when it accommodated guests and attracted visitors' praise. Writing to her husband to describe a recent ball she reflected on their impressive rooms:

I can not tell you how magnificent the

house was, the apartments were in a blaze of light and never in a crowd altho' there were more than two hundred and fifty people by the porters account, the carpets looked beautiful & everybody came up to me to envy my having had an opportunity of getting such Rich & Elegant things.[24]

This preoccupation with sociability may appear ample explanation for the emergence of visual representations of interiors. Surely a domestic background would be the predictable choice for those seeking to emphasize their social selves? Significantly, however, artists were equally skilled at depicting social interaction without intricate interior detail. This is illustrated in Richard Collins's *A Family of Three at Tea* (see pl.5.14) and Thomas Rowlandson's *A Tea Party* (see pl.5.15). Both are essentially domestic scenes. However, aside from a few pieces of key furniture, both are remarkably devoid of any reference to the fabric of those interiors. The existence of social scenes that *lack*

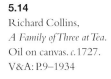

5.14
Richard Collins,
A Family of Three at Tea.
Oil on canvas. *c.*1727.
V&A: P.9–1934

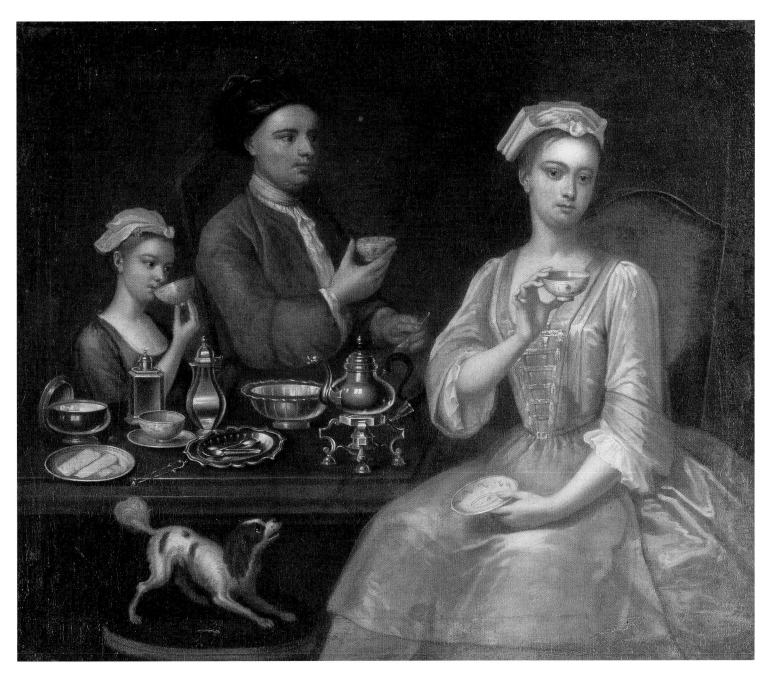

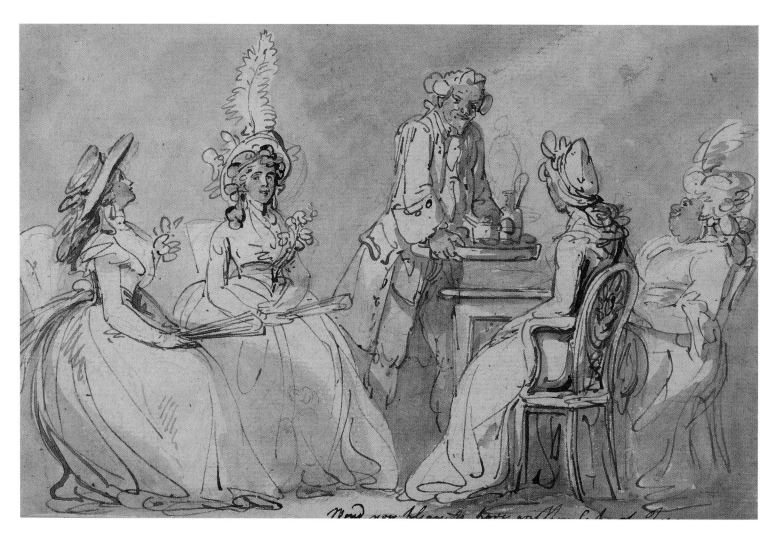

references to domestic interiors warns against presuming that a concern with social activity automatically heralded an increased visual preoccupation with interior space.

Moreover, the domestic interior in paintings was not only deployed to demonstrate sociability. The common use of interior scenes in eighteenth-century portraits of individuals testifies to use in other contexts. As well as completing many conversation pieces that depicted social groups, Devis also painted a host of individual portraits in similar interior scenes. *A Lady in a Drawing Room* (see pl.5.16) and *An Unknown Man Seated at a Table* (see pl.5.17) both show individuals at ease in an interior. Although not directly illustrating social action, these portraits nonetheless emphasize personal association with an interior setting. As with conversation pieces, the interior details are awarded the same artistic attention as the features of the sitters and their attire.

Whether associated with group interaction or individual display, the proudly polite and commercial culture of the eighteenth century was not without its critics. The diversification and increased availability of consumables brought their own pressures. In the wake of the new range of goods that were sold across the country grew a concern about 'taste'. The distinction between gentility and vulgarity, between 'good' and 'bad' taste, was worryingly blurred in the contemporary imagination.[25] The domestic interior, it was believed, was particularly at risk and an all too convenient setting for offensive show. As the author of the poem *The Woman of Taste* warned in 1733,

> Wou'd you then please and be a toast of note
> Though *Kitty* wants a frock and *Charles* a coat,
> Spare no expense to make your *Villa* fine,

5.15
Thomas Rowlandson,
A Tea Party.
Pen, ink, pencil and watercolour
on paper. *c.*1790–5.
Yale Center for British Art,
Paul Mellon Collection

5.16
Arthur Devis,
A Lady in a Drawing Room.
Oil on canvas. *c.*1740–1.
Yale Center for British Art,
Paul Mellon Collection

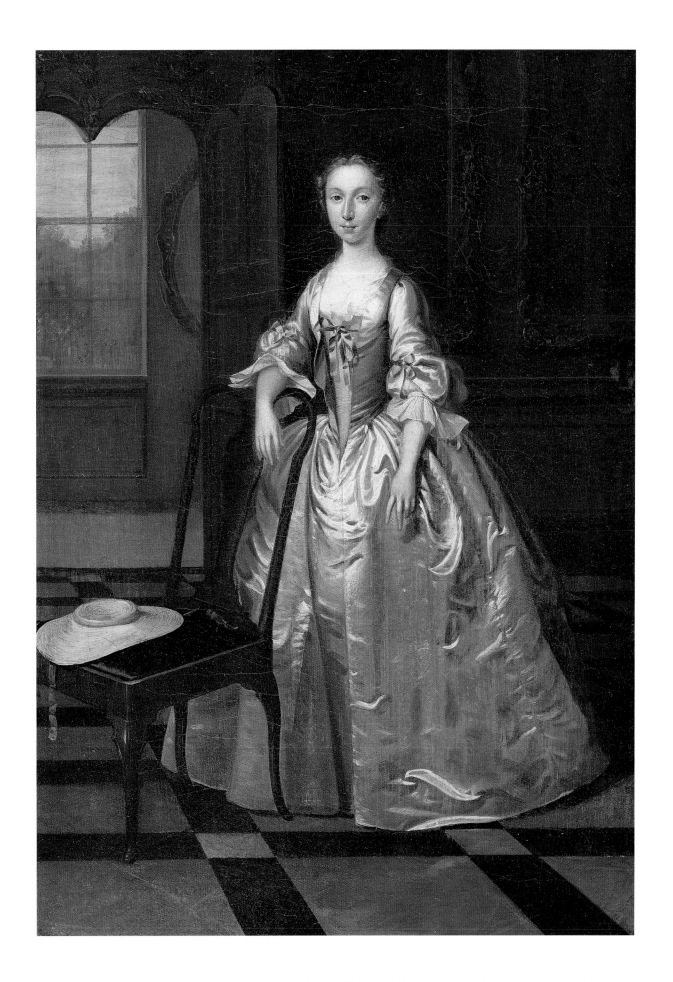

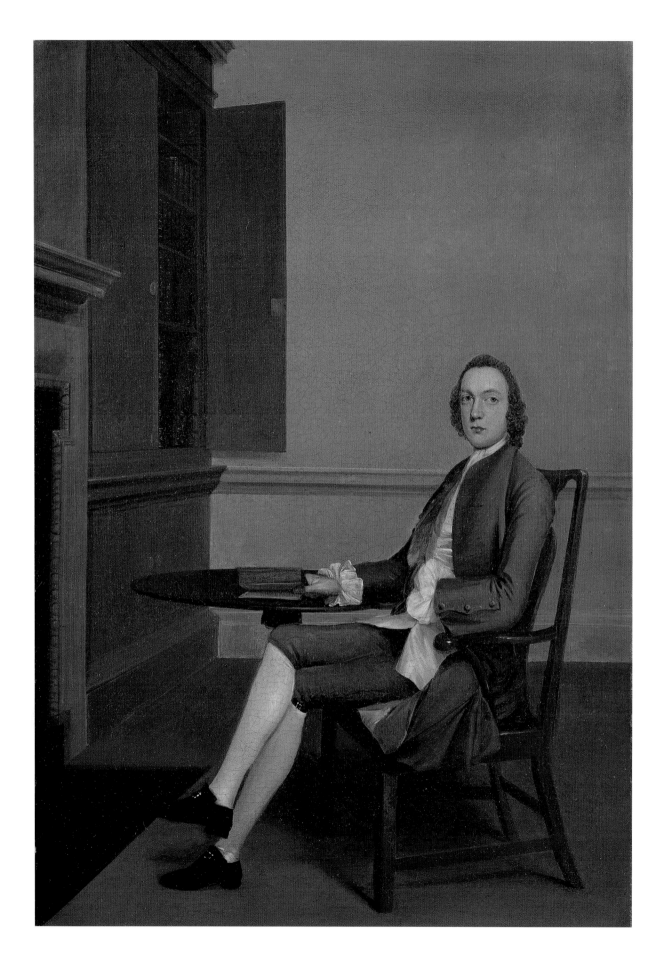

O'er gay walls let *Holben's* pictures shine,
China her jars, and costly vases shew,
Load the gilt chimney, and japan'd bureau,
On every floor, in every chamber seen,
Persia's rich carpet, *India's* imagined screen,
The *Lombard* pencil and the *Asian* loom,
Contending which shall best adorn you room,
Your frugal guineas with much wisdom spent,
To deck a closet, with one manour's rent.[26]

Surviving correspondence reveals that the ability to demonstrate a refined taste within the domestic interior was a major preoccupation amongst those responsible for furnishing the home. This was, for example, a concern for Mrs Boscawen, who noted in December 1747: 'I have tried at china ornaments for my chimney-pieces, which demand them in great quantities, but I have not been able yet to raise myself to the price of anything good and I don't care for a parcel of trumpery – like some chimney-pieces we know of'.[27]

When furnishing a new family house in London in the 1710s, the Countess of Strafford was similarly watchful of the appropriateness of furniture and decorative effects. Monitoring the preferences of London's élite, she was quick to correct her husband if he proposed an out-moded style, sent updates of what was 'quite the fashion' and negotiated with her husband to ensure certain accoutrements appeared in their home. The Countess was as contemptuous of those she believed failed to meet the standard, as she was anxious to follow the latest style. For example, describing the accommodation chosen by their acquaintances the Marshalls, she reported:

I wonder Mr Marshall can talk of his great living here, for they had a very indifferent Lodging in St James's Street, & the house was kept the Nastiest I ever see a House … & she sat in the first room with a Cole fire and Tallow candles which I know was made a great jest on.[28]

The possibility of a similar social *faux pas* was clearly on Sarah, Lady Cowper's mind when she recorded in her diary a dispute with her husband over the appearance and use of reception rooms. Writing in 1705 she noted:

We have now gott a Drawing Room hung with Damask and furnish'd well enough, so I propos'd there might be a Billet kindled every afternoon and if no Vistant come by 4 a clock the Usual time I go forth the fire wou'd be soon laid by, but Sir W[illiam Cowper] Said No, that was very expensive, 'twere better light it when Company came in being Soon done, to which my reply was I cou'd not Expose myself So as to be Calling out Fire when La[dies] were there … and if that was to be his way I chose rather to Sit by a Cole fire in the Parlour.[29]

Personal accounts such as these imply that good taste and judgement were not only attained through the display of certain choice ornaments but also extended through a broader range of objects and practices. Both Sarah, Lady Cowper and the Countess of Strafford revealed that there were many stages and elements to the complicated performance of gentility and status – the correct type of fuel for a fire in the correct room, which was appropriately decorated, appropriately situated within the house and appropriately used by its occupants.

It was not only murmured confessions within contemporary diaries and letters that reveal such concerns. Artists also reflected upon the problems that faced the eighteenth-century consumer and used images of interiors to showcase their concerns. Although Hogarth painted a number of conversation pieces, many of his paintings and subsequent prints, such as *A Midnight Modern Conversation* (1733), *A Harlot's Progress* (1732) and *Marriage à la Mode* (1745), portrayed the risks of sociability, the superficiality of politeness, the decadence and criminality of urban life, and the horrors of vulgarity in equal measure. In each famous Hogarth series, images of the interior were a key narrative device, often inverting the stylistic codes of the conversation piece to invoke disorderly and immoral domestic scenes. The framing devices and themes privileged in the conversation piece also provided ample fodder for the vicious wit of caricaturists towards the end of the century and into the early 1800s. Robert Dighton's *The Harmonious Family* (see pl.5.18) and Thomas Rowlandson's *Miseries Personal* (see pl.5.19), for example, illustrated informal social groups engaged in music-making and dining. The details of the interior are drawn with the same attention as the features of the figures. However, whereas the interiors shown in conversation pieces were strikingly commodious, easily accommodating polite sociability, in Dighton and Rowlandson's images the interior space is too small for such activities, rendering the interior crowded and the occupants clumsy.

As this begins to reveal, when studying representations of the English domestic interior it is important to note that ideals of politeness, consumption and good taste were not uncon-tested in the eighteenth century. It was not simply that visual or textual representations were either 'for' or 'against' prescriptions of polite-ness, sociability or active consumption. Certain representations were shaped by (and conveyed) the contradictory messages of the age, and both embraced consumer culture whilst distancing the subject from its more problematic associa-tions. Although famous for their interiors, Devis's portraits, for example, have on occasion been dismissed by historians and art historians as rather idiosyncratic examples of the conver-sation piece genre. In comparison to the work of other artists, Devis's interiors are simple, sparsely furnished and, it has been claimed, unimaginative and uninspired.[30] However, rather than representing a bizarre deviation, Devis's imagery can also be read as a powerful expression of the pressures felt by contempo-raries, pressures engendered by the broader discourses surrounding politeness and taste.

On comparing a range of Devis's portraits,

5.18
Robert Dighton, *The Harmonious Family*. Pen and black ink and brush and grey ink over grey and black washes on laid paper. Yale Center for British Art, Paul Mellon Collection

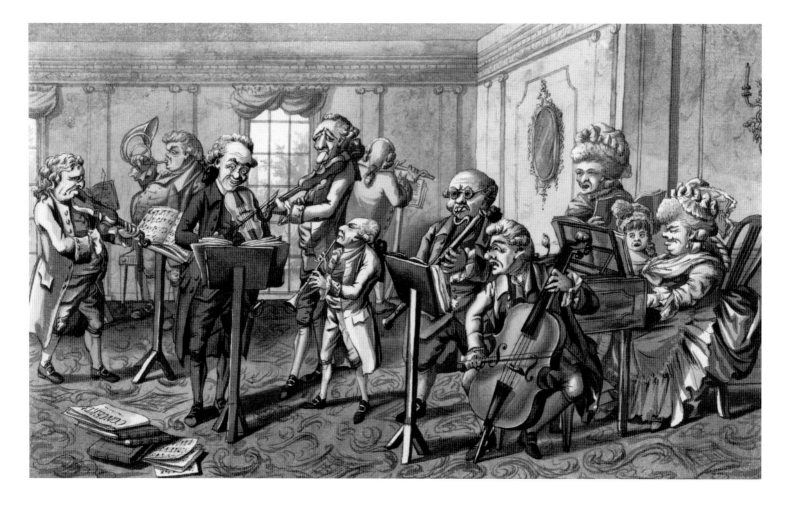

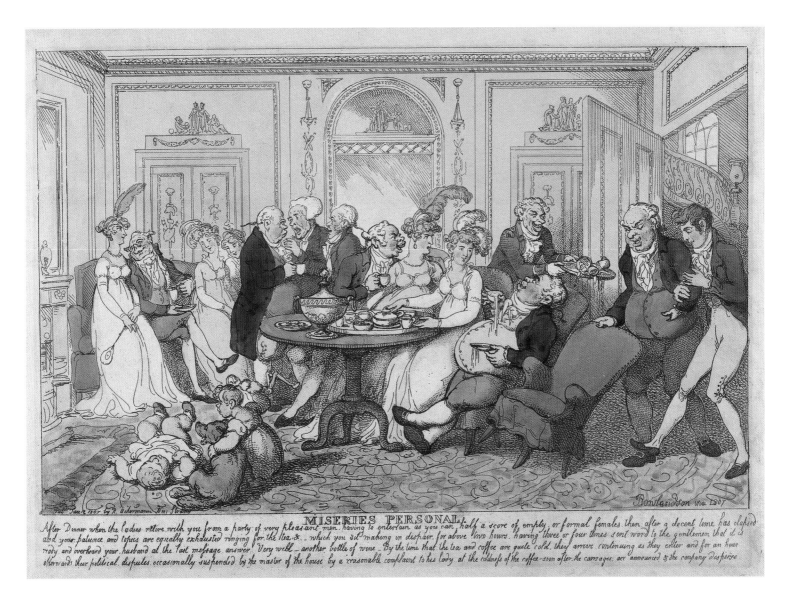

MISERIES PERSONAL. *After Dinner when the ladies retire with you from a party of very pleasant men, having to entertain as you can, half a score of, empty, or formal females then after a decent time has elapsed and your patience and topics are equally exhausted ringing for the Tea &c. — which you sit making in despair, for above two hours, having three or four times sent word to the gentlemen that it is ready, and overhear your husband at the last message answer, Very well — another bottle of wine — By the time that the tea and coffee are quite cold, they arrive, continuing as they enter and for an hour afterwards their political disputes occasionally suspended by the master of the house by a reasonable complaint to his lady at the coldness of the coffee — soon after the carriages are announced & the company disperse*

5.19

Thomas Rowlandson,
Miseries Personal.
Coloured etching. *c.*1790–5.
Yale Center for British Art,
Gift of Mrs Paul Moore

which are set in an interior, with paintings in the same genre by other artists, certain distinguishing features emerge. Whereas Zoffany, Greenwood and Philips, for example, sought to convey the scale of the interior, Devis more often depicted only a corner of a room, setting the group or individual in a much smaller interior space than was the convention.[31] The interiors and figures shown in the majority of Devis's portraits are noticeably stripped of any ornament that might be considered excessive. The sitter's dress is often simple and unadorned, devoid of the bejewelled show favoured by Zoffany. Heavy gilt candelabras, glittering mirrors, expensively decorated china or yards of luxurious drapery are rarely found in Devis's compositions.

When viewed in the light of complex contemporary debates, such imagery emerges as strategic rather than eccentric. Devis's conversation pieces enabled his clients to be depicted in a modish form of portraiture set within an interior. Yet, by keeping the interior scene bare and simple, Devis successfully defended them against accusations of flashy show or gaudy bad taste. Devis's portraits of individuals seem to offer a similar defensive strategy. Again the fashionable interior scene was detailed, but by showing an individual alone, the client was clearly protected from contemporary concerns about the superficiality and vulgarity of constant group activity. Notably, whilst Devis's style appealed to a broad range of patrons – and he claimed a fair share of the titled élite in his

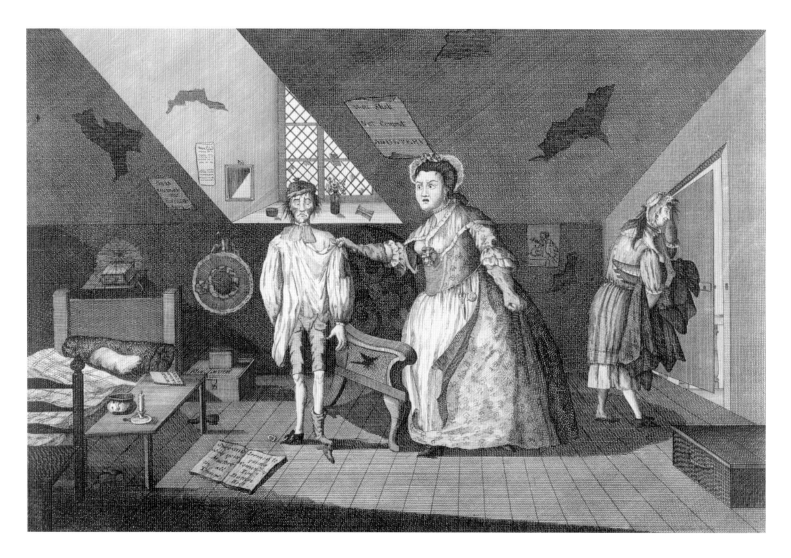

5.20
Artist unknown (Cabbage),
*The Methodist Taylor Caught in
Adultery*. Engraving. 1768.
Yale Center for British Art,
Paul Mellon Collection

books – one of his major client groups was wealthy northern merchant families. This group kept abreast of metropolitan fashions and changing tastes, and were proudly knowledgeable of what was modish. Yet they distanced themselves from fashion's extremes.[32] It is this combination of knowledge and restraint that is carefully captured and reflected in Devis's images of interiors.

Almost all of the representations discussed thus far, both visual and textual, were preoccupied with patterns of the consumption of élite and middling groups. It is, of course, the records of the wealthy that have most frequently survived. The lives of the majority of the population, particularly the poorest, are harder to trace. Although rarer than the conversation pieces and prints that portray the élite, images of the poorer sections of society, their lifestyles and homes, do feature within the spectrum of

eighteenth-century representations. Some of the most famous images of the poor from this period are squalid street or market scenes, for example Hogarth's *Gin Lane* (1751). In these, the poor are portrayed as uncontained and uncontainable, existing beyond the constraints and discipline imposed by a walled domestic environment. However, within this genre, a small number of interior views can also be identified. Better known examples include *The Poet's Lodgings* and *A Harlot's Progress*. Equally arresting are lesser known prints such as *The Methodist Taylor Caught in Adultery* (see pl.5.20) and *The Hen Peckt Husband* (see pl.5.21).

Although a considerable range of furnishings are detailed, both images show the interior in a state of shabby decay, a stark contrast to the polished settings of the conversation piece. These representations depicted very different interior spaces, the garret and the kitchen.

These rooms were absent from portrayals of the élite, which focused almost exclusively on grand reception rooms. Moreover, the ordered, genteel and harmonious family units of the élite conversation piece were not reflected in these representations. Instead, the gendered nature of domestic authority and management was laid bare.

The range of representations available for the eighteenth century is such that written descriptions of interiors can be found to echo sentiments suggested in visual forms, and vice versa. For every Hogarth image criticizing excessive consumption, supporting textual arguments can be found. For every testimony of glorious domesticity in a letter, a suitably showy portrait of an owner relaxing in their resplendent house can be produced. Yet, in one regard,

5.21
Unknown, *The Hen Peckt Husband*. Line engraving. 1768. Yale Center for British Art, Paul Mellon Collection

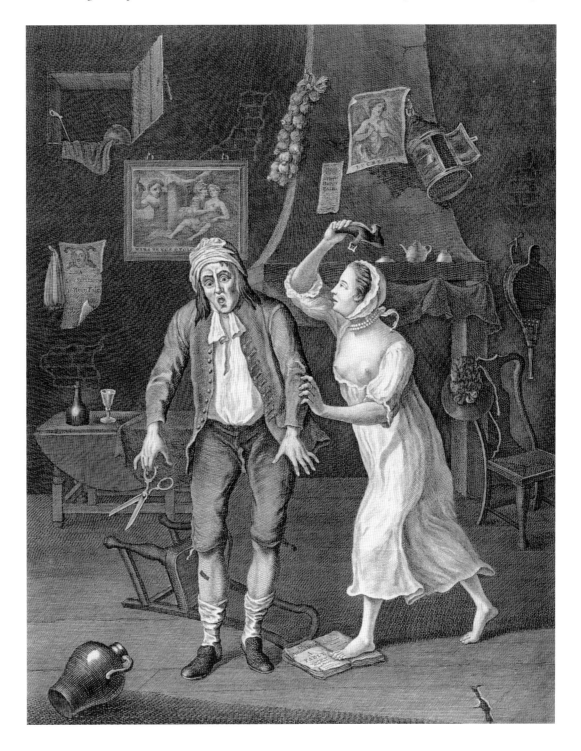

certain visual and textual representations of interiors were fundamentally different. Within letters and diaries written by contemporaries (which survive in both published and unpublished forms today) the domestic interior was routinely described as demanding renovation and repair. It was a space that had to be built, furnished, redecorated, refurbished and rebuilt over time. Consequently, these writings portrayed the domestic interior in a starkly different way to visual portrayals, which show the interior as furnished and complete.

A marked concern with domestic management is so commonplace that it appears mundane and unremarkable within personal papers. Building accounts for extensions to houses, and the costs and nature of successive alterations, can be drawn from many a collection of family records. Surviving receipts and bills from upholsterers, cabinet-makers and even window cleaners testify to domestic interiors that are worn with use. Between January and June 1772, for example, the Earl Spencer spent £93 on the interior upkeep of Spencer House, London.[33] Fire screens, music stands, lanterns, chairs, dressing tables, beds, carpets, dining tables, a tea kettle, sofas and sideboards were all mended. Curtains were ordered, sewn and hung. A bathing machine was fitted. Paintings were commissioned and carefully positioned, and every item of the interior, from pewter kitchenware to marble statues, was scrutinized and repaired as necessary. Contemporary letters, diaries, account books, memoirs, bills and trade cards all detailed incomplete interiors in need of constant attention.

This apparently routine concern with refurbishment in personal papers and manuscripts appears noteworthy when contrasted with visual representations. Prints, drawings and paintings predominantly portrayed fully furnished and complete interiors. Images of incomplete interiors (excluding architectural and technical drawings) are rare. A frontispiece to *The Chimneypiece Maker's Daily Assistant*, represented an interior under construction (see pl.5.22). Here, however, the incomplete interior is used to showcase the skills of a particular trade. In this regard, then, it is distinct from the incomplete interiors described in letters, diaries and accounts, which are associated with the owners and residents. An anonymous print from 1786, titled *Frederick Elegantly Furnishing a Large House* (see pl.5.23), is therefore

5.22
Frontispiece to *The Chimney-piece Maker's Daily Assistant*. 1766. NAL: 34.B.62

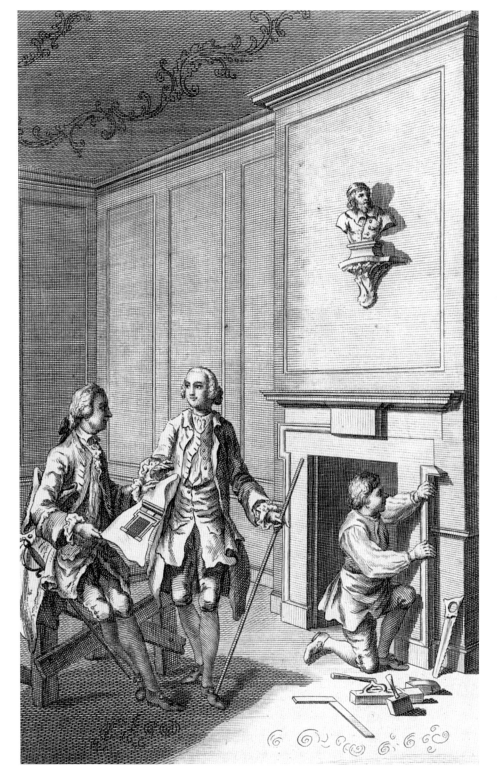

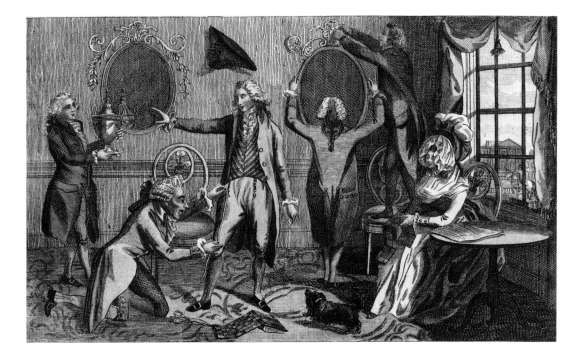

5.23
Anon., *Frederick Elegantly Furnishing a Large House*. Etching and engraving with hand colouring. 1786. Lewis Walpole Library, Yale University

extremely unusual in its portrayal of a property being furnished by its residents. Here the dressing of 'Frederick' occurs alongside the dressing of the interior. That such a major preoccupation of textual representations was so rarely considered in visual forms is remarkable. It reveals that, although they were often comparable, representations of interiors in eighteenth-century image and text were not always identical and offered, in many ways, fundamentally different portrayals.

Overall the range of themes addressed in eighteenth-century English representations of interiors is impressive. Celebrations of the glory of the well-furnished home coexisted with stark warnings about the perils of excessive consumption. Endorsements of the benefits of sociability ran alongside anxieties about its superficiality, and concerns that sociability undermined business and familial affairs. These conflicting messages together created a multi-layered discourse that was reflected and mediated within contemporary representations of the interior.

Certainly, different forms of representation would have reached different audiences. The painted conversation piece, proudly hung in a family home, would have been viewed differently by contemporaries to caricatures clustered in the print shop window. Personal notes in diaries, or letters to family members describing purchases, were fundamentally different to the bills and receipts presented by tradesmen to consumers for domestic goods. Yet together the constellation of visual and textual references to interiors from the eighteenth century brings into focus contemporary preoccupations with domestic space.

Representations of interiors reflected and also shaped the new consumer culture and new conceptions of property current to the age. Rather than being ascribed to any single cause – be it the emulation of European precedents, the precepts of politeness, the growth of urban space or the boom in consumer goods – the centrality of the interior within contemporary representations drew on all of these influences. Some interiors depicted were direct representations of real homes. Others were artistic imaginings. Nevertheless, many in eighteenth-century England chose to be portrayed in a domestic setting and such domestic imagery was available, in both image and text, in a broad range of forms. Indeed, that some of the interiors were aspirational, or idealized, merely highlights further the centrality of the interior to eighteenth-century evaluations of status and identity.

Representing Rooms: plans and other drawings

Michael Snodin

Before the sixteenth century representations of interiors other than by artists were surprisingly rare. The different ways of showing interiors as plans, elevations, sections and perspectives, which seem so self-evident today, fully emerged only in the mid-sixteenth century as architects (a new profession) gradually took control of the whole design of buildings both inside and out. From the later seventeenth century onwards such drawings became more common with the development of the totally designed interior, with matching wall decoration, furniture and furnishings, and the emergence of the interior designer. The mode of representation has always been closely linked to the function of the drawing. Measured drawings to scale only became essential when proportion became a key element in architecture, with exteriors and interiors being required to match and work together. The main measurable method was the orthographic (i.e. non-perspectival) plan, elevation and section, which directly demonstrated proportions and the distribution of elements. Orthographic interior drawings appeared in Italy in the sixteenth century: they reached Britain in the next century with the work of Inigo Jones and his pupil John Webb. Interior elevation drawings could also show elements cut through in section, such as the ceiling beams and mouldings

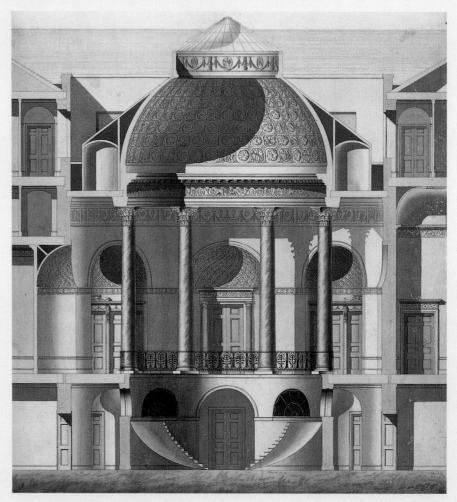

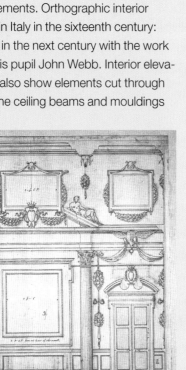

in Webb's design shown here (see pl.5.24), giving an illusion of reality. In fact orthographic drawings show what we know is there rather than what we actually see, which would of course be in perspective. This idea was developed into a way of showing buildings cut open in section. They were often virtuoso exercises in calculated shading and perspective, such as James Paine's exhibition drawing illustrated here (see pl.5.25).

For most of the eighteenth century, however, British architects preferred to use another drawing convention, namely the laid-out interior. This combined a ground plan with orthographic wall elevations radiating from it. According to the architect

5.24
John Webb, *Design for an interior*. Pen, ink and wash. *c*.1640–60. V&A: 3436.66

5.25
James Paine, *Section of Wardour Castle, Wiltshire, from South to North*. Pen, ink and wash. *c*.1770. V&A: 8416.3

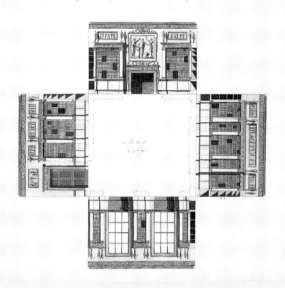

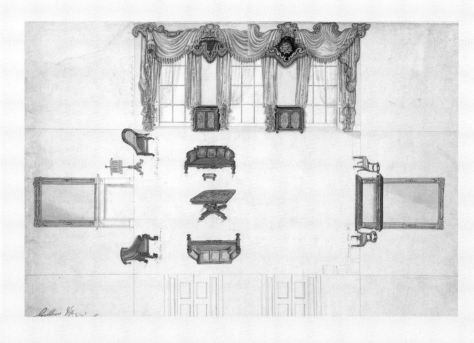

Isaac Ware in 1768, such drawings greatly aided the designing of rooms in which the four walls had to match in proportion and decoration. It was also possible, he maintained, to 'raise them perpendicularly' in the imagination, and 'see the room in miniature; divested of its ceiling'. Difficult as this feat is, it lay behind the use of such drawings to show interior design schemes to the clients of the Adam brothers and Gillow and Co., the interior decorators. Gillow's odd mix of orthographic elevations and furniture in perspective and at all angles shows the convention taken to its furthest point (see pl.5.27).

Although artists had shown interiors in perspective since the fifteenth century, it did not become a convention in designing interiors until the second half of the eighteenth century, encouraged by the need for alluring architectural views and interior design schemes in publications and public exhibitions. Its growth was matched by a fashion for drawing 'portraits' of existing rooms, such as those commissioned by Horace Walpole in the 1780s to show his collection-filled interiors at Strawberry Hill. The artists making them may have had the use of William Storer's 'Delineator', a camera obscura drawing device acquired by Walpole in 1777 and promoted by its inventor as being suitable for 'persons, or prospects, or the insides of rooms' (see pl.5.28).

5.26
Robert Adam, *Presentation Design for the Library at Mamhead House, Devon*. Pen, ink and wash. 1766. V&A: D.2174–1896

5.27
Gillow and Co., *Design for furnishing a room, with alternative suggestions*. Pen, ink and watercolour. 1819. V&A: E.17–1952

5.28
Thomas Sandby, Paul Sandby and Edward Edwards, *The Gallery at Strawberry Hill, Middlesex*. Pen, ink and wash. Completed by Edward Edwards in 1781. V&A: D.1837–1904

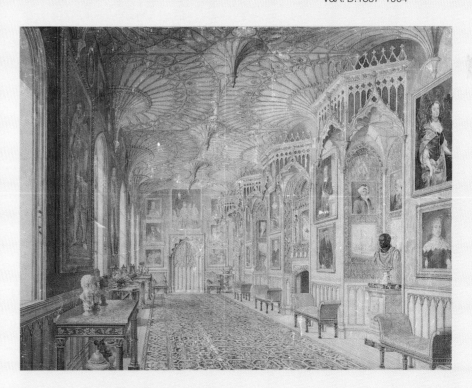

Inside the Interior: furniture and its inner spaces in eighteenth-century France

Carolyn Sargentson

Furniture made for eighteenth-century Europe's aristocratic and commercial élite was as much about the arrangement of the internal space it enclosed as the way it was perceived from the exterior – closed, static and unrevealing of its inner complexity. French furniture was particularly intricate in its design, especially in the case of forms made specifically for women, including toilet tables, jewel caskets and writing tables. Such objects often combined two or more functions, allowing (just as in the case of room use at this period) the potential for flexibility and the temporary transformation of space according to the activity that was taking place in it. Within a number of possible contexts of intimacy and privacy, furniture expressed simultaneously the possibility of exposure – revealing interior writing surfaces, drawer fronts and other decorative and functional features which might be used in the semi-public space of salon or boudoir (see

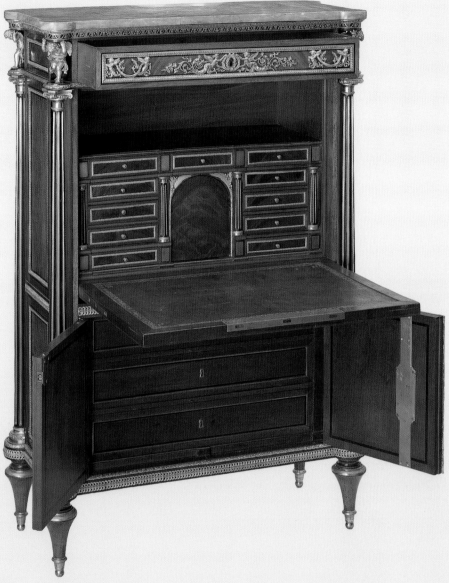

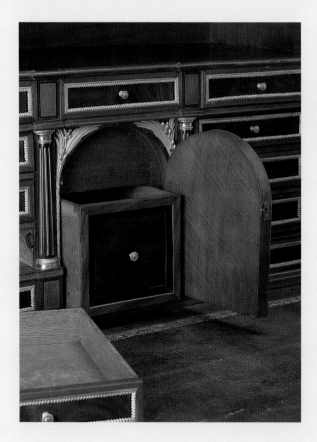

pl.5.29) – and of concealment – through devices such as locks, springs and other triggers which protected in secure spaces and secret compartments items of symbolic or monetary value (see pl.5.30). Only the owner, in principle, could have understood the full relationship between these two aspects, the latter being only guessed at by family members, household servants and domestic audiences alike.

To support both public and private use, furniture

5.29
Above: Attributed to Guillaume Benneman, secrétaire. Oak veneered with mahogany, gilt bronze mounts, marble slab. 1785–90. V&A: W.23–1958

5.30
Left: (detail of 5.29)

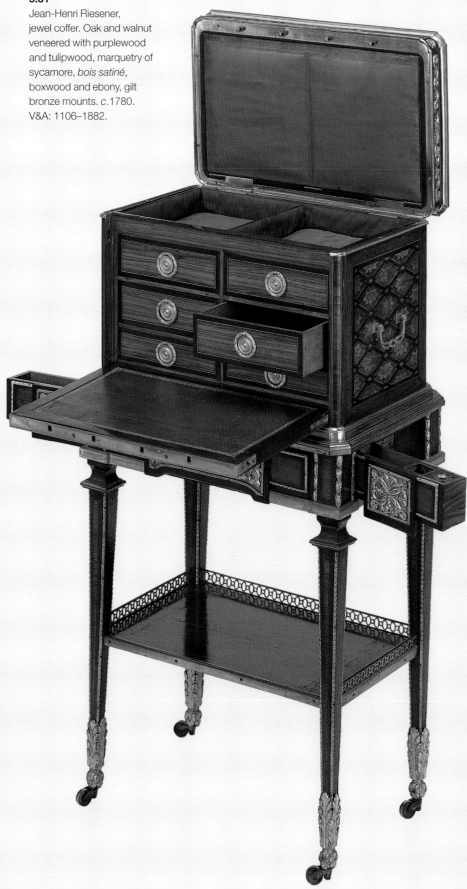

was constructed with a number of tiers, or layers, of vertical and horizontal space (see pl.5.31). Like buildings, it was designed with complex inner spatial arrangements and routes (a series of entrances, exits and doors including some to storage areas, some with locks, some without, and some only accessible to the initiated). Hence furniture-making demanded more than an understanding of the properties of wood and metal, calling also on artisanal ingenuity to conceptualize the inner space of objects in new ways. Architect and furniture-maker shared (as, of course, did their clients) preoccupations with concealment and security as well as more predictable concerns for usefulness and comfort. Indeed, in 1783 in *Le Tableau de Paris* Mercier observed of buildings

> Two hundred years ago no one could have visualised the hidden secret stairs, the little unsuspected cabinets, the false doors which conceal the true exits, the floors which could be made to rise and fall, and the labyrinths in which one can hide and put off inquisitive servants whilst indulging one's tastes….

The successful navigation of furniture's interior spaces depended on the one hand on the knowledge or anticipation of hidden space and on the other on the delicate operation of keys, locks and hidden triggers. In plate 5.30, for example, a button within the drawer cavity (on the left) controls the opening of the arched door which conceals the central drawer. Beneath this is hidden a secret compartment and further drawers. The holder of the physical and intellectual keys to the inner arrangement and secrets of the object held the enviable ability to manipulate access to and protection of his or her belongings. Such strategies were valuable not only to protect possessions from visitors to the house (social, professional and occasionally uninvited) but also to withhold private material from householders (notably staff and spouses). In these ways, the design and operation of furniture related closely to the development of specialized, flexible spaces within the home, as well as to the development of subtly different levels of access to space, and its control, within the household environment.

Eroticizing the Interior

Karen Harvey

British eighteenth-century erotica used metaphor and suggestion to create the illusion that bodies were concealed and that sexual activity was deferred. A range of metaphors were employed, but several key metaphors used the dimension of space to depict bodies. Male and female bodies had a great deal in common, but women's bodies were distinguished in part by their interior spaces. As the popular sex manual *Aristotle's Masterpiece* (11th edn., 1725) described, 'Women are but Men turn'd Out-side-in'. This practice of defining women's bodies by their interior spaces was consolidated in erotica by the locations in which sex was situated. Scenes of sexual intimacy invariably took place in women's rooms, as in the poem *Kick Him Jenny: A Tale* (1737). Roger bounds into Jenny's room to have sex, but is observed by Jenny's mistress at the door. In the accompanying illustration, he strains towards the door and is clearly an intruder in this woman's space (see pl.5.32). In contrast, Jenny is part of the space as the folds in her dress blend with her buttocks into the soft folds of the bed fabric.

The feminine locations for sex shared key features. Screened chambers and tester beds, groves and grottoes, caves and gulfs: these dark, enclosed and shady locations were perfect places for illicit encounters in erotica. They were also common in documentary evidence, such as the depiction of 'Lady Anne Foley, Lord Peterborough and the Oak Tree', from *The Cuckold's Chronicle: Being Select Trials for Adultery, Incest, Imbecility, Ravishment &c.* (see pl.5.35). And eroticized outdoor spaces shared the same features as indoor spaces. In fictional writing, these spaces were described as soft and inviting: rooms were furnished with luxurious fabrics; grottoes were lined with velvety down. Crucially, such features were also noted as distinctive physical characteristics of female bodies. The title of the illustration 'The Peeper; or, a Stolen View of Lady C-'s Premises', from *A Voyage to Lethe* (1741) puns on this relationship between Lady C's body and the architectural space in which she is situated (see pl.5.34).

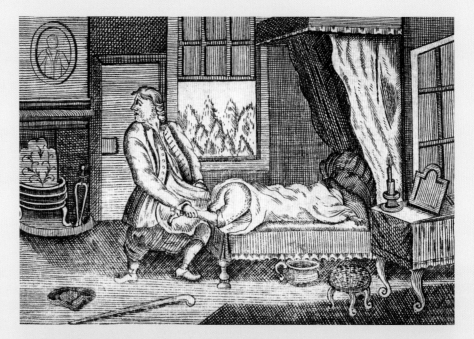

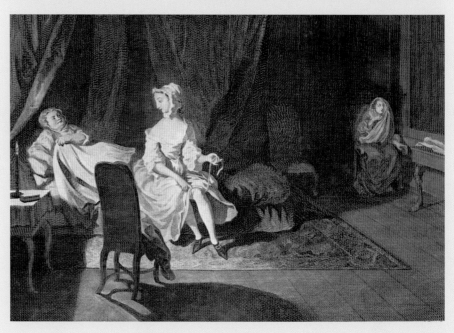

5.32
'Roger and Jenny' from
Kick Him Jenny: A Tale. 1737.
The British Library, London

5.33
Louis Truchy after Joseph
Highmore, 'Pamela
Undressing Herself'. 1762.
V&A: E.2040–1919

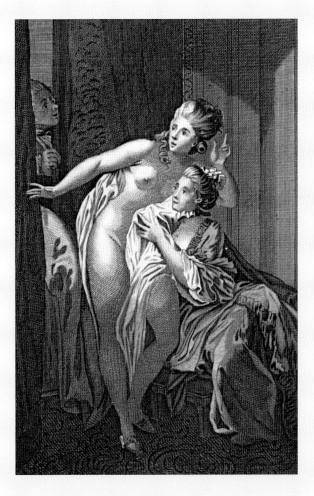

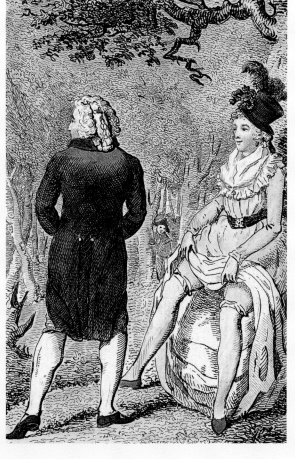

5.34
'The Peeper; or, a Stolen
View of Lady C–'s Premises'
from *A Voyage to Lethe* by
Samuel Cock. 1741. The
British Library, London

5.35
'Lady Anne Foley, Lord
Peterborough and the Oak
Tree' from *The Cuckold's
Chronicle: Being Select Trials
for Adultery, Incest, Imbecility,
Ravishment &c.* 1793.
The British Library, London

This association between femininity and secluded interior spaces infused popular literature. In Samuel Richardson's novel *Pamela* (1740–41), Mr B.'s repeated attacks on Pamela's virtue are echoed in his invasion of her private spaces. The illustration 'Pamela Undressing Herself', by Louis Truchy after Joseph Highmore (1762), depicts the scene in which Mr B. disguises himself as the maid Nan in Pamela's bedchamber, before joining Pamela in bed (see pl.5.33). The frisson of the scantily clad woman, the location of a woman's supposedly private space and voyeurism are classic erotic elements. Much of the frisson of erotica arises from the sense of observing what should be hidden. This voyeurism of the reader or viewer is made manifest in these images through

the presence or suggestion of a spy or intruder, thus exposing the processes of constructing and consuming erotic images as representation.

In many different genres of eighteenth-century text, ranging from pornographic works such as *Fanny Hill* (1748–9) to descriptions of landscape gardens, there is an identification between the female body and interior spaces both inside and outside. Through projecting desire into these interior, feminized spaces, male authors and artists contained sexual desire and distanced themselves from its potentially effeminizing effects. At the same time, sex was situated in enclosed, warm, soft and secluded feminine spaces, eroticizing the relationship between women, the interior and privacy.

6

'One's self, and one's house, one's furniture': from object to interior in British fiction, 1720–1900

Charlotte Grant

What shall we call our 'self'? Where does it begin? Where does it end? It overflows into everything that belongs to us – and then it flows back again. I know a large part of myself is in the clothes I choose to wear. I've a great respect for *things*! One's self, and one's house, one's furniture, one's garments, the books one reads, the company one keeps – these things are all expressive.[1]

THE ASSERTION MADE HERE by the cynical, materialistic and manipulative Madame Merle in Henry James's *The Portrait of a Lady* (1881) depends on an association between character and environment which is almost automatic for a reader in the early twenty-first century. Whilst we may not entirely share Merle's view of a permeable self, we take for granted the idea that the things we choose to have around us are 'expressive'. Whole industries rely on the concept that the way in which we, as well as others, see ourselves is affected by our clothes, houses and furniture as much as, or more than, by the books we read and the company we keep. It seems logical that when writers depict characters they frequently turn to descriptions of the things and the places around them. Descriptions of houses, interiors

and objects feature with varying degrees of detail and different rhetorical effect from the early prose fiction of the eighteenth century through to contemporary novels. Such descriptions are 'expressive' not merely in material terms. This chapter argues that the novel, as it developed between 1720 and 1920, is a key form for representing and imagining the domestic interior, and that the novel's development is, at many points, bound up with ideas of the home, its interior, and the social practices associated with it.

Other forms of writing of course also represent domestic interiors in this period: periodicals and other non-fictional prose, especially conduct literature, continued to comment on the household, its management, physical and personal structures. In eighteenth-century Britain, due in part to Sir Robert Walpole's 1737 Licensing Act, drama's capacity to represent the contemporary was severely curtailed, whereas depictions of the domestic proliferate in nineteenth-century European theatre. The domestic, and domestic labour in particular, is, I shall argue, an important theme in British eighteenth-century poetry, and one taken up by the novel in the nineteenth century. Whilst prose fiction of varying lengths produced before 1720, in such genres as romance, scandal narratives and confessional texts, refers to the domestic interior, it is the novel, as it developed through the eighteenth and nineteenth centuries, that is arguably the written form most closely associated with the domestic interior, and this association fuels persuasive metaphors around the house, fiction and the interior.

In his 1909 preface to *The Portrait of a Lady*, James develops a striking extended metaphor describing the current state of 'the house of fiction'. Authors look at the outside world through the windows of a house: 'The spreading field, the human scene, is the "choice of subject", the pierced aperture, whether broad or balconied or slit-like and low-browed, is the "literary form" but they are, singly, or together, as nothing without the presence of the watcher—without, in other words, the consciousness of the artist.'[2] Each author sees differently according to the viewpoint their window gives them, and their own experience. Fiction does not merely depict houses and interiors, it is, for James, itself a house. The same analogy fuels 'The Novel Démeublé', an essay by Willa Cather, who complains about the level of detail in nineteenth-century depictions of the interior: 'The novel', she writes in 1936,

> … for a long while, has been over-furnished. The property man has been too busy about the pages, the importance of material objects and their vivid presentation have been so stressed, that we take for granted whoever can observe, and can write the English language, can write a novel.[3] …

Whilst bemoaning the extent and level of detail of description, Cather nevertheless maintains the metaphor, at the end of the essay calling for a return to 'drama and four walls'.

Realism, the interior and interiority

When did fiction become a house? And what distinguishes the novel from earlier forms of fiction? Clara Reeve, writing in 1785 on 'The Progress of Romance', argues that novels describe real experience and encourage the reader to identify with characters and events.

> The Novel gives a familiar relation of such things, as pass every day before our eyes, such as may happen to our friend, or to ourselves; and the perfection of it, is to represent every scene, in so easy and natural a manner, and to make them appear so probable, as to deceive us into a persuasion (at least while we are reading) that all is real, until we are affected by the joys or distresses, of the persons in the story, as if they were our own.[4]

Identification as Reeve describes it is a key to the readers' experience. A different form of identification also operates within the novel, as Madame Merle suggests, to link character and environment. If fiction figures as a house for both Henry James and Willa Cather, then its interiors frequently figure interiority, operating as a means for the writer to tell us about the characters' inner thoughts and feelings. The association between the representation in fiction of a character's internal mental state, self-awareness or interiority, and a focus on the interior, specifically the domestic interior, appears pervasive and sustained. Historian John Lukacs claims that 'The interior furniture of houses appeared together with the interior furniture of minds'.[5] This assertion is corroborated, according to Lukacs, by the fact that a whole series of words denoting 'the interior landscape' of our minds appeared in roughly the same period as an increase in the furnishings of the interior. Medieval scholars might contest both Lukacs' statement that: 'As the self-consciousness of medieval people was spare, the interiors of their houses were bare, including the halls of nobles and of kings',[6] and the assumption of a lack of self-consciousness before the vocabulary he points to. It is however irrefutable that there are important shifts in the imagining of the home, of ideas of privacy, comfort and the differentiation of room use, between 1400 and 1700, and that there is, broadly, a series of lin-

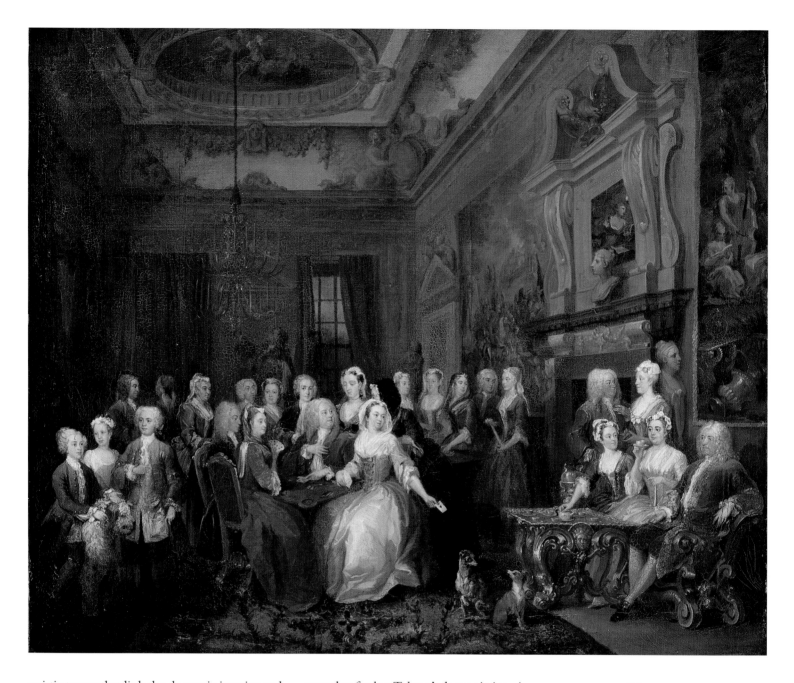

guistic tropes that link the domestic interior and its furniture to the interior of the mind.[7] In the essay quoted above, Willa Cather allows that Tolstoy's depictions of the interior, for example in such novels as *War and Peace* (1863–9) and *Anna Karenina* (1873–7), achieve a crucial fusion: 'the clothes, the dishes, the haunting interiors of those old Moscow houses are always so much a part of the emotions of the people that they are perfectly synthesized; they seem to exist not so much in the author's mind as in the emotional penumbra of the characters themselves'.[8]

Cather's phrase 'emotional penumbra' sug-

gests that for her Tolstoy's domestic interiors are satisfying representations precisely because, much as Madame Merle describes, he blurs the boundary between self and things to such an extent that his descriptions seem a part of his characters' emotions, rather than imposed on the narrative by the author. In 1936 the future of fiction lay for Cather not in verisimilitude, but in simplification: 'following the development of modern painting … to present the scene by suggestion rather than by enumeration'. Cather, with her plea to 'throw all the furniture out of the window, and along with it,

6.1

William Hogarth, *Assembly at Wanstead House*. Oil on canvas. 1728–31. Philadelphia Museum of Art all the meaningless reiterations concerning physical sensations'[9] advocates a turn from the enumeration of objects and the evidence of the senses towards abstraction. Her essay, looking back from the 1930s over two centuries of the novel, simultaneously acknowledges and rejects the centrality of literal descriptions, arguing instead for a return, on behalf of the reader as much the writer, to the power of imagination.

If we look at the etymology of the word 'interior', dating, according to the OED, from 1490, its earliest meanings relate to the mental, appearing as a synonym for 'inward' in 1513. References to the interior meaning 'inland' occur from the 1770s; the OED cites meanings referring to the inside of a building or room,

or 'a picture or representation', from the 1820s. At around this date the interior is established as itself a subject, rather than context, in visual representations. If we compare paintings by Hogarth and Turner of social gatherings in the interiors of country houses (see pl.6.1–6.2) the differences in representation are not merely about style, but also a question of focus. Whilst, typically, Hogarth's protagonists are set off by the grand interior he represents, Turner's bodies and surroundings blur. Turner's views of Petworth also include unpopulated interiors such as plate 6.3, where the room itself is clearly the subject of the composition. But when does a comparable shift from context to subject occur in depictions from novels?

6.2
J.M.W. Turner, *The White Library*. Watercolour, bodycolour and pen and ink on paper. 1827. Tate, London

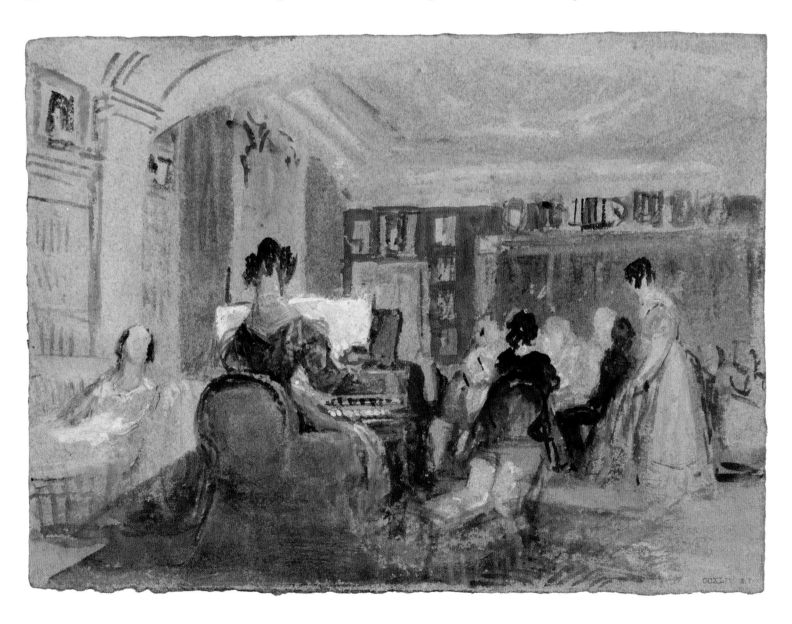

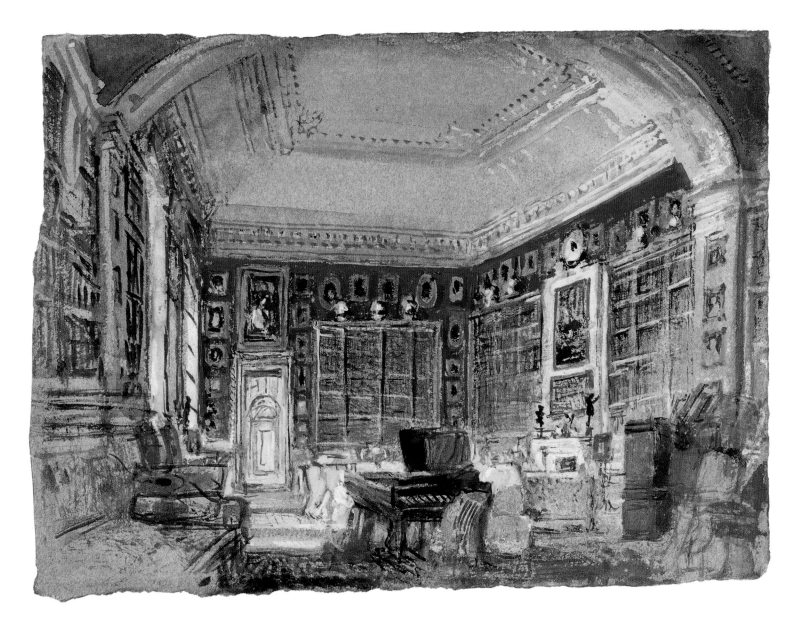

6.3
J.M.W. Turner, *Music in the White Library*. Gouache and watercolour on paper. 1827. Tate, London

Of the various accounts of the growth of the British novel, one of the earliest, Ian Watt's *The Rise of the Novel* (1957), is still influential. Like Clara Reeve's 'easy and natural a manner', Watt argues for what he terms 'formal realism' as the defining characteristic of the new type of fiction produced by, initially, Daniel Defoe, Samuel Richardson and Henry Fielding. Watt refers to philosophy: 'modern realism, of course, begins from the position that truth can be discovered by the individual through his senses: it has its origins in Descartes and Locke, and received its first full formulation by Thomas Reid in the middle of the eighteenth century.' Watt proposes a 'concept of realistic particularity' and states: 'two ... aspects suggest themselves as of especial importance in the novel – characterisation and presentation of background.'[10]

If we accept Watt's link between realism in the novel and empiricist philosophy, it is not surprising that authors give us increasingly detailed descriptions of their protagonists' material culture. In, for example, Daniel Defoe's persuasive retelling of a ghost story, *A True Relation of the Apparition of One Mrs Veal* (1706), several of his many authenticating devices evoke his characters' immediate material surroundings. As the ghostly Mrs Veal 'who was in a Riding Habit' arrives, 'the clock struck Twelve at Noon'. Later Mrs Veal tells Mrs Bargrave that her 'Gown sleeve' is 'a Scower'd Silk, and newly made up.'[11] In this short narrative, as in Defoe's extended fiction, we get a sense of the rooms or houses in which action takes place through Defoe's depiction of objects. According to Watt, 'Defoe would seem to be the first of our writers who visualized the whole of his narrative as though it occurred in an actual physical environment', although he acknowledges that 'this solidity of setting is particularly noticeable in Defoe's treatment of moveable objects in the physical world.'[12]

Robinson Crusoe describes building his house and his 'castle', but our sense of those spaces derives from the objects in them. Similarly in *Moll Flanders* (1722), the narrative dwells more on the articles of plate and fabrics Moll acquires, and the streets through which she flees her pursuers, than the spaces she inhabits. In his later *Roxana* (1724), Defoe again evokes rather than describes spaces. Defoe lingers on Roxana's clothes and the other portable personal objects that constitute her fortune, rather than on her surroundings. Much of the action in the central section of the novel takes place in a 'good House, and well-furnish'd'[13] belonging to a Quaker woman 'in a Court in the Minories'[14] (a street near the Tower of London) where Roxana secrets herself after leaving her glamorous but dissolute West End life. We get some sense of the layout of the house, as when Roxana, who has been sitting in her landlady's 'Chamber up-stairs' tells us 'I went down a Pair of Back-stairs with her, and into a Dining-Room, next to the Parlour in which he was',[15] a room already described as 'a very handsome Parlour below-stairs'.[16] Such moments, whilst recording use and movement through the house, do little to relate the characters to their surroundings. A different kind of identification operates in the frontispiece to *Roxana* (see pl.6.4) where the protagonist stands in the Turkish dress which gives her the name 'Roxana' against a backdrop of opening doorways. The scene evokes the entertainment spaces of her West End house, but whilst theatrical, gives few details of the interior. Here, her body seems to stand for the pleasures promised in the rooms beyond, of which the sight of her (and, it is implied in the narrative, for the Prince alone, the touch of her) is itself the chief pleasure on offer.

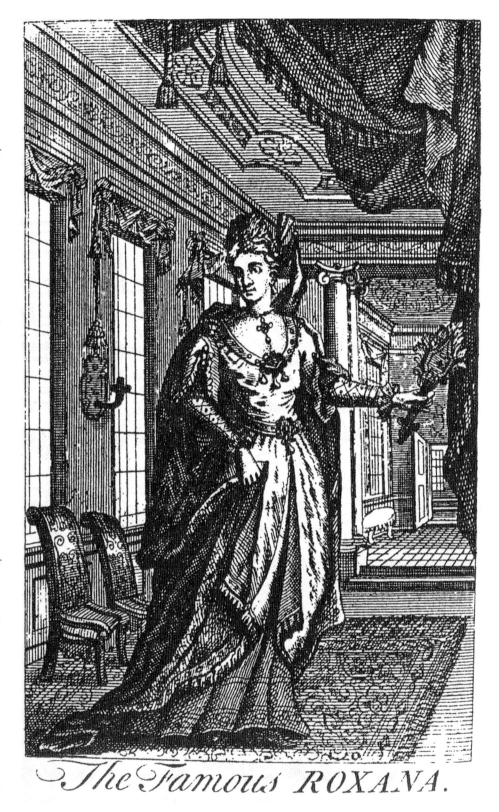

6.4
Frontispiece to *Roxana* by Daniel Defoe. 1724.
The British Library, London

In depictions of the interior, the drive to represent the real is paralleled by a desire for insight into characters' minds, the synthesis that makes the difference for Cather. But when does this identification occur? Samuel Richardson's novels of the 1740s and '50s identify individuals closely with their surroundings. Richardson offers a new level of detail and intensity to his descriptions of the interior in both *Pamela* (1742) and *Clarissa* (1747–9). Both are epistolary novels where the text is made up of characters' letters, giving a narrative immediacy described as 'writing to the moment'. The house carries important ideological weight in the battles over Richardson's female characters' lives and depictions of the interior are increasingly freighted through his work. Pamela is a lady's maid whose mistress dies and whose new master, the lady's son, attempts to seduce her. She foils him and through maintaining her virtue against the odds, reforms and marries him. Her story is intimately related to the house in which she worked and which she eventually becomes mistress, to domestic labour and domestic duty, and to the complex hierarchy of spaces in the mid-eighteenth-century wealthy home. The little-read second volume, much of it narrated through Pamela's journal, records the trials and tribulations of her married life, providing a detailed account of household management and domestic duty. Richardson's male protagonists' struggles over the female bodies they desire are mapped onto the intimate details of the domestic interior. These are domestic dramas and depend on the evocation of domestic space. These spaces are intrinsically hierarchical: library, closet, bed-chamber, dining room, summer house all suggest particular modes of behaviour that Richardson frequently has his protagonists transgress to dramatic effect. The closet, typically a private, feminine space, becomes in *Clarissa* a room of utmost importance, described by critic Emma Clery as 'a workshop of the mind, a laboratory of the soul'.[17]

Pamela was so successful it went through six editions in two years and, given Richardson's heady evocation of context, it is perhaps not surprising that attempts to visualize the narrative followed. Richardson himself published an illustrated edition with prints designed by the English artist Francis Hayman and engraved by the prominent French engraver Hubert-François Gravelot. This was an expensive edition, and did not sell well. The prints (see pl.6.5–6.6) are rather static. Figures stand, or more frequently sit, and occupy roughly half the picture plane. As in these examples, corners of rooms are often shown. In plate 6.5, the first image in the book, Mr B. finds Pamela writing to her parents, and examines her letter. In the heady style of moment by moment narrative Richardson developed, Pamela writes breathlessly: 'I have been scared out of my Senses; for just now, as I was folding up this letter in my Lady's Dressing-Room, in comes my young Master!'

Hayman's image, whilst it conveys Pamela's alluring modesty, does little to capture the drama of the text. Pamela's expression is similar to that in one of the later images in which she tells a story to her assembled children in the nursery, 'this happy Retirement' (see pl.6.6). Richardson's evocation of the scene, in Pamela's letter to Lady G, suggests the extent to which his narrative is spatially aware, as Pamela recounts the exact position and details of the furniture each of her children occupies. The eldest, Miss Godwin, is her husband's illegitimate daughter whom Pamela benevolently welcomes into the family.

[Miss Godwin sits] on my Right-hand sitting on a Velvet Stool, because she is the eldest and a Miss: *Billy* on my Left, in a little Cane Elbow-Chair, because he is the eldest, and a good Boy: My *Davers*, and my sparkling-ey'd *Pamela*, with my *Charley* between them, on little silken Cushions at my Feet, hand-in-hand, their pleased Eyes looking up to my more delighted ones, and my sweet-natur'd promising *Jemmy* in my Lap; the Nurses and the Cradle just behind us, and the Nursery Maids delightedly pursuing some useful Needlework, for the dear Charmers of my Heart.[18]

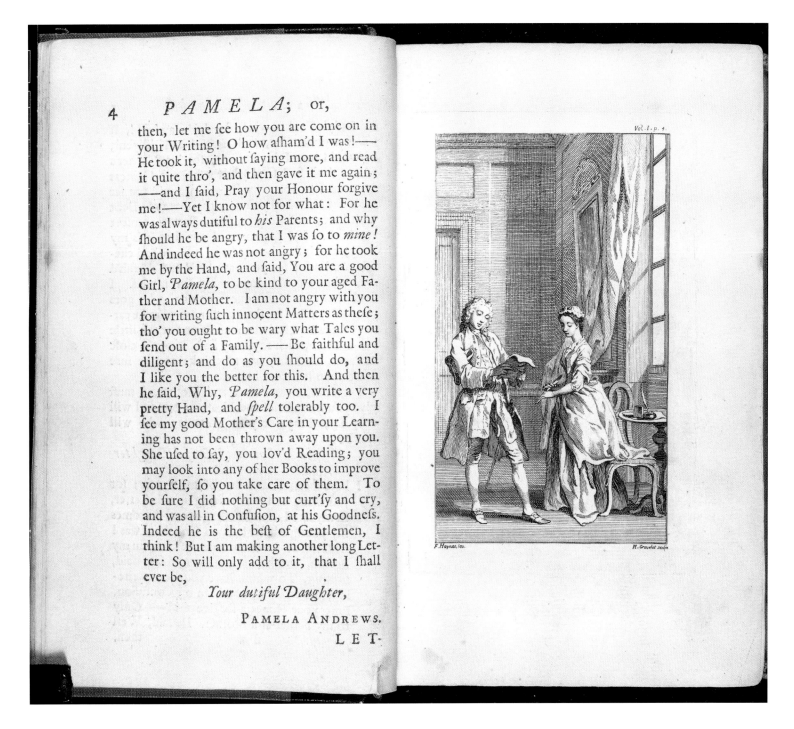

PAMELA; or,

then, let me see how you are come on in your Writing! O how afham'd I was!——He took it, without faying more, and read it quite thro', and then gave it me again;——and I faid, Pray your Honour forgive me!——Yet I know not for what: For he was always dutiful to *his* Parents; and why fhould he be angry, that I was fo to *mine!* And indeed he was not angry; for he took me by the Hand, and faid, You are a good Girl, *Pamela,* to be kind to your aged Father and Mother. I am not angry with you for writing fuch innocent Matters as thefe; tho' you ought to be wary what Tales you fend out of a Family.——Be faithful and diligent; and do as you fhould do, and I like you the better for this. And then he faid, Why, *Pamela,* you write a very pretty Hand, and *fpell* tolerably too. I fee my good Mother's Care in your Learning has not been thrown away upon you. She ufed to fay, you lov'd Reading; you may look into any of her Books to improve yourfelf, fo you take care of them. To be fure I did nothing but curt'fy and cry, and was all in Confufion, at his Goodnefs. Indeed he is the beft of Gentlemen, I think! But I am making another long Letter: So will only add to it, that I fhall ever be,

Your dutiful Daughter,

PAMELA ANDREWS.

LET-

6.5

Pages from *Pamela* – Volume I by Samuel Richardson with illustrations by Gravelot and Hayman. 1740–41. The British Library, London

A livelier series of illustrations followed. Joseph Highmore took *Pamela* as his inspiration for a series of 12 paintings. Highmore's paintings tend to focus on more dramatic moments in the story, such as Pamela's attempted seduction by Mr B., and were highly visible through their engraved versions (see pl.5.33). The images relate closely to the contemporary genre of the conversation piece – small scale, frequently domestic portraits discussed in chapter 5 above.

A comparison of the same scenes as Hayman illustrated, Pamela caught writing to her parents (see pl.6.7) and then later reading to the family (see pl.6.8), shows how the interiors are more realized, and Highmore draws attention to the ways in which Pamela is constantly under observation – in the first scene scrutinized by Mr B., later by the visiting ladies who watch her perform the role of perfect mother.

Richardson was instrumental both in

promoting the novel form and in stressing its potential as a moral force. Whilst conveying a firm moral message, and insisting at all times on the fact that Pamela represents 'virtue rewarded', the text was open to other readings focusing on the titillating aspects of the narrative rather than its claimed virtuous intent. Fielding's *Shamela* mocks Richardson's emphasis on material culture as well as his heroine's insistence on her virtue. Richardson was also mocked in visual responses: Philip Mercier's scurrilous print shows Pamela as an unambiguously erotic subject. Richardson's fictions appealed to a morality grounded in the evocation of feeling and strove, despite their focus on scenes of attempted seduction, to distance themselves from the scandal literature that preceded them. Depictions of interiors, especially scenes of seduction, had featured in the Restoration scandalous narratives by Delariviere Manly and Eliza Haywood.[19] Richardson, a publisher as well as writer, took pains to distinguish his ostensibly moral narratives from such scandalous predecessors, adopting the term 'history' rather than 'novel'. His writing practice reveals him to have been very conscious of his readership, gathering a group of virtuous female acquaintance around him who commented on *Clarissa* as it was written.[20] The virtuous reader of *Clarissa* is exemplified by Reynolds' portrait of Theophilia Palmer, where a named sitter is shown absorbed in her reading. The close-up allows for little hint of her surroundings, but serves to emphasize rather a process of virtuous readerly identification of the kind envisaged by Clara Reeve.

Womens' novel reading, especially among the young and impressionable, was frequently perceived as a cause of anxiety through the eighteenth century. James Northcote's illustration to William Hayley's poem 'The Triumphs of Temper' shows the heroine, Serena, being discovered with a novel by her aunt, who then removes it to read it herself. The section of the poem illustrated describes the novel infiltrating the domestic space: 'Beneath the pillow, not completely hid./ The novel lay- She saw – She seiz'd – she chid;/ With rage and glee her glaring eye-balls flash,/ Ah wicked age! She cries, ah filthy trash!'[21]

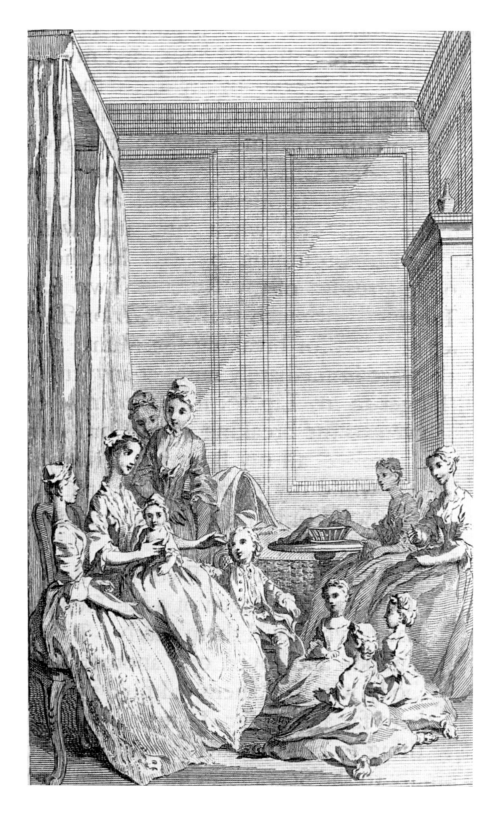

6.6
'Pamela reading to the children' from *Pamela* – Volume IV by Samuel Richardson with illustrations by Gravelot and Hayman. 1740–41. The British Library, London

The poem puns on the possibilities of over-identification and confusion that female readers were perceived as being particularly prone to. Delusion by fiction is an old theme explored in Charlotte Lennox's 1752 novel *The Female Quixote*. Perhaps precisely because novels were typically read in a domestic, though often not a solitary context, and their structure invites identification, they were frequently cited as encouraging inappropriate behaviour and fantasy – even though there is plenty of evidence of virtuous, rational and critically engaged reading practices among both women and men.[22]

Writing, poetry and labour

Whilst the representation of the domestic interior is fundamental to the novel as it developed through the eighteenth and nineteenth centuries, the domestic also figures in eighteenth-century poetry, although the evocation of a domestic ideal is more common than detailed depictions of the interior. Much poetry of the period draws on the idea of retirement, where the act of writing simultaneously offers and represents a refuge from the rigours of public life, following classical models derived from Horace.[23] Whilst this retreat is

6.7
Joseph Highmore, *1: Mr B. Finds Pamela Writing*. Oil on canvas. 1743–4. Tate, London

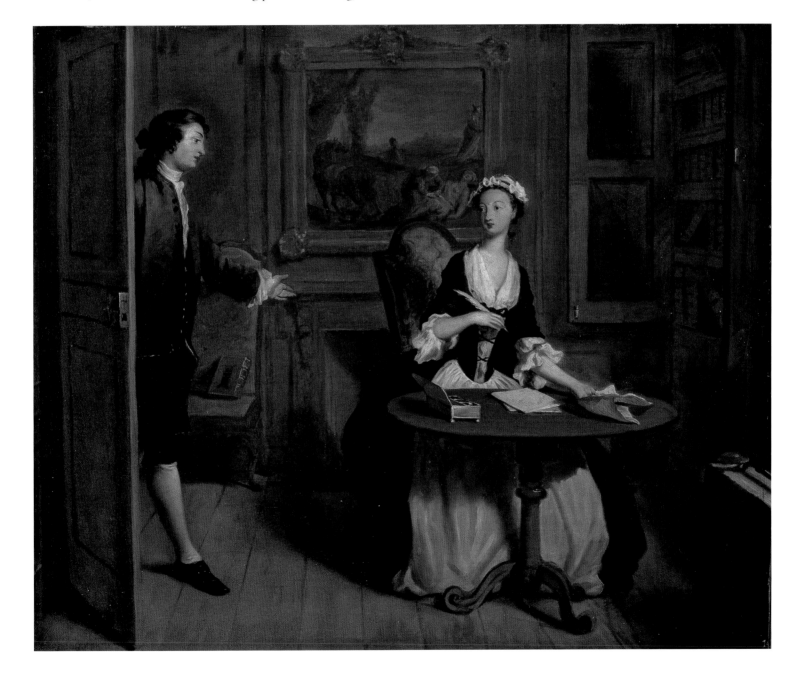

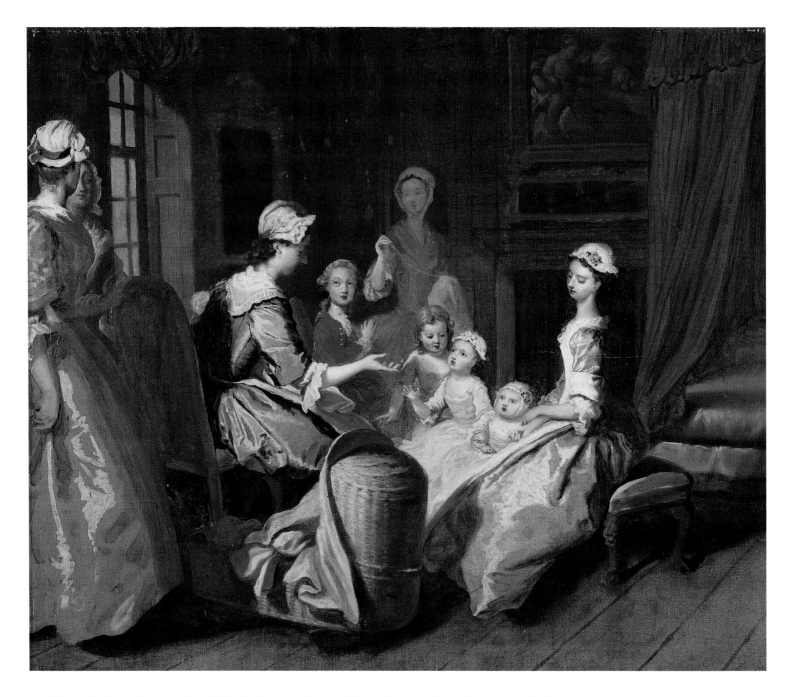

traditionally figured as rural, and lies behind much landscape poetry of the period, it is possible to trace a development that similarly sees the domestic interior as a refuge. For example, Coleridge's 'conversation' poems of the 1790s juxtapose the outside public world with the domestic. In 'Frost at Midnight' (1798) Coleridge uses the firelight flickering on the hearth as a visual prompt to meditate on his sleeping son, and wishes him a freer, more domestic childhood than his own has been. Here the domestic and the rural are conflated into an ideal of retreat from the urban, which owes as much to Cowper's long poem 'The Task' (1785) as it does to the classical Horatian model. Cowper's poem in four long books, much beloved of Jane Austen, is a domestic reverie which, opening in the domestic interior ('I sing the sofa'), reaches out from its core to encompass the traditional modes of urban and rural georgic, praising Britain and its productivity from a solid, explicitly domestic base.

If reading figures as a potentially problematic activity for women, so too did writing.

6.8
Joseph Highmore, *Pamela Tells a Nursery Tale*. Oil on canvas. *c.*1744. Fitzwilliam Museum, Cambridge

From the opening of the century onwards women poets were at pains to assert their right to write. Esther Lewis, writing in 1748, imagined eavesdropping on her acquaintance, both male and female, condemning her literary ambition. 'The men', she suggests 'are mightily apt to say, / This silly girl has lost her way … she ought to mind domestic cares, the sex were made for such affairs.' She goes on to ask, in a complaint couched in highly conventional terms, 'Why are the needle and the pen / Thought incompatible by men? / May we not sometimes use the quill, / And yet be careful housewives still?'[24]

Throughout the period, women poets sought to reconcile poetic and domestic labour. Mary Barber (*c.*1690–1757) was, according to Roger Lonsdale, 'perhaps the first woman poet to make a virtue out of the original educational purposes of her poems [for her sons] and the domestic context of many of them'.[25] Domestic duty is embodied and celebrated by Barber, providing a model for much later poetry by women.

Whilst Barber apparently embraces the limitations of the domestic, other female poets in the course of the century challenged their position in different ways. This is particularly true of a number of labouring class poets, including Mary Leapor, Mary Collier, Ann Yearsley and Phillis Wheatley. This tradition looks at the domestic interior from a different angle, as a contested space of labour and duty, and helps us question the easy association of 'one's self' and 'one's house' that Madame Merle makes in assuming 'one's' ownership of one's surroundings and surrounding objects.

The mid-century's culture of Sensibility privileged sensation and the senses over reason as a means to a moral end. It grew from empiricism's emphasis on the prime importance of sensory experience, and embraced the fascination with feeling manifested in Richardson's novels. For the reader possessed of a 'feeling heart', 'unlettered' poets offered an authentic record of experience, which, properly mediated, could benefit the reader of higher social status. The first such writer, Stephen Duck, bemoaned the hard life of an agricultural labourer in 'The

Thresher's Labour' of 1730. In 1739 a response came from Mary Collier who argued in 'The Woman's Labour: An Epistle to Mr. Stephen Duck' that the working woman has an even harder lot than the labourers Duck describes. Collier points out that when male and female agricultural labourers leave the fields to return home, women's work merely continues:

> When Ev'ning does approach,
>   we homeward hie,
> And our domestic Toils incessant ply:
> Against your coming Home prepare to get
> Our Work all done,
>   our House in order set;
> *Bacon* and *Dumpling* in the Pot we boil,
> Our Beds we make,
>   our Swine we feed the while;
> Then wait at Door
>   to see you coming Home,
> And set the Table out against you come;
> Early next Morning we on you attend;
> Our Children dress and feed,
>   their Clothes we mend;
> And in the Field our daily Task renew,
> Soon as the rising Sun
>   has dry'd the Dew.[26]

Much of the labour Collier describes also happens out of doors, but an unusual picture of female domestic labour emerges in Mary Leapor's 'Crumble-Hall' (1751). Leapor worked as a housemaid and the experience gives a very particular perspective on the country house: a maid washing up is described with an immediate physicality:

> But now her Dish-kettle began
> To boil and blubber
>   with the foaming Bran.
> The greasy Apron round her
>   Hips she ties,
> And to each Plate
>   the scalding Clout applies:
> The purging Bath
>   each glowing Dish refines,
> And once again
>   the polish'd Pewter shines.[27]

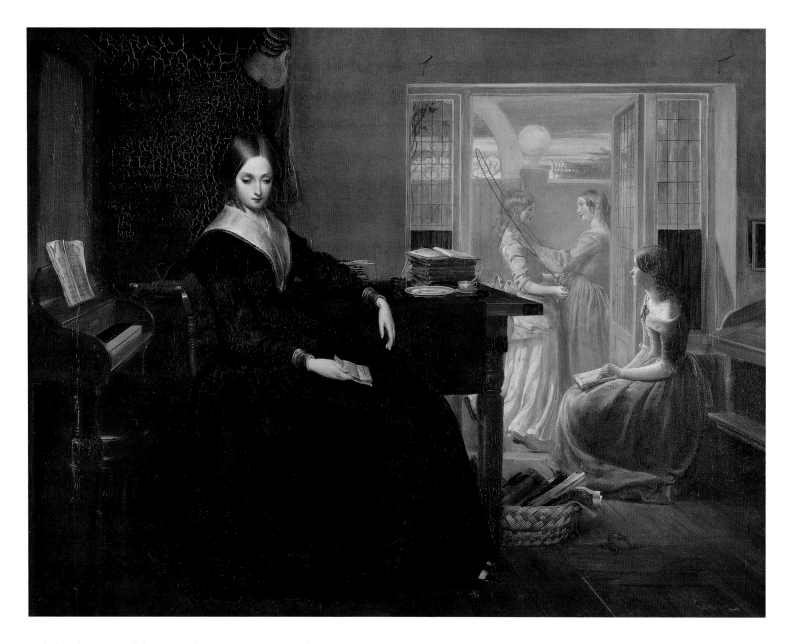

Whilst domestic labour and poverty is an important theme, particularly for women poets in the eighteenth century and despite the fact that Richardson's Pamela, a key early figure, is a housemaid, labour does not become a central concern of the novel until the following century. One ambiguous figure in the domestic economy, the governess, becomes particularly important. Marginal in eighteenth-century fiction, the role of the governess is variously discussed in Austen's *Emma* (1816). Jane Fairfax looks forward to when she will have to work as a governess, 'With the fortitude of a devoted noviciate, she had resolved at one-and twenty to complete the sacrifice, and retire

from all the pleasures of life, of rational intercourse, equal society, peace and hope, to penance and mortification for ever'.[28] It is in the novels of the Brontës in the 1840s, who themselves had direct experience of working as governesses, that the role takes centre stage.[29] The governess also became a key figure in Victorian paintings of the domestic interior, as in *The Governess* (see pl.6.9) by Richard Redgrave. Exhibited in 1845 at the Royal Academy, the catalogue stresses the central figure's alienation from the ideal of home: 'She sees no kind domestic visage here'. Like Pamela before her, she is connected to the outside world through the letter she holds, although the scene suggests

6.9
Richard Redgrave, *The Governess*. Oil on canvas. 1844. V&A: FA.168

no possibility of her redemption. She is linked to another figure who looks up from her reading, the girl in pink by the window who gazes out beyond her sunlit companions, a book in her lap, but no indication that she might identify, or sympathize with the governess.

Realizing character: interiors and interiority

By what point has the identification of character and interior seen in Richardson become a narrative given? It is clear if we look at the interiors described by Austen in *Mansfield Park* (1814) that they are of considerable significance. The sparse but distinct details of furnishings in Fanny's East Room suggest contemporary aesthetics, the taste for the picturesque, and Fanny's place in the family pecking order, as well as her own values.

> The comfort of it in her hours of leisure was extreme. She could go there after any thing unpleasant below, and find immediate consolation in some pursuit, or some train of thought at hand.— Her plants, her books—of which she had been a collector, from the first hour of her commanding a shilling—her writing desk, and her works of charity and ingenuity, were all within her reach; —or if indisposed for employment, if nothing but musing would do, she could scarcely see an object in that room which had not an interesting remembrance connected with it.— Every thing was a friend, or bore her thoughts to a friend….The room was most dear to her, and she would not have changed its furniture for the handsomest in the house, though what had been originally plain, had suffered all the ill-usage of children—and its greatest elegancies and ornaments were a faded foot-stool of Julia's work, too ill done for the drawing-room, three transparencies, made in a range for transparencies, for the three lower panes of one window,

where Tintern Abbey held its station between a cave in Italy, and a moonlight lake in Cumberland; a collection of family profiles thought unworthy of being anywhere else, over the mantle piece, and by their side and pinned against the wall, a small sketch of a ship sent four years ago from the Mediterranean by William, with H.M.S. Antwerp at the bottom, in letters as tall as the main-mast.[30]

If descriptions of domestic interiors can tell the reader about character, and here about Fanny's sense of herself, they are also employed to inform (and often warn) fictional characters about others. Early on in George Eliot's *Middlemarch* (1871–2) the heroine, Dorothea, visits her future husband, Mr Casaubon, at home and, unlike her sister, 'found the house and grounds all that she could wish: the dark book-shelves in the long library, the carpets and curtains with colours subdued by time, the curious old maps and bird's-eye views on the walls of the corridor, with here and there an old vase below, had no oppression for her'.[31]

Dorothea may not feel it, but the 'oppression' is there, lurking at the end of the sentence to confirm the reader's suspicions. Another heroine who makes an unfortunate marriage, Isabel Archer in Henry James' *The Portrait of a Lady*, ignores the feeling of disquiet and oppression provoked by her first visit to the Italian home of Gilbert Osmond, her future husband: 'His kindness almost surprised our young friend, who wondered why he should take so much trouble for her; and she was oppressed at last with the accumulation of beauty and knowledge to which she found herself introduced'.[32] A very different impression is generated by an earlier heroine inspecting the home of her future husband. When Elizabeth Bennett visits Pemberley in Austen's *Pride and Prejudice* (1813) she finds herself in an interior with 'lofty and handsome' rooms and furniture of 'real elegance' and meets the housekeeper who gives her master an extraordinarily glowing character reference. Elizabeth's visit does more than confirm Darcy's socio-economic status; he is not merely Austen's wealthiest hero, his house confirms his possession of taste and moral probity. Pemberley, with its 'well-proportioned' rooms and 'prospects', provides Elizabeth with clarity; her seeing Darcy's portrait in the context of the family gallery and praised by his housekeeper places Darcy in a far more favourable light than she has ever seen him.[33]

In contrast Dorothea's visit in *Middlemarch* to Casaubon's appropriately named house, Lowick, offers anything but clarity. Instead it is defined in negatives: unlike her uncle's, Casaubon's relations have not been travellers, so there is no hint of a European, Catholic sensuality to offend Dorothea's 'puritan' sensibilities. There is in fact, as the reader is meant to notice, no hint of vitality. Dorothea reads, or rather interprets Casaubon as a text, and sees any lacks as her own: 'She filled up all blanks with unmanifested perfections, interpreting him as she interpreted the works of Providence, and accounting for seeming discords by her own deafness to the higher harmonies'.[34] Where Austen's interiors are relatively transparent, if often generalized, offering for both protagonist and reader an insight into the taste, which for her signifies moral as much as aesthetic choices, Eliot's scope is wider. Middlemarch is, after all, a town rather than a house, and the interconnections of its rural and urban life require an appreciation of the complexities of social and economic interaction Austen sidelines. Eliot also demands of her readers a capacity for abstraction, for interpretation and imagination. As she puts it in *Middlemarch*: 'We are all of us imaginative in some form or other, for images are the brood of desire'.[35]

Dorothea is, Eliot implies in her prelude, 'a modern St Theresa', and, as Eliot points out, whereas the original 'found her epos in the reform of a religious order', since then 'Many Theresas have been born who found for themselves no epic life'.[36] Eliot refers to 'the meanness of opportunity' for modern women; Dorothea hopes her life with Casaubon will give her intellectual and spiritual scope. His house should have told her otherwise: it is dark and subdued, and, later, trapped by it, she repeatedly gazes out down the alleyway of trees, searching for an escape from her husband whose pedantry and bigoted myopia threaten to suffocate her. Early on in the novel, Dorothea demonstrates her benevolent intentions in her plans for workers' cottages. It is the bluff but benevolent Sir James Chettam, however, who, having been turned down by her, marries her sister and puts her plans into action rather than her husband-to-be Casaubon. 'Mr Casaubon apparently did not care about building cottages, and diverted the talk to the extremely narrow accommodation which was to be had in the dwellings of the ancient Egyptians, as if to check a too high standard'.[37]

Between Richardson and Eliot, then, depictions of the interior are established as an important tool in the novelists' construction of character as well as of background. If we look for sustained descriptions of the interior, one genre in particular, the gothic novel, stands out. Gothic themes of incarceration, familial disharmony and dynastic secrets are frequently played out against detailed evocations of interior spaces, above all in the fiction of Ann Radcliffe. Cynthia Wall argues that 'Where Richardson pioneered details of interior space, Ann Radcliffe opened up narrative landscape (as well as interiors) in similarly detailed and surface-loving ways.'[38] Radcliffe was celebrated (and occasionally mocked) for her expansive depictions of landscape and interior scenes in which character is mapped onto picturesque detail in a novelistic realization of the pathetic fallacy. As Wall puts it, 'Radcliffe pioneered both description as setting, creating a visual space to be entered, when finished, by characters and events, and description that maps psychology directly onto landscape or interior. Both would become stock conventions of the nineteenth-century novel.[39]

Wall points to Sir Walter Scott's admiration of Radcliffe, which 'translates into his own version of detailed historical description of place'. And it is in Scott and other Scottish and Irish novelists that, Margot Finn argues, the most consistently realized depictions of the interior occur in Romantic period novels.[40]

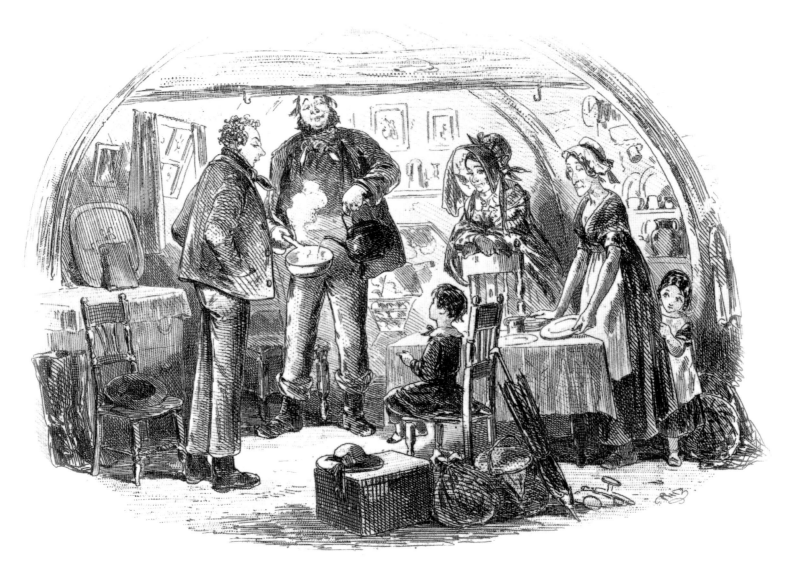

The gothic remains an important theme for many nineteenth-century descriptions of the domestic interior at their most vivid, for example in the novels of sensation, and earlier in Charles Dickens. Dickens employs depictions of the domestic interior to great symbolic effect, as in, for example, his extraordinary descriptions of Miss Havisham's nightmare interior in *Great Expectations* (1861). Pip describes a mummified room in which character and surroundings threaten to collapse into each other, achieving a synthesis brought about by decay that results in a terrifying still-life or, even more appropriately in the French, *nature morte*:

I knocked, and was told from within to enter. I entered, therefore, and found myself in a pretty large room, well lighted with wax candles. No glimpse of daylight was to be seen in it. It was a dressing-room, as I supposed from the furniture, though much of it was of forms and uses then quite unknown to me. But prominent in it was a draped table with a gilded looking-glass, and that I made out at first sight to be a fine lady's dressing-table.

Whether I should have made out this object so soon, if there had been no fine lady sitting at it, I cannot say. In an armchair, with an elbow resting on the table and her head leaning on that hand, sat the strangest lady I have ever seen, or shall ever see.

She was dressed in rich materials – satins, and lace, and silks – all of white. Her shoes were white. And she had a long white veil dependent from her hair,

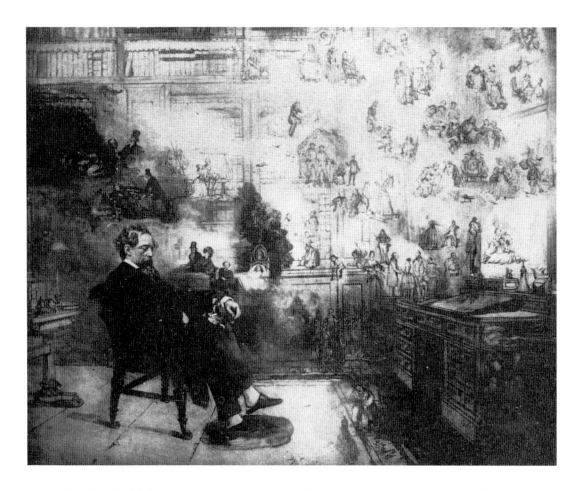

6.11
From an unfinished painting
by R.W. Buss, *A Souvenir of
Charles Dickens. c.*1875.
The British Library, London

and she had bridal flowers in her hair, but her hair was white. Some bright jewels sparkled on her neck and on her hands, and some other jewels lay sparkling on the table. Dresses, less splendid than the dress she wore, and half-packed trunks, were scattered about… It was not in the first moments that I saw all these things, though I saw more of them in the first moments than might be supposed. But, I saw that everything within my view which ought to be white, had been white long ago, and had lost its lustre, and was faded and yellow.[41]

Here Dickens manipulates the novel's ability to convey experience over time, the richness of his description simultaneously registering initial and repeated impressions with Pip's fascinated horror suggested by the excess of detail. Dickens's more benevolent interiors, frequently, as in *David Copperfield* and *Barnaby Rudge*, where the most

domestic spaces are in improvised accommodations such as houseboats rather than houses, also operate on an ideological level. Dickens is a key figure in the nineteenth century's construction of an idealized image of the home. On his first visit to Peggotty's houseboat David states: 'If it had ever been meant to be lived in, I might have thought it small, or inconvenient, or lonely; but never having been designed for any such use, it became a perfect abode' (see pl.6.10).[42] If, as I've suggested, the domestic interior by the 1820s comes to figure a kind of interiority, then the Victorian period saw an increased emphasis on the domestic as offering a special kind of interiority, a refuge from the increasingly dominant external world of industry and labour. Critic Allan Grant identifies Dickens's 'characteristic insistence on the simple virtues of domesticity and family home life' as what stamps him as a Victorian writer.[43] Grant describes Dickens as the theme's 'most successful and influential promoter in imaginative terms', and refers to Ruskin's characterization of 'home' in the context of a discussion about the place of women in his *Sesame and Lilies* (1865) as a typical mid-Victorian example of what lies behind Dickens's portrayal of families.

> This is the true nature of home – it is the place of Peace; the shelter, not only from all injury, but from all terror, doubt and division. … roof and fire are types duly of a nobler shade and light, – shade as of the rock in a weary land, and light as of the Pharos in the stormy sea;– so far it vindicates the name, and fulfils the praise of Home.[44]

Few of the homes Dickens portrays, whether loveless or loving, conform to Ruskin's radical disjunction between the 'outer world' and the interior, except perhaps Wemmick's fortified castle in *Great Expectations,* and, as we've seen, Dickens relishes a nightmarish vision of the home in the same novel. Ruskin renders his interior sacred, its physical characteristics of roof and hearth elevated to ideal and symbolic function. Whilst Ruskin's description is clearly highly mediated and determined by a very specific cultural moment, his vocabulary grounds his view in the authority of a classical past through reducing the idea of home to its central metonymic components of 'roof' and 'hearth'. His idealization simultaneously evokes a biblical and, by implication, Christian world view.

Not only is the depiction of domestic interiors central to Dickens's novels' concerns with the related themes of home and childhood, which are such an important part of the enduring legacy of his fiction, but the ways in which his novels were circulated and read also tells us a lot about how the home was conceived of in the period. Many of Dickens's mature novels were published in serial form, either weekly or monthly, and the complete novel published to coincide with the final issue. For example, the first issue of *Great Expectations* appeared in December 1860 in *All Year Round*, the magazine Dickens edited and published from 1859.

In his later years Dickens became famous for his live readings from his novels, but the model of serial publication remained key to both composition and reception of his fiction.[45] And serial publication has, as Dickens was keen to emphasize, a very particular and immediate relationship to its reading audience. Whilst early serial publications such as Joseph Addison and Richard Steele's *The Spectator* (1711–12) saw their audience as occupying a public reading space, specifically the coffee house, Dickens's rhetorical strategy is to imagine his readers at home. From 1850, until its incorporation into *All Year Round*, he edited the pertinently named periodical *Household Words* which included his own and others' serialized fiction; for example *Hard Times* appeared weekly in 1854, and was then published in book form in the same year. *Household Words* described itself as 'the gentle mouthpiece of reform'; Dickens termed himself its 'Conductor', and led a sustained attack on current social abuses, crusading on behalf of education, sanitary reform, prison reform,

6.12
Charles Dickens's Legacy to England. 1870.
The British Library, London

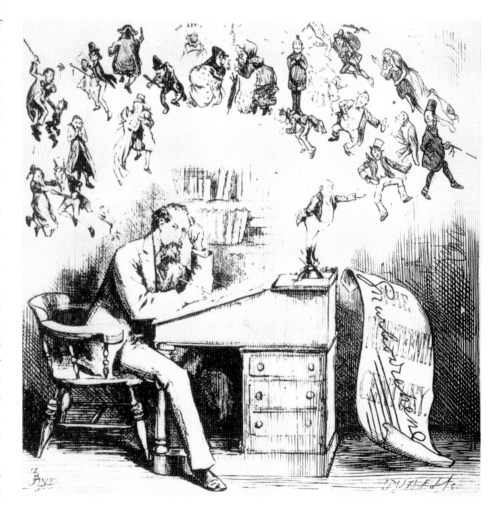

decent houses for the poor and safety in factories.[46] This identification with the domestic is visible in the series of commemorative portraits of Dickens that appeared after his death in 1870. Following a portrait by R.W. Buss (see pl.6.11) in which domestic detail is mixed with fantasy as Dickens's characters appear to him, the newspapers carried a series of images of either him writing or his empty chair (see pl.6.12–6.13).

Narrative style

One reason that descriptions of the domestic interior in fiction can do so much might be related to the many different narrative styles available to the novelist. And those narrative modes that exploit the association between the interior and the viewing subject's interiority are especially fruitful. It is, of course, not merely that descriptions tell us about a character's environment and, by extension, socio-economic status and aesthetic concerns, it is, as I've suggested, a spectacularly rich vein for revealing a protagonist's response to others. In Dickens's *Little Dorrit* (1755–7) we see Mrs Clennam's house through the eyes of both Little Dorrit, the maid coming to the big house to sew, and Arthur Clennam, the henpecked son returning from 20 years in China. The house, central to the plot, collapses in the course of the narrative, but until that point acts as a focus of different characters' experiences. Arthur finds the house dark, lugubrious, imposing, stifling and confining. Walking up through the 'old close house' Arthur comes to a large garret bedroom described as 'Meagre and spare, like all the other rooms, it was even uglier and grimmer than the rest'.[47] Little Dorrit, brought up in the Marshalsea prison for debtors, finds the house brighter and less stuffy than Arthur. We not only get a rich image of an interior from two perspectives, we also get an insight into those characters and their experiences. If we look again at Dickens's narrative style in the above passage, we see it follows closely the thoughts and speech patterns of his characters. In the opening of Chapter 14 Dickens makes the identity of his viewpoint explicit:

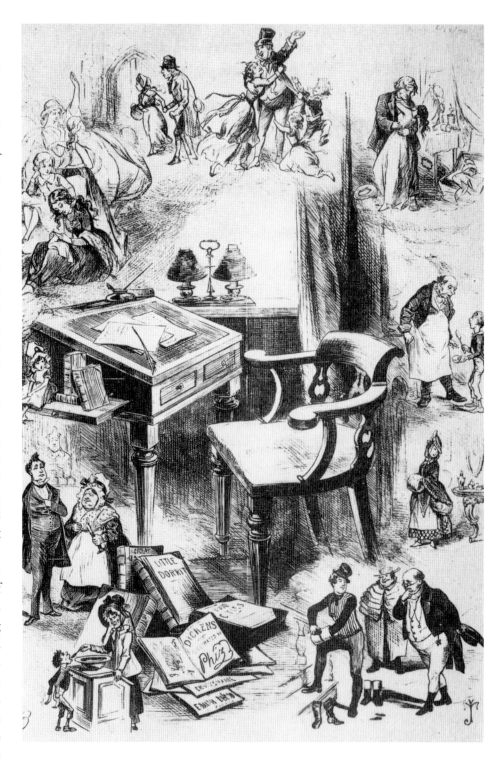

6.13
The Empty Chair. 1870.
The British Library, London

This history must sometimes see with Little Dorrit's eyes… . Little Dorrit looked into a dim room, which seemed a spacious one to her, and grandly furnished. Courtly ideas of Covent Garden, as a place with famous coffee-houses, where gentlemen wearing gold-laced coats and swords had quarrelled and fought duels; costly ideas of Covent Garden … all confused together, – made the room dimmer than it was, in Little Dorrit's eyes, as they timidly saw it from the door.[48]

Free indirect discourse, or style, is the term given to that type of third person narration which takes the linguistic characteristics of the perceiving character. Associated with, amongst others, Jane Austen and Gustave Flaubert, it is a highly appropriate mode for the description of interiors. The effect is similar to the direct correlation between narrative voice and perceiving subject achieved by Richardson's use of the letter form. Returning to the description of Fanny Price's East Room in *Mansfield Park*, for example, Austen's observing eye and language are those of her heroine:

> To this nest of comforts Fanny now walked down to try its influence on an agitated, doubting spirit – to see if by looking at Edmund's profile she could catch any of his counsel, or by giving air to her geraniums she might inhale a breeze of mental strength herself. But she had more than fears of her own perseverance to remove; she had begun to feel undecided as to what she *ought to do*; and as she walked round the room her doubts were increasing. Was she *right* in refusing what was so warmly asked, so strongly wished for?'[49]

Here Austen follows Fanny's thought patterns in relation to what she sees in her room. This mode of narrative feeds into the narrative style termed, not entirely satisfactorily, 'stream of consciousness' explored in the early twentieth century by, amongst others, James Joyce, Virginia Woolf and Dorothy Richardson. In Woolf's celebrated evocation of the Ramseys' summer house in *To The Lighthouse* (1927) we are taken on a mental tour of the house, her concerns about its inhabitants and her own life, by Mrs Ramsey as she tries to measure her son's leg in order to take clothes to the lighthouse keeper's children. The narrative voice follows Mrs Ramsey's own thoughts and associations:

> She looked up – what demon possessed him, her youngest, her cherished? – and saw the room, saw the chairs, thought them fearfully shabby. Their entrails, as Andrew said the other day, were all over the floor; but then what was the point; she asked herself, of buying good chairs to let them spoil up here all through the winter when the house, with only one old woman to see to it, positively dripped with wet?[50]

The multiple narrative voices available to the novelist and, in particular, the techniques of free indirect style and stream of consciousness allow for exceptionally engaged depictions of the domestic interior. These depictions reveal for the reader the processes of that other, older version of the interior, the mind, and confirm Madame Merle's sense of the self flowing into and returning out of objects and surroundings that 'belong[s] to us'. Thus as descriptions move from object to interior, from Defoe's focus on objects towards Woolf's evocation of an interior, via the nineteenth century's fascination with the minutiae of domestic interiors, that shift is facilitated in part by changing narrative techniques. The novel's structural versatility allows the author to describe interiors through the characters' perceptions, and to engage in so doing with characters' pasts and futures in a way that is difficult in other media. These narrative modes are of course available (and used) in describing other scenes and locations. However, particularly in novels focusing on women's experience, houses often play a key role in the narrative, and serve as indicators of past experience (childhood, for example) as well as offering clues to a series of potential futures. There is a sustained link between 'self' and house or home, whether owner, labourer or visitor. The domestic interior is, through this period, established as a powerfully 'expressive' site, and nowhere more so than in its representation and imagination by novelists.

Picturing Domesticity: the cottage genre in late eighteenth-century Britain

John Styles

In Britain, painterly idealizations of cottage life came to prominence in the work of Thomas Gainsborough. His influential series of cottage scenes in the 1770s and 1780s suggest the domestic satisfactions of the simple rural life (see pl.6.15). Gainsborough evoked those satisfactions by portraying humble family groups outside their cottages in picturesque woodland settings, not by itemizing the material details of their indoor domestic routines. The many painters who worked in the cottage genre after Gainsborough continued to focus on the exterior.

Depictions of cottage interiors were fewer. They tended to offer a more didactic, moralizing message than Gainsborough's generalized evocations of sympathy for the life of peasant mothers and their ragged, yet healthy and carefree children. George Morland in his contrast paintings *The Comforts of Industry* and *The Miseries of Idleness* (both 1790) juxtaposes two cottage interiors to inculcate a stark moral lesson (see pl.6.17 and 6.18). Here the cottage is envisaged as a site of domestic accounting. Ragged clothes, torn curtains and disarrayed furniture signify improvidence, not Gainsborough's rustic wholesomeness. Improbably fine clothing, ample provisions and well-ordered furnishings signal proper domestic economy. Morland's two paintings conspire to secure a judgement of approval or disapproval, not human sympathy.

William Redmore Bigg's *Poor Old Woman's Comfort* (1793) envisages a cottage interior in a less obviously didactic way (see pl.6.14). The old woman's stare is melancholy but tranquil, the sadnesses of old age mitigated by the material comforts that populate her cottage. Comfort became a key term in late eighteenth-century social thought, one that was particularly associated with the snug confines of the cottage. Previously comfort had meant emotional support at a time of misfortune. Now its meaning came to embrace absence of material want, a sense of physical wellbeing and the minor luxuries that sustained it. In Bigg's painting the old woman's comforts include a table and chairs, a fire and a candlestick, a clock, an

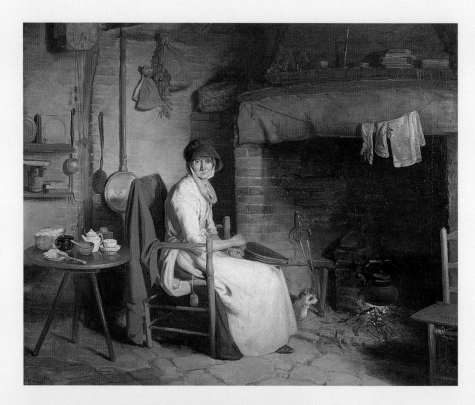

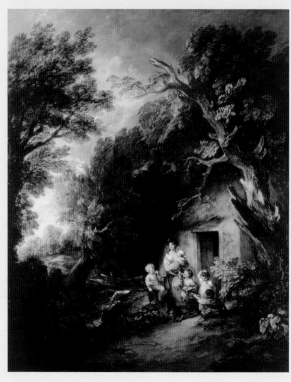

6.14
William Redmore Bigg,
Poor Old Woman's Comfort.
Oil on canvas. 1793.
V&A: 199–1885

6.15
Thomas Gainsborough,
Cottage Door. Oil on canvas.
c.1780. The Huntington Art
Collection, San Marino,
California

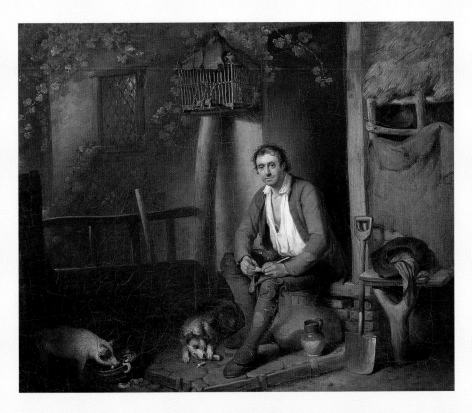

often appear in inventories of the goods owned by paupers in the south of England compiled in the late eighteenth century. And Bigg's painting highlights consumer goods that had recently become common among the rural poor, such as tea wares and clocks.

Bigg's conception of the deserving poor is more generous than Morland's. The old woman is portrayed as no less worthy of her little luxuries than Morland's industrious cottagers, but her entitlement, rather than being a reward for industry, is rooted in time-honoured sympathy for the hardships of old age. Moreover, Bigg's sympathy embraces novel comforts such as tea and white bread that were disparaged by patrician critics obsessed with pauper extravagance. Nevertheless, it is deeply conservative in its understanding of the relationship between women, men and the domestic interior. At the Royal Academy exhibition in 1794 where Bigg exhibited *Poor Old Woman's Comfort*, he showed a companion piece, *The Husbandman's Enjoyment* (see pl.6.16). The contrast is striking. The husbandman secures enjoyment, not comfort. He takes it at the cottage door, not at the cottage hearth. It involves different material things – tobacco, not tea; beer, not bread. In the juxtaposition of these two paintings, the cottage interior acquires a distinct identity. It emerges as the territory, indeed the sanctuary, of the old, the vulnerable and, above all, the female.

6.16
William Redmore Bigg. *The Husbandman's Enjoyment*. Oil on canvas. 1793. V&A: 198–1885

6.17
George Morland, *The Comforts of Industry*. Oil on canvas. 1790. National Galleries of Scotland, Edinburgh

6.18
George Morland, *The Miseries of Idleness*. Oil on canvas. 1790. National Galleries of Scotland, Edinburgh

earthenware teapot, tea cup and tea saucer, a tea caddy, a tea spoon, white bread and butter. These modest possessions, neatly grouped by Bigg around the fireplace, provide no hint of the brutal privation suffered by many among the rural poor in the 1790s, but they are not inaccurate. Objects such as these

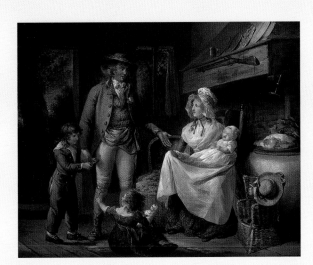

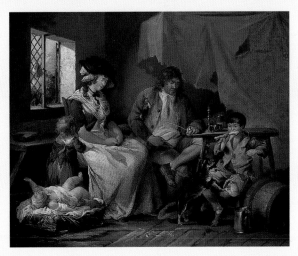

Modelling Houses:
the Killer Cabinet House

Halina Pasierbska

In the 1830s, John Egerton Killer, a prosperous Manchester physician, ordered a copy to be made of a favourite eighteenth-century cabinet in his collection. On the outside, it looked like a piece of furniture. Inside, however, was a representation in miniature of an English gentleman's home of the early 1800s (see pl.6.19). There is some uncertainty as to which member of the Killer household the cabinet was originally intended for, but his daughters must have enjoyed furnishing the doll or 'baby' (meaning 'small') house.

Known as the Killer Cabinet House, this elaborate cabinet is a particular example of an enduringly popular form of three-dimensional representation of the domestic interior. The cabinet is lacquered and decorated in the Chinese style, fashionable at the time, with gold on the outer doors and red and gold on the inside. The oriental feeling is repeated in the sumptuous floral wallpapers in the two reception rooms, which perhaps were samples from the

decorating of Dr Killer's real home. The furnishings are sparse, reflecting actual rooms of the period, and an air of easy elegance hangs about the house.

The Killer Cabinet House was furnished with a mixture of objects, some of which were made at home. The greatest delight of all, however, was to send away for dolls' house furnishings, a luxury afforded only by the prosperous classes. By the end of the eighteenth century articles for furnishing dolls' dwellings were available from a rapidly increasing number of toy shops, such as Hamleys of London, founded in 1760.

The Killer Cabinet House is strongly reminiscent of cabinets in vogue in the Netherlands in the seventeenth and eighteenth centuries. The cabinets were often elegant pieces of furniture in which china, cloth or rare and unusual treasures were stored and displayed. Amongst these were the finely appointed baby households commissioned by the wealthy wives

6.19
Killer Cabinet House with doors open. Lacquered wood. *c.*1830.
V&A: W.15–1936

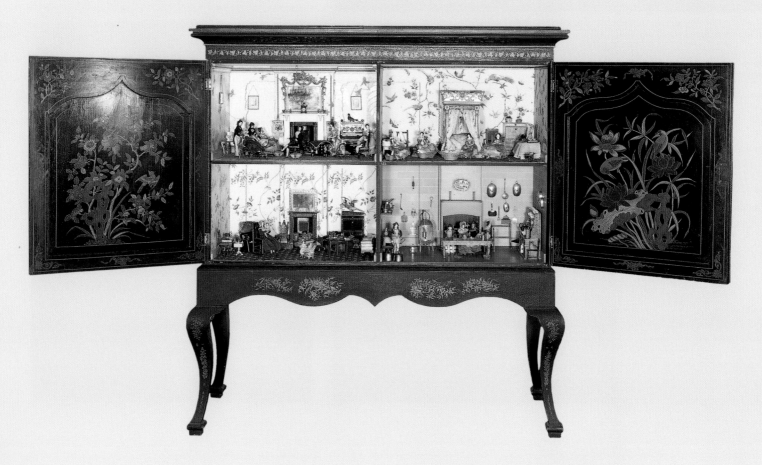

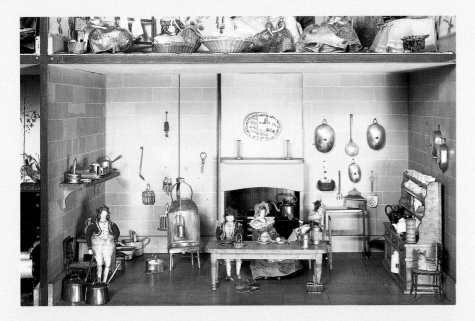

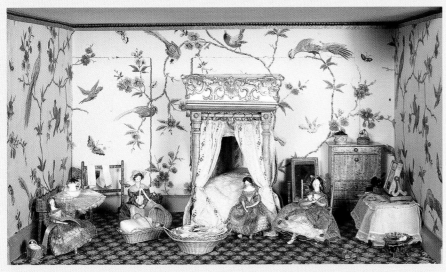

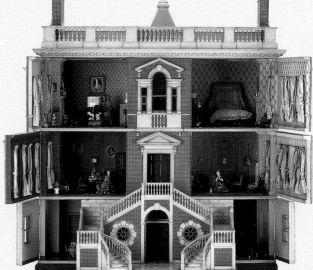

6.22
The Tate Baby House. Wood.
*c.*1760. V&A: W.9–1930

6.20
Killer Cabinet House, kitchen.
Lacquered wood. *c.*1830.
V&A: W.15–1936

6.21
Killer Cabinet House,
bedroom. Lacquered wood.
*c.*1830. V&A: W.15–1936

of Dutch merchants, who often spent huge amounts of time and money on miniature paintings, ivory, porcelain, silver and gold. Collectors such as Sara Ploos van Amstel, whose walnut cabinet house was made in 1745 by Jan Meiijer (now at the Gemeentemuseum at The Hague), kept a precise record of all the objects bought, their arrangement and the names of all the craftsmen involved. These tiny worlds provide an important record of the domestic surroundings of seventeenth- and eighteenth-century Dutch households.

English taste was for the miniature building rather than the cabinet house, resulting in the construction of many fine baby or dolls houses including The Tate Baby House at Bethnal Green's Museum of Childhood (see pl.6.22), Uppark Baby House at Uppark

(1730–40), The Blackett Baby House at the Museum of London (1740) and the Nostell Priory Baby House at Nostell Priory in Yorkshire (1735–40). As a result of this trend few British cabinet and cupboard houses such as the Killer Cabinet House were made in the 1800s.

Unlike the more complex and detailed Dutch cabinets, only four rooms were chosen to be represented in the Killer Cabinet House: the kitchen (see pl.6.20), the drawing room, the morning room and the bedroom (see pl.6.21) or lying-in room. Its owners did not aim at emulating the high standards of ostentation of the Dutch examples, being more concerned, as suggested in a letter offering to donate the house to the V&A in 1931, to present an informal portrait of stylish 'dress and life in a gentleman's house of 1830'.

Temperance and the Domestic Ideal

Mark Jones

The development of the nuclear family, which created a new ideal vision of the domestic interior, has an important origin in the Temperance Movement: a mass movement that in the nineteenth century was more popular than Chartism, Radicalism, Trade-Unionism or Socialism.

Drink was the mainstay of social life in early nineteenth-century Britain. In most towns there were more drinksellers than there were butchers, bakers, fishmongers, greengrocers, cheesemongers and grocers combined. Children at home and at school, patients in hospital, prisoners, soldiers and sailors were all provided with copious quantities of beer as a matter of course. Turning your back on drink, as the Temperance Movement advocated, involved a rejection of the norms and forms of society.

What was to replace these? Tea meetings, soirées and fêtes – and Friendly Societies such as the Independent Order of Rechabites and the Good Templars, with their highly structured social life and opportunities for display and advancement – were part of the answer. But more important by far was the invention and propagation of a new vision of domestic life.

Temperance literature and the visual aids used at temperance meetings are rich in images of domestic bliss. They describe the homes of the respectable working class, and as such offer an enormously valuable source of information about the construction of a new domestic ideal for mass popular consumption. George Cruikshank's *The Bottle* was the most commonly used visual aid at temperance meetings. It begins by showing a happy, temperate household (see pl.6.23). Not a wealthy household, their life is conducted in one room, but one in which, as J.W. McCall's accompanying text has it, 'evidences

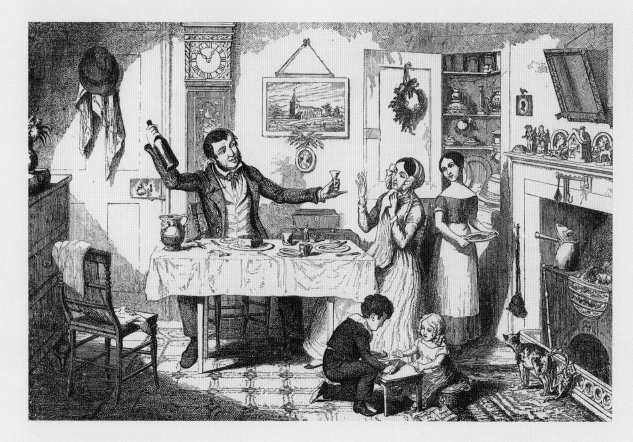

6.23
George Cruikshank,
The Bottle. Plate I.
Etching. 1847.
V&A: 9927.1

of plenty abound, and shew what skill and industry have been doing for years'. A fire burns in the hearth, the table is set with good things, there are chairs for the married couple and their elder daughter, a longcase clock, pictures on the wall, ornaments and portraits on the mantelpiece and an array of crockery and metalware proudly displayed in the open cupboard. A well fed cat and kitten play on a hearth-rug before the fire, there are bright fire-irons beside it and a carpet covers much of the floor. This ideal worker's home is explicitly contrasted with the lack of material possessions that characterizes the same family's home when drink has taken hold (see pl.6.25). The same room is now bare and comfortless and their youngest child is dead.

Popular medals propagated a similar message (see pl.6.24). The temperate home is a cosy haven from the outside world, populated by both parents and by never less than three or more than four children. This is a family sufficient unto itself. It eats together and engages in harmless or improving recreation together. It has no need of the glaring lights and tinsel pleasures of the Gin Palace. Interestingly, the new home is home only to the nuclear family, which will define its success by the acquisition of an array of material possessions so attractive and comforting that children will stay there to be read to and parents will stay in to play with their children.

This image was sufficiently compelling to be appropriated by the middle classes who, guided by Arts and Crafts architects, abandoned formal façades and high-ceilinged rooms for the cottagey cosiness of the new domestic ideal pioneered by the working and lower middle classes. The idea of home-building, of the 'family house' centred on living room and kitchen, was to dominate Western cultures through much of the twentieth century. It is only with its decline in the late twentieth and early twenty-first centuries and its partial replacement by other varieties of household, interestingly coincident with changed attitudes to the social consumption of alcohol, that the bold originality and widespread influence of Temperance notions of the ideal domestic space have become apparent.

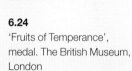

6.24
'Fruits of Temperance', medal. The British Museum, London

6.25
George Cruikshank, *The Bottle*. Plate V. Etching. 1847. V&A: 9927.5

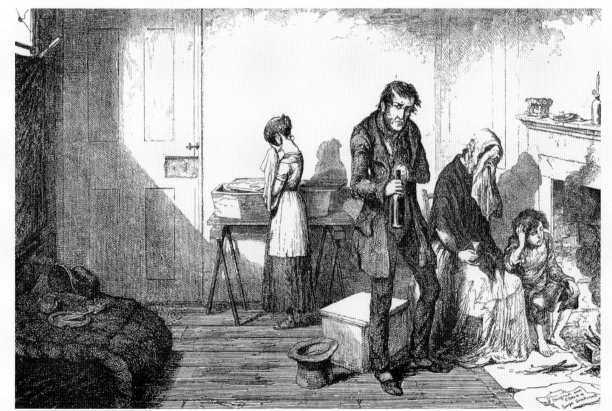

Lived Perspectives: the art of the French nineteenth-century interior

Francesca Berry

Writing in Paris in the 1930s the German literary and cultural historian Walter Benjamin placed the domestic interior at the centre of nineteenth-century French society. Benjamin's unfinished account of the nineteenth century has proved influential in its insights and representation of the domestic interior which he saw as refuge for the bourgeois imagination, describing it as 'not just the universe but also the *étui* [casing] of the private individual.'[1] From his twentieth-century perspective Benjamin identified in the rich material culture of the early to mid-nineteenth-century bourgeois home the origins of a popular new literary genre: detective fiction. 'To dwell means to leave traces' Benjamin claimed.[2] 'In the interior, these are accentuated. Coverlets and antimacassars, cases and containers are devised in abundance; in these, the traces of the most ordinary objects of use are imprinted. In just the same way, the traces of the inhabitant are imprinted in the interior.'[3]

Despite the perceptive acuity of his account and the extent to which it has informed subsequent analysis of the nineteenth-century interior, Benjamin devoted little of his manuscript to 'the universe of the private individual'. Moreover, his account constituted just one aspect of a wider re-evaluation of the nineteenth-century interior from a twentieth-century perspective. Benjamin's fellow countryman, the Surrealist artist Max Ernst, who was also working in Paris at this time, produced a pictorial analogue to Benjamin's text with his serialized 'collage novel' of 1934, *A Week of Kindness (Une Semaine de bonté)*.[4] Domestic interiors constitute a significant plot device in a book designed to parody the overblown romantic narratives and minutely observed scenes that form the backbone of nineteenth-century popular fiction. At first glance these interiors, inhabited by generic bourgeois characters and other more fantastical creatures, assume the familiar appearance of those seen in the previous century's illustrated literature, from which the collage fragments were gleaned. However, absurd elements of a suggestively erotic nature erupt with uncanny effect into domestic scenes typical of the nineteenth century, leading art historian Hal Foster to suggest these collages capture 'the psychic unrest of the bourgeois interior'.[5] In a salon scenario, a young bourgeois woman is depicted asleep on a *chaise-longue*, watched by a man of possibly Central Asian extraction who appears to be accompanied by a similarly out-of-place dragon. In a familiar pictorial trope, a bourgeois man is separated from this group and depicted at the window, drawing back its lace curtains to look out of the apartment (see pl.7.1). In another plate depicting a bedroom scenario, an ideal female nude reclines asleep

7.1

Max Ernst, plate from 'The Dragon's Court', from *Une Semaine de bonté*. Volume III. Engraving. 1934. NAL: Fischer 43 (i-v)

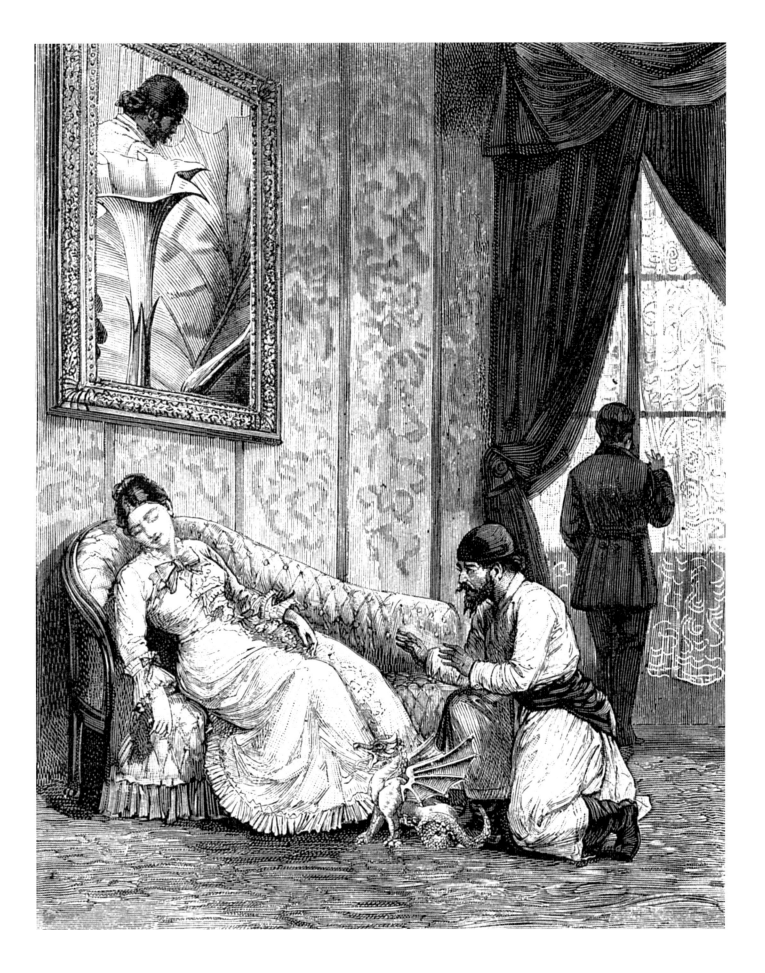

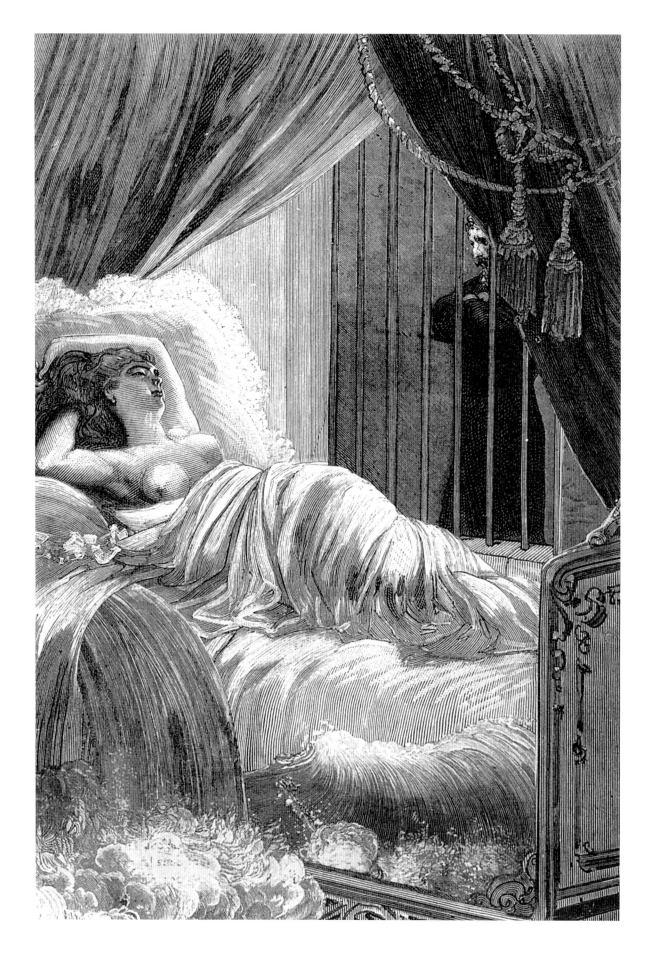

7.2
Max Ernst, plate from
'Water', from *Une Semaine
de bonté*. Volume II.
Engraving. 1934.
NAL: Fischer 43 (i–v)

on a luxurious bed of breaking waves, watched with considerable intensity by a bourgeois man from behind the bars of a cell (see pl.7.2). In the plates that follow, the male figure surfs the waves of his watery bedroom encounter, whilst other men appear to drown. Despite, or even as a result of, the novel's bizarre and humorous elements, Ernst encapsulated aspects of the bourgeois interior and its visual representation that are pertinent to our analysis. Produced from cheap nineteenth-century wood engravings in a period when the Modernist interior and its more 'sophisticated' modes of representation were coming to the fore, these collages are testaments to the pervasiveness of nineteenth-century domestic visual culture and to the nineteenth-century interior itself as a lasting historical remnant – a space in which many

people continued to live.[6] Moreover, Ernst produced a remarkable visual take on the fantasy life of bourgeois men and women that suggests the psychological currents bubbling under the surface of the bourgeois interior were simultaneously elaborate and banal. Seen through the lens of Freudian psychoanalysis, Ernst's collages simultaneously tell us about the 1930s and highlight the nineteenth century's developing concern for the psychology of domestic life, a topic explored in some depth in the textual and visual culture of the *fin de siècle*.

Artistic interiors
Interestingly, the bedroom scene featured in Ernst's collage novel invites comparison with a significant nineteenth-century modern-life painting of a frustrated sexual encounter –

7.3
Edgar Degas, *Interior*.
Oil on canvas. *c*.1868–9.
Philadelphia Museum of Art

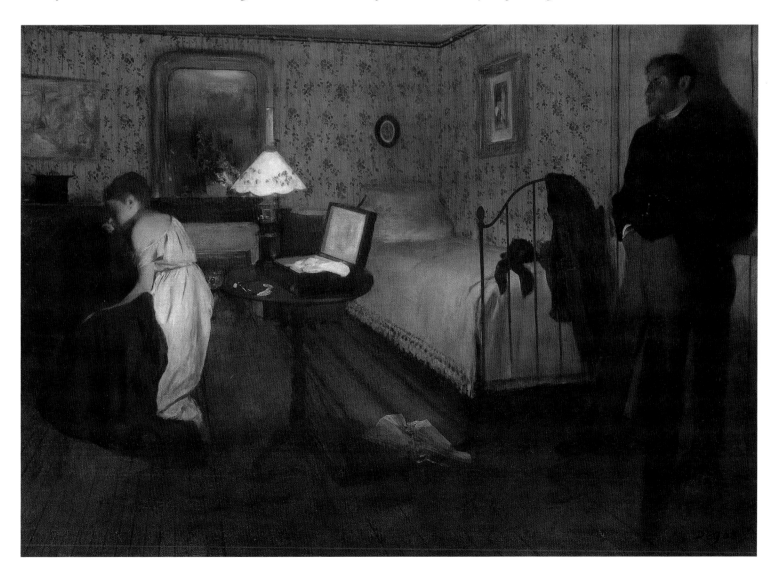

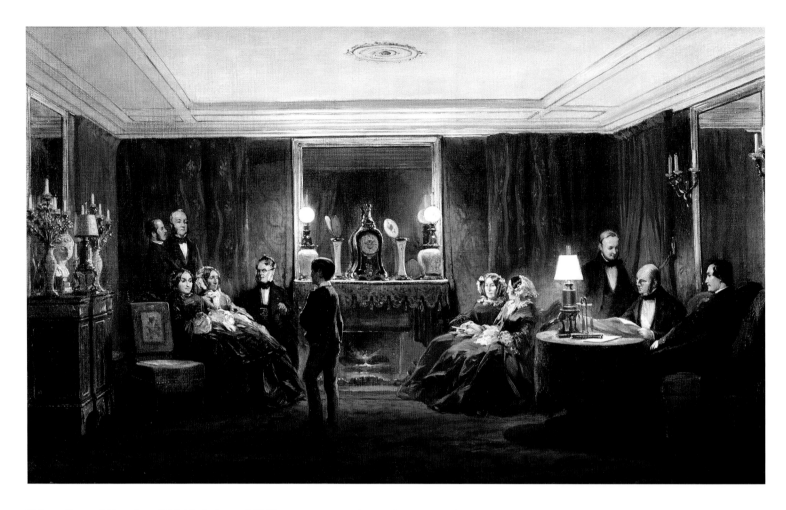

Edgar Degas' *Interior* of 1868–9 (see pl.7.3).
Previously interpreted as depicting the aftermath of a cross-class rape, this painting has
recently been re-defined by Susan Sidlauskas as
a painting on the theme of failed sexual desire
within bourgeois marriage.[7] As with Ernst's
collage, the male and female figures are arranged
around the intimate primal scene of a bed, but
the theme of frustrated pleasure in the Degas
painting is represented using less obviously
psycho-symbolic means. Unusually for a nineteenth-century domestic scene, meaning is not
conveyed using the conventional mechanisms
of genre painting (overt symbolism, moral
didacticism and legible social types), but in slight
manipulations of the pictorial conventions for
representing figures in internal space. The walls
and floor that in more conventional paintings
produce a stage-like box on which figures
perform (see pl.7.4), have been twisted side-
wards and upwards and the room's perspective
telescoped to produce an unusually dynamic,

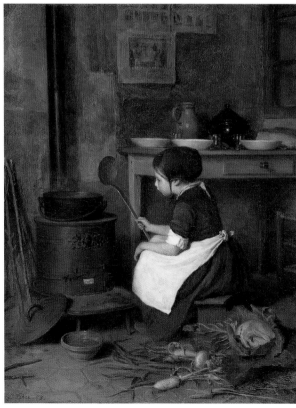

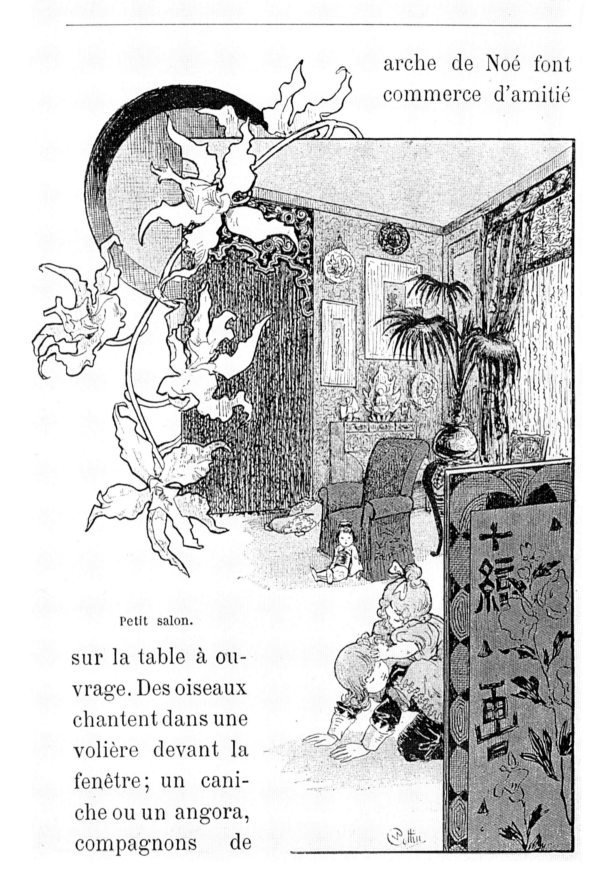

arche de Noé font
commerce d'amitié

7.6
Plate from *Le Goût dans
l'ameublement* by Henri de
Noussanne. 1896.
NAL: 502.N.233

Petit salon.

sur la table à ou-
vrage. Des oiseaux
chantent dans une
volière devant la
fenêtre; un cani-
che ou un angora,
compagnons   de

triangular space. Standard bedroom items such as the bed and the small table expand aggressively towards the viewer. Indeed, the table, a motif that tends in domestic genre paintings and family portraits to constitute the locus around which the protagonists gather, here performs the contradictory act of spinning the figures out towards the boundaries of the room. These slight but significant compositional manipulations produce unstable relationships between the figures, the objects and the space. Sidlauskas suggests that it is these charged encounters that induce an uncomfortable bodily empathy on behalf of the viewer and that help to convey to the viewer signs of the protagonists' anxiety; the signs of something unusual going on inside.[8]

As a set of practices and discourses, modern-life painting in mid- to late nineteenth-century France developed new pictorial means for representing the emotional and psychological life of the individual in relation to the bourgeois interior. Resulting from technological developments in the capacity for reproduction and distribution, the interior in image and text proliferated during the nineteenth century. As a representational motif, the interior continued to function as the context for various domestic and familial activities but increasingly operated as the actual subject of representation in the form of prescriptive and commercial illustrations and literature, such as furnishing catalogues, domestic advice manuals and guides to interior decoration (see pl.7.6). Whilst this chapter will explore representative depictions of the bourgeois interior sourced from the wealth of general textual and visual culture produced to represent the interior in the period, it will focuus on the urban bourgeois interior as it was more exceptionally represented in modern life paintings. Though working-class domestic life in rural and urban settings garnered increased attention during the century, most notably from sociologists, artists (see pl.7.5), novelists and illustrators (see pl.7.7), it was the urban bourgeois apartment interior that dominated the representational field.

Marked by the vicissitudes of time and use, actual domestic spaces were constantly changing, something that static images have struggled to represent. Historians tend to rely upon textual media such as novels, diaries and letters to represent temporal shifts and more personal, experiential accounts of domestic life. Though more exceptional than representative, this chapter will demonstrate that modern-life paintings are unusual in offering significant visual means of understanding, even 'experiencing', the nineteenth-century domestic interior in terms

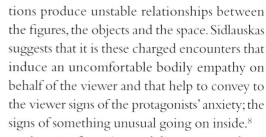

7.7
Georges Bellenger, 'The Death of Lalie'. Etching from *L'Assommoir* by Emile Zola. 1878. Bibliothèque nationale de France, Paris

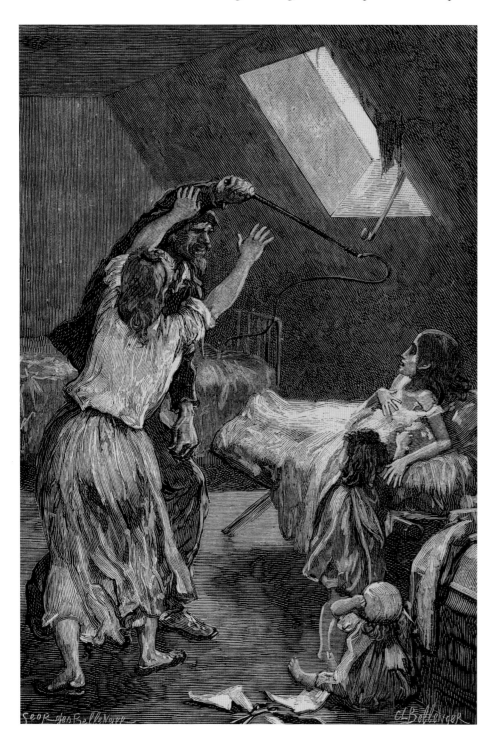

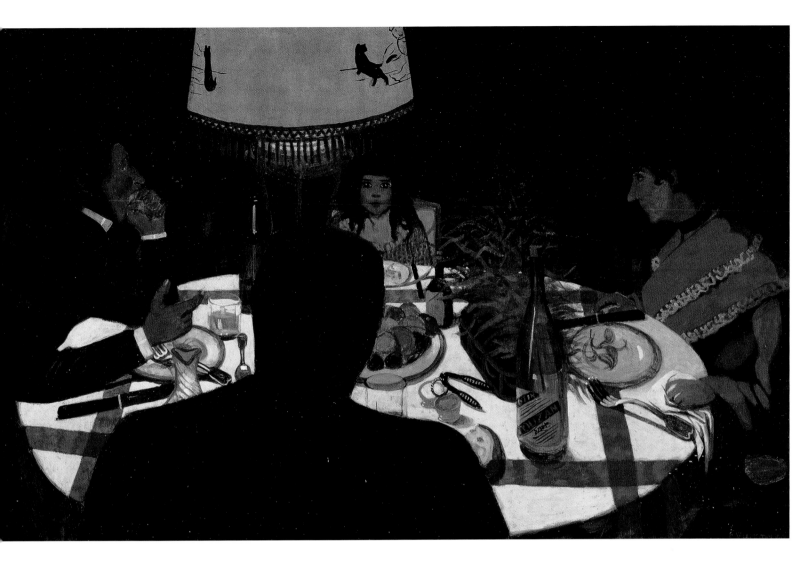

of spatial, temporal and emotional character. Such representations can be personal in tone, particularly in the latter part of the century when many modern-life painters turned towards personal subjects – their family in the interiors they inhabited. At the same time, modern-life paintings were subject to pictorial conventions that made these images meaningful to wider audiences. As a result, certain traceable representational tropes, such as the *à table* scene (see pl.7.8) and the *à la fenêtre* scene (see pl.7.9), emerge and re-occur as forms of pictorial shorthand for certain ways of being in the interior. These and other tropes re-occur in Ernst's collages (see pl.7.1) and their persistence suggests that even when referring to the interior life of the individual they can tell us something about shared modes of domestic experience.

Urban apartments

Multi-storey buildings consisting of ground-level shops, communal staircases and self-contained apartments occupied by single households were first constructed in Paris during the 1820s as the means to house a rapidly expanding bourgeois population.[9] In the following decades the urban apartment building and its living spaces flourished as representational motifs in a range of luxury and cheaper media including architectural treatises, paintings, novels, *physiologies* (cheap serialized pamphlets caricaturing a single social type) and illustrated periodicals.[10] 'The Parisian Housewife' featured in an 1841 *physiologie* lived in a modest apartment at the top of a new Parisian apartment building. As the author pointed out, readers would clearly interpret this location, together with the site of the cooking stove in a small

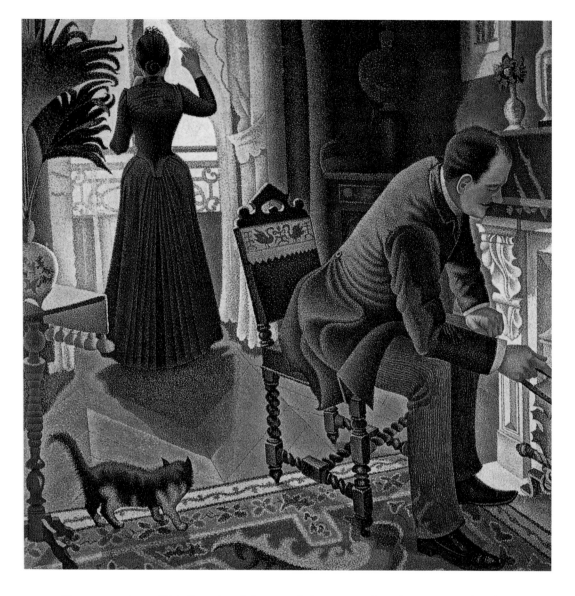

7.9
Paul Signac, *Un dimanche*.
Oil on canvas. 1889-90.
Private collection

room of its own, as signs of this figure's *petit-bour-geois* identity.[11] Whilst cooking in working-class households tended to be carried out in the same room as a number of other activities, including sleeping, the occupants of the new apartment buildings were classified as belonging to the *petit-*, *moyen-* or *haut-bourgeoisie* according to their apartment's height from the street.[12] An 1845 illustration from a leading magazine, 'The Levels of Parisian Society' (see pl.7.10), satirizes this form of social classification using the representational strategy of bisecting a typical apartment building. The street level is occupied by the jolly family of the concierge, who appear to be moving up the social scale by virtue of this man's authority within the building and their proximity to its bourgeois inhabitants.[13] The first floor

belongs to an *haut-bourgeois* couple who relax in opulent, if alienating, surroundings. On the second floor, three generations of a content *moyen-bourgeois* family are assembled around the core motifs of the parents and the circular dining table. As the building rises to the smaller apartments on the upper floors, its occupants become more socially ambiguous and their claims to bourgeois domesticity more tenuous. Amongst them an elderly couple possess some of the same domestic objects as the *moyen-bourgeois* family on the floor below, though their *petit-bourgeois* status is suggested by the furniture's less sophisticated appearance and more confined setting.

As well as suggesting how interiors and domestic objects communicated social identity, these satirical slices of apartment building life

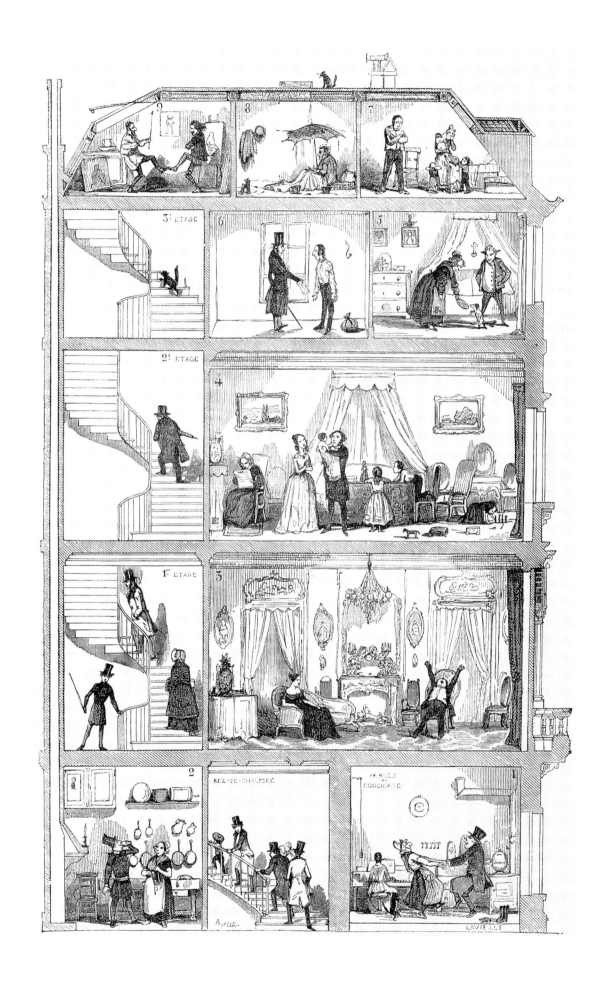

7.10
'The Levels of Parisian Society'
from *L'Illustration*. 11 January
1845. NAL: PP.10

attempted to apply order to a changing urban population. The same is true of the *physiologies* that emerged in the 1840s as attempts to produce recognizable social types such as the 'The Parisian Housewife' and 'The Mistress of the House'. Evidently, these two were thought to represent the extremes of bourgeois femininity. Certainly, they engage in very different domestic roles that represent changing models of domestic femininity. 'The Parisian Housewife' pre-empts an early twentieth-century ideal, as she works without a servant to produce for her family an ordered interior in whose sparkling surfaces her reflection is made visible.[14] In contrast, 'The Mistress of the House' looks back to an eighteenth-century ideal. A salon hostess, she uses her apartment (even her bedroom) for social events, a role demanding the considerable household income of 50,000 francs per year and reportedly made all the more difficult by the layout of the new apartments where rooms for reception and for living were now combined.[15]

Separate spheres

Popular representations of apartment buildings and their inhabitants dating from the 1840s were characterized by the transparency of their spatial boundaries, both within the apartment and between the apartment and the city. Whilst the salon hostess allowed her bedroom to be used for social events, the façades of modern apartment buildings were removed to reveal the material and even emotional status of their typical inhabitants. 'The Parisian Housewife' and 'The Mistress of the House' models of domestic femininity were as much a part of the social fabric of the modern city as iconic masculine types such as 'The Ragpicker' and 'The Flâneur'. Since the late 1970s 'separate spheres analysis' deriving from feminist historical scholarship and, in part, a critique of Walter Benjamin has dominated discussion of the nineteenth-century interior.[16] In brief, 'separate spheres analysis' foregrounds the historical emphasis given to gendered distinctions between public life, associated with the masculine world of commerce, and private life, associated with the

feminine world of domesticity. Whilst it was clear to many historians that such demarcations were never absolute, recent research, including that by literature historian Sharon Marcus, suggests that the conceptualization of the domestic interior as a space distinct from urban space was historically unusual – emerging in Paris during the 1850s as a function of Haussmannization, the changes in the urban fabric of Paris initiated by Baron Haussmann, the civic planner associated with the rebuilding of Paris in the 1850s and 1860s.[17] Certainly, opinion seems to have hardened around the mid century, with a consensus proclaiming women's 'natural' domesticity whilst insisting, in the manner of the Larousse dictionary, that the domestic interior was an 'inviolable' feminine space distinct from the masculine space of the street.[18] In 1856 the moral philosopher Paul Janet published a collection of lectures that was to be re-issued many times, *The Family: Lessons in Moral Philosophy*. In it he re-defined 'The Mistress of the House', who relinquished the role of salon hostess in favour of managing the production of an orderly and welcoming household for her male companion, 'The Head of the Family'.[19]

Others developed a seemingly more pragmatic understanding of domestic space, positing it as a microcosm of a well-ordered society structured by gender differences and a distinction between public and private life. According to César Daly, architect and author of the most significant treatise on Second Empire Parisian domestic architecture, the ideal residence should reflect the duality of existence by being divided into three distinct spaces: reception rooms, family rooms and domestic areas equipped to service the individual requirements of public and private domestic life.[20] Daly's understanding of domestic space may have been more socially inclusive but it acted to formalize spatial demarcations, with both public and service areas functioning as buffers protecting a private core. Interestingly, Daly simultaneously identified the private core of bourgeois domestic life with a commitment to the immediate family and to 'liberty and secrecy', pointing to his belief that the family could really only be itself when not being its public self.

The Naturalist writer Émile Zola satirized pretensions to spatial demarcations in his Parisian apartment building novel *Pot-Bouille* (1884) that tapped into the existing popular imagery of apartment buildings, while offering a biting revelation of moral hypocrisy beneath a façade of bourgeois respectability. Architecturally at least, the building was divided according to Daly's principles: between the (faux) neo-classical luxury of the grand staircase that appears to accord with public decorum, the social and familial rooms of the individual apartments that aspire to mark distinctions between public and private life and, finally, the service areas including the kitchens, back staircase and attic bedrooms. But the boundaries between the outward respectability of public life and the inner sanctity of private life are consistently flouted by the sexual dalliances of the bourgeois residents and further exploited by the servants who use the kitchen windows opening onto the building's filthy inner courtyard to exchange gossip about the 'private' lives of their employers.[21]

Bourgeois families

The debate continues as to whether the ideology of separate spheres functioned purely in the field of representation or was also a matter of lived experience. It is likely that practice always exceeded the boundaries of prescription. Despite claims to the opposite, the bourgeois household with its cohort of servants directed by 'The Mistress of the House' operated within the world of work and commerce. Indeed, it could be argued that the new emphasis placed upon the demarcation of spaces into gendered spheres was a symptomatic reaction to a perceived erosion of social barriers. Whether a matter simply of prescription or also of practice, it is true to say that bourgeois models of domesticity came to dominate the representational field. Ironically, numerous texts and images located the bourgeois family in the bourgeois interior at the centre of public

discourses on the sanctity of private life. This is nowhere more ably exemplified than in a *carte-de-visite* photograph of the emperor Napoleon III and his family (see pl.7.11). Produced in around 1860 from a negative of *c*.1857, these photographs exploited the legibility of the bourgeois family as a symbol of moral pre-eminence as much as they exploited the new reproducibility of the photographic print and its expanding distribution networks.[22] All the appropriate signs for bourgeois identity are present: the familial but hierarchical triangle of father, mother and child; the stiff poses of the figures and the matching outward gazes of father and son that subtly undercut the authority of the empress Eugénie whose gaze is maternal; the figure of the emperor soberly dressed in bourgeois black and resting one hand on a book and the other on his wife's chair, strikes just the right balance of paternal benevolence and authority. A studio construct, the rich but unostentatious interior plays a mere

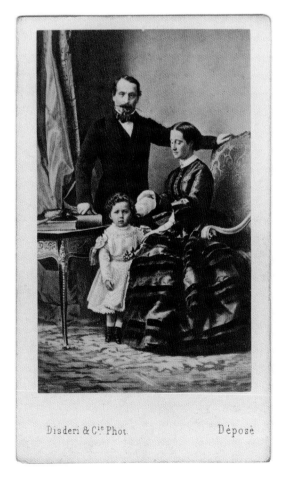

7.11
Disderi, *Napoleon III, Eugène Louis Jean Joseph Napoleon and Empress Eugénie*. Albumen *carte-de-visite*. *c*.1860. National Portrait Gallery, London

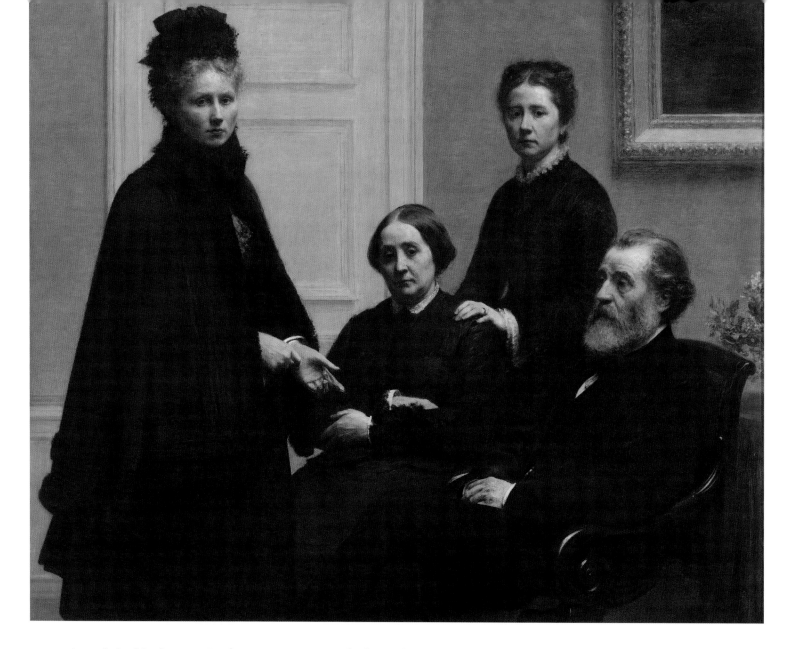

supporting role in this photograph – but a crucial role nonetheless. The heavy curtain, the small round table, the upholstered armchair, the thick carpet and the play of shadows are all actors in the staging of *haut-bourgeois* domesticity. Signifiers of material wealth, bodily comfort and muffled sound, the cropped objects police the edges of the scene to shelter the intimate family unit in this most public of images.

Similar conventions are at play in a family portrait painting of 1878, Henri Fantin-Latour's *The Dubourg Family* (see pl.7.12). The artist includes cropped signs of bourgeois domestic life – the dining chair, the bouquet of flowers and the framed painting – to focus the viewer on the family, the seated maternal figure in particular, towards whom the other figures gravitate. This is a public portrait of a personal subject, the artist's new wife (left) and her family, exhibited at the Paris Salon and London Royal Academy. Interestingly, it seems to exemplify Daly's attitude towards the ideology of separate spheres, using the door, the centrifugal arrangement of the figures and the coming together of hands to refer to the private life of the intimate family unit. The sombre attire and direct gazes of the female figures suggest, nonetheless, that this family is putting on its public face; an effect that drew negative responses from those critics looking for a more intimate view of bourgeois family life.[23]

At the table

In 1876 Gustave Caillebotte produced a more intimate painting of the bourgeois family. *Luncheon* (see pl.7.13) is at once personal and

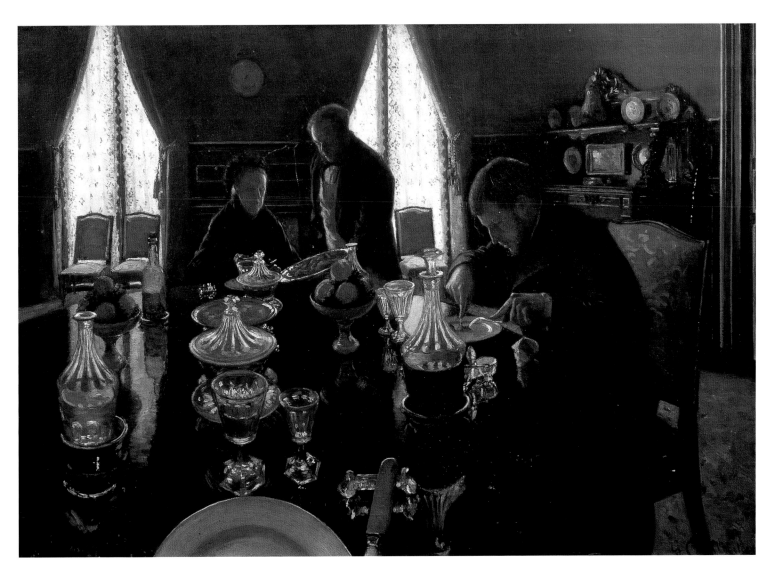

7.13
Gustave Caillebotte,
Luncheon. Oil on canvas. 1876.
Private collection/
Bridgeman Art Library

generic – an unacknowledged portrait of his mother and brother being served and eating lunch and, as such, a painting of everyday *haut-bourgeois* domestic life. Caillebotte employed a standard representational trope in this painting – the *à table* scene – newly composed of figures tightly framed around a table located close to the forward plane of the composition. Popular with artists of the period, the *à table* scene functioned as a stage for the performance of the family in two guises: either as an atomized unit or as an extending social entity.[24] As a representational trope the *à table* scene straddles Daly's demarcation of domestic life into public and private spheres. One particularly dramatic example of the latter is Félix Vallotton's *Dinner, by Lamplight* (see pl.7.8) of 1899, where the lamplight creates a brilliant spotlight on the surface of the table

evoking, together with the central silhouetted figure and the lampshade's black cat motif, the Parisian shadow-puppet plays of the period. All eyes are on the dark-eyed little girl gazing at the mysterious silhouetted figure, who is neither fully a part of the scene nor fully excluded from it and with whom the viewer of this painting might identify as a guest at the table. Caillebotte's earlier use of the *à table* trope may be less theatrically staged than Vallotton's, but it is even more engaging. In this instance the viewer is invited to imagine sitting at the table, but less as a mysterious guest and more as a member of the family – a substitute for the artist. As art historian Michael Fried has written, the painting is divided into 'distinct but continuous spatial zones keyed to various angles of embodied vision', such that the viewer begins by looking down at the plate and progressively raises their head until their gaze reaches the opposite end of the room.[25] Unusually, different formulas for the representation of objects in space have been deployed within the same painting. Shifts from 'lived perspective' to normative single-point perspective can be registered in the development from the circular form of the cropped plate, to the progressively more oval forms of the wine glass and serving dishes, and back to the circular form of the clock hanging on the wall between the windows.[26] In this respect, viewing was envisaged as spatially located and extended over time. It might even be that this embodied and temporal viewing experience invokes a knock-on series of imaginative sensory effects, such that the viewer is invited to imagine not only how sitting at this table over a period of time might actually feel, but also how the space might smell and sound. Although aural experience in this palpably muted environment is likely to be limited to the clinking of cutlery and the ticking of the clock.

Caillebotte's *The Luncheon* was exhibited in Paris at the second Impressionist exhibition of 1876. At the same time and quite possibly in response to this exhibition, the art critic Louis Edmond Duranty published a pamphlet essay, 'The New Painting', defending and theorizing the subjects and representational strategies of modern-life painting. Duranty identified the apartment interior as a key motif, partly because this and the urban street were considered to be *the* settings of modern existence and partly because, as the 1840s *physiologies* already knew, the interior offered clues to the status of its inhabitants.[27] Whilst Duranty's enthusiasm for naturalistic paintings of figures in interiors is pertinent to our analysis, of real interest is his conceptualization of the new strategies being developed for representing the interior that made it capable of conveying in a pictorial medium the experience of being in an interior; the visceral experience of inhabiting three-dimensional space. In order to communicate embodied spatial experience, Duranty argued that paintings of interiors should accommodate the subjectivity of vision:

In real life views of things and people are manifested in a thousand unexpected ways. Our vantage point is not always located in the centre of a room whose two side walls converge toward the back wall; the lines of sight and angles of cornices do not always join with mathematical regularity and symmetry … Sometimes our viewpoint is very high, sometimes very low; as a result we lose sight of the ceiling, and everything crowds into our immediate field of vision, and furniture is abruptly cropped. Our peripheral vision is restricted at a certain distance from us, as if limited by a frame, and we see objects to the side only as permitted by the edge of this frame.[28]

Duranty could have been describing Caillebotte's *The Luncheon* (he may well have been), with its curious mix of fidelity to the *haut-bourgeois* material world (of fine crystal, smooth table surfaces and diffused light) and commitment to subjective experience conveyed in perspectival manipulations, close-ups and abrupt framing. Not that Caillebotte was the first to employ such strategies in interiors paintings, nor Duranty the first to formulate them. We have already noted their use almost a decade earlier in Degas' *Interior* (see pl.7.3), where the distorted space and its looming objects were as much protagonists in the depiction of sexual and psychological disharmony as the two figures. Susan Sidlauskas has shown how Degas and Duranty were informed by a new teaching method being developed in the 1850s and 1860s outside the official arena of the École des Beaux-Arts. This approach taught art students to create a 'perspective of feeling' capable of 'expressing the maker's subjectivity and engaging the spectator's response' by softening and distorting the geometric rules of perspective.[29] It was in 1876, however, that Caillebotte manipulated perspective to implicate, as never before, the viewer as an embodied and subjective presence.

The Luncheon has produced its own debate about how to interpret Caillebotte's depiction of bourgeois family life. For some, this is a painting about emotional poverty amidst material wealth, where individual alienation has been linked to the figures' lack of communication.[30] But it might equally be a painting about emotional comfort borne of familiarity, in that nobody feels compelled to speak to each other. At the very least, Caillebotte's *à table* scene finds a way to visualize, without recourse to melodrama, a developing cultural interest in the psychological or interior life of the individual that is separate from the private life of the family. Like Degas' *Interior*, it is a painting that provides answers to the question how were paintings or other pictorial forms of representation able to signal psychological interiority when devoid of the rhetorical devices, such as internal dialogue, that were otherwise available to writers? In an era committed to representational naturalism, where overt symbolism and theatrical gestures will no longer do, *The Luncheon* depicts figures individually absorbed in tasks requiring the minimum of conscious effort and focuses on bodies that reveal little on the outside but signal psychological interiority by being closed-off to the viewer and to each other within a contained space.[31] We noted above how César Daly identified the private sphere of the bourgeois interior with the 'secrecy and freedom' that enabled the family to be its 'true' self. In the early 1880s architectural reformers looking to soften the formality of Daly's model of domestic space did so by privileging the private life of the individual over that of the family, a model that seems to fit more readily with Caillebotte's approach. According to these treatises, whilst the outside of the apartment building should conform to public decorum, in the interior the inhabitant should enjoy the freedom, borne of privacy, to express their individuality. Reformers such as Henry Havard linked the spatial interiority of the interior and the physical and psychological interiority of the individual, employing bodily metaphors that equated the apartment building to the body as both surfaces and containers. Havard extended his bodily metaphor by comparing the outside of the apartment building to

a black suit and shirt front, and the apartment interior to clothes worn inside where 'we are free, if we feel like it, to wear flannel or not'.[32] Imaginatively implicated as an embodied and subjective presence within the scene, the viewer of *The Luncheon* is unable ultimately to penetrate the impassive façades of the room's occupants, becoming acutely conscious of the private psychological life of the figures by what each is seen to be withholding.

At the window

As a representational trope the *à table* scene functioned as pictorial shorthand for being an individual whilst also being *en famille*. A further representational trope employed by artists in this period was the 'at the window' scene, most potently deployed when featuring a male and female figure in a confined setting, as in Caillebotte's *Interior, Woman at a Window* of 1880 (see pl.7.14) and subsequently in Paul Signac's *A Sunday* of 1890 (see pl.7.9). Both paintings depict a seated male figure and a female figure individually absorbed and incommunicative, the latter gazing out of an apartment window (the location signalled concisely in each by the external balustrade). Though the positions of the male and female figures have been exchanged, Max Ernst's post-Freudian take on this representational trope (see pl.7.1) pointed to sexual frustration within bourgeois marriage as the specific theme of these and related images. Whether specifically about sexual frustration or more broadly about conjugal ambivalence, Caillebotte took a nuanced approach compared to Signac whose representation of the figures' alienation within a specific period of (leisure) time is theatrically, even parodically staged by the body. In Caillebotte's *Interior, Woman at a Window* a slight tension is detected in the corseted female figure's stance, particularly when juxtaposed in such confined circumstances with the unknowing ease of her male companion. Unusually, the viewer of this painting is not invited to identify with the male figure but with the woman at the window, whose act of looking 'through' a framed aperture the viewer replicates.[33] In this context, the

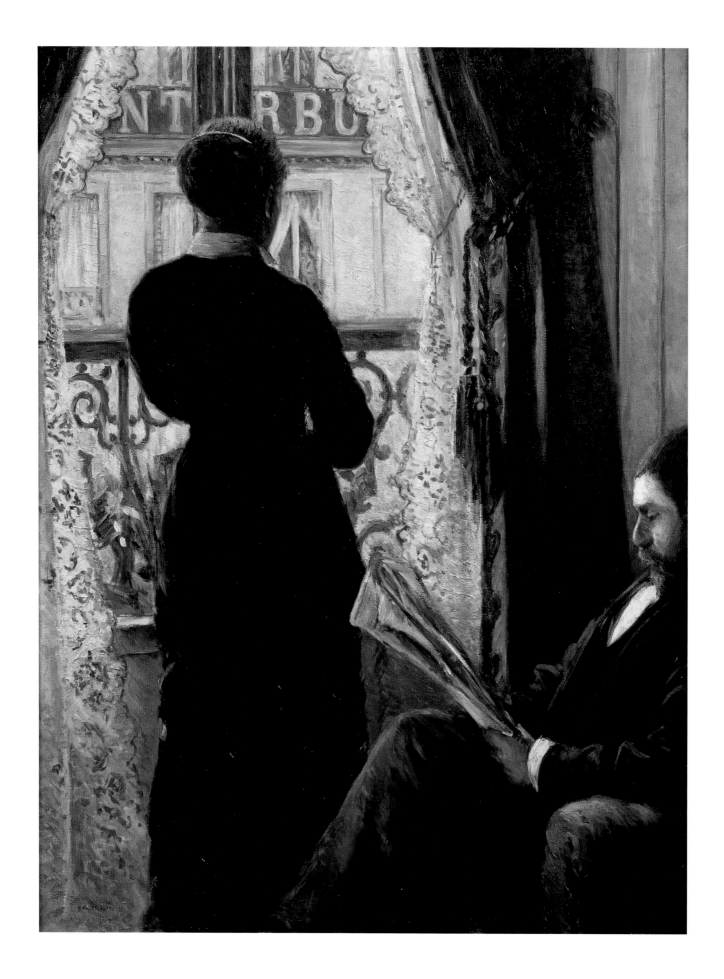

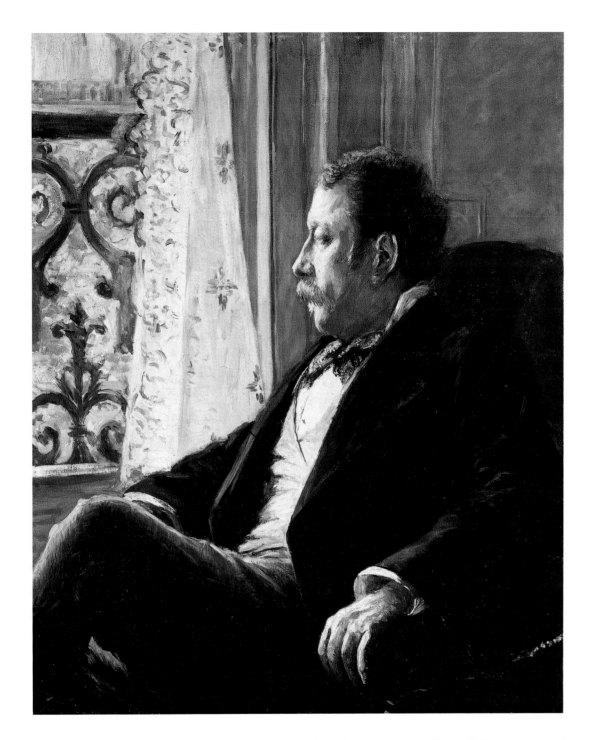

7.14
Gustave Caillebotte,
Interior, Woman at a Window.
Oil on canvas. 1880.
Private collection/
Bridgeman Art Library

7.15
Gustave Caillebotte,
Portrait of a Man.
Oil on canvas. 1880.
Private collection, Giraudon/
Bridgeman Art Library

window appears to function as a transparent boundary, a symbol as much of the female figure's exteriorizing gaze and transcendent imagination as of her bodily confinement. The mirroring of the female figure's position by the figure at the window of the apartment opposite suggests the situation is not specific but generic.

With the tense couple removed, the 'at the window' scene took on a different complexion altogether. In paintings by Caillebotte, *Portrait of a Man* (see pl.7.15), and, previously, Berthe Morisot, *Young Woman at her Window* (see pl.7.16), a further aspect of this trope emerges: solitary figures seated close to windows opening onto urban scenes. In each the figure, whether male or female, adopts a similarly contemplative pose, except that the male figure gazes abstractly outside whilst the female figure looks down at her fan. Each appears melancholic more than

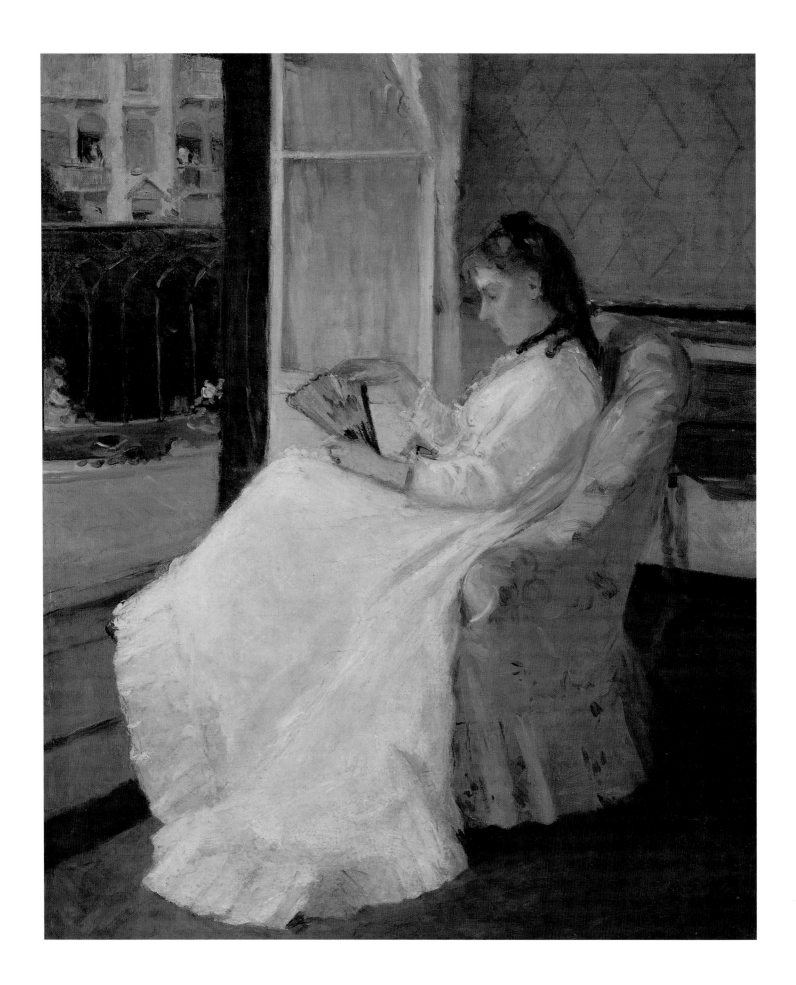

tense, but, as with *The Luncheon*, ultimately each is psychologically inaccessible. Ironically, the open window seems to signal the private psychological life of the individual. Each figure is positioned close to the world visible through the openings in the apartment building's façade and yet removed from it, acknowledging and yet refusing the exteriority it promises. Paintings of female figures located close to spatial, particularly domestic, boundaries were more common in this period and have been interpreted by feminist art historians as representations of bourgeois women's sequesterment in feminized space, here emphasized by the female figure's downward gaze.[34] As Gloria Groom has noted, paintings of inactive male figures ensconced in interiors and usurping their place within the city were unusual.[35] Nonetheless, during the closing decades of the nineteenth century it was certainly more common to associate masculine, as opposed to feminine, subjectivity with domestic interiority.

Subjective interiors

We have already registered a change of attitude occurring in the early 1880s. As noted above, architectural reformers such as Henry Havard argued for a more personalized approach to interior decoration and linked this to the deconstruction of internal divisions between public and private life together with a renewed distinction between inside and outside. Havard was not alone in promoting subjective interior decoration. Produced by, yet claiming to react against, the expanding market for domestic consumer goods, guides to interior decoration critiqued the generic banality of Haussmann apartments, urging readers to offer visitors an intimate psychological encounter such that they will 'meet this *je ne sais quoi* that is intimate, personal, pleasing to the eye or to the spirit, which will be like a mark, the individual representation, even the genius of the owner.'[36] Attitudes to subjective interior decoration were, however, gendered. Texts specifically aimed at bourgeois women, even those written with the intention of encouraging them to become more creatively involved in the decorative arts movement, tended to portray the interior as another female accoutrement, a cosmetic extension of the female body.[37] Links between subjectivity and the interior also became the focus of professional psychological interest. In popular magazines doctors promoted the interior as a refuge from nervous disorders, such as neurasthenia, that were thought to plague modern urban existence.[38] At the same time they warned women of the detrimental effects that unsympathetic decoration and exuberant colour would have upon women's already fragile nervous systems.[39] Others, most notoriously the novelist and art critic Joris-Karl Huysmans, celebrated the psycho-active possibilities and

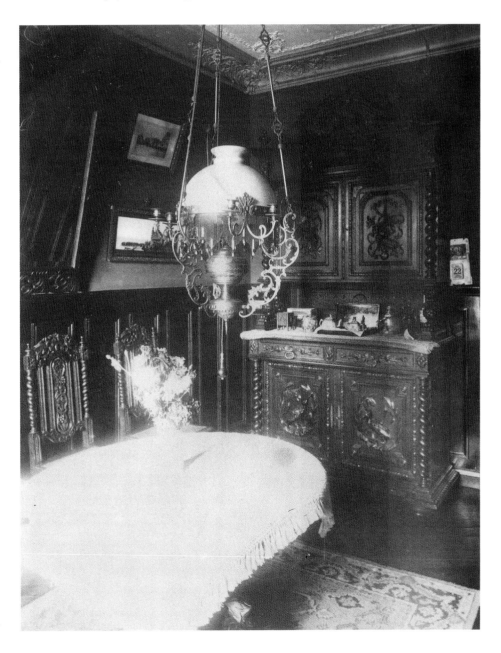

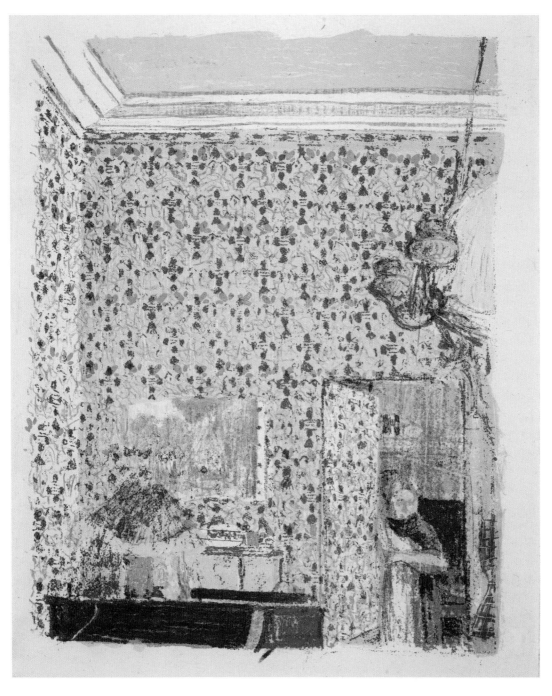

7.18
Edouard Vuillard,
Pink Interior I. Lithograph
published in *Landscapes and
Interiors* album. 1899.
The British Museum, London

7.19
Edouard Vuillard,
Pink Interior III. Lithograph.
published in *Landscapes and
Interiors* album. 1899.
The British Museum, London

risks of the subjective interior in his 1884 novel *Against Nature*. Frequently aesthetes and taste professionals conceived of women as the servants to a male fantasy of absolute interiority, as was the case with the Art Nouveau architect Frantz Jourdain who described a dream of living alone in a completely self-contained and silent house, serviced by 'mute blonde women dressed in pink gowns.'[40]

This fantasy seems to have found a pictorial equivalent in the work of the Symbolist artist Edouard Vuillard who focused the majority of his 1890s work on the *moyen-bourgeois* apartments he shared with his mother. These are the kinds of apartments analyzed in the turn-of-the-century photographs of Eugène Atget who produced an album of *Parisian Interiors*, categorizing each photograph by the location of the apartment and the professional status of its inhabitant. We might compare Atget's photograph of a hat-maker's dining room (see pl.7.17) to Vuillard's lithograph of a dining

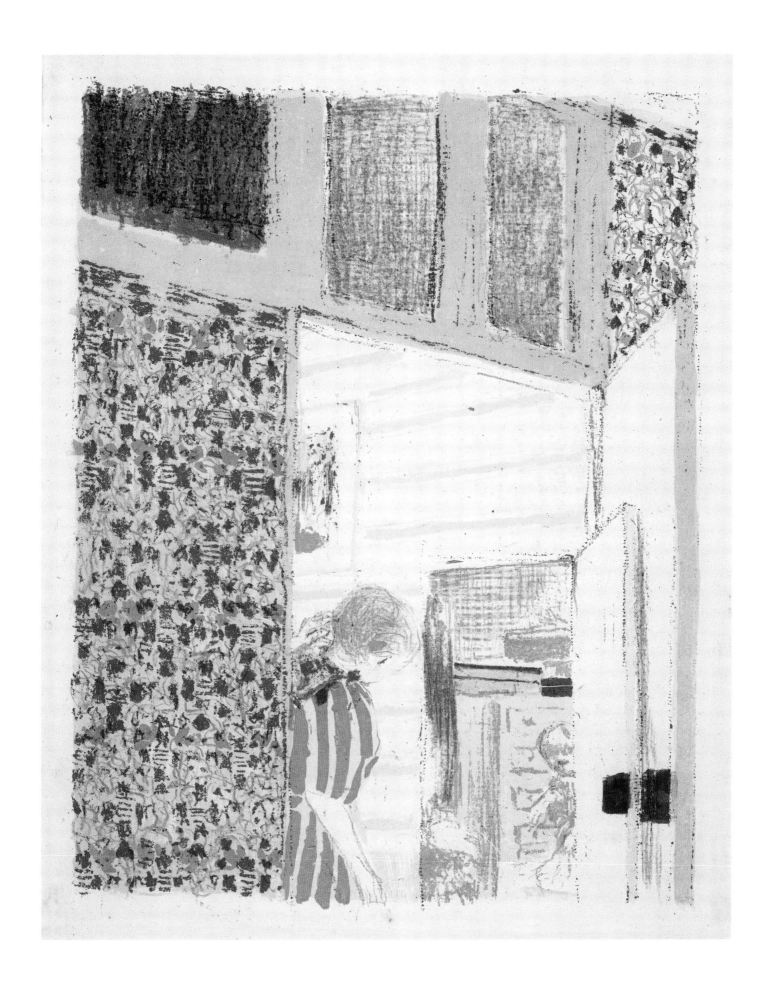

room (see pl.7.18) in which the figure of his corset-maker mother is visible in the doorway. Each features the central hanging lamp that defined the normative function of this room. But here the similarity ends. From the corner of the room the photograph inventories the objects, spatial arrangements, sources of daylight and other factors thought to define an inhabitant's status.[41] In this respect, Atget's album of interiors tapped into the tradition represented by apartment-building cross-sections (these continued late into the century as a popular representational form), compiling a less satirical microcosm of typical Parisian society according to the possession of material things. On the other hand, Vuillard's lithograph took the pictorial theme of the figure absorbed in enclosed space to its logical conclusion. The viewer of *Pink Interior I* is clearly implicated at the centre of the room by the looming presence of the hanging lamp, which makes the dining table above which these lamps normally hang seem viscerally present whilst being pictorially absent. The web of fine lines employed in the lithograph to represent the dense patterns and textures of late nineteenth-century domestic space further contributes to a palpable sense of the body extending into a contained space; a blurring of the boundaries between interior and self.

Vuillard developed other strategies for enhancing embodied experiences of spatial interiority, as seen in a lithograph from the same series, *Pink Interior III* (see pl.7.19), where the viewer is offered a view into not one but two further internal spaces, with the door of one room curiously folding back onto the door to another. Other images, such as *The Linen Cupboard* (see pl.7.20), used decorative figures trapped behind folding screens to produce a sense of bodies extending into and contained within intimate space. Indeed, the folding screen emerged in the period as a trope in its own right for suggesting intimate space, as seen in the illustration for a 'Small Salon' published in an interior decoration manual of 1896 (see pl.7.6). As *The Linen Cupboard* and related images suggest, cupboards were objects

of some significance in Vuillard's work and might be said to have encapsulated metaphorically the spatial interiority of the apartment. This is interesting because apartment buildings were sometimes likened to cupboards.[42] It is possible that this association stemmed from the popular cross-sections representing the apartment building as a social entity, but the perspectival blindness and textural overload of Vuillard's interiors urges association with the more current fantasy of an apartment isolated from those that surrounded it.

Female figures almost exclusively occupy Vuillard's interiors where his decorative approach to the representation of figures in space, unlike Caillebotte's illusionistically three-dimensional approach, causes figure and milieu, subject and object, psychological interior and spatial interior to be seen as co-extensive.[43] As such Vuillard's apartment interiors represent the end of our journey. They are the culmination of a developing mid- to late nineteenth-century concern for the domestic interior as an atomized space, removed from the spaces surrounding it, but in which individual subjectivity might be free to reside. Of course, the belief that the domestic interior could house individual subjectivity was an idealistic fantasy. Moreover, the increasingly public nature in which the domestic interior was represented in paintings, novels, architectural treatises, decoration manuals, magazines and so on as a private and subjective space betrayed any pretensions to such an ideal. But this did not prevent the novelist Marcel Proust, amongst other early twentieth-century commentators, returning to the nineteenth-century interior, the interiors of his childhood, as profound repositories of memory – the origins of his subjectivity.[44] Nor did it prevent Walter Benjamin and Max Ernst doing the same, albeit more critically, a generation later when the nineteenth-century interior and its representational forms remained as outmoded historical remnants. After all, like their nineteenth-century predecessors, Benjamin and Ernst recognized that 'to dwell means to leave traces'.

7.20
Edouard Vuillard, *The Linen Cupboard*. Oil on cardboard. *c.*1892-5. Musée d'Orsay, Paris

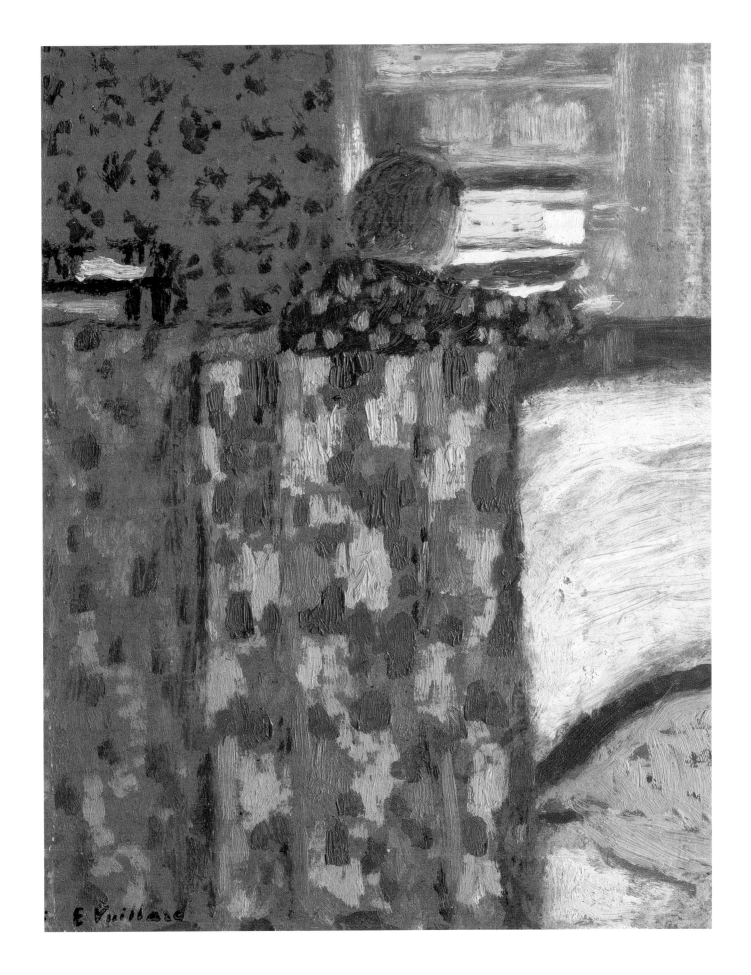

Managing and Making the Home: domestic advice books

Jane Hamlett

The publication of advice on how to manage and decorate the home expanded in the second half of the nineteenth century, offering readers a new way of imagining the home. Household advice manuals such as *Cassell's Household Guide* and Mrs Beeton's *The Book of Household Management* were published in the 1860s, and included suggestions that ranged from fashioning gothic furniture and embroidering antimacassars to ideas for window decorations (see pl.7.21). While women were associated with overall domestic management, men were also expected to contribute to practical home improvement. Alongside a wealth of tips for the cleaning and maintenance of the interior, full-scale decorative schemes were occasionally put forward.

Full of references to material goods, these manuals were aimed at the expanding Victorian middle classes and contrasted starkly with the more spartan literature aimed at the working class. The latter emphasized the moral meaning of home and promoted an altogether more evangelical ethos that informed home management rather than interior decoration. The monthly periodical *The Mother's Treasury* for January 1864, for example, urged wives to be 'frugal' and cautioned against buying domestic goods on credit. Working-class mothers were encouraged to read the Bible to children at home (see pl.7.22). Illustrations could be surprisingly grand, conflicting with the nature of the working-class home implied in the text. They encouraged working-class readers to imagine themselves in the middle-class domestic interior and assume the values of the middle-class home.

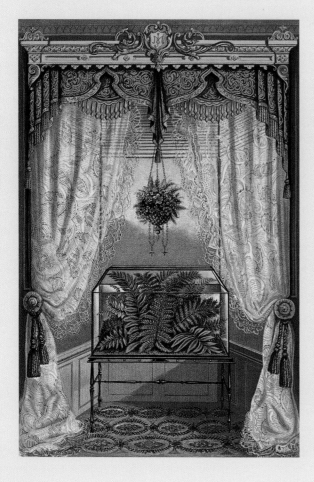

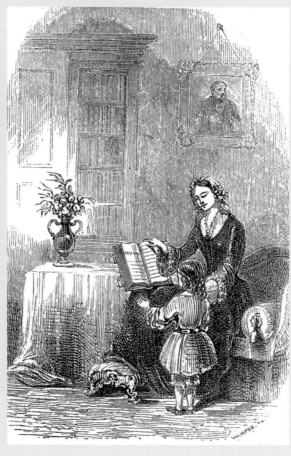

7.21
'Scheme for window decoration', frontispiece from *Cassell's Household Guide*, Volume IV. *c*.1869–71.
NAL: 20.Y.26

7.22
'A mother reads the Bible to her child' from *The Mother's Treasury*. *c*.1864.
NAL: 862.AA.0522

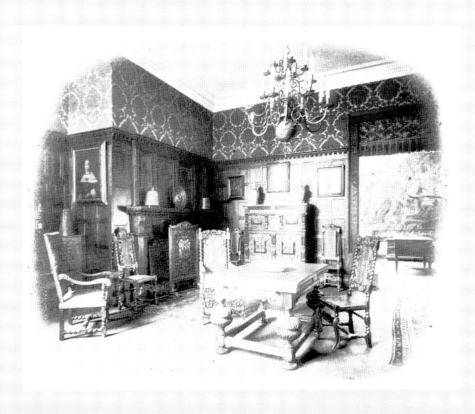

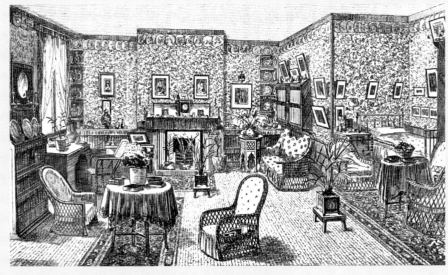

A number of advice manuals that dealt explicitly with decorative choice were published slightly later, led by Charles Eastlake's *Hints on Household Taste,* first published in 1868. Many of these books consisted of articles that were first serialized in magazines; Eastlake's commentary was first published in the weekly magazine *The Queen* under the pseudonym Jack Easle. There was also an exchange between the USA and Britain. Some illustrations for the widely read *Art at Home* series were drawn from American advice manuals. These books were more concerned with design than household management, and reflected the gendered nature of society. Homes were divided between the 'masculine' dining room and the 'feminine' drawing room. Recommendations for the drawing room included the use of light colours and the French style, while schemes for dining rooms, studies, libraries and smoking rooms were darker, often featuring heavy furniture and animal skins (see pl.7.23).

While later books on household management borrowed Eastlake's decorative emphasis, they played on the notion of authentic female domestic expertise. Jane Ellen Panton, an artist's daughter, for example, was a highly successful proponent of this genre. She was particularly concerned to define feminine spaces in the home. Rather than expend limited space on a study for the man of the house, she argued that the mistress should have her own morning room for the familial pursuit of hobbies and informal entertainment. In her second manual, *Nooks and Corners* of 1889, she designed a scheme for a boudoir-bedroom for the daughter of the house and argued that girls should be given their own distinct space within the home (see pl.7.24). Panton continued to write household management books until the 1920s. In her later works she reflected on the changes in the gendered division of space within the home and charted the rise of the sitting room as a shared space.

7.23
'A dining room furnished in the "masculine" style'
from *Our Homes*
by H. J. Jennings. 1892.
The British Library, London

7.24
'A boudoir-bedroom for a young girl' from *Nooks and corners* by J.E. Panton.
1889.
NAL: 47.W.250

Advertising Interiors and Interiors in Advertising

Amanda Girling-Budd

In Victorian England art and commerce became inextricably intertwined. The design reform movement encouraged manufacturers to apply art to their commercial products to make them more competitive. The Great Exhibition of 1851 fed the public appetite for artistic products, and technological advances in printing made it possible for works of art to be reproduced cheaply in magazine form, so bringing them to a wider audience. The epithet 'artistic' became synonymous with fashionability and desirability in the home.

Mass public awareness of art was a useful tool for those selling products and services. In 1876, the designer Bruce Talbert published *Examples of Ancient and Modern Furniture and Metalwork, Tapestries and Decorations* (see pl.7.26). As the title suggests, the work contains illustrations of actual historic interiors as well as new interior schemes designed by Talbert, but

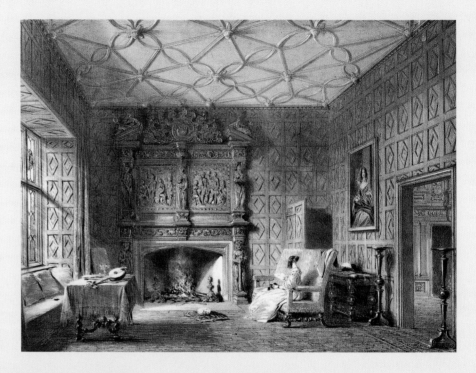

7.25
'Small Drawing Room, Levens Hall, Westmoreland' from *The Mansions of England in the Olden Time* by Joseph Nash, Volume IV. 1839–49.
NAL: 51.H.45

7.26
'Drawing Room' from *Examples of Ancient and Modern Furniture and Metalwork, Tapestries and Decorations* by Bruce Talbert. 1876.
NAL: 57.F.38

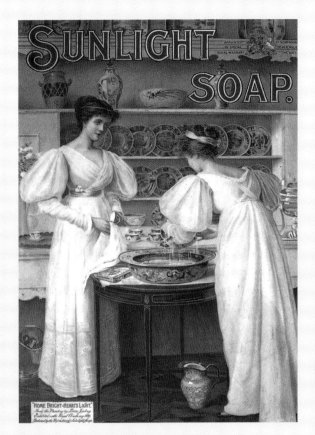

7.27
Louise Jopling,
Home Bright Hearts Light.
Sunlight Soap poster. 1896.
Unilever Archive,
Port Sunlight

not yet realized. *Examples* is therefore a hybrid text, combining elements of architectural treatise and pattern book. Its form borrows directly from Joseph Nash's *The Mansions of England in the Olden Time*, a four-volume set of drawings of the interiors of Elizabethan and later houses, published between 1839 and 1849 (see pl.7.25). Nash was a painter and architectural draughtsman who pioneered a populist approach to the depiction of historic architecture and interiors. His mansions were accurate renderings of existing buildings, but the costumed figures that inhabited them were of Nash's imagining. They looked somewhat like Victorians in fancy dress, but they fulfilled their purpose, adding drama and romance to bare architectural bones, allowing the Victorian middle classes to inhabit, imaginatively at least, England in 'the Olden Time'. Talbert not only used Nash's style of architectural perspective drawing, but also included figures in several of the plates. This was novel for a pattern book, but worked in the same way as Nash's figures, allowing the viewer to enter the scene imaginatively. In this case, though, the purpose was to

stimulate a desire to consume the product, namely the interiors designed in historical revival styles.

Art was also used by the great innovators of advertising, the soap manufacturers. In the first half of the nineteenth century soap was usually locally made and sold, and even still made in the home in some rural areas, but large-scale manufacturers with national and international distribution networks emerged towards the end of the century. Soap was packaged and branded and the consumer was faced with a choice for the first time. One of the more successful marketing strategies was to buy and adapt popular paintings by well-known artists. A. & F. Pears caused outrage in the art world by their hijacking of John Everett Millais' painting *Bubbles* as a soap advertisement. Sentimental paintings of children had an obvious appeal, but William Hesketh Lever also bought pictures of domestic interiors to adapt into advertisements for Sunlight Soap, Lever Brothers' main product and a soap for household use. Louise Jopling's *Home Bright, Hearts Light* (see pl.7.27), bought by Lever in 1896 and immediately adapted into a poster, appealed to consumers on various levels. The first woman to exhibit work at the Royal Academy, Jopling was a well-known figure in artistic circles. The setting of *Home Bright, Hearts Light* was domestic. The 'aesthetic interior' depicted was unequivocally middle class, and fashionably furnished, with white painted furniture displaying 'artistic' blue and white china. The female figures, in their classically inspired costume, were not servants, and their labour seemed genteel and recreational, certainly not the drudgery of housework, making this an early pictorial example of aspirational advertising. The direct appropriation of works of fine art for advertising was a relatively short-lived phenomenon, with paintings finally being put beyond the reach of advertisers by a change in the law in 1911 that allowed artists to reserve copyright on their works. However, the association between art and advertising endures into the present.

3

DISPLAYING THE MODERN HOME, 1850 TO THE PRESENT

I N THE LAST TWO CENTURIES, the domestic interior has become the subject of increasing public interest. From the Great Exhibition of 1851 to the Festival of Britain in 1951, the Daily Mail Ideal Home Exhibition and its imitators in Britain since 1908, to world fairs in America and Europe, the domestic interior has been the object of mass, public curiosity and consumption. This has been facilitated by new means of transport, first the railways, shipping and the motorcar, then air travel on a worldwide scale.

The public interest in domestic interiors has been reflected in their collection as artefacts and their incorporation both into the private residencies of the wealthy and the 'period rooms' of public art museums and galleries. The model interior, designed according to moral as well as aesthetic principles, became a potent symbol for a future, better society. Architecture and politics met in the aspirations of Modernism, a cultural response to modernity, and its public and private successes and failures. This is also the period of planned housing developments, from charitable trusts in late nineteenth-century Britain to the post-World War II reconstruction of Europe and North America.

Throughout this period, technology played an increasingly important part in the representation of the home, as well as its running. Through lithography and photography, the mass production and consumption of images was encouraged by the sheer scale and number of representations of the interior and their circulation in diverse contexts. We reflect on magazines, advertisements and exhibitions, and in the two final chapters, on film, television and new information technologies. More than any other medium, the moving image has transformed our imagination of interiors, and their images in both documentary and fictional form are available to millions in a world context. Such international representation is matched by a global market for the trappings of interiors; we can buy the identical, mass-produced kitchen across Europe and North America, and beyond, and do so in our millions.

Joseph Byron, *Photographer's Studio. c.*1898. The Byron Collection, Museum of the City of New York

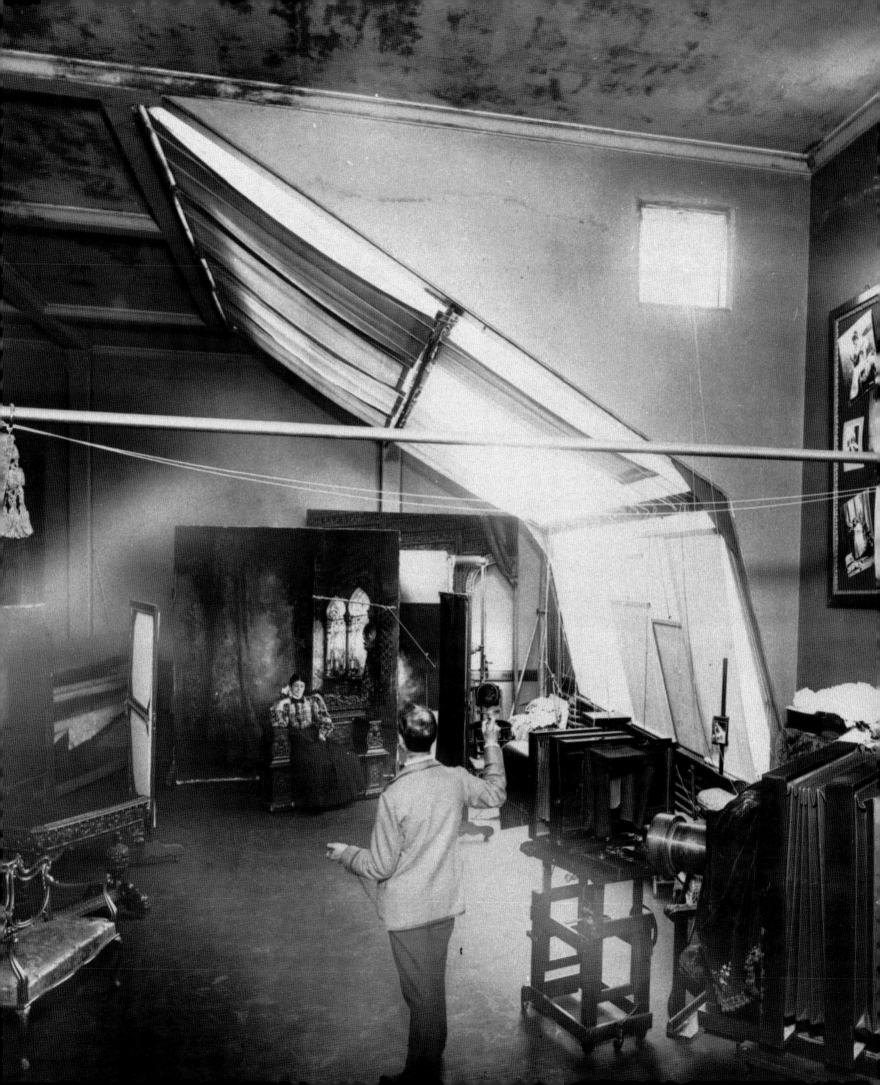

8

Displaying Designs for the Domestic Interior in Europe and America, 1850–1950

Jeremy Aynsley

STRATEGIES TO PRESENT designs for the domestic interior to a professional and public audience developed rapidly between 1850 and 1950 in Europe and the United States of America, a period when the idea of the modern home was subject to major experiment and re-evaluation from many directions. Publications, exhibitions, museums and shops all introduced significantly new ways of displaying the domestic interior. The years were marked by an increasing awareness of the implications of commodity culture on the domestic imagination as witnessed by the burgeoning mass media of newspapers, magazines and advertising. At the same time, the home took on an increasingly ideological and social significance. Designers and architects themselves responded variously to such challenges. Some embraced commercial idioms enthused by the ability to reach a wide audience through a variety of representations; others recoiled from such overt publicity, guided by moral or aesthetic principles. Indeed, the Viennese architect Adolf Loos, commenting on the growth in publications on interior design at the turn of the twentieth century, went so far as to say: 'There are designers who make interiors not so that people can live well in them, but so that they look good in photographs. These are the so-called graphic interiors, whose mechanical assemblies of lines of shadows and light best suit another mechanical contrivance: the camera obscura.[1]

Such reservations were not unusual, as this essay will reveal. Troubled by the commodification of the interior, Loos introduced a dichotomy between the representation of ideal designed interiors and their actual reality which would be a leitmotiv of the century to follow. This chapter will consider some of the interconnections between various forms of display of the domestic interior, and in so doing, explore the implications of making a private world public through design.

Great Exhibitions

By 1900, most modern forms of print communication had developed and together they formed the first stages of a mass media. Newspapers, books and magazines circulated among the public on an increasing scale, while advertisements appeared in many such publications, and also in the streets in the form of large-scale posters on billboards, as signs and leaflets, as well as smaller point of sale material in shops. A second stage of media, even more visual, was made available through developments in technology. As the century developed, this included the popularization of radio and film in the 1920s, and the advent of television, largely a phenomenon of the post-war years.[2]

Before such mediated representation was available to the public, however, many events depended on the first-hand experience of visiting sites and actually being there. For example, the universal exhibitions, held throughout the second half of the nineteenth century, became a major public venue for the display of the domestic interior. Furthermore, they were events on an unprecedented scale. The first of these, the Great Exhibition of 1851 at the Crystal Palace in South Kensington, had an official visitor attendance of 16 million people.[3] Although various nations had previously held exhibitions of their own indigenous manufacture, Crystal Palace was distinctive because here, assembled under one roof, to the design

of Joseph Paxton, was the 'wealth of nations' of all 32 exhibiting countries, organized around a grand aisle with its Medieval Court. Such a 'cathedral to consumption', as it later was to be interpreted, heralded a chain of similar events in other major cities of the world. The exhibitions combined instruction with entertainment as part of a modern spectacle. A central purpose was to display a nation's prowess in manufacture through skill and technique. Exhibits ranged from raw materials, through machinery and mechanical inventions, to the products of these machines in the form of all manner of goods, including the fine and plastic arts. The overall effect was of a veritable phantasmogoria, as the German cultural philosopher Walter Benjamin would later write.[4] In specific connection with the interior on display, the

8.1
Joseph Nash,
'Hardware at the Great
Exhibition' from *Dickinson's
Comprehensive Pictures of the
Great Exhibition of 1851.*
Colour lithograph. 1852.
NAL: 46.K.4

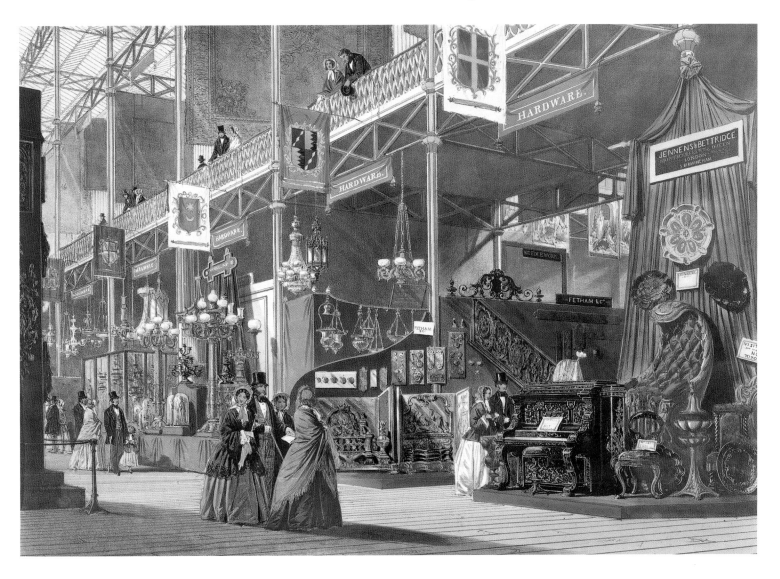

historian Thomas Richards has suggested, 'So awestruck were people by the design of the Crystal Palace that they actually began to believe in the transformative power of interior decoration'.[5] The event was known about not just through visiting, but also from the commemorative publications it provoked, including full-colour lithographic prints, peopled with imaginary visitors, such as those by H.C. Pidgeon and Joseph Nash (see pl.8.1).

In 1851, Prince Albert, a major force in promoting the exhibition, showed a model of a workers' house for four families, a scheme subsequently realized by a Dr A. Penot in Mühlhausen. The expositions in Paris of 1867 and Vienna of 1873 extended this theme of house displays. In Paris, for example, these encompassed a collection of Russian houses, an Austrian village and a *cottage anglais*. With novelty as their driving force, such displays emphasized regional and national distinctiveness. Also in the Paris exhibition, a total of 40 workers' houses were erected on the *Champ de Mars* site.[6] Although exhibition visitors could enter such houses, emphasis lay on their architectural form, rather than the fixtures, fittings and furniture. The accompanying catalogues and guides stressed room arrangement and costs in their commentaries, indicating that improvements in the provision of housing for the labour force of these industrialized countries had become a priority (see pl.8.2).

For those visitors interested to scrutinize individual details of furniture design at the universal exhibitions, other forms of display were available beyond the frame of the house as built

8.2
A. de Bar, 'A pair of model workers' houses' from *L'Exposition universelle de 1867 à Paris*. 1867.
NAL: 504.G.41

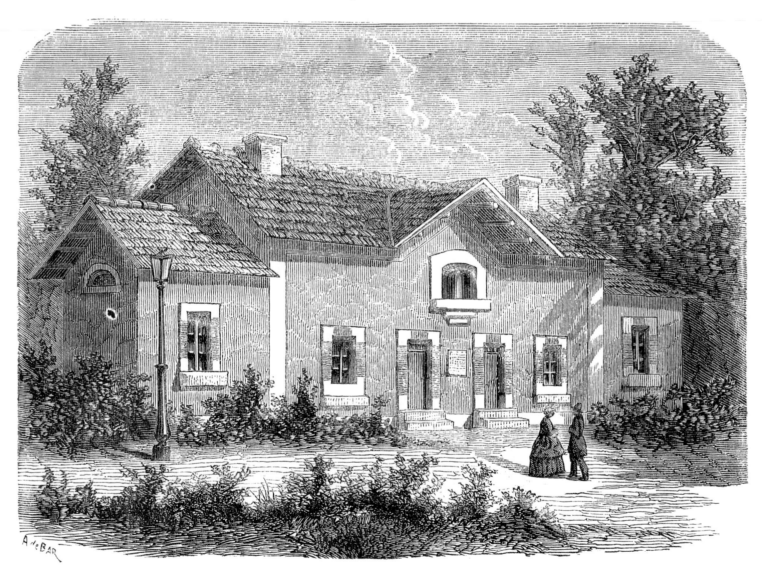

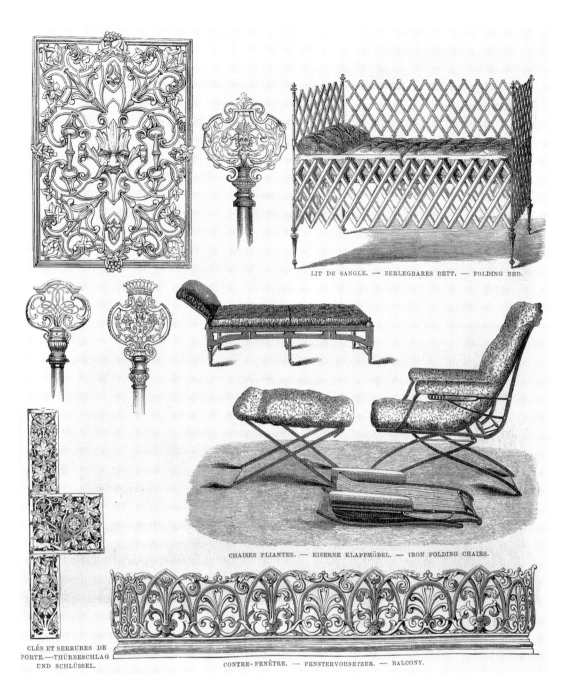

8.3
Page from *Museum für modernen Kunstindustrie*. 1873.
NAL: 58.B.31

LIT DE SANGLE. — ZERLEGBARES BETT. — FOLDING BED.

CHAISES PLIANTES. — EISERNE KLAPPMÖBEL. — IRON FOLDING CHAIRS.

CLÉS ET SERRURES DE
PORTE.—THÜRBESCHLAG
UND SCHLÜSSEL.

CONTRE-FENÊTRE. — FENSTERVORSETZER. — BALCONY.

form. At the 1873 Vienna Universal Exhibition, for example, among renowned British furniture manufacturers, Holland and Sons, Gillow and Co., and Heal and Son were invited to show their goods under the headings of the 'Wood Industry'. Other sections including furniture and designs for the home more generally, were 'Designs for Manufactures and Decorations', 'Furniture and Decorations, with Designs', and the more specialized 'School Fittings and Furniture'.[7] In such cases, the exhibits would usually appear as an array of goods,

displayed in a somewhat sporadic manner, juxtaposed but often disconnected. It becomes clear that in the early years of the exhibitions, no readily understood concept of 'the interior' was being employed by which to organize the material (see pl.8.3).

The Crystal Palace introduced a vast visiting public to the conventions of exhibition arrangement and their various representational strategies. Techniques of display developed that would become standard for many other events that involved viewing objects in public space.

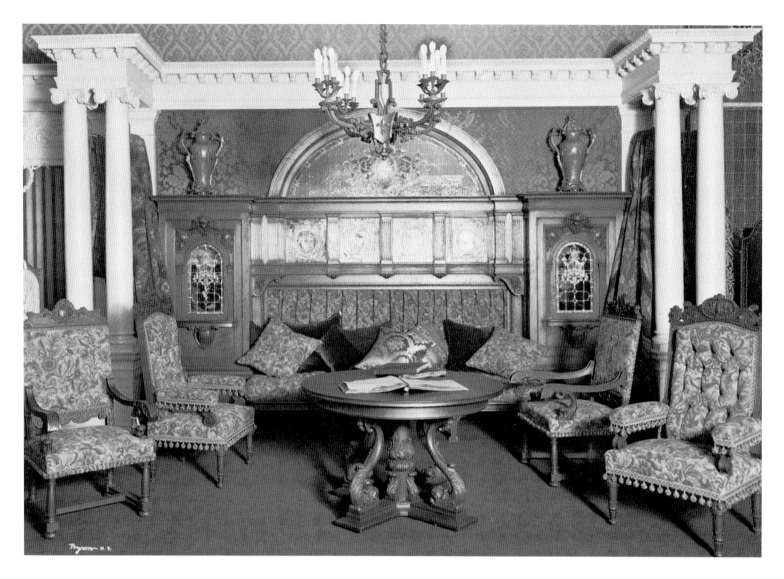

8.4
Joseph Byron, 'Display Area in the W. & J. Sloane Store, 884 Broadway' from *Photographs of New York interiors at the turn of the century*. 1902. The Byron Collection, Museum of the City of New York

Indeed, such an activity became an important aspect of modern life, whether in smaller, specialized exhibitions in galleries and museums, or in the new department stores that were springing up in the centres of big cities. Fundamental features included a climate-controlled landscape, often under expanses of glass and flooded with natural and artificial light by day or night. In this, the public was guided by a restricted circulation route, marked out by focal points and frequently organized by department or section.[8] Crucially, priority was given to the visual as a means to understanding, above other senses (see pl.8.4).

The artefacts on display included exhibition pieces on a remarkable scale, many of them involving a quality of workmanship not usually found in more everyday items. A testament to the artistic knowledge devoted to these was in the references made to historical styles, or *les Styles*; known as such for their origin in the French decorative arts. Much of the work therefore took on a composite, eclectic and often exaggerated character. As is well known, the 1851 exhibition prompted a reaction to what was perceived as this excess of ornament and recourse to historicism.

Among the first exponents of design reform were Sir Henry Cole, the leading figure behind the 1851 exhibition, Owen Jones, John Ruskin and William Morris. A common strategy was to teach, by example, what they understood to be 'true and false' principles of design, through writings, exhibitions and by assembling museum collections – as well as, in many cases, by their own design theories. The model of design schools, established to teach future designers of manufactured goods and linked with newly founded museums of decorative and applied arts, took off in many countries in Europe and the United States. The campaign was multi-layered. For along with the manufacturers themselves, the message needed to reach future artisans, decorators, upholsterers and all the specialist trades associated with making the home, and those responsible for selling goods in the retail trades. Among the home-occupiers, women in particular were identified as a growing audience, consumers with especially important responsibilities for the domestic sphere. Designs for the home had entered centre stage.

Design reform

[A] revival of interest in the dwelling–house is absolutely essential if the applied arts are to persist in their renewed activity and to thrive. The house is their only possible home; the sole aim of any Arts and Crafts movement must be to furnish the dwelling–place and house.[9]

Within the Arts and Crafts movement, what William Morris himself had termed the 'lesser'

and 'useful' arts became the focus of attention, replacing the fine arts. For the domestic interior, this meant attention was given to all its aspects, whether textiles, wallpaper, furniture, stained-glass, ceramics and glass, or metalwork, as the reflections of the Prussian civil servant Hermann Muthesius in his important study of the English house a generation later indicated above. Looking back over the previous 40 years, Muthesius identified a comprehensive approach to the design of the entire aestheticized interior which proved to be highly influential across Europe and North America (see pl.8.5).

In a related sphere, the 1870s and 1880s witnessed a significant increase in prescriptive texts dedicated to informing readers in what to purchase and how to arrange the home, some directly informed by Arts and Crafts principles, others less so. In these, the interior came to be represented as a primary area of aesthetic and moral concern. One of the first to strike the critical high-ground adopted was Charles Eastlake, author of the popular and influential *Hints on Household Taste in furniture, upholstery, and other details* of 1868, a book that had reached six editions in the USA by 1881 (see pl.8.6).[10] Earlier, Eastlake contributed an article to the *Cornhill*

8.5

C.F.A. Voysey, 'Garden hallway and furnishings' from *Das Englische Haus* by Hermann Muthesius, Volume III. 1905.

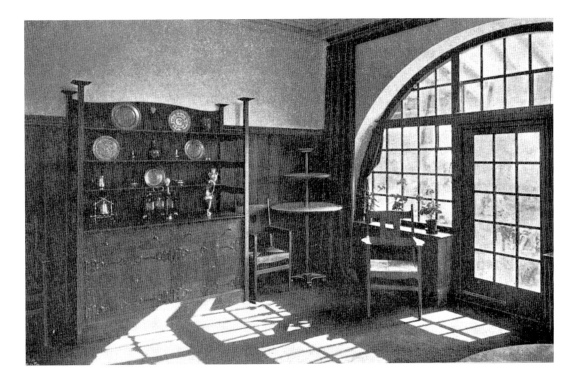

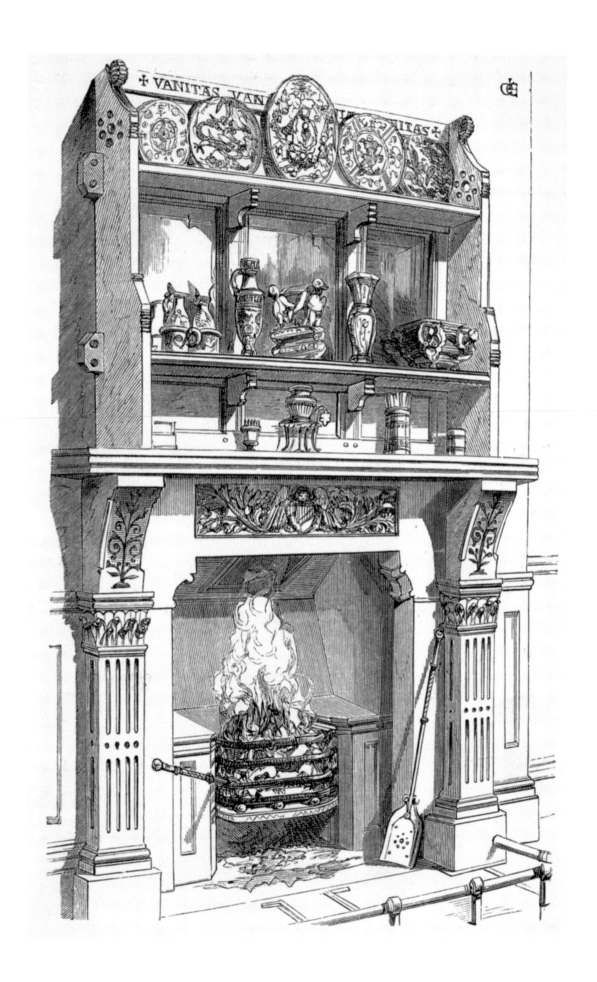

8.6
Charles Eastlake, 'Mantel-piece
Shelves' from *Hints on household
taste in furniture, upholstery and
other details*. 1868.
NAL: 47.E.13

Magazine in May 1864 entitled 'The Fashion of Furniture'. He wrote, 'There is a direct analogy between the spirit which induces a vulgar woman to dress beyond her station in life as a sacrifice of more necessary requirements, and the silly demand of small householders that the fittings of their dwellings should ape those of a much higher rent'.[11]

If one point of concern was emulation, in his book Eastlake also advised against unnecessary ornament. In particular, he criticized the retailer as advisor on matters of taste, and sought to define fundamental principles of good taste, themes that would recur throughout the next century. It was hoped that this initiative would protect the process of selecting items of furniture for the home from the vagaries of the fashion system. No doubt informed by Social Darwinism, many of the writers betrayed a belief in the evolution of taste, from the simplicity of medieval times to the ornate of their own century. If the reformers were to have their way and their message prove successful, they would witness a return to simplicity. In the years that followed, women writers also took up the mantle of advisors, some echoing Eastlake's tastes and preferences, others quite openly critical of what they perceived to be his condescension.[12]

Collecting rooms

Alongside the proliferation of texts devoted to the theme of the domestic interior, newly established museums of the decorative arts began to collect, preserve and interpret actual historical rooms. The first room acquired in 1869 by what was then the South Kensington Museum (known since 1899 as the Victoria and Albert Museum) was the Serilly Cabinet of 1778 from the Hôtel de Serilly of the Marais district of Paris (see pl.8.7).[13] It complemented the Museum's interests in assembling examples of high-style French furniture and woodwork at the time. By contrast, the collection of rooms started at the Metropolitan Museum of Art, New York in 1903 with the acquisition of the Pompeii bedroom, the Bosco Reale Room of 40–30 BC. This was followed by a wood-

panelled chamber from Flims in Switzerland with its magnificent stove (1644–5), and an eighteenth-century bedroom from the Palazzo Sagredo in Venice, notably all important interiors of significant European origin.[14] In many respects, a time-warp existed between the contemporary concerns that inspired the foundation of these museums and their subsequent collecting policies.

8.7
Serilly Cabinet, V&A Museum. 1778. V&A: 1736–1869

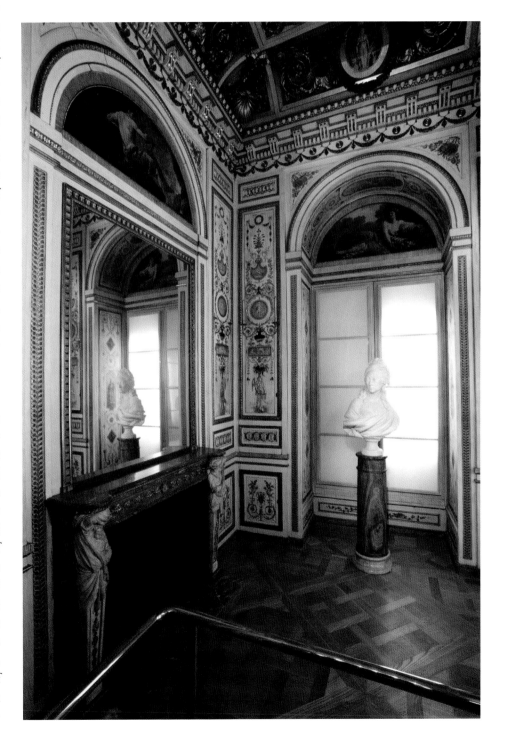

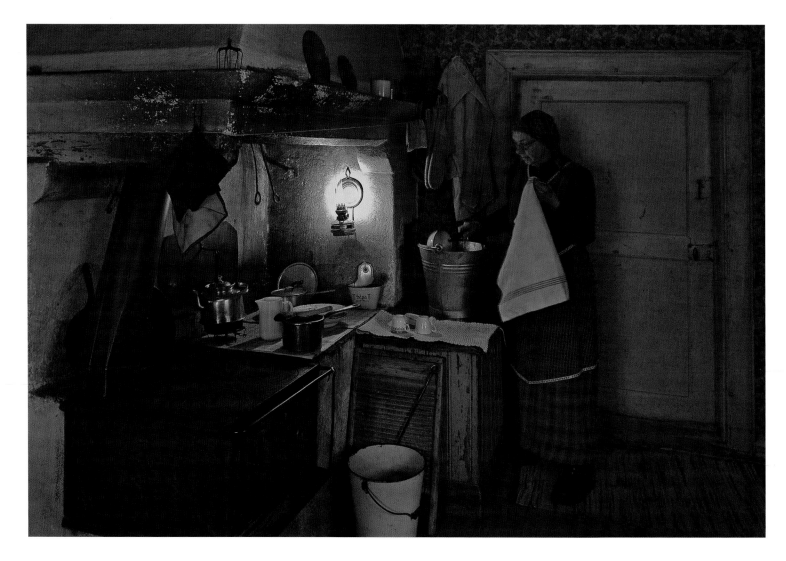

In terms of representational strategies, the orthodoxy of the period room was to look on to the interior, as if the fourth wall were removed, which was also often actually the case. As such, it betrayed its origins in the nineteenth century, when realism was a dominant cultural force. Few museums allowed the visitor to enter each room and in this sense the experience of looking on to a naturalist setting of an un-peopled room was not totally removed from viewing its depiction on the published page.

A distinction can be made between the collecting of rooms by such decorative arts museums, and those in a new form of museum, the living, open-air museum, which originated in Sweden. Skansen, the first museum of its kind, was founded in 1891 by Artur Hazelius for the purpose of showing how people had lived and worked in different parts of Sweden

in earlier times.[15] For his original museum, Hazelius created folk life pictures and tableaux of daily life which he took to the great exhibitions of Philadelphia in 1876 and Paris in 1878.[16] Hazelius realized the need to rescue relics and traditional activities by which it would be possible to present a continuity with the past in Swedish civilization. Since its foundation, visitors to the houses and farmsteads at Skansen have been met by hosts and hostesses in period costume who demonstrate domestic occupations such as weaving or spinning, or other rural artisanal skills or perform traditional music (see pl.8.8). While Skansen clearly was concerned to collect and interpret houses that were a product of the past, through its emphasis on everyday life and the democratic, non-élite character, the Nordic domestic interior became defined by practice rather than mere appearance.

8.8
Kitchen interior, farm labourer's cottage. Contemporary photograph. Skansen Museum, Stockholm

Promoting artistic interiors

The Aesthetic Movement had its strong advocates in the press. A rash of new titles began in the 1890s, some to publish for over 30 years, while others only proved to be short-lived. The influential London-based magazine *The Studio*, which was established in 1893, covered both the fine and applied arts, whereas more specialist titles devoted to interior design soon appeared, especially in Germany. There, leading examples included *Dekorative Kunst* in Munich (1891–1929), which became *Das Schöne Heim* between 1929 and 41, and *Innendekoration* (1890–1944) and *Deutsche Kunst und Dekoration* (1897–1932) in Darmstadt. They were joined, among others, by *Das Interieur* (1900–1915) in Vienna, *Art et Décoration* (1897–) in Paris, and *House Beautiful* which was published in Chicago (1896–1930) and in New York (1896–).[17] These magazines circulated internationally and their impact can be measured by the second generation of magazines, often similar in format, that were formed in their mould in the years to follow (see pl.8.9).

While the editorial blend of each title was individual, sufficient common characteristics suggest that by 1900 they had become a defined genre of magazine publishing that in many respects continues on similar lines today. To take the Chicago-based monthly magazine *House Beautiful* in 1904 as an example of this new kind of consumer-oriented magazine, its typical interests combined profiles of individual houses with detailed descriptions of their room arrangements, furnishings and gardens. In many instances, these would have fulfilled the aspirational desires of the reader, rather than presenting an actually achievable or affordable home. Alongside these were articles offering useful hints in home-making and decorating, at a more practical and down-to-earth level, although American readers of women's magazines may have found similar articles in the *Ladies' Home Journal* and *Woman's Home Companion,* or later *Good Housekeeping*. Some articles were syndicated, allowing them to appear in more than one context, sometimes with different illustrations, crossing the Atlantic in both directions to reach wider readerships (see pl.8.10).

Occasionally lectures or polemical articles gave guidance in matters of taste, or aired issues to do with the 'Woman Question', the role of women in home and beyond, which arose from the debate on early feminism and Suffrage. Thematic articles on furniture offered solutions, as for example, 'What to put on a Library Wall' or how to install 'A Yellow Dining Room', in this instance, for a particular Frank Lloyd Wright house.[18] In keeping with its editorial sympathies, *House Beautiful* in March 1904 stressed the small and inexpensive, rather than the overt luxury of conspicuous consumption. Advertisements in the

8.9
Title-page from
Innen-dekoration. 1908.
NAL: PP.40.Z

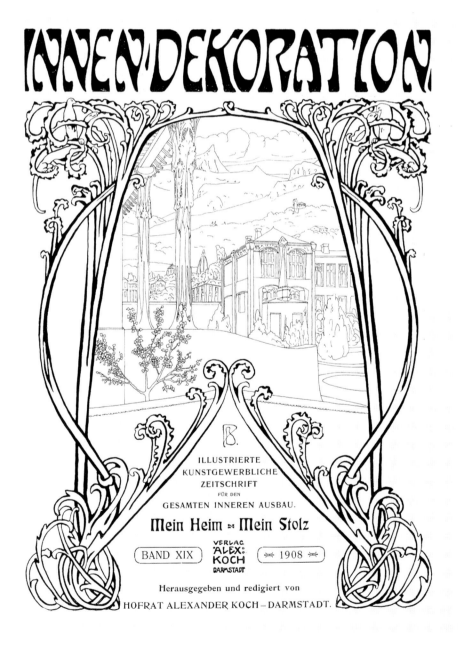

beads. The history of Nos. 5, 6, 7, and 8 is unknown.

And last, in No. 9, as if in humble proof that the deeds of all women are much the same, is shown the little bead bag of some Minnehaha, who laughed and dimpled in the sunshine of sixty years ago. The workmanship on the buck-skin is ruder, but the beads seem to be the same as those used in the "pokes" of the "pale face" sisters.

The majority of these old reticules are very tender, and apt to shatter the beads if roughly touched, but handled with care, they are still good for many years of prosperous and interesting existence in the possession of the collectors of unconsidered trifles of the past.

THE DECORATION OF A CITY HOUSE

By JOHN EDNIE

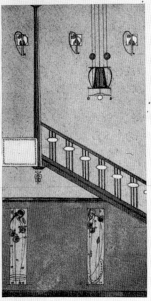

THE HALL—STAIRWAY

[The editors deeply regret the failure of the competition for the decoration of a city house of the conventional three-story and basement type, which was projected some time ago. The good designs received could not possibly have been worked out for the five hundred dollars, which was made the limit of cost. Nevertheless, some of these are eminently worthy of consideration by the readers of HOUSE BEAUTIFUL. The one printed herewith is the work of Mr. John Ednie of Edinburgh, Scotland. Though his estimate of the cost of this kind of work in America is much too low, the scheme itself is novel and attractive. It is unfortunate that it cannot be reproduced in color, as black and white necessarily takes away much of its charm.]

THE sum of five hundred dollars seems a fairly adequate allowance for decorating a house of seven apartments, but if we would be original, and deviate from the beaten track, we must needs economize, for with the appropriation at our disposal, we have to supply floor coverings as well as the wall decorations. If, however, we add thought and artistic taste to the allotted sum, it is quite possible to make the city house beautiful to behold.

A house of this description generally falls into the unsympathetic hands of the local painter, who contrives to render the wall decoration as ugly as possible, by throwing on yards upon yards of embossed papers, at a price out of all proportion to the size of the house.

My proposal, then, is to be simple, to use the simplest of materials, and expend more time and thought on the matter than is usually given to it. It is not the house-

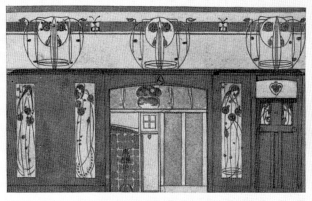

THE HALL, LOOKING TOWARD THE DRAWING-ROOM

painter who is condemned to spend his days among the monstrosities which he perpetrates, it is the individual owner.

Very few owners study the house as a whole. Your local painter advises you to have maybe a blue room, a red room, a white room, etc., etc. You spend a mint of money on this idea, and yet you experience no satisfaction when the work is completed. The most noticeable effect that it produces is that it is brand new. This undesirable state of affairs is due to the fact that the house has not been studied as a picture—a composition in which each component part must harmonize with the others.

In the ground-floor plan of the brownstone front there is the entrance hall and staircase, the hall leading directly into the drawing-room, or front parlor, which in turn gives access into the back parlor, and thence into the dining-room. The rooms of this suite are divided from each other principally by double doors, and when desired, can be thrown into one large apartment by sliding these doors open. This planning gives the designer ample opportunity for considering a scheme of decoration that will be harmonious. The first or bedroom floor should also be recognized by a somewhat similar decorative treatment, but the necessity here is not so great, because the rooms are private apartments and cannot be seen as a whole. My idea is, then, that in viewing one room from the other, the quality and value of color be preserved, and that all the apartments harmonize with each other.

The lower walls of the entrance hall are covered with a gray-green colored canvas called Fab-ri-co-na, to a height of eight feet. This canvas is absolutely hygienic, and its surface is specially prepared for wall decoration. It should be pasted hard to the plaster wall, to which it will adhere firmly. I have purposely adopted the green color for the predominating tone, because I have calculated that in a house of this size the existing woodwork will probably be stained or painted in brown. The green therefore will form a natural harmony with the brown, and will greatly assist us in the conception of the general color scheme.

Above the filling is carried a frieze of

---

magazine offered advice on whose services might be available. These ranged from craftsman-built furniture to new inventions such as an adjustable table for bedtime reading, or the purchase of a Remington typewriter for use in the home. Fashionable and faddish hobbies, such as pyrography,– fire painting on wood – were promoted, while particularly distinctive to the American market were the Navajo blankets or Hupa and Klamath basketry that could be ordered for adorning the home in an artistic manner.

As historians of the magazine suggest, it is impossible to tell with complete assurance what a reader would have gained from the experience of browsing or reading more fully such a periodical press.[19] No doubt, as today, the impact depended on the kinds of interest and knowledge that the reader brought to the process. However, we can recover a sense of how magazines matched their readers through the 1892 novel *The Diary of a Nobody* by George and Weedon Grossmith, first published in serialized form in the magazine *Punch,* then subsequently as a book. It opened,

My dear wife Carrie and I have just been a week in our new house, 'The Laurels', Brickfield Terrace, Holloway – a nice six-roomed residence, not counting basement, with a front breakfast-parlour…. After my work in the City, I like to be at home. What's the good of a home, if you are never in it? 'Home, Sweet Home', that's my motto. I am always in of an evening. Our old friend Gowing may drop in without ceremony; so may Cummings, who lives opposite. My dear wife

8.10

'The Decoration of a City House' from *House Beautiful.* 1903. NAL: SZ.0183

Caroline and I are pleased to see them, if they like to drop in on us. But Carrie and I can manage to pass our evenings together without friends. There is always something to be done: a tin-tack here, a Venetian blind to put straight, a fan to nail up, or part of a carpet to nail down – all of which I can do with my pipe in my mouth; while Carrie is not above putting a button on a shirt, mending a pillow-case, or practising the 'Sylvia Gavotte' on our new cottage piano (on three years' system), manufactured by W. Bilkson (in small letters), from Collard and Collard (in very large letters).[20]

The book continues by giving a full description of the pastimes and pre-occupations of one Henry Pooter, who epitomizes the suburban resident. Through his concern to keep up appearances by, among other things, decorating 'The Laurels', Pooter takes note of current commercial strategies of the advertisers, paying attention to brand names and adopting the advice of magazines, which he exchanges with neighbours, in a wish to introduce his desired effect of homeliness (see pl.8.11).

As well as the monthly publications that presented the domestic interior, there were more prestigious art and design publications, often exclusively produced in limited editions and available through subscription. In late nineteenth- and early twentieth-century Germany, Alexander Koch was a particularly prolific publisher of such works. As a young man, Koch had worked for the typefoundry and printer Flinsch of Offenbach am Main. His own drawing skills and experience of typography and ornament meant that he took an active interest in the design of his journals, and he commissioned many prominent designers of the *Jugendstil* generation for his projects. He was the figure behind *Deutsche Kunst und Dekoration* and *Innendekoration*, as well as numerous thematic books about interior design.

One editorial strategy Koch shared with *The Studio* and *Art et Décoration* was to run

APRIL 26.—Got some more red enamel paint (red, to my mind, being the best colour), and painted

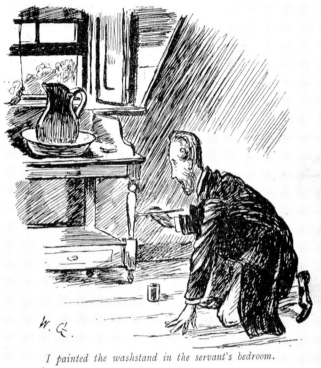

I painted the washstand in the servant's bedroom.

the coal-scuttle, and the backs of our *Shakspeare,* the binding of which had almost worn out.

8.11
'I painted the washstand in the servant's bedroom' from *The Diary of a Nobody* by George Grossmith. *c.*1892. The British Library, London

competitions for amateurs and professionals in his magazines. No doubt these were for both attracting readers or subscribers and generating editorial content, with female readers especially targeted. They began with a poster design competition for the journals and the competition, 'How can our women undertake the decoration of our living rooms?' (Wie können unsere Frauen zur Ausschmückung der Wohnräume beitragen?) which ran between 1891 and 1906 in *Innendekoration.* The most prominent competition was for 'Ideas for artistic and original designs for a House for an Art Lover', a competition that drew responses from a range of internationally based designers, announced in December 1900. Although no first prize was awarded, the results were published in *Deutsche Kunst und Dekoration* as well as featured in the

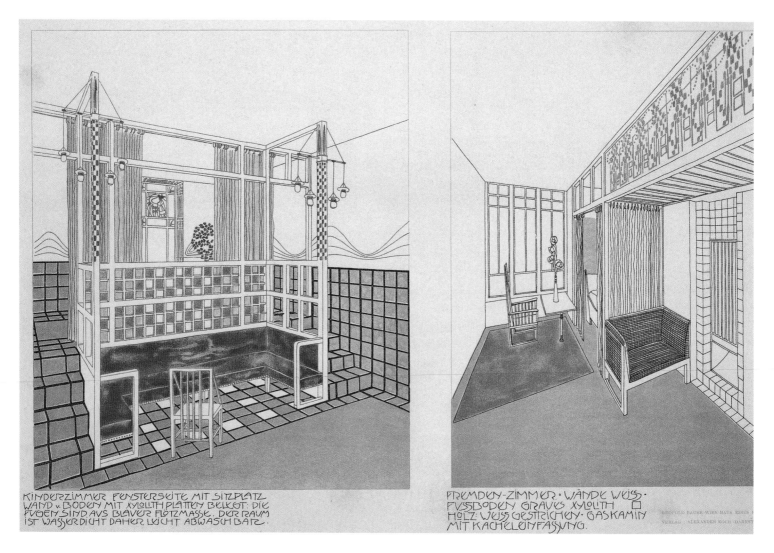

KINDERZIMMER FENSTERSEITE MIT SITZPLATZ
WAND v. BODEN MIT XYLOLITH PLATTEN BELEGT DIE
FUGEN SIND AUS BLAUER FLOTZMASSE. DER RAUM
IST WASSERDICHT DAHER LEICHT ABWASCHBAR.

FREMDEN-ZIMMER · WÄNDE WEIS ·
FUSSBODEN GRAUES XYLOLITH
HOLZ: WEISS GESTRICHEN · GASKAMIN
MIT KACHELEINFASSUNG.

celebrated portfolios *die Mappenwerke – Haus eines Kunst-Freundes* of 1902 (see pl.8.12).[21]

Monographs on architects' and artists' houses became a distinct genre and an important source of inspiration. A similar high-profile representation of a domestic idyll, for instance, on this occasion the Sundborn home of the Swedish artists Carl and Karin Larsson, also depended on publication for its international significance. In their case, the home had been designed by themselves and popularized in the book *Ett Hem* (A Home), first published in 1899 with Carl's watercolours showing the activities of an artistic, family life.[22] The book promoted a simple approach to decorating the home, combining non-élite designs with a gentle neo-classicism that proved extremely influential in Sweden, as well as other parts of Europe and the United States (see pl.8.13).

Changes in the representation of the domestic interior could be driven by technical circumstances, just as much as by cultural and social forces. Developments in printing presses, reproductive processes, the chemistry of inks and paper manufacture, as well as innovations in binding in the late nineteenth century, all activities of major industries, made available to the publisher or art editor an unprecedented range of possibilities. This meant that the visual language of books and magazines was by no means singular, but instead, their art directors and editors could exploit a multitude of novel printing effects. Like the subject of interiors themselves, however, publication design became an active area of debate and discussion, and also a site of reform. The initial convention was for magazines to appear like books, with double columns of dense text with some inte-

8.12

Leopold Bauer, designs from *Das Haus eines Kunst-Freundes* by Felix Commichau. 1902

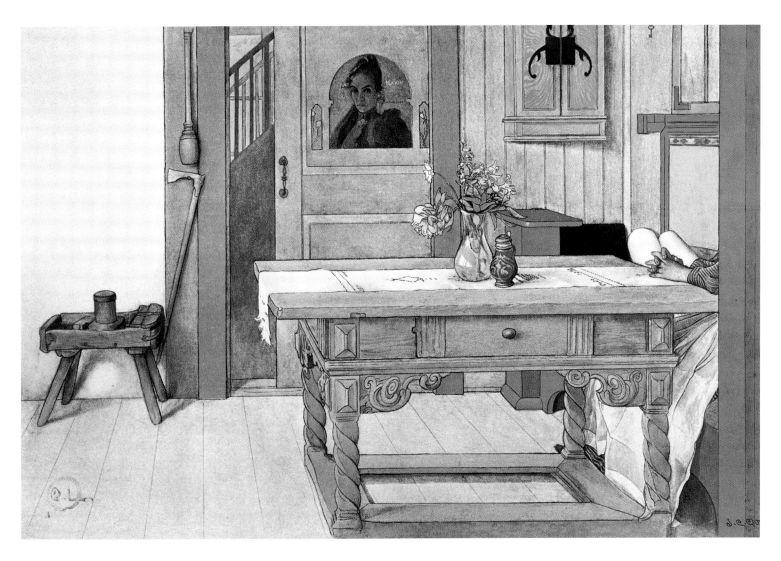

8.13
Carl Larsson, 'Sondag'.
Watercolour, from
Ett Hem. 1899.
NAL: 60.V.240

grated images, and others in full-colour tipped in separate plates. Gradually, in line with developments in all magazine publishing, an independent magazine layout emerged that dedicated more space to the arrangement of the text and image, and through this magazines in general became more distinguishable from books. Typographic reform led to the design of new typefaces for the foundries. The impact was particularly strong in examples from Art Nouveau and Art Deco, when page layouts self-consciously echoed the featured designs of the interiors, form and content merging into a unified aesthetic arrangement (see pl.8.14). Also, advertising was important as a major source of revenue and became a dominant feature in many titles, often leading the way in terms of quality of illustration, use of colour and novelty of design. It fell to the art director to

reconcile the balance between editorial and advertising contents, the relative significance of their texts, and to harmonize their sometimes conflicting visual appearance.[23]

Illustrations, in the case of interiors magazines, ranged across reproductions of full-colour paintings to specially prepared lithographic prints of interiors. Designers' and architects' original drawings were reproduced alongside renditions by commissioned commercial illustrators. A familiar trope was to show the same room 'before' and 'after' the intervention of the interior designer. For many years, black and white photographs were combined with colour, hand-rendered illustrations. It was not until the 1930s that colour photography was introduced as an effective form of reproduction, eventually challenging the primary role of the illustrator's art.

Les Jolis Boudoirs

PAR

HENRY ROUJON
DE L'ACADEMIE FRANÇAISE

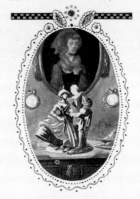

VOULONS-NOUS une définition du mot « boudoir »?

Littré répond : « Cabinet élégant attenant à l'appartement d'une dame. » Mais pourquoi « boudoir »? Le savant lexicographe ajoute : « Ainsi dit parce que les dames se retirent dans leur boudoir lorsqu'elles veulent être seules. » N'en déplaise à Littré, que Thiers appelait justement « le prince de la Grammaire », c'est là répondre à la question par la question. Et puis, convient il d'allier nécessairement l'idée maussade de bouderie au réduit le plus coquettement aménagé d'une habitation féminine? Littré semble croire que pour bien bouder il faut être seule; en est il bien sûr? A quoi bouder servirait il s il n'y avait point aux pieds de la boudeuse quelqu'un pour en souffrir? En tout cas, si cette étymologie a été exacte, elle ne l'est plus. L idée de boudoir n'évoque dans l histoire de la galanterie que de gracieuses images et de souriants souvenirs.

L'on est d accord pour fixer l'origine du boudoir à l'époque de la Régence. Est-ce à dire qu'avant cette période les femmes françaises n'aient pas su se réserver dans leur logis un coin de prédilection? Non, sans doute; mais c'est dans l'embrasure d'une fenêtre ogivale sur un lac que s'imagine la châtelaine du moyen âge. Les princesses de la Renaissance, une Marie Stuart, une Marguerite de Valois, nous nous les figurons dans le demi-jour d'un oratoire. Le cabinet de Louise de Vaudemont, tendu de velours noir, avait pour meuble principal un prie-Dieu. Aux « cabinets » des Précieuses, chez la divine Arthénice et sa fille Julie, les livres et les manuscrits voisinaient avec les miroirs. Avec le règne radieux de Louise de la Vallière, le « cabinet », sans mériter encore le nom de « boudoir », devient à la fois intime et somptueux. Louis XIV fit meubler pour la jeune favorite deux petites pièces: une « de riche broderie fond d or, manière de velours à arabesques, rouge cramoisy, consistant en six fauteuils, six chaises, six pliants et une grande tapisserie »; dans la seconde, les meubles étaient de velours rouge et de brocart lamé d'or, avec des franges d'or et d'argent. Mme de Montespan, l'altière Vasthi de

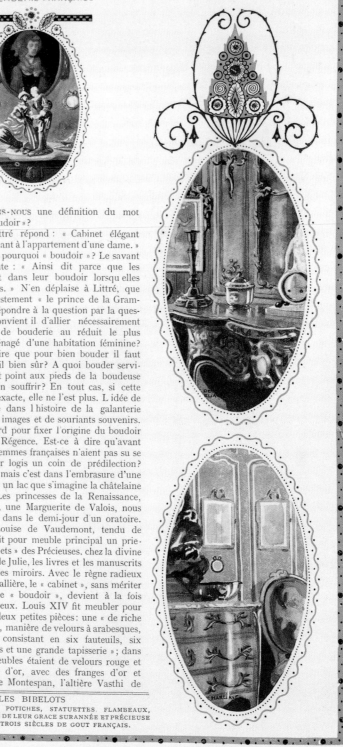

(A gauche et à droite.) LES BIBELOTS
RELIQUES DU PASSÉ, POTICHES, STATUETTES, FLAMBEAUX, ANIMENT LES BOUDOIRS DE LEUR GRACE SURANNÉE ET PRÉCIEUSE OU SE REFLÈTENT TROIS SIÈCLES DE GOUT FRANÇAIS.

The Modernist interior

If the first 50 years of design publishing were spent consolidating genres in the field, the subsequent years, from 1920 onwards, were driven by two important forces that were sometimes at odds with one another: avant-garde design ideals and commercial publishing practices. In the first decades of the twentieth century, in artistic and design circles, tremendous experimentation took place in the movements of Cubism, Futurism, Expressionism, Suprematism and Constructivism.[24] Following the First World War and its unprecedented scale of mass destruction, a belief in making a new world was manifested in a broad range of social, political and cultural developments. In the British context, for instance, one response was to lead a campaign to provide 'Homes fit for heroes', to house the returning soldiers and their families.[25] An urgent need for social housing was felt across many parts of Europe, with particular intensity in Holland, Germany and the countries of central Europe, where not only the devastation of war but also the migration of rural populations to the cities increased the pressure of demand. Among the avant-garde designers, it was strongly felt that a new artistic language should be applied to such projects. The 'new' became a prefix for all their initiatives, as in Het Nieuwe Bouwen (the new building) in the Netherlands, or die neue Wohnkultur (the new living culture) in German-speaking lands and L'Esprit Nouveau (the new spirit) in France.[26] In particular, through joining forces as groups, writing manifestos and collaborating in exhibitions, an international movement adopted an experimental visual language and the rudiments of geometry as the necessary way forward for progressive design. Crucially for the domestic interior, their plans involved breaking up conventional forms of composition to investigate abstraction, whether in painting and sculpture, a piece of design or an entire environment. For a number of years it was a case of projecting a Utopian future, rather than producing actual realized designs, and in this sense it could be seen as a period of living in the picture. By the mid-1920s,

however, with the stabilization of the economy, building could again resume and design projects be realized.

The move to abstraction freed design from traditional conceptions of space within the domestic interior, ones that were vehemently dismissed by Modernists for being symptomatic of a bourgeois lifestyle they sought to avoid. Radical elements within the designs included collapsing conventional distinctions between interior and exterior, with extensive use of balconies, terraces and roof gardens. Double-height rooms, built-in furniture, and multi-purpose spaces challenged conventional definitions of the interior and its boundaries. Wherever possible new construction materials, especially glass and metal, stressed transparency and light. New graphic ideas were used to present the designs, including photomontage, modern photography exceptionally in colour (see pl.8.15) and the asymmetrical layouts of the new typography.[27]

Many Modernist initiatives were originally directed towards the minimum dwelling and mass-housing based on the urban apartment module, intended for the industrialized city worker, within a small family unit. In these, ideals of standardization of furniture and other fittings were applied. At the same time, the domestic interior and how people lived became the subject of rational scrutiny and scientific investigation. As so many of the initiatives and the underlying social vision were informed by Socialist and Communist principles, it is paradoxical that another important source of ideas was the American efficiency movement, in particular the writings of Christine Frederick. Frederick had studied the organization and arrangement of the home to consider better planning for daily activities, with the American housewife particularly in mind. The ideas of household management and time/motion studies were set out in her books, *Housekeeping: Efficiency Studies in Home Management* (1913) and *Household Engineering and Scientific Management in the Home* (1919), which were translated into several European languages.[28] In particular, circulation routes to

8.14

'Les Jolis Boudoirs' from *Fémina*, December 1913. NAL: PP.6.C

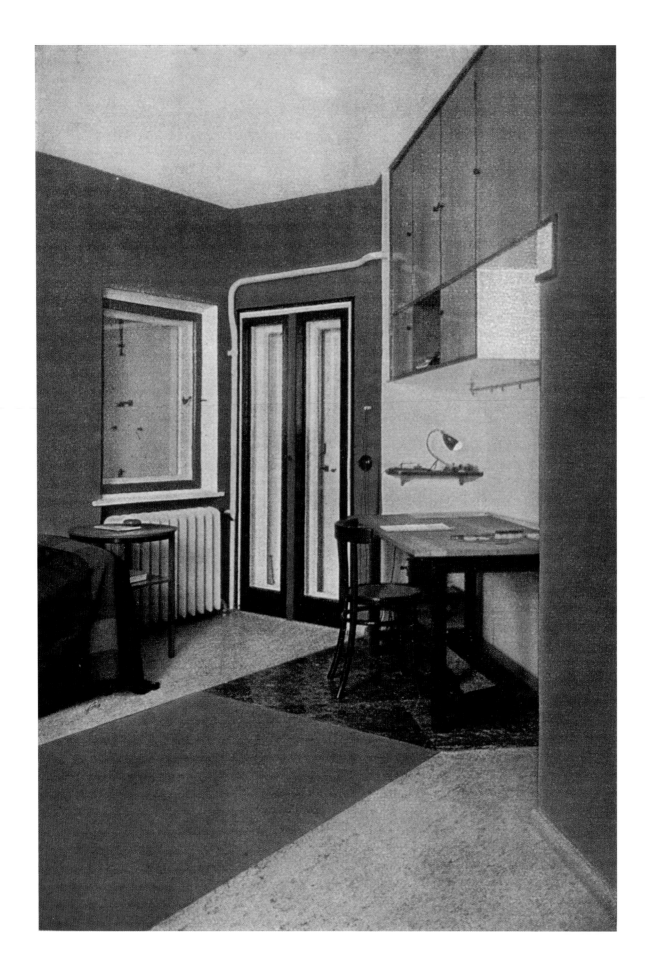

8.15
Colour plate from *Ein Wohnhaus* by Bruno Taut. 1927. NAL: 34.C.77

justify the arrangement of rooms became the norm. By the 1920s and '30s, from Moscow to Berlin, Budapest to Paris, and Stockholm to Milan, publications on 'the new dwelling' circulated with plans, diagrams, charts, tabulated figures and statistics, all developing from such studies (see pl.8.16).

One of the exponents of this new built form, the architect Hannes Meyer wrote in 1926,

> The surest sign of true community is the satisfaction of the same needs by the same means. The upshot of such a collective demand is the standard product. The folding chair, roll-top desk, light bulb, bath tub and portable gramophone are typical standard products manufactured internationally and showing a uniform design. They are apparatus in the mechanisation of our daily life. They are manufactured in quantity as a mass-produced article, as a mass-produced device, as a mass-produced structural element, as a mass-produced house.[29]

Even more than the Arts and Crafts movement before it, a major quarrel for Modernism was with the immediate past. This is revealed in the case of The Deutscher Werkbund exhibition *Die Wohnung* (The Dwelling) which opened between July and September 1927 in Stuttgart, subsequently known by the title of its location, Am Weissenhof.[30] The Werkbund had formed in 1907 as an association to promote design and good relations between designers, retailers and manufacturers. Weissenhof acted as an international building exhibition with an array of Modernist architects contributing, among them Le Corbusier, Mies van der Rohe, Walter Gropius, Mart Stam and J.J.P. Oud – indeed, it was a major source for the term 'International Style' to be coined in New York in 1932.[31] The poster for the exhibition, designed by the graphic designer Willi Baumeister, made a clear attack on historicism (see pl.8.17). Accompanying the question *Wie Wohnen?* (How to live?)

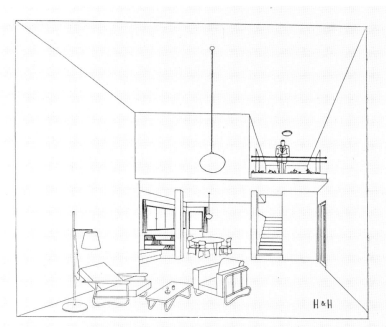

Pohled do obývacího pokoje vily na Smíchově

Vila na Smíchově

Pro zajímavost přinášíme několik dokumentů z průběhu úředního jednání o povolení této vily.

Zápis sepsaný v Magistrátní komisi dne 21. ledna 1929 v Praze.

Dle parcel. podmínek bylo výslovně stanoveno zastavění v uvedeném bloku budovami s normální střechou. N a p r o t i t o m u p o s t a v e n í b u d o v y d l e p ř e d l o ž. p l á n u v ú p l n ě m o d e r n í m s l o h u v n e s e n b y b y l ú p l n ě c i z o r o d ý p r v e k, k t e r ý b y p ů s o b i l r u š i v ě n a v ý s t a v b u c e l é h o b l o k u, což patrno by bylo, vzhledem k tomu, že se jedná o budovy na náhorní rovině, patrné se všech stran, zejména z protějšího

19

three versions of the poster appeared with photographs, one of a Jugendstil interior and two of historicist interiors struck out by a strident red cross. The formula proved controversial, as at least one of the designs could be identified. Accompanying the negative propaganda of this poster, an entire graphic system of tickets, guide and accompanying book was arranged in the clearly modern style of the 'new typography' of Baumeister's design.[32]

Just as the new design challenged conventional perspective through recourse to abstraction, so too, experimental exhibition design challenged the illusionism of the

8.16

Interior plan from *Stavby a Plany* by Josef Havlíček and Karel Teige. 1931. NAL: 502.K.94

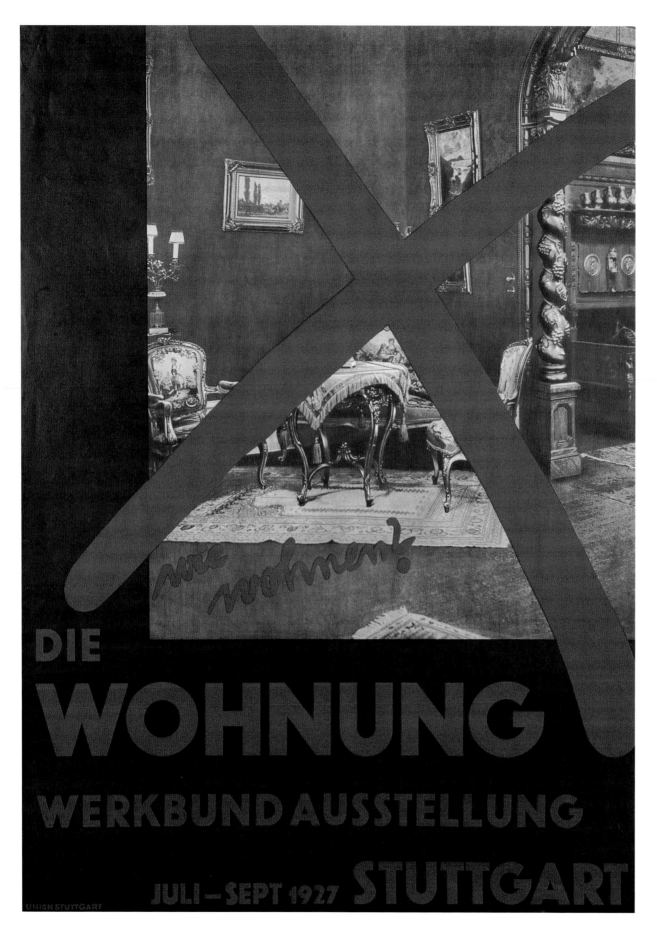

8.17
Willi Baumeister,
Wie Wohnen?,
Lithograph. 1937.
V&A:E.266–2005

conventional room display of the museum and department store. Such was the case, for example, in the installation of the German contribution to the exhibition of the Société des Artistes Décorateurs Français at the Grand Palais in Paris, 1930. Amidst a sequence of traditional ensemble room installations suggesting a mis-en-scène, former Bauhaus staff Herbert Bayer, Marcel Breuer and László Moholy-Nagy, under the direction of Walter Gropius, developed an alternative mode of display in which they stressed furniture as a serial object and exactly repeatable idiom. In its abstraction, the display attempted to connect the exhibited objects with the everyday world of the factory and the shop.[33] The full display, which included room settings for a modern apartment block, incorporating a collective

social space and gymnasium equipped with tubular steel furniture manufactured by Thonet, indicated their resolve to move away from conventional bourgeois lifestyles. The most striking section featured chairs suspended from the wall in vertical series. These serial design objects were arranged to parallel strategies current in modern window displays and avant-garde film (see pl.8.18).

Popular interiors

The representation of the modernist domestic interior gained prominence through a wealth of promotional material in the form of books, exhibitions as well as the actual designs. In this respect, their high profile was out of proportion to the initial impact of Modernism on everyday life. A more representative kind of living, asso-

8.18
Herbert Bayer, 'Arrangement of room with enlarged photos of modern building and modern types of chairs' from *Die Form.* 1930. NAL: PP.74.A

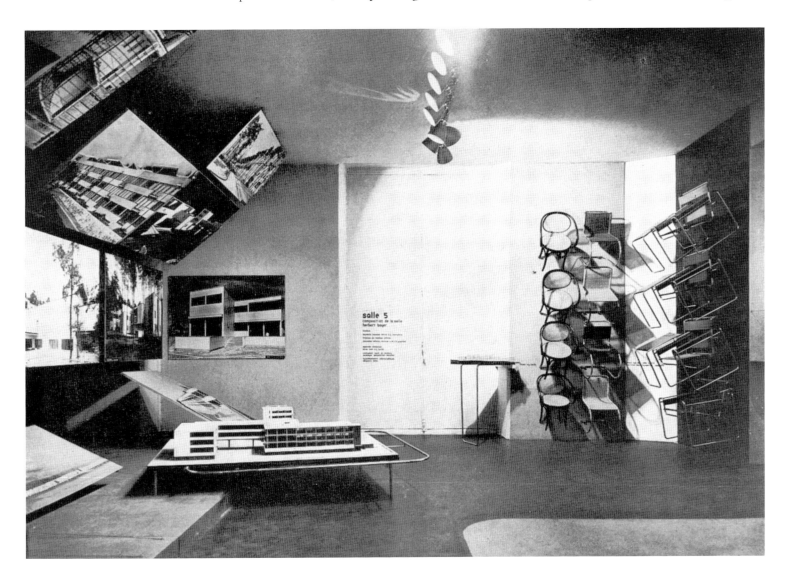

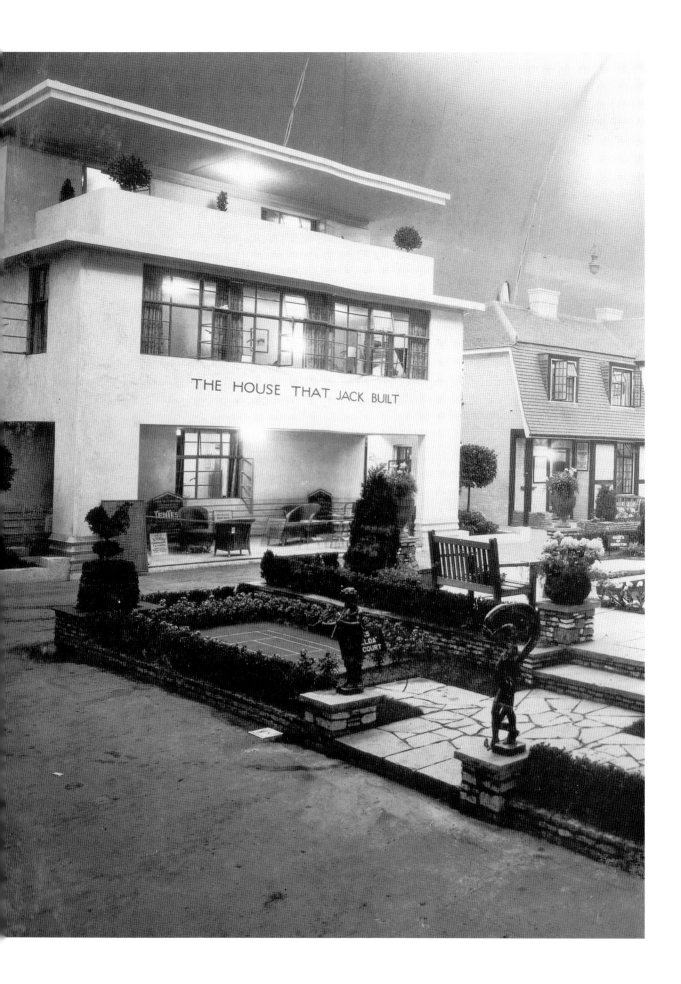

THE HOUSE THAT JACK BUILT

8.19
Thomas Dalgleish McLean, *The House That Jack Built. Daily Mail* Ideal Home Exhibition, 1931. NAL: NC.98.1028

ciated with the United States and increasingly developed in Europe, instead took the form of suburban modernity which allowed for a variety of lifestyles. This would carry global significance by the late twentieth century.

Here, instead of seeking a collective experience informed by ideals of social progressiveness, individual and private pleasures of the home were stressed as a universal goal. Often, new technologies were embraced, such as electricity as a source of power for labour saving devices and car ownership, all organized in spaces to increase the well-being of the nuclear family. Commentators on such suburban modernity have stressed how in many respects this vision of the home could be interpreted as a feminization of the domestic sphere, reinforcing a separation between work and the home. Accordingly, the mode of address in many advertisements and magazines was directed towards the housewife. Often, they contained a central opposition between the modern techniques, goods and services used to equip and run such homes, and the social or political values encapsulated in them, which maintained the traditional or status-quo. As such, they offered what might be called a 'conservative modernity'.[34]

A characteristic element of such modernity was that it, too, was promoted through consumer magazines, advertising, exhibitions and representations in popular culture. To take one example, in Britain in 1908, the *Ideal Home* exhibitions began with the collaboration between the newspaper proprietor of the *Daily Mail*, Lord Beaverbrook, and manufacturing companies in trades allied to the building and maintaining of homes. These annual displays offered accessible ways to imagine and create future domestic scenarios.[35] As well as the model homes constructed on site in various architectural styles, from Tudorbethan to Moderne, staff at display stands promoted consumer goods, gadgetry and new inventions (see pl.8.19). At a time of increasing home ownership, made available through house-building schemes and the introduction of mortgages as a standard way of purchasing, a broader range of social classes sought to own

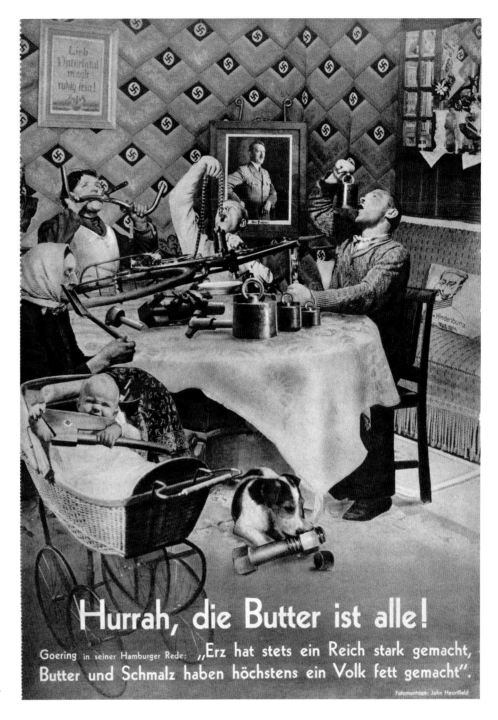

Hurrah, die Butter ist alle!

Goering in seiner Hamburger Rede: „Erz hat stets ein Reich stark gemacht, Butter und Schmalz haben höchstens ein Volk fett gemacht".

Fotomontage: John Heartfield

their own homes. The suburban locations depicted in advertisements suggested the home could be a refuge from the city. An abundant use of pattern and ornament reinforced this message, with many motifs drawn from nature, with references to Englishness or royalty in the names of product ranges.

As we have seen, the politicization of the home was already apparent in Modernism, when the domestic interior was purposely used

8.20
John Heartfield, *Hurrah, die Butter ist alle!* (Hurrah the butter is finished! Goering in his Hamburg speech: 'Iron has always made a country strong, butter and lard only make people fat') from *Arbeiter Illustrierte Zeitung*, Issue 26. 1935. George Eastman House

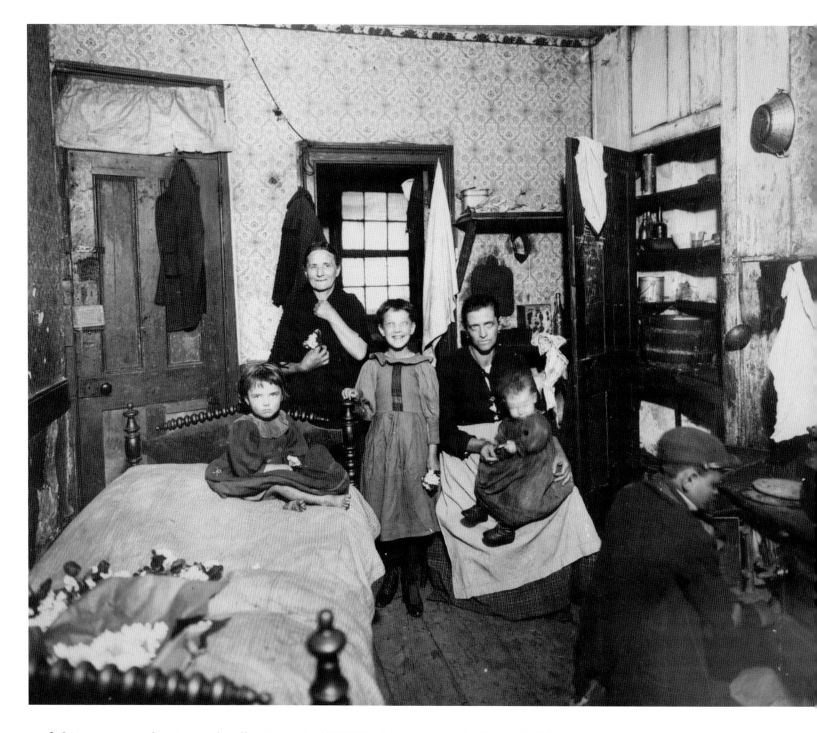

to fashion more egalitarian and collective ideals. This escalated in the 1930s on a number of fronts. In many instances, a correlation between national formation and the organization of domestic life was promoted by governments of various persuasions. In Sweden, for example, the concept of the State as a 'home of the people', the '*folkhemmet*', was promoted in the key political motto formulated by the Social Democrat leader Per Albin Hansson

in 1928.[36] In this case, a massive house-building scheme followed, providing a continuity in democratic ideals that lasted until the 1980s. Swedish designs for the domestic interior stressed natural materials and practicality that were generally less austere than the Functionalism of the 1920s, although they shared many of its social goals.

By contrast, under National Socialism in Germany after 1933, the home was used strate-

8.21
Joseph Byron, *Slum Interior*. 1896. The Byron Collection, Museum of the City of New York

gically to promote ideological messages about the role of the family in national life. Through Nazi propaganda, a particular type of modern domestic interior of the previous Weimar period was ridiculed and denounced. In its place, already popular elements were promoted through the use of indigenous woods and stone, or decorative motifs, many with *Völkisch* associations.[37] New technology, such as the radio in the form of the *Volksempfänger* (people's receiver), was incorporated in the modern interior for propagandist as well as entertainment purposes and used as a medium to alter modes of private life. The significance of such campaigns is highlighted by the counter-attack in the photomontages of the acerbic German Communist John Heartfield, who sought to disclose the hypocrisy of Nazi domestic and foreign policy (see pl.8.20).[38]

From rooms to ruins

Many of the representations in this chapter contributed to a dominant impetus of the modern period to make the domestic interior a site of consumption, both as a place to consume and in which to consume. Their role in the domestic imagination was therefore viewed as positive and life-enhancing, contributing to a sense of identity, comfort and leisure – in short, a place of homeliness and belonging. In the first half of the twentieth century another tradition emerged, which had its origins in movements of social concern and reform. These had led people to record the plight of the poor, the dispossessed and the migrant, motivated by philanthropy, self-help, or, sometimes, as a form of control. Whether in words or pictures, attention turned to inadequate housing and slum conditions. Literature provided one obvious way to record such lives as the working-class biography and autobiography became a distinct genre in the twentieth century. Another method was the documentary photograph, deemed an effective form of reportage, as in the *Slum Interior* by Joseph Byron (see pl.8.21). In the United States, Lewis Hine was one of the first professional photographers to work for charities, for instance, when in 1908 he took

on a project for the National Child Labor Committee, reporting on conditions, including the accommodation, of poor labourers, a role he continued until the Depression years. Jacob Riis, a fellow photographer, compiled *Battle with the Slum* and *How the Other Half Lives: studies among the tenements of New York*.[39]

At the end of the 1930s, what for Britain has been called the 'Devil's Decade', the outbreak of the Second World War was to force the domestic interior through another set of contortions and displacements.[40] In the face of the decline of Empire and world war, an imaginative space opened for a change of meaning for the home and domestic interior. Gone was the immediacy of effective design solutions. In their place a neo-Romantic sensibility came to the fore. Bill Brandt, the photographer, put this into words and pictures in three studies, *The English at Home* and *A Night in London* in 1936 and 1938 respectively, and *Camera in London* of 1948 (see pl.8.22). Reflecting on war-torn London, Brandt wrote,

> Everyone has at some time or other felt the atmosphere of a room. If one comes with a heightened awareness, prepared to lay oneself open to their influence, other places too can exert the same power of association. It may be of association with a person, with simple human emotions, with the past or some building looked at long ago, or even with a scene only imagined or dreamed of. This sense of association can be so sharp that it arouses an emotion almost like nostalgia. And it is this that gives drama or atmosphere to a picture.[41]

Brandt's approach to layout was often to pose two contrasting images that commented on the social mores, habits and customs of the people who interested him. Looking to the future, he wrote,

> Under the soft light of the moon the blacked-out town had a new beauty. The houses looked flat like painted

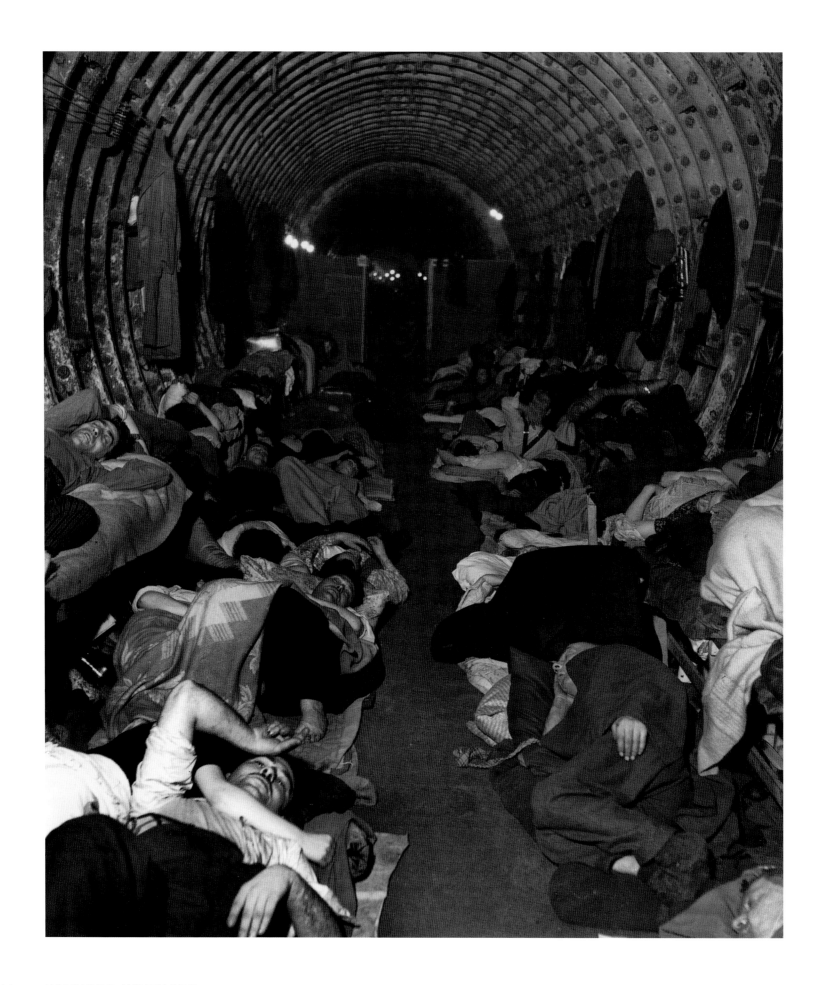

scenery and the bombed ruins made strangely shaped silhouettes. Through the gaps new vistas opened and for the first time the Londoner caught the full view of St Paul's Cathedral. And perhaps out of the ruins of war will rise new buildings which will rival those of Wren. I hope that will be in the not too distant future, because I want to be there to photograph them.[42]

Indeed, out of the ashes and ruins of devastated Europe a new vision did arise, propelled by a second generation of modernist designers. In Britain, for example, in 1942, Abram Games, himself a graphic designer informed by Euro-pean Modernism, predicted the situation in a poster, *Your Britain, Fight for it Now!* (see pl.8.23).[43] In this, he contrasted the Victorian slum with a model of future domestic housing. This message was reinforced in the 'Plan for Britain' published as a special issue of the magazine *Picture Post* in January 1941. Here lay the foundations of the Welfare State.[44] It included Elizabeth Denby's article 'Plan the Home' announcing the 'All-Europe House'. Once again, the metaphor of the nation as home was invoked to unify a people at war and after in a shared purpose. The future of the domestic interior in the immediate postwar years looked set to undergo a further complex negotiation of cultural, historical and social questions.

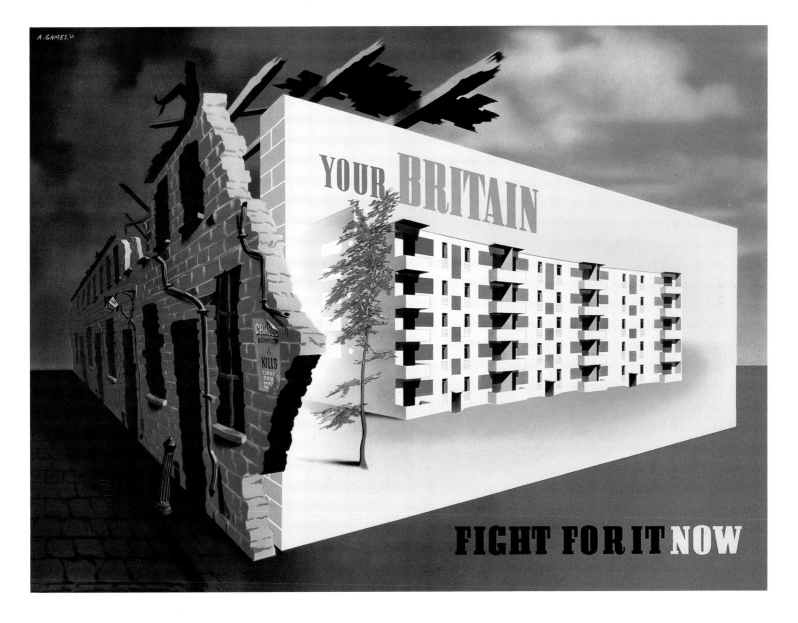

Reading, the Child and the Home: illustrated children's books in late nineteenth-century Britain

Rebecca Preston

Illustrated children's books were not a nineteenth-century phenomenon, but the social, demographic and economic changes that had occurred by the middle of the century prompted demand for a greater variety of juvenile literature. The number and range of titles published for an increasingly literate and visually sophisticated young audience further accelerated with technological improvements after 1860. These books were new in quality and overall design as well as in how they addressed the idea of childhood. The images of children in the interior shown here indicate both the tenacity of older forms of representing the child, reading and the home, and some of the new ways in which these relationships were conceived. They suggest the different manner in which authors and illustrators engaged with the idea of the child at

home between 1860 and 1900, and the material importance of books and reading to representations of childhood.

Literary and graphic representations of children at home were prominent in particular types of books, including anonymous moralizing Christian stories published in cheap illustrated 'reward books' throughout the century (see pl.8.24). These belonged to an older tradition of children's reading matter and many tales intended as prizes for obedient children had a domestic setting, with accompanying vignettes that often made use of interior features to frame the family at home.

Popular 'family chronicles' written by middle-class women formed a second group of books representing the child at home in the mid- to late nineteenth

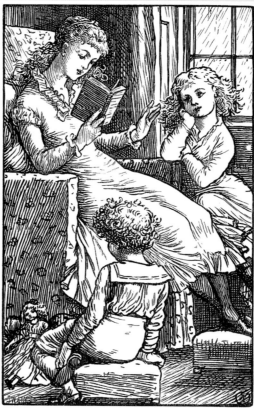

8.24
'The Pear'. Engraving from *Dean's Pictorial Reward Books* by Dean Thomas. 1868. The British Library, London

8.25
Walter Crane, 'Now be quiet all of you, I'm going to begin'. Woodcut illustration from *'Carrots': Just an Ordinary Boy* by Mrs Molesworth. 1884. NAL: 60.X.179A

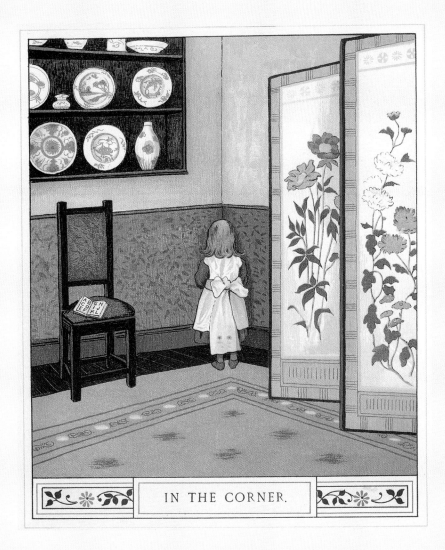

IN THE CORNER.

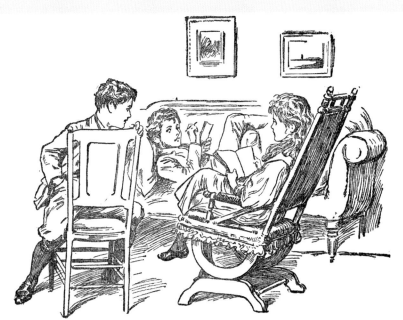

IT WAS NOT TILL NEXT DAY THAT HE OWNED THAT THE TYPEWRITER HAD BEEN
A FIEND IN DISGUISE.

8.26
'In the Corner'. Coloured
lithograph from *At Home* by
J.G. Sowerby and Thomas
Crane. NAL: 60.U.22

8.27
Gordon Browne, 'It was not
till next day that he owned
that the typewriter had been
a fiend in disguise' from
New Treasure Seekers
by E. Nesbit. 1904.
NAL: 861.AA.1261

century. These stories had moral and religious
undertones but were intended to entertain as well as
instruct, to inspire rather than chasten their subjects
into proper behaviour. What bestselling writer
Charlotte Yonge called her 'domestic record of home
events' provided familiar settings for working out
themes of exploration and self-discovery in equal but
different fashion to adventure stories set beyond the
home. Illustrated volumes in this vein increasingly
introduced a stronger relationship between text and
image, writer and illustrator, producing favourites such
as Mrs Molesworth's more relaxed children's fiction
series illustrated by Walter Crane (see pl.8.25).

The work of Crane and other Arts and Crafts
illustrators created a third group of picture books for
children in which illustration was integral to the book's
design. They presented a fantasy, nursery-rhyme
childhood in which adults were peripheral or simply
ridiculous. Plate 8.26 is from a similarly conceived art
book illustrated by J.G. Sowerby and Thomas Crane,
At Home of 1881, which makes a direct and
humorous analogy between childhood, home and
book. It opens into a Queen Anne-style house of the
type associated with the Aesthetic Movement where,
page by page, the young reader is led through
its rooms, finding little Lettice aged three who,
distracted by her Aesthetic surroundings, refuses
to learn her ABC.

In plate 8.27 Gordon Browne captures E. Nesbit's
portrayal of self-reliant, physically and intellectually
adventurous children in her *New Treasure Seekers*
(1904). In addition to showing changes in interior
arrangement and use, these examples illustrate how
depictions of home and book moved from being
primarily a means of correcting children to
encouraging self-discipline, exploration and fun –
within a tradition of picturing children reading at home.

Photographing Home

Trevor Keeble

During the nineteenth century the domestic interior posed specific challenges and opportunities for photography. From the outset of its development, photographic technology sought to harness and control the role of light in the photographic process. The restricting conditions of the interior impeded the exposure of light required by the earliest methods of photography. Nevertheless, the domestic interior and the objects of the interior did figure in the first publication to use photographic illustration, William Henry Fox Talbot's *The Pencil of Nature,* published between 1844 and 1846. Talbot, the English pioneer of photography, used these works to showcase his 'calotype' process. Among the 24 images were photographs of domestic objects such as glassware, porcelain and even of photographs themselves, which were presented as an objective reality of material things. Talbot's 'A Scene in a Library' demonstrates the difficulty in photographing interior space at this time. The image depicts its subject not as a spatial environment but as a flat, two-dimensional elevation and yet the representation of spatial relationships was central to Talbot's concern. Taking its cues from seventeenth-century Dutch domestic painting, 'The Open Door' is a picturesque arrangement that provides a glimpse across the threshold into a darkened interior beyond (see pl.8.28).

In spite of this allusion to a genre of painting, during this period photography was emphatically viewed by many as a technology rather than as an art, and subsequently its evolution provided opportunities for the domestic realm and its inhabitants. Excluded from the privileged arena of the gallery or academy, photography flourished as a representational medium for the masses. In 1857, Lady Eastlake, a notable early commentator on photography, went so far as to

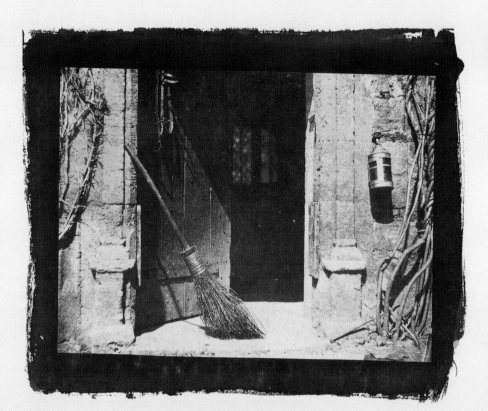

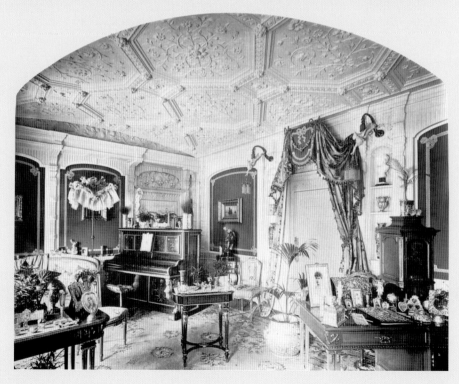

8.28
William Henry Fox Talbot,
'The Open Door'.
Black and white photograph.
1843. Private collection/
Bridgeman Art Library

8.29
Harold Palmer,
'The Boudoir' from *Souvenir of Wickham Hall*. 1897.
London Borough of Bromley

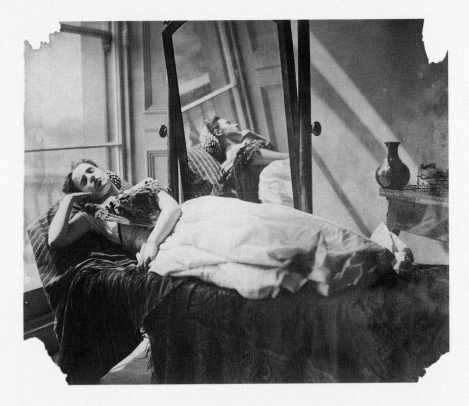

representation delivered a new democracy of representation (see pl.8.29).

By the 1860s and '70s professional photographers and photographic studios were commonplace in most British towns and cities. For the first time ordinary people and their interior environments were visually represented in a widely accessible form. This was a potentially paradoxical act, at once deeply personal and private, and yet also explicitly revealing and potentially public in nature (see pl.8.30). Nowhere is this conflict more evident than in professional studio portraits, where the impersonality of the studio was disguised by the domestic traces of tables, desks and curtains (see pl.8.31). On the one hand, as a medium, photography compromised the supposed privacy of the domestic space, and it is not surprising that as it developed through the century the photographic gaze was more commonly directed away from the familiar surroundings of the home towards more exotic locations often associated with travel and tourism. On the other hand, the consumer demand of the period, with its insatiable appetite for representation, meant that photographing home was no longer a personal act of the individual but a commercial strategy for manufacturers, retailers and design professionals (see pl.8.32). As printing and reproduction technologies improved the possibilities for the dissemination of the domestic photograph were boundless.

describe this increasingly omnipresent technology as a 'household want'. Her enthusiasm for photography stemmed from its exclusion from art. For Lady Eastlake the photograph would be a 'sworn witness' of 'facts' but unlike painting and its preoccupation with beauty, the facts of photography might be '*minor* things'. In time this prophecy of everyday

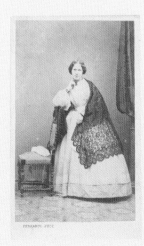

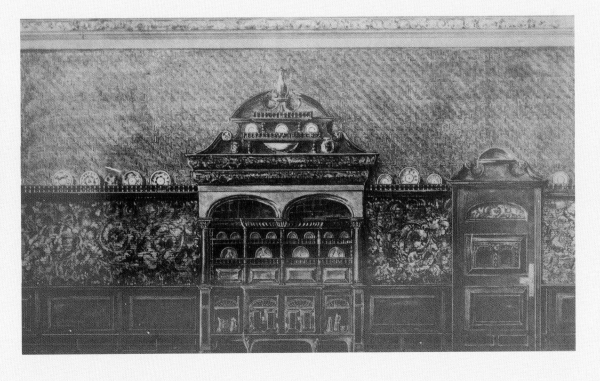

9

The Twentieth-Century Architectural Interior: representing Modernity

Tim Benton

THE THEORY AND PRACTICE of what is now called Modernist architecture developed in parallel with the transformation of the nature and distribution of media of representation, irreversibly changing the relationship between the unique work and its representations.[1] In particular, the technical development of architectural photography and its establishment as the almost universal medium of architectural representation and distribution has created new design parameters for the architect and a completely transformed domain for critics and historians. Translating the experience of visiting a building into a photograph, and one which for most of the twentieth century has been almost exclusively monochrome, has not been welcomed by many architects. The designer and architect Adolf Loos wrote, in 1910:

> However, I contend: a real building makes no impression as an illustration reproduced two-dimensionally. It is my greatest pride that the interiors which I have created are totally ineffective in photographs. I am proud of the fact that the inhabitants of my spaces do not recognise their own apartments in the photographs, just as the owner of a Monet painting would not recognise it at Kastan's [a former Viennese waxwork gallery].[2]

Loos was writing about the houses and apartments he had designed in the ten years previous to his article. With their walls lined in mahogany or marble, their reproduction Biedermeier or Chippendale furniture, their oriental rugs and plentiful works of art and musical instruments they must have been a nightmare to photograph.[3] While taking the opportunity to complain about the refusal of architectural journals to publish photographs of his buildings, Loos is making the Kantian statement that each art is particular to itself and cannot be translated into another medium: 'It is a well-known fact that every work of art possesses such strong internal laws that it can only appear in its own form… The mark of a building which is truly established is that it remains ineffective in two dimensions.'[4]

A novel which can be turned into a play, Loos argues, is a bad novel, just as Clement Greenberg later argued that, 'the task of self-criticism became to eliminate from the specific effects of each art any and every effect that might conceivably be borrowed from or by the medium of another art'.[5] Hence Loos's satisfaction that any two-dimensional representation of his interiors would fail to satisfy. Similarly, Le Corbusier insisted that real buildings could only properly be experienced in three dimensions, from a moving viewpoint.[6] Like most Modernist architects, Le Corbusier was an inveterate traveller with an

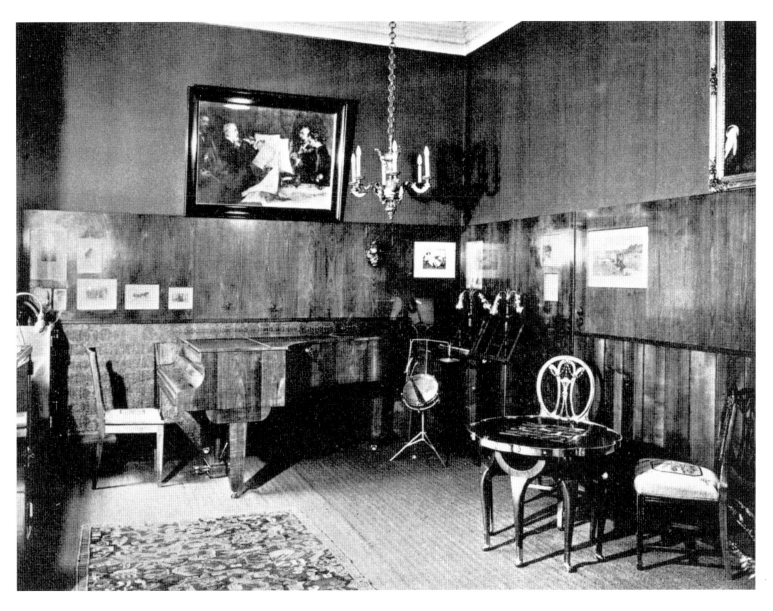

9.1
Adolf Loos, Musikzimmer,
Apartment for Arthur
Friedman, Bellariastrasse.
Photograph by Atelier Gerlach
from *Bauforum*. 1970.
NAL: PP.65.G

unquenchable curiosity for good solutions wherever they could be found (particularly in vernacular architecture). But, as Walter Benjamin put it, in a tantalizing fragment for an essay, 'The medium through which works of art continue to influence later ages is always different from the ones in which they affect their own age'.[7]

Architecture in general, and Modernist architecture in particular, has obeyed the law of transposition of media. The rapid global spread of the 'modern movement' in architecture passed predominantly along the monochrome two-dimensional channel of half-tone photographic illustrations. And the history and criticism of modern architecture, including that of recent writers such as Beatriz Colomina, has

been largely a history of its (black and white) representations, 'Until the advent of photography, and earlier lithography, the audience of architecture was the user. With photography, the illustrated magazine, and tourism, architecture's reception began to occur through an additional social form: consumption.'[8]

Apart from the obvious ways in which this is untrue (buildings have always been visited by non-users and have been 'consumed' in a variety of media at least since the development of mercantilism and printing in the early modern period), there is a sense in which photography in the twentieth century has created a new discipline for architects to master.[9] In other words, apart from the impact on criticism and history,

photography and the other media of representation have had an impact on architectural
design. For example, Modernist buildings have
all been designed with photographic representation in mind as one at least of the necessary
representations of the design. And when their
interiors have not come out well in photographs, architects have made every effort to
suppress their publication.

Whereas most Modernist architects claimed
that façade and visual effects were less important than social utility and structural
rationalism, a current view is that Modernism
was above all an exploitation of surface effects.
For example, Janet Ward begins her book
Weimar Surfaces by considering the twentieth
century as the period 'in which content yielded
to form, text to image, depth to façade and *Sein*
to *Schein…*' (from being to appearing).[10] She
goes on to attribute to the founders of Modernism a more significant role: 'It would not be
an exaggeration to claim for the culture (or
cult) of surface in 1920s Germany the status of
the visual embodiment of the modern per se'.[11]
For Colomina and Ward, the emphasis on the
visual, on surface effects and spectacle, trans-
mitted above all by photography and film,
represents the commodification of architecture.

I will return to photography but first want
to place photographic representations of Modernist interiors into some context.[12] An
underlying theme in this essay is the curiosity
about the eternal conflict in architectural interiors between 'Art' and 'Life', that is, between
the expectations and aesthetic ambitions of
architects and the lived experience of inhabitants. It is a conflict that spills over into every
aspect of discussion of the interior, from living
in rooms to discussing photographs.

The emphasis on the photograph, with
which I began, must be qualified somewhat.
Plans, renderings (and especially axonometric
projections), models and full-size installations
have also been important means of diffusion of
Modernist architecture. Success for an architect
in the twentieth century depended more on
creating exhibitable or publishable plans, renderings, models, installations and above all

photographs than on meeting the practical and
psychological needs of clients.[13] All have influenced architectural design to some extent, to
the point where the different media with
which architects felt comfortable formed part
of the parameters of their architectural imagination. We might almost say that if Baillie Scott
imagined his buildings as watercolours, Van
Doesburg conceived of his as coloured axonometric renderings and Richard Neutra
dreamed of his in the deep-toned hues of Julius
Shulman's photographs.

Understanding the determining influence
of the media is one of the challenges for the
historian of Modernist architecture. Of course,
buildings are themselves also representations of
architectural ideas (among other things), and
there is an interesting history of the architectural visit, of the effect that buildings themselves
have had on Modernist architects, critics and
historians.[14] Many of the most influential buildings in the Modernist canon were visited by a
very small number of architects and critics.
I doubt that Loos's houses in Vienna were
visited much by foreigners before the 1970s.[15]
But others, such as Le Corbusier's Maison La
Roche or Gropius's Bauhaus buildings and
Masters' houses, were visited by a significant
cross-section of influential architects.

Exhibition buildings present particular
issues. Relatively few architects or critics
visited Le Corbusier's L'Esprit Nouveau Pavilion (Paris, 1925) or Mies's German Pavilion
(Barcelona 1929, see pl.9.15), and the diffusion
of these important buildings was managed
largely by a handful of very influential photographs directed and selected by the architects.[16]
On the other hand, the Weissenhof Siedlung in
Stuttgart (1927), where 15 leading Modernist
architects from 5 countries built their houses,
was visited by a generation of international
architects and critics, and the particular qualities
of these demonstration interiors have been disproportionately influential. This impression was
only amplified by the books and magazine cov-
erage publicising the exhibition.[17]

Alfred Barr claimed in 1932 that 'Expositions and exhibitions have perhaps changed the

9.2
Margarete Schütte-Lihotzky,
Factory workers' house plan. 1929

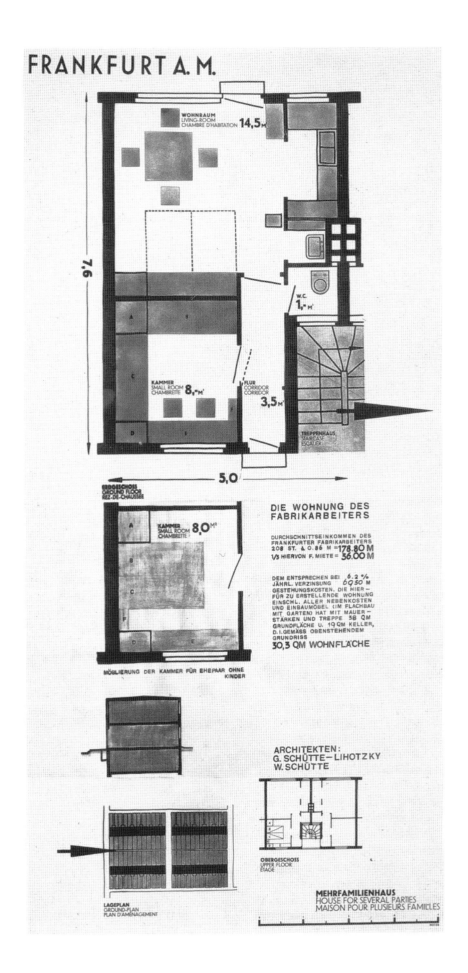

FRANKFURT A. M.

WOHNRAUM
LIVING-ROOM
CHAMBRE D'HABITATION 14,5 M

7,6

W.C.
1,- M²

KAMMER
SMALL ROOM
CHAMBRETTE 8,- M²

FLUR
CORRIDOR
CORRIDOR
3,5 M

TREPPENHAUS
STAIRCASE
ESCALIER

5,0

ERDGESCHOSS
GROUND FLOOR
REZ-DE-CHAUSSÉE

DIE WOHNUNG DES
FABRIKARBEITERS

KAMMER
SMALL ROOM
CHAMBRETTE 8,0 M²

DURCHSCHNITTSEINKOMMEN DES
FRANKFURTER FABRIKARBEITERS
208 ST. à 0,86 M = 178.80 M
1/5 HIERVON F. MIETE = 36.00 M

DEM ENTSPRECHEN BEI 6.2 %
JÄHRL. VERZINSUNG 6050 M
GESTEHUNGSKOSTEN. DIE HIER—
FÜR ZU ERSTELLENDE WOHNUNG
EINSCHL. ALLER NEBENKOSTEN
UND EINBAUMÖBEL (IM FLACHBAU
MIT GARTEN) HAT MIT MAUER—
STÄRKEN UND TREPPE 58 QM
GRUNDFLÄCHE U. 19 QM KELLER,
D.I.GEMÄSS OBENSTEHENDEM
GRUNDRISS
30,3 QM WOHNFLÄCHE

MÖBLIERUNG DER KAMMER FÜR EHEPAAR OHNE
KINDER

ARCHITEKTEN:
G. SCHÜTTE–LIHOTZKY
W. SCHÜTTE

OBERGESCHOSS
UPPER FLOOR
ÉTAGE

LAGEPLAN
GROUND-PLAN
PLAN D'AMÉNAGEMENT

MEHRFAMILIENHAUS
HOUSE FOR SEVERAL PARTIES
MAISON POUR PLUSIEURS FAMILLES

character of American architecture of the last forty years more than any other factor'.[18] In an American context, where many of the innovative buildings between the wars were remote from New York (in the mid-West, California or Europe, for example), the impact of the Chicago Century of Progress Exhibition of 1933–4 and of the New York Worlds' Fair in 1939 was particularly important.[19] Perhaps the fact that Modernism, despite making less 'official' headway in America compared to Europe, acquired a popular base by the end of the 1930s far in advance of that in Europe was in part due to these exhibitions.

Similarly, the exhibition houses in the popular domestic exhibitions, such as the Daily Mail Ideal Home in London and the Salon des Arts Ménagers in Paris, introduced large numbers of people to the direct experience of walking through different homes. The history of these exhibition houses is curiously out of sync with the historiography of modern architecture. For example, the Ideal Home exhibition included a modern house in 1928 that, while reflecting the progress of Modernism in Europe, was more 'advanced' than anything built in England at that time.[20]

Plans and models

By contrast with the full-size building or installation, the most abstract form of representation of the domestic interior is the plan. Modernist architects struggling with the problem of rehousing the maximum number of people with the minimum of means, focused on the so-called *Existenzminimum* plan. The Congrès Internationaux d'Architecture Moderne (CIAM) organized its first major conference in Frankfurt in 1929 around the minimum plan, presenting an exhibition where over 100 plans, all drawn to the same scale and conventions, were exhibited on large panels side by side (see pl.9.2). Iñaki Àbalos sees these plans as the highest expression of reductivist positivist thinking.[21] Although Positivism had only a weak influence on Modernism, which was largely Idealist in its orientation, there is something in the attention given to the floor plan

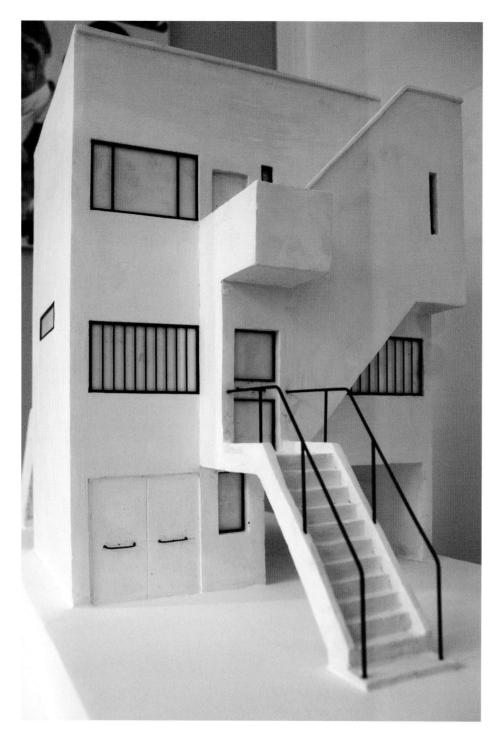

9.3
Le Corbusier, *Maison Ribot*
model. 1923.

consisted of a plan and a perspective sketch of the exterior.[22] The interior is probably too personal to promote commercially. Everyone likes to feel that their interior is their own. What they are buying in the Sears and Roebuck catalogue is a category of house at a price, with the convenience and flexibility offered for individual innovation offered by that category. The exterior appearance is crucial because it represents the chief public value of the investment, and the future owner can have less control over it.

Some forms of architectural representation are particularly hostile to the representation of the interior. From 1922–3, when the theory and practice of Modernism was forged, one of the most significant forms of representation of domestic architecture was the plaster model. For example, Le Corbusier discovered that large white models of his designs would be given excellent exposure at the Salon d'Automne (see pl.9.3).[23] These models were also an occasion for deep reflection on the aesthetic success of his early Purist designs. Looking back to the Citrohan model, he wrote, in 1929:

> This plaster model at the 1922 Salon d'Automne represented a significant demonstration of architectural aesthetics. Some very precise problems were given revolutionary solutions: the roof garden, the suppression of the cornice, the horizontal window, the house in the air … this categorical feeling of purity, candour, total commitment and loyalty. Reinforced concrete produced the novelty of an absolutely pure envelope expressing, all on its own, *the decisive eloquence of architectural volume.*[24]

among Modernist architects which gives food for thought. The insistence on the plan certainly contributed to Modernism's reputation for dehumanizing the domestic.

Interestingly, although the highly developed commercialism of the American housing market has consistently promoted individualism throughout the twentieth century, the paradigmatic form of the housing catalogue has always

It is difficult to imagine a discourse (and a medium of representation) more removed from the design of the modern interior. The year 1923 was an *annus mirabilis* for the plaster model. For example, since almost nothing had been built by then the International Architecture exhibition at the Weimar Bauhaus from July to September 1923 consisted largely of

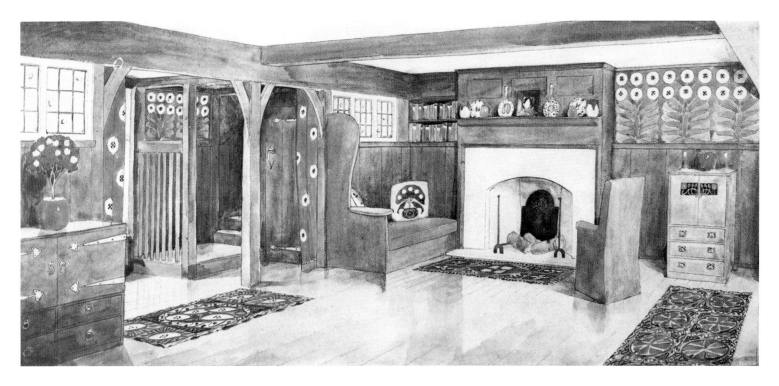

9.4
M.H. Baillie Scott, 'Falkewood,
the Dining Hall' from *Houses
and Gardens*. 1906.
NAL: 34.A.110

plaster models and drawings. In October 1923 the de Stijl exhibition at the Leonce Rosenberg galleries in Paris featured the models of Theo van Doesburg and Cornelis van Eesteren.[25] The 'battle of the models' fixed certain features of evolving Modernism in the attempt to create formal interest without ornament. All this formal apparatus pre-existed the development of the modern plan and had a determining influence on Modernist houses when they started to appear in quantity around 1925. Only after 1925 did Modernist houses begin to be illustrated photographically in the architectural press.[26]

The standard medium for publication in the nineteenth century was the woodcut, and to a lesser extent the chromolithograph. The Aesthetic and Arts and Crafts movements threw this into crisis, because of the desire to control colour and line without the mediation of the engraver.[27] A comparison between Baillie Scott's warm and soft-edged rendering of the dining hall at Falkewood (see pl.9.4) and Gerlach's black and white photograph of Loos's Friedman apartment (see pl.9.1) points to some of the difficulties of representing Arts and Crafts interiors.[28] Colour, texture and the sense of touch were important to both architects, but

richly textured interiors with relatively small windows are notoriously difficult to photograph. Interiors were usually photographed with the curtains drawn or with the windows seen at an oblique angle to avoid the daylight burning out the negative. By contrast, the watercolourist can choose his viewpoint with equanimity, to bring out the colour scheme and fill the interior with coloured light. Baillie Scott clearly felt happier illustrating his interiors in colour, but used black and white photographs of executed buildings as a form of self-promotion.[29] The watercolour perspectives also allowed him to create wide angle views which were not then practical for photographers.[30]

Children in the home

Kate Greenaway's hugely successful and influential *Under the Window* (1878 pl.9.5) helped to shape an idea of the domestic for generations to come.[31] This book of 'innocent' poems (one of her role models was William Blake) is set among backgrounds drawn from the English village and suburb; she later settled in the leafy suburb of Hampstead. Although there are no interior views in this book, Greenaway captures many of the themes of the Modernist domestic interior which would recur throughout the twentieth century. The childlike and the vernacular are represented as organically linked. The paradigmatic metaphor is one of children growing up among flowers and plants, with mother indoors, mostly unseen but present as observer. Although rare in Modernist representations, this trope is repeated in a drawing of the agricultural family in the industrially produced *Ferme radieuse* in 1934 (see pl.9.6).[32] While the farm workers, still in clogs, relax after their labours, two children play among the flowers and their mother looks on from the balcony.

The place of children in the Modernist interior has been insufficiently studied, despite the de Stijl children's furniture designed by Gerrit Rietveld, or the Bauhaus children's furniture at the Haus am Horn exhibition (1923) or even Giuseppe Terragni's tubular steel miniature chairs in the Asile infantile, Como (1936). Many Modernist houses and apartments were commissioned by young couples with children, but the forms of representation developed by Modernism not only excluded children (and indeed people in general) from photographs but also any messy signs of their presence.

A publication that did associate children with interiors, watercolour renderings and Arts and Crafts values was Carl Larsson's *Ett Hem* (*A Home*, 1899). In Germany, the widely

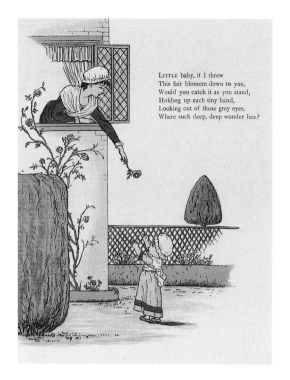

LITTLE baby, if I threw
This fair blossom down to you,
Would you catch it as you stand,
Holding up each tiny hand,
Looking out of those grey eyes,
Where such deep, deep wonder lies?

distributed *Blaue Bücher* reprinted a German edition of Larsson's book in 1922 (with additional illustrations, see pl.9.7).[33] Books like this, emphasising the 'homely' qualities of the domestic interior, often using coloured illustrations and usually advocating a return to the countryside and the simple life, continued to be published throughout the Modernist period and form a significant backdrop to it. Many writers have argued that, despite the inroads

9.5
Kate Greenaway, plate from *Under the Window*.
Colour wood engraving. 1878.
NAL: 60.U.13

9.6
Drawing of the agricultural family from *Ferme radieuse*. 1934.

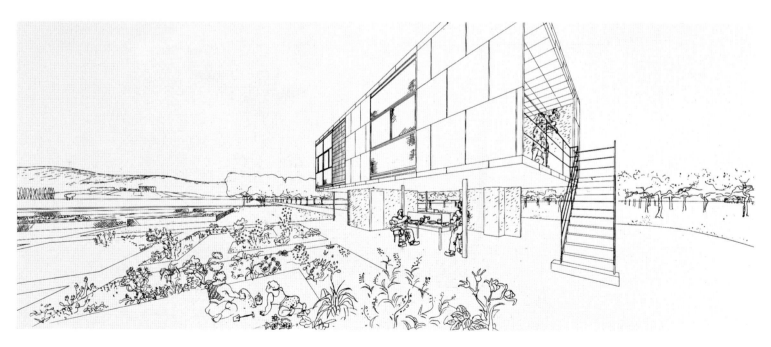

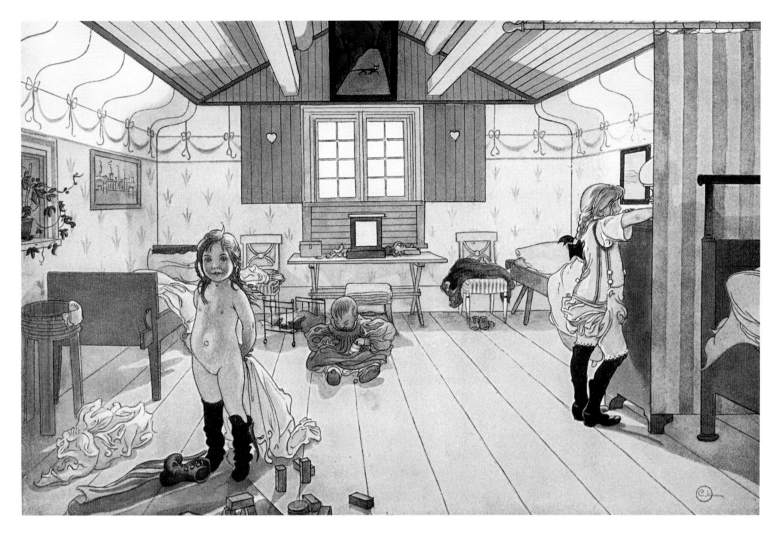

9.7
Carl Larsson, 'In the little girls'
bedroom'. Watercolour from
Ett Hem. 1922. NAL: 399.B.33

of Modernism in the design of homes, the archetypes of traditional houses remain fixed in the imagination. Children living in blocks of flats still draw 'home' as a cottage with pitched roof and smoke curling from the chimney.[34] First exhibited in America in 1895, the watercolours for this book remained continuously in print as postcards, prints and book illustrations throughout the twentieth century.[35] They constitute a hymn of praise to the Arts and Crafts ideal of creative labour, family life and the celebration of personal and social pleasures.[36] The stripped and painted pine floors, brightly illuminated interiors, lacquered furniture and delicate antiques in the style popularized by Gustav III (1746–92), together with the close relationship to nature, can be read both as a metaphor for the innocence of childhood and the production of a childlike commodity. This is rustic primitivism without the poverty, fear

and blinding smoke of the real thing, filled with light, colour and freedom. In this context, the distinctive thing about this kind of illustration is that the message of formal 'reform' is interpreted for the viewer by a dream of intimate family life. This is precisely what most representations of Modernism did not attempt.

The human touch

People are normally excluded from the representations of the modern interior in architectural publications. In the case of photography, there are technical reasons for this; it was not until the 1970s that fast films allowed the camera to come off the tripod in architectural photography, allowing images that both gave a reasonable rendering of spatial enclosures and allowed for the informal presence of people. And this took place during the swelling backlash against Modernism in the 1970s. Photographs showing people in interiors belong almost exclusively to the world of cinema, interior design and fashion magazines. Significantly, however, the 'modern' interiors that feature in this kind of photo story are eclectic, classical or Art Deco, as opposed to Modernist and for this reason I have not looked at examples of this kind.

In Modernist drawings, by contrast, token human figures are often reproduced for scale, and Le Corbusier, and indeed many other architects, drew sketches for their prospective clients showing what an inhabitant would see in his or her house.[37] An association was soon formed between technical functionalism (stripping away unnecessary weight and clutter) and nudity, and not only in the mouths of hostile critics. When Buckminster Fuller exhibited a model of his Dymaxion house (1927) in The Marshall Field's department store in Chicago in 1929, he populated it not only with a figurine of a naked woman lying on a bed, but also some apparently joyous sun bathers on the roof terrace (see pl.9.8). While Fuller solemnly explains that the figurine is there to demon-

strate the perfect temperature control of his house, the titillating contrast between the solemn and suited inventor and the nude benefactors of his design reinforces a standard but repressed Modernist trope. Man (outside) disposes and woman (preferably naked) lies or stands inside, exposed. Modern architects did not invent 'her indoors', and in fact occasionally celebrated women as progressive.[38] Some women, such as Charlotte Perriand, combined a personal preference for outdoor exercise (and nudism) with their interior design work, going out of their way to embed signs of physical exercise in their projects.[39]

A photograph that uses (female) figures to express the lifestyle that the design of the interior is intended to serve is the iconic view of Marcel Breuer's interior for a gym instructress (1930, pl.9.9). When women were represented photographically in the interior, it was most typically in the kitchen (often in the form of a domestic servant), demonstrating the rational organization of storage, streamlined circulation and mechanical equipment.[40] A 1928 film by

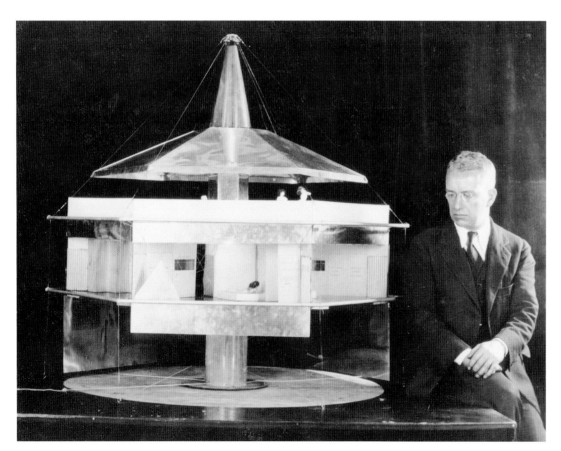

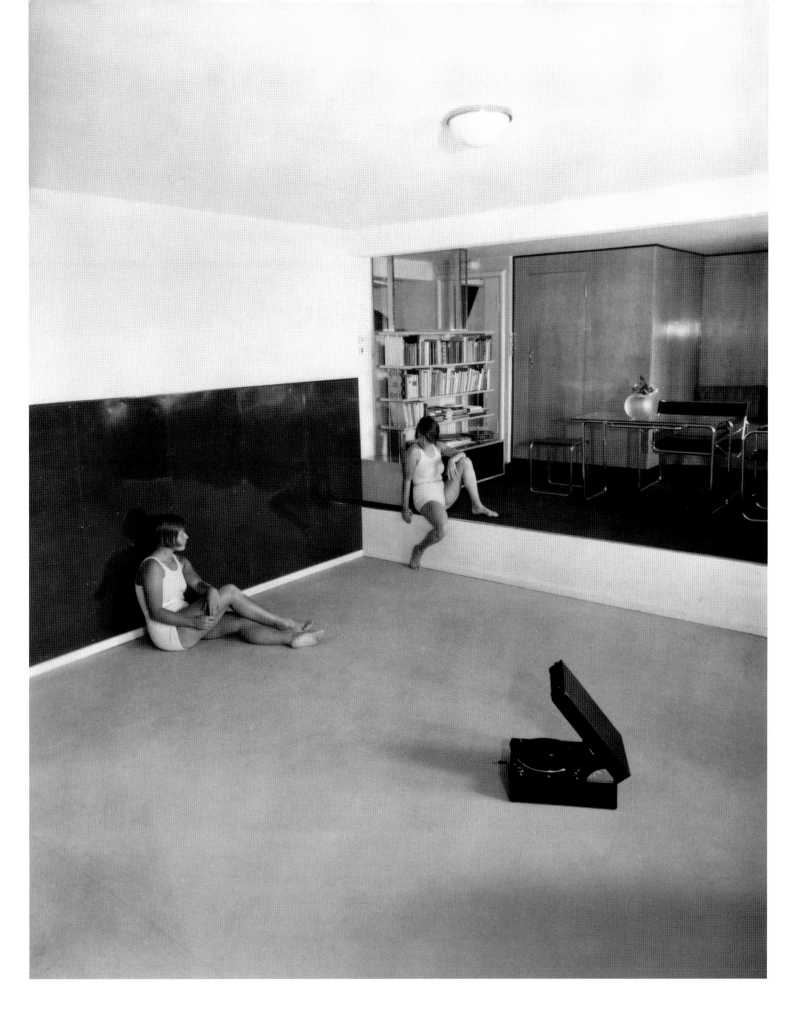

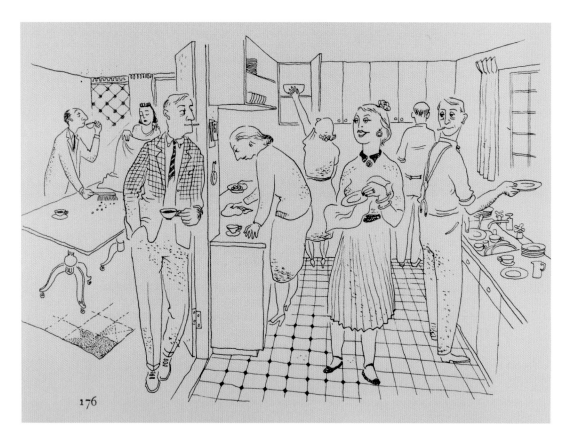

9.10
Mary Wright, 'Cleanup can even be part of the evening's pleasures' from *Guide to Easier Living* by Mary and Russel Wright. 1951. The British Library, London

Paul Wolff, for example, shows a servant putting the Frankfurt kitchen (designed by Margarete Schütte-Lihotzky in 1926) through its paces, while another film shows a maid putting things away in the cupboards of Walter Gropius's house in Dessau (1925).[41] This genre was amusingly developed in graphic form in 1939 by Gordon Cullen, illustrating the work of Tecton, as well as the house in Newton Road, Paddington, by Denys Lasdun.[42] Cullen invented a style of drawing combining photographs with analytical cut-away drawings and human incident. The technique of collage was adapted from Modernist art practice to explain interiors in terms of space, structure, functions and human use. Interestingly, Lasdun's interior was also presented as 'an experiment in furnishing design', showing the same interiors in three states: unfurnished, furnished with antiques and with modern furniture.[43]

A further extension of the humanization of the interior can be found in the witty and stylish drawings of Mary and Russel Wright, whose *Guide to Easier Living* (1951) places people and human comfort at centre stage (see pl.9.10).[44]

The book exemplifies a number of changes that had taken place in the popularization of modern design and architecture in America in the later 1930s. Several points should be made about this book. The title page photograph is in colour and shows a modern couple in their living room, thus breaking two conventions of Modernist representation of the interior.[45] Secondly, although the drawings that fill the book have a fully Modernist message (opening out the space of the interior, rationalizing domestic routines and so on), they use perspective and colour to create the sense of space and comfort. Many of the drawings are 'analytical', for example seen from above, to show a whole room and its fittings, and most of them include people, comfortably relaxing or socialising. Finally 'life' values determine the artistic ones: great emphasis is placed on storage and the detail of everyday routines. The text is fully in line with the Taylorization of the domestic, including almost military style lists and tables of things to do or put in order, but the representation is a million miles away from the abstract plans with their dotted lines showing circulation patterns

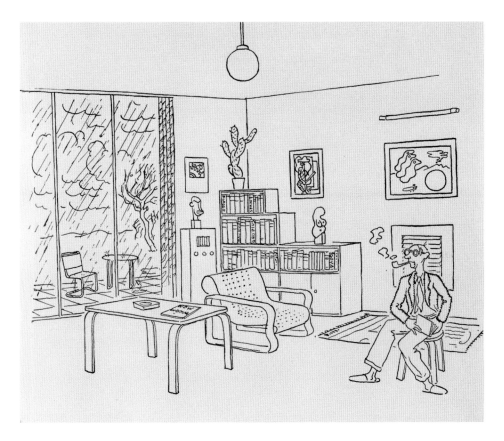

9.11
'The Functional Interior' from
Homes Sweet Homes by Osbert
Lancaster. 1939.
NAL: 47.V.59

of the interiors of Loos and Le Corbusier) has been held against Modernism in the recent literature.[49] Osbert Lancaster, astute observer of the frailties of the Modernist ideal (see pl.9.11), noted in 1939 the 'apparent failure of the reformers in the realm of domestic architecture [to eliminate the object]…' since 'in the home logic has always been at a discount'.

> The vast majority, even including many readers of *The New Statesman*, crave their knick-knacks, though not in Victorian abundance, and are perfectly willing to pay the price in prolonged activities with broom and duster. At the moment there are signs that many of the leaders of the school, though not of course the more strict, are compromising, and a selected assortment of *objets d'art et de vertu* are being once more admitted.[50]

favoured by Christine Frederick and her followers. Compared to interwar Modernist designers, who promised a revolution and democratization of lifestyle, the Wrights exemplify the actual revolution in etiquette that allowed for self-service kitchen buffets and communal washing-up at the end of the evening. It is worth reflecting how the standard means of representation favoured by Modernism were incapable of illustrating this revolution of domestic practice, in so far as it had made headway before the Second World War.

The Modernist architectural interior is intolerant of objects (especially in photographs).[46] For Walter Benjamin, this was one of the revolutionary implications of an architecture of steel and glass (which is how he described the work of Loos and Le Corbusier): 'Glass is such a hard and flat material that nothing settles on it…. It is above all the enemy of secrets. It is the enemy of possessions'.[47] The accomplishment of the new steel and glass rooms, then, is that 'it is difficult to leave a trace'.[48] This radical observation (which betrays a lack of close observation on Benjamin's part

Objects never disappeared completely from the Modernist interior, even if photographers were at pains to reduce or eliminate them in the interests of formal values. Many architects collected natural objects and artefacts to display alongside works of art in their own domestic interiors.[51] For example, Le Corbusier became increasingly tolerant of personal objects and clutter as his work moved towards the use of natural materials and *objets trouvés*. By the time that he designed the Maisons Jaoul in 1951–5, he had both accepted the charm of incorporating his clients' collection of artworks and antique furniture and gone a considerable distance to celebrating the personal and idiosyncratic culture of the domestic space (see pl.9.12). Ledges and niches were provided for the display of objects. Fenestration was carefully controlled to illuminate walls to best effect and avoid glare for the inhabitants. Wall surfaces were provided for hanging pictures. These are interiors crying out to be illustrated in colour, as indeed they were.[52]

Colour was a kind of test for the understanding of Modernism. Those who visited the domestic work of Le Corbusier, J.J.P. Oud, Hans

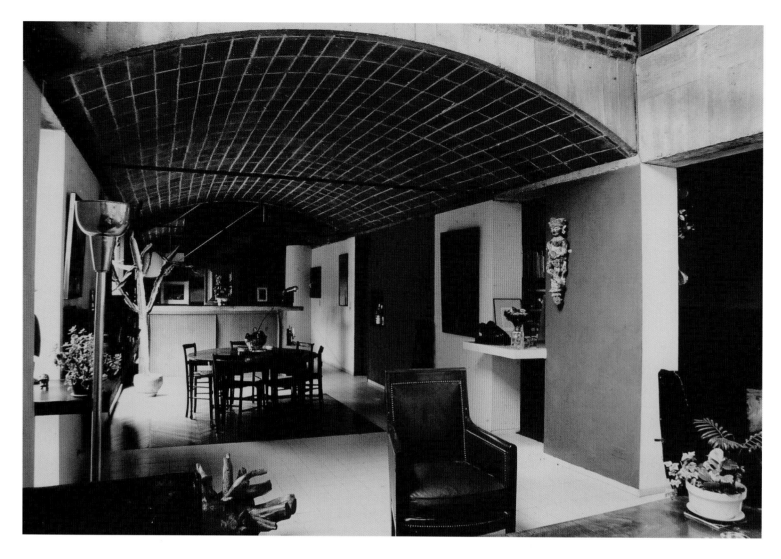

9.12
Le Corbusier, interior of
Maisons Jaoul, in *Maison et
Jardin*, 1956

Scharoun, Bruno Taut, Gerrit Rietveld or Kees Van der Vlught would have known that colour played a crucially important role in their interiors. But those whose experience was based on black and white illustrations formed an opinion of Modernism as colourless and inhuman.

Colour illustrations can be associated with a 'humane' populism, representing homes in all their characteristic warmth. This, for example, was the motivation for books such as Derek Patmore's *Colour schemes for the modern home* (1933).[53] But colour could also play on the other side of the 'Art' and 'Life' divide. The coloured axonometric rendering has a particular place in representations of the Modernist interior.[54] For the de Stijl architects, the axonometric was a means of representing top and bottom, front and back as weightless and abstract equivalents.[55]

It has been repeatedly claimed that the idea of comfort is at odds with the Modernist conception of the interior as 'a new realism of space and time'.[56] A widespread 'puritanical' movement just before and after the First World War in Germany led to a stripping away of ornament and objects and a lightening of the interior.[57] Old furniture (usually inherited) was wrong because it made outdated claims for social distinction, because it encouraged the preservation of the traditions of an older generation, because it caused unnecessary labour for the housewife and, most crucially in this context, because it messed up Modernist architectural space. This process accelerated in the 1920s, under the influence of the avant-garde art movements, towards an increasingly abstract and 'pure' interior, defined by walls, ceilings and floors and little else.

Representing architectural space

The problem with representing the modern interior, as the aesthetic of Modernism developed in the twentieth century, was that emphasis was laid on intangible qualities: space, movement through space and transparency. Hermann Muthesius had already hinted at this in the third volume of *Das Englische Haus* (1905):

> The interior is a whole, the essence of which lies, in fact in its totality, in its quality as space. In conceiving the interior as a work of art, therefore, the artist must first think of it as a space, that is, as the over-all form and the interrelationships of the space-enclosing surfaces.[58]

But representing 'over-all form' and 'space-enclosing surfaces' was not a simple matter. Jane Becket has traced the development of the interior conceived of as abstract space.[59] For architects, trying to represent as much as possible of their interiors led to a 'stretching' of space.

Le Corbusier's perspective drawings of his houses have come under scrutiny in recent literature.[60] Le Corbusier followed no precise rule of perspective. He combined a field of view of around 100° (or wider) with a treatment of the middle- and background viewed from a closer viewpoint. This avoided the excessive effect of tunnel vision that a very wide angled viewpoint should give. An extreme example of Le Corbusier's instinctive desire to open out the space in his renderings can be seen in a marginal sketch on the first of his drawings for the Villa Savoye (see pl.9.13).[61] In Le Corbusier's sketch, an impossible panoramic view is obtained whereby the wall on the right is pulled right round so that the window (extreme right) is actually directly behind the viewer and would join up with the near end of the window on the left.

The stripped out and space-expanded interior created difficulties for the photographer. A rarely reproduced interior of Mies's Lange House (1927–30, see pl.9.14) illustrates the problem. Despite the sculptures and paintings on the wall, a splendid oriental rug, built-in bookcases and a few examples of Lange's traditional furniture, the interior looks unavoidably empty in the black and white photograph.[62] What interests me here, however, is the technical problems of photographic representation and the difficulty of making these empty spaces aesthetically satisfying. Mies himself clearly believed that this, and almost all the other interior views of his 1920s houses, were unsatisfactory and refused to allow them to be published.[63] He made every effort to ensure that the photographic images that represented him in exhibitions and publications were those of the German Pavilion in Barcelona, the Tugendhat House (both 1929) and the exhibition house and apartment for a bachelor at the Bauausstellung exhibition, Berlin 1931. Furthermore, he ensured that all visual clutter, including even the chromed steel and glass doors that closed off the entrances to the

9.13
Le Corbusier, *marginal sketch of the Villa Savoye.* 1928. Fondation Le Corbusier, Paris

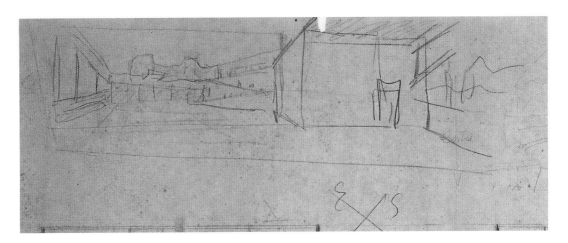

Barcelona Pavilion, were removed for the photographs.

The abstract interior

The modern architectural photograph of the domestic interior is typically taken with a wide-angle lens at an oblique angle, creating its formal effects through sharply inclined orthogonals, the play of light on surfaces and the contrast of reflective, matte or textured materials. Although not a house at all, the Barcelona Pavilion belongs to the genre of Mies's domestic architecture of the late 1920s and informed both the Tugendhat House, Brno (1929) and the single storey house he contributed to the Bauausstellung, Berlin, 1931. The architectural photograph tending towards formal abstraction best represents interiors in which the domes-

tic has been reduced to zero.[64] In the much reproduced photograph of the entrance (see pl.9.15), there is a lack of separation of outside and inside; at night, folding steel and glass doors were installed to close off the interior (three black marks in the ceiling reveal their location). Every conventional means of enclosure is rejected, just as the interior lacks any fixtures or identifying signs to indicate human usage. But in this photograph, the interior is indicated metaphorically by the contrast between green marble and glass and by the shadow line projected by the roof slab.

Mies had given the most evocative definition of the *Zeitgeist* principle in July 1923: 'Building art is the spatially apprehended will of the epoch. Alive. Changing. New.'[65] But how could space be represented?[66] In drawings, Mies

9.14
Mies van der Rohe,
Lange House, interior. 1927–30

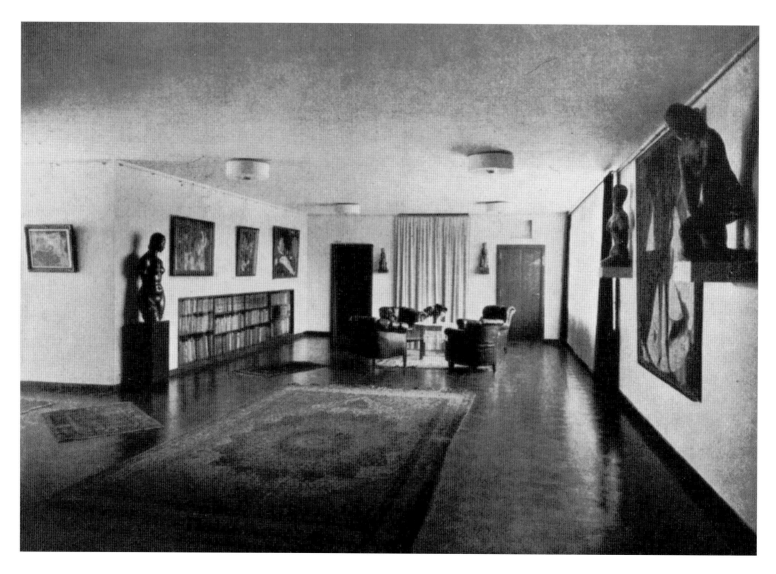

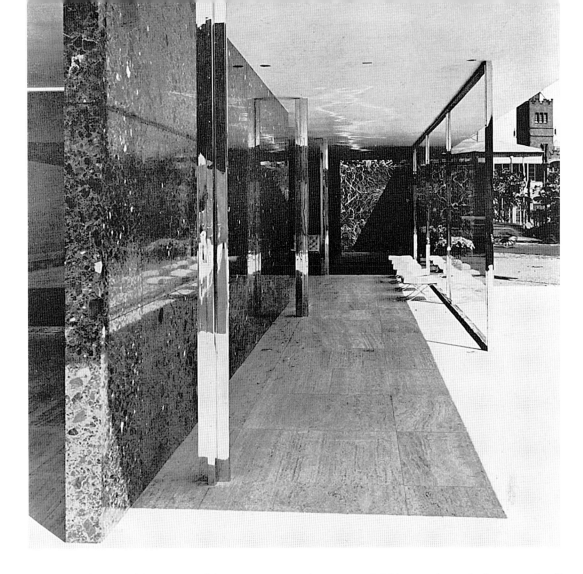

could use the visual language of abstract art to accentuate the transparency and mystery of the spatial envelope to the maximum. In Mies's presentation drawings, delicately rendered in chalk or charcoal, he strove for effects of transparency, setting diagonally aligned walls of glass against plain walls and thin stanchions, all indicated in the most minimal possible way (see pl.9.16).

Mastering nature

An extreme representation of a Mies interior was the collage designed for Mr and Mrs Resor in America.[67] The main feature of the house was a rectangular living room with a picture window overlooking the Snake River in Jackson Hole, Wyoming. Mies represented this as a photograph of the view to the North surrounded by the ghostly presence of two thin stanchions and an implied spatial envelope indicated by a few lines in pencil (see pl.9.17). In another rendering, the view to the South is

shown, overlaid by a coloured photograph of Paul Klee's *Bunte Mahlzeit* (1928) and a strip of mahogany wood veneer.[68] Interiority is defined as a contemplation of nature from the detachment of an abstract interior.

For photographers, the problem has always been how to balance the bright light of an exterior with the interior. One approach, similar to Mies's Resor House collage, is to concentrate on the landscape, framed by the window.

In the wide open spaces of the American West, European architects such as Richard Neutra developed the opening out of the interior to extreme lengths, perfectly captured in the photographs of Julius Shulman. In one of the drawings for the James Moore house (1952), Neutra sketched this semi-glazed porch from the outside, showing the (male) client sitting under the overhang (outside) while two women stand inside.[69] The 'point of command' of the landscape from the indeterminate space of the porch or the

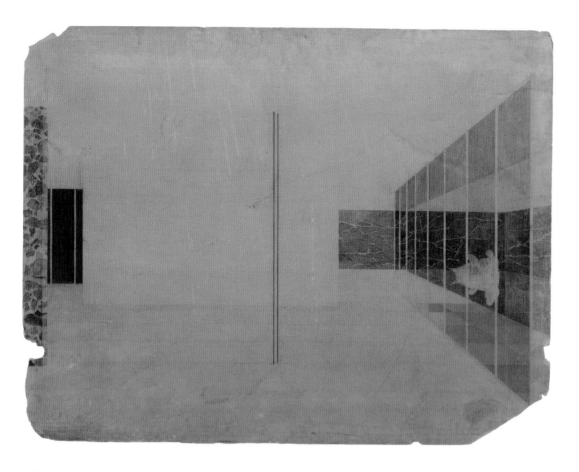

9.16
Mies van der Rohe, Barcelona
Pavilion. Presentation drawing.
1929. The Museum of Modern
Art, New York

fully glazed (and opening) window is a fundamental attribute of Modernist Utopia and is
represented photographically as if from behind
the viewer (see pl.9.19).[70] Lavin cites the client's
wife, Orline Moore, as identifying this corner
with 'the inter-relation of Nature without and
living within' which was capable of eradicating
the 'depression which we feel'.[71] Among Neutra's Californian clients, many of them committed
environmentalists with a range of spiritual and
psychological interests ranging from Krishna-
murti to Wilhelm Reich, exposure to landscape
was both a therapeutic comfort and a challenge.[72]
Neutra developed a theory of 'careful studies and
experiments on subjective comfort, physiologi-
cally analyzed'.[73] But many Modernist clients
would have agreed with Anastasia Clother's
heart-felt cry:

> In fact from the inside of a Neutra
> house, one has the feeling of being
> outside inside, if you get what I mean.
> I don't exactly. That's my trouble with
> Neutra. I don't want to be outside. I

don't want to be one of my neighbors.
Maybe as a well adjusted person in this
contemporary world, I just don't fit.[74]

Modern photography could gratify architects
by the representation of extreme transparency.
And Modernist architects set challenges to
photographers by their desire to represent their
interiors in increasingly wide-angle views.
Richard Neutra explored the physiological
psychology of architecture and, by implication,
of architectural photographs in particular, in a
fascinating book of photographs by Julius Shulman, *Mystery and Realities of the Site*, supported
by extended captions.[75] Architecture existed to
place man in direct contact with an unpopulated nature, whose therapeutic value on the
devitalized modern man would be certain and
regenerative.[76] This experience of nature was
to be controlled to reinforce the 'neurologically
salubrious agents' and avoid disturbing, disor-
ganized or dangerous features of the outside
world. In the terms in which he expressed
this principle, it is clear how closely Neutra

associated the architectural sensations he strove for with the physical state of nakedness.

> There is a natural gratification in feeling visually unimpeded and in being free for action, at liberty, not caged and incarcerated. A person may look at large view windows of a living room with their unobstructed panoramic possibilities, and every time he does so he may feel like taking a breath of relaxation, gratification and relief.[77]

He extended this approach to the interior, advocating the provision of 'continuous, *smooth and even* distribution of stimuli' across wall and floor surfaces.[78] 'Sociologically, nearness, if undesired, connotes oppression, perhaps danger, or infringement on privacy' and distress could be produced by 'visual conflict, friction … visual collision … optical litter'.[79] Leaving aside the revealing sexual implications of these views, coming from a notorious misogynist, the nature of the task for his photographer becomes clearer. He had to reduce 'visual conflict, friction … visual collision' in his architectural views. One mechanism was that of controlling the sense of distance, contrasting smooth surfaces close to the camera with more textured effects in the background, manipulating perceptual illusion.

A photograph that has escaped from its original context to stand for a whole attitude to architecture and architectural photography is Julius Shulman's view of Neutra's Kaufman House (see pl.9.18).[80] Simon Niedenthal makes the undeniable statement, 'The Kaufman house is perhaps one of the most striking examples of the way in which a house can become identified with its photographic image. As such it offers an irresistible entry point into the current debate on representation.'[81] Niedenthal demonstrates how this photograph, one of many taken during a three-day shoot, was first published in America in *Architectural Forum* in December 1949, after two years of discussions in which Henry Wright, the journal's editor, had played a crucial role.[82] Of the two spreads, the first shows external views (including this one) while the second illustrated plans and interiors, including one of Shulman's characteristic views towards the landscape through a plate glass window, with a table in the foreground indicating the place of the viewer. When *Life* published the twilight view, however, on 11 April 1949, it occupied a two-page bleed, over the heading 'glamourized houses'. Here, the photograph has broken free from its physical object; the subject of the piece is Shulman, and his ability to make houses 'look dramatic'.[83] It was from this moment that the photograph began its life as a cult image. Why has it been so influential? There are aesthetic reasons: the mysterious lighting,

9.17

Mies van der Rohe, *Resor House: Interior perspective of living room (view through north glass wall)*. 1938. The Museum of Modern Art, New York

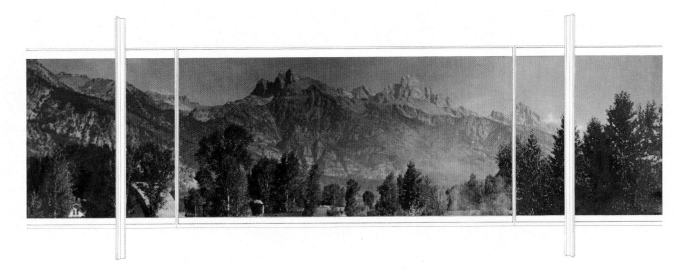

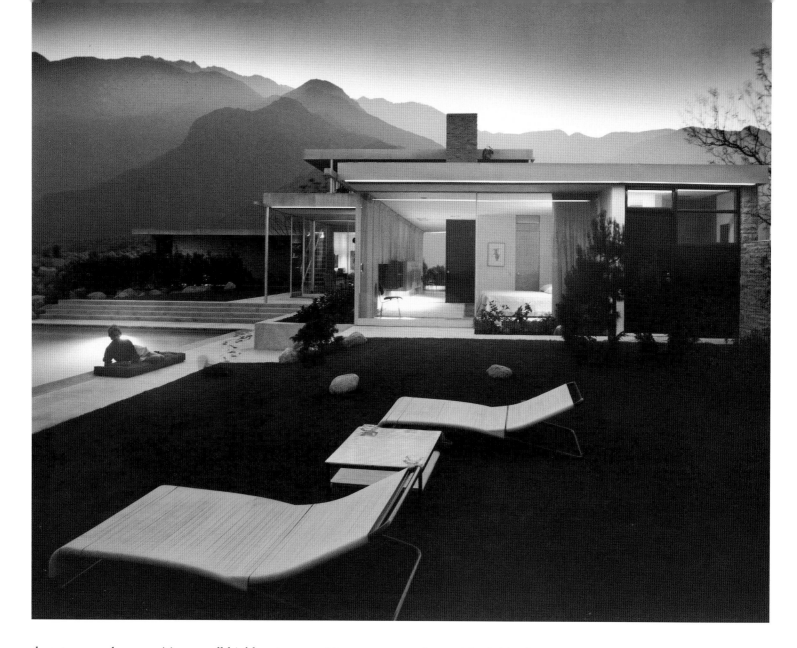

deep tones and composition are all highly satisfying. To create the illusion of a perfect balance between dwindling daylight and artificial light, Shulman resorted to trickery, taking three separate exposures, registering the natural light in a long exposure before turning on the house lights for a shorter, second exposure. For the third exposure, he switched on the pool lights and asked Mrs Kaufman to pose on a mattress to mask off the glare. Psychologically, the photograph drives home the analogy between the transparent house and the female body. The carefully posed white daybeds in the foreground, reinforced by the horizontal body framed by the pool, more than hints at the gratification of sensual pleasure.[84] The brightly illuminated interior becomes a voyeuristic architectural metaphor.

Neutra seems to have picked this photograph from all the others of the Kaufman house even before the *Life* issue.[85] Since, as Dione Neutra said, 'All the clients came through publications, I would say', Neutra clearly identified the image he thought would bring him most work.[86] Like all architects, Neutra made it clear that a photograph is only a fixed and 'frozen' moment, whereas, 'Architecture is not frozen music – it is nothing frozen at all! It plays on us in time, the vivid time of our living responses which melt one moment into the next'.[87] But he was ready to admit that a good photograph could make his design intention 'appear again, clearly hinted at least, in a still picture'.[88] The history and criticism of Modernism have turned around images which have 'hinted' at architectural design intentions.

9.18
Richard Neutra, Kaufman House. Photograph by Julius Shulman. 1946.

9.19
Richard Neutra, Porch, James Moore House, Ojai. Photograph by Julius Shulman. 1952.

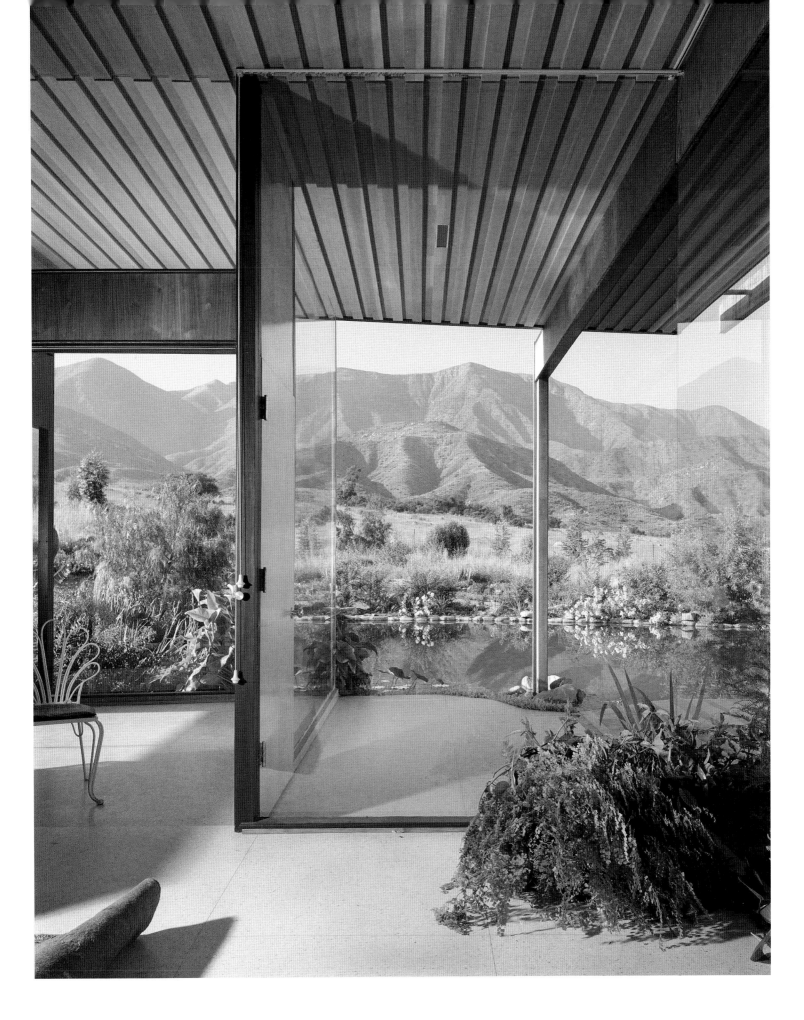

Hollywood Studio Design: the Great Hall of Xanadu

Christopher Frayling

In 1926, the architect and interior designer Robert Mallet-Stevens wrote of the big sets of Hollywood films (only recently emancipated from the flat back-drops and fixed viewpoints of the theatre) that 'the décor ought to present the character even before he or she appears – to indicate the character's social situation, tastes, habits, way of life, personality. The décor ought to be an integral part of the narrative and the action, and can become its organising principle...'. These prophetic thoughts were later reprinted as *L'Art cinematographique*. Sometimes, enough drawings, photographs and studio memos have survived, to guide historians in detail through all stages of this still under-researched design process in the studio era.

One such case is Orson Welles's *Citizen Kane* (1941; supervising art director Van Nest Polglase; 'associate' – the real designer – Perry Ferguson). The cavernous Great Hall of Charles Foster Kane's palace of Xanadu, assembled at RKO studio, consisted of an imposing stone staircase, a vast fireplace flanked by

9.20 and **9.21**
Orson Welles, *Citizen Kane*,
Mercury / RKO Radio. 1941

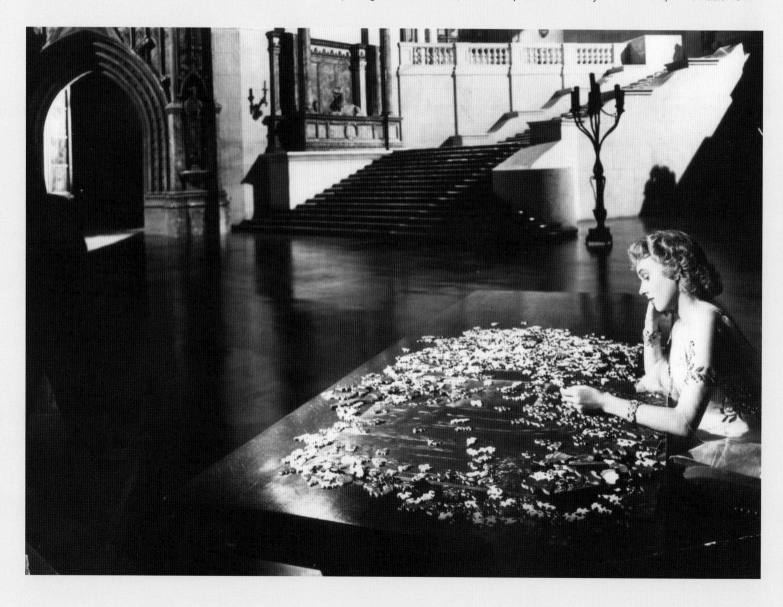

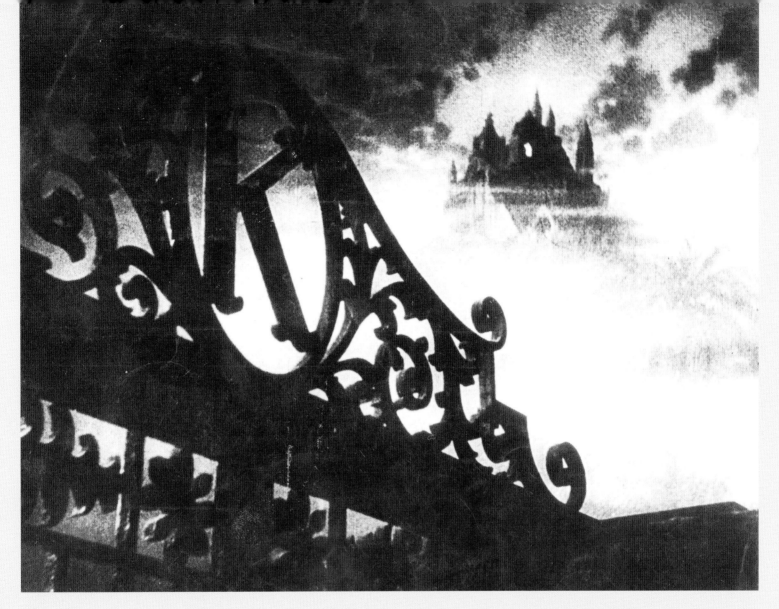

classical sculptures (loosely based on the equivalent in the Great Dining Hall of William Randolph Hearst's San Simeon) and a Gothic cathedral-style entrance – all of them evidence of Kane's mania for collecting on a grand and eclectic scale. The original script had explicitly referred to 'Int. Great Hall … massive renaissance fireplace, baroque candelabra … [and] vast Gothic windows'. In turning these words into preliminary drawings, the art department went through studio reference files (under 'Palaces – Italian Renaissance') and found two illustrations – of a forecourt and staircase, and a hallway – in William J. Anderson's *The Architecture of the Renaissance in Italy*. Some of the resultant drawings were 'okayed' for further development, but as they became a practicable set various modifications occurred – partly for budgetary reasons. An existing staircase and cathedral entrance were found somewhere on the RKO lot, and two interiors in the script – a living room and a hallway – were combined, with the 8-m (25-ft)

wide neo-Renaissance fireplace (made in the RKO plaster shop) serving as a kind of proscenium arch for scenes of the Kanes's disintegrating marriage. While Susan plays jigsaws on the shiny floor (RKO was producing Fred Astaire musicals at the time), husband Charles walks yards across the vast emptiness just to reach his favourite chair. 'Our home is *here*, Susan', echoes his voice, and it has a hollow ring to it. The gaps between the big props were filled with rolls of black velvet, which registered on film as deep space. As Perry Ferguson wrote, after the release of *Citizen Kane*, 'the camera's powers of suggestion' did the rest, especially when incongruous sculptures (a gargoyle, a classical goddess) were carefully placed in the foreground. Ferguson concluded that this 'much-discussed set' combined economy with appropriateness to the characters and story, by suggesting much more than really met the eye. It was a distinctive form of interior design, separate from – but related to – design in the real world.

Designing Lifestyles: retail catalogues

Harriet McKay

In Britain and North America furniture retailing in the nineteenth century grew dynamically. A rise in middle-class interest in expressing status through home furnishings brought about changes in distribution essential to meeting demand through urban outlets, particularly the department stores and specialist furniture shops, which began to lead the market after 1870. To capitalize on the purchasing power of the newly wealthy social group to whom they appealed, retailers were concerned to develop strategies for keeping ahead of the market. Window displays and room-sets provided examples of ready-made interiors that would boost the confidence of the potential but uncertain purchaser; suppliers frequently also offered a complete showroom-based interior decoration service, a tradition that went back to the beginning of the nineteenth century.

During this period too, with the advent of cheaply available printing methods, the illustrated retail catalogue was realized as an important selling technique. Complete with estimates for the various available schemes, these pamphlets offered both flexibility and accessibility, through mail-order services and easily understood pricing.

Catalogues were to prove particularly successful in the United States where both the burgeoning population and attendant building boom created a vibrant market and geographical distance made mail-order an attractive option. Most prominently, the Montgomery Ward and Sears, Roebuck & Co. (see pl.9.22) catalogues offered to deliver any item of furniture anywhere in the country.

Attempting to ship furniture over even greater distances, the British firm Heal and Sons (established in 1834) had produced a catalogue during the 1860s illustrating 'Bedsteads, Bedding, and Bedroom Furniture for India, China and the Colonies', and as early as the 1840s, John Harris, Heal and Sons' founder, had realized the value of catalogue retailing. In two canny moves to maintain public profile and increase sales, advertisements for the United

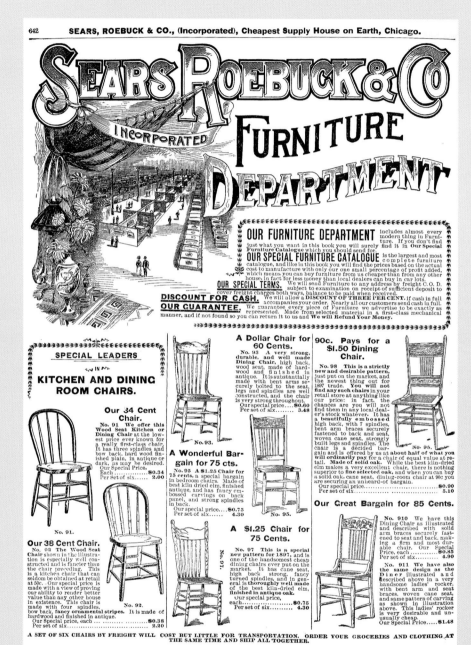

Kingdom market, pioneering the idea of using room sets as illustrative material, were placed in many of the instalments of Charles Dickens's publications from the 1830s onwards and during the Depression years, Heals launched economy lines (see pl.9.23).

The trend established by the furniture stores, and

9.22
'The Furniture Department' from *Sears, Roebuck & Co. Catalogue*. 1897.
NAL: 603.AB.1080

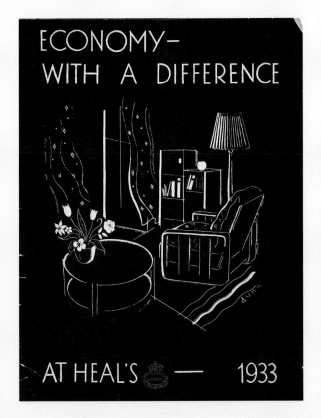

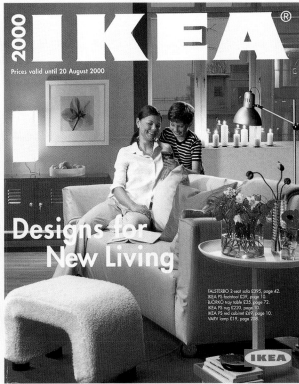

cemented by catalogues for creating holistic schemes was to continue in Britain in the second half of the twentieth century with the arrival of the 'concept' store. Just as in the previous century, new shops – amongst which Terence Conran's Habitat, founded in 1964, was foremost – arose to service a recently affluent generation of consumers, intent on purchasing a cost-efficient interior, presented to them as room-sets to accommodate a lifestyle. First published in 1966, the Habitat catalogue was uniquely tied in with the history and development of the wider company. It was conceived, like the shop itself, as selling a complete environment and 'not only as a selling tool but a guide to decorating a home and a statement about lifestyle' (see pl.9.25).

Also employing the room-set device to illustrate its tens of thousands of home furnishings and domestic items, the Swedish company IKEA was to dominate the global market in the late twentieth century (see pl.9.24). The design group, founded by Ingrar Kamrad in 1943, produced its first catalogue in 1951 and by 2002 had a distribution figure of 110 million across 34 languages. Writing in the *Guardian* in June 2004, Oliver Burkeman summed up the British relationship with

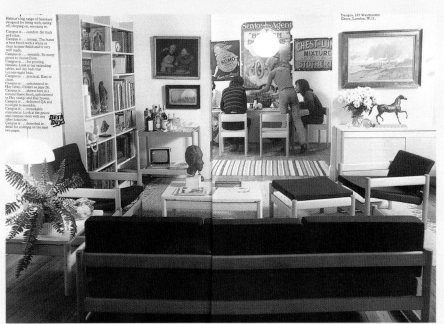

lifestyle consumption of the domestic interior through the IKEA model: 'for a broad demographic swathe of Britain, Ikea has designed our lives…. We love it and hate it, rely on it and satirise it … as if it were not a shop at all but something far more emotively substantial: a football team … or the government.'

10

'Anthropology at Home': domestic interiors in British film and fiction of the 1930s and 1940s

Rod Mengham

AT SOME TIME BETWEEN the publication of Walter Greenwood's novel *Love on the Dole,* in 1933, and the release of the film version, directed by John Baxter, in 1941, a quiet revolution had taken place in the representation of the British domestic interior. Novel and film are both set in Salford, and commence with a reflection on the northern working-class home. The film dwells carefully on the arrangements of what D.H. Lawrence would have called the 'house-place', a kitchen and living room combined. In the film, this room is dominated by a massive kitchen range, initially screened by a housewife with her back to the camera, holding a newspaper in front of the range to create a draught of air. The newspaper catches fire, suggesting immediately that nothing works straightforwardly in this environment, that merely inhabiting this space and functioning in it from day to day requires a certain amount of ingenuity and inventiveness: a state of constant adaptability. Baxter's 'house-place' is an extremely crowded and disordered space, with a mixture of decorative and serviceable objects hanging on the walls or standing on individual, purpose-built shelves. Clearly, everything has its place and seems to be there for a reason, but the whole ensemble is visually chaotic. The effect of disorder is a powerful marker of specific histories; the mess has been created by particular individuals, by personal preferences, interests and habits. It is very striking that, during a period when the threat of standardization was felt to issue from a left-wing politics associated with proletarian life-styles, Baxter's working-class domestic interior seems to offer itself as a guarantee of individualism.

The single most important difference between the opening of the film and the opening of the novel is that none of the descriptive details of 'mess' is present in the original fiction. Greenwood's narrative focuses not on the domestic interior but on what one might call the domestic exterior:

> The doorsteps and window-sills of the houses are worn hollow. Once a week, sometimes twice, the women clean them with brown or white rubbing stone; the same with portions of the pavement immediately outside their front doors. And they glare at any pedestrians who unavoidably muddy their handiwork in traversing the strip. Some women there are whose lives are dedicated to an everlasting battle with the forces of soot and grime.[1]

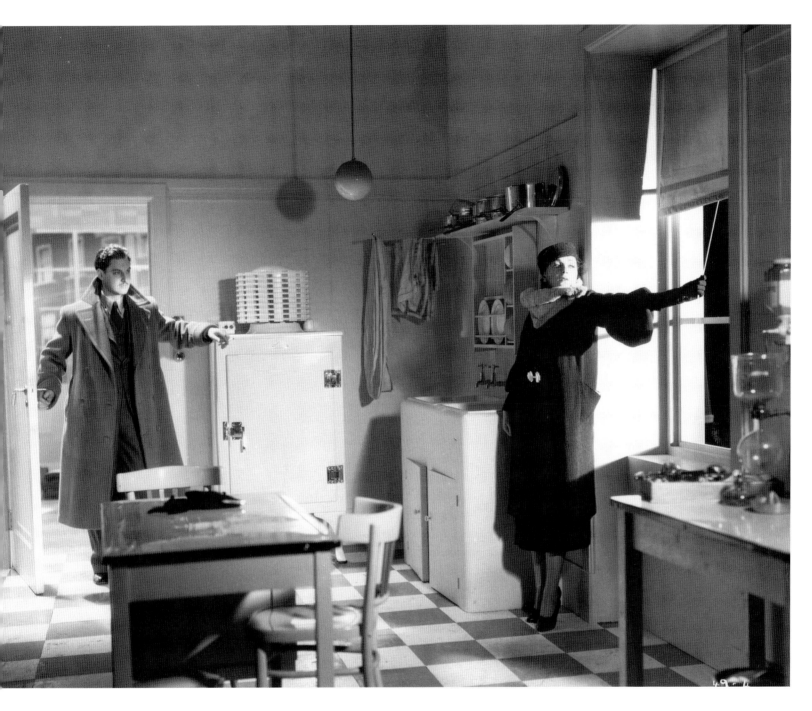

10.1

Alfred Hitchcock, *The Thirty Nine Steps*. Gaumont-British Picture Corporation. 1935

This contrast can be accounted for by the fact that during the period between the publication of the novel and the release of the film, British film and fiction went indoors with a vengeance, both literally and conceptually. This cultural introversion was not confined to film and fiction, but was equally apparent in poetry and photography, as well as in the genre of social reportage that became especially popular during the 1930s. It is possible to speak of an 'ethnographic turn' occurring in a wide range of cultural activities, with film and fiction in particular sharing a project that involved the observation of the English, in a way that perceived them as if for the first time, as if from the point of view of the anthropological stranger.

One of the most celebrated examples of this form of enquiry was George Orwell's *The Road to Wigan Pier*, first published in 1937. Some 11 of its 32 badly reproduced photographic plates featured working-class domestic interiors in London – in Poplar, Stepney, Bethnal Green,

Limehouse – as well as various locations in South Wales. In the same year, the social survey movement 'Mass Observation' was launched with a manifesto entitled 'Anthropology at Home.'[2] One year earlier, Bill Brandt's career as cultural observer had started with the publication of an album of photographs entitled *The English at Home*. Structured in terms of pairs of images, this book offered a series of pointed contrasts between the living conditions of rich and poor.

But perhaps the single most influential and authoritative means by which the 'ethnographic turn' made its presence felt was the development of documentary film. Numerically, documentaries represented a small proportion of the British film industry's output, and the audiences involved were relatively limited. But the conceptual impact of documentary film was considerable, with many of its aims and procedures being absorbed into mainstream cinema, as well as into other art forms.

Legal and financial pressures on the British film industry also contributed to an emphasis on British culture during the 1930s. The Cinematograph Films Act of 1927 required a quota of the films shown on British screens to be British-made. The 1938 Act of the same name reduced that quota quite substantially. The period in between was an unusually rich one for British cinema, not only in the number of productions but also in terms of the range of different kinds of films produced: there were historical costume dramas, musicals, thrillers and melodramas, as well as documentaries. There was also a popular demand for British films. In terms of production companies, the second most popular source of films during the 1930s in Britain was Gaumont-British, coming second only to MGM, despite the fact that its output was roughly a quarter of that of the major Hollywood producers.[3] Documentaries were not the most popular films of the decade in terms of box-office success, but the principles of documentary infiltrated many of the other genres of film being screened.

What were the 'principles of documentary'? This was the subject, and the title, of an essay by John Grierson, a key figure in the establishment and development of the British documentary movement. Grierson focused on three desiderata. First, the documentary method would involve photographing the 'living scene and the living story', as opposed to the studio practice of photographing acted stories against artificial backgrounds. Secondly, the 'original (or native)' actor and scene should be regarded as the best guides to a 'screen interpretation of the modern world.' Lastly, Grierson believed in the power and scope of the unprompted gesture; his formulation is worth quoting at some length:

> We believe that the materials and the stories thus taken from the raw can be finer (more real in the philosophic sense) than the acted article. Spontaneous gesture has a special value on the screen. Cinema has a sensational capacity for enhancing the movement which tradition has formed or time worn smooth. Its arbitrary rectangle specially reveals movement; it gives it maximum pattern in space and time. Add to this that documentary can achieve an intimacy of knowledge and effect impossible to the shimsham mechanics of the studio, and the lily-fingered interpretations of the metropolitan actor.[4]

Grierson was completely uninterested in the expressive capacity of gesture to reveal clues about individual psychology, focusing instead on the way that bodies could be read in relation to a shared culture, a collective repertoire of gestures. His own distinction between 'romantic' documentary, drawn towards examples of the 'noble savage' – a classic instance being Robert Flaherty's *Nanook of the North* (1921) – and 'realistic' documentary, concerned mostly with modern, urban social content, involves a perception of the former as celebrating the individual, while the latter is understood as subduing this emphasis. The demarcation, however, is an unstable one. In a similar fashion, Grierson was to insist that young directors should choose whether to 'go documentary' or 'go studio', in the firm belief that they could not do both, whereas the history of British cinema has shown a tendency towards mixture and ambivalence. Greenwood's *Love on the Dole* was only one of a number of novels published in the late 1920s and early 1930s that were felt to constitute a proletarian school of literature. Readers might expect such books to prioritize typical, rather than individual, experience, and yet, as we have seen, John Baxter was to exploit Greenwood's settings for resisting and even reversing some of the usual expectations. In other novels of the same period, this complex attitude towards the domestic interior was already in place, as in John Hampson's *Saturday Night at the Greyhound* (1931): 'The Greyhound kitchen was full of relics. Incoming people brought this thing, outgoing folk left that. Mrs Tapin knew everything in the room, and its history. Skelts left behind the shining Welsh dresser with its lustre jugs and blue china'.[5]

Mrs Tapin, charwoman at the Greyhound Inn, has seen a succession of landlords come and go. The household articles compose a palimpsest of their arrivals and departures. In a culture of relative impoverishment, the acquisition of every object is an event, and the individual's relationship with the object is one of unusual intensity. With this in mind, it is perhaps unsurprising that the relationship between the well-off and their domestic interiors should be much less intimate, and may even involve indifference. Henry Green's novel *Party Going* (1939) suggests that a uniformity of taste is much less likely to stem from a Marxist-inspired proletarian culture, than from conditions of affluence:

> Amabel's flat had been decorated by the same people Max had his flat done by, her furniture was like his, his walls like hers, their chair coverings were alike and even their ash trays were the same. There were in London at this time more than one hundred rooms identical with these. Even what few

books there were bore the same titles and these were dummies…. If their houses were burned down they had only to go to the same man they all thought best to get another built, if they lost anything or even if it was mislaid the few shops they went to would be glad to lend whatever it might be, up to elephants or rhinos, until what had been missed could be replaced.[6]

Despite this staggering degree of uniformity, Green's narrator is at pains to point out that the replication of home furnishings is no guarantee of the replication of sensibilities. Standardization says precisely nothing about individual backgrounds; what it does speak to, however, is the projection of identical aspirations, of converging desires: 'and by so doing they proclaimed their service to the kind of way they lived or rather to the kind of way they passed their time.'[7] These up-to-the-minute domestic interiors have no history, precisely because what they lay claim to is a way of managing the future.

Something very similar is being proposed by Alfred Hitchcock's 1935 film version of John Buchan's novel *The Thirty-Nine Steps* (1915). Buchan's original text begins with a chapter entitled 'The Man Who Died', set mostly in Richard Hannay's London bachelor-flat. Almost no details are provided in the description of this apartment, whose location is given as 'the first floor in a new block behind Langham Place.'[8] References are made to a 'smoking room' and a 'tray of drinks', but to little else, and there is nothing to consolidate an effect of novelty in this recently furnished interior. Hitchcock's departure from the text is decisive, as it often is with regard to both plot and setting. The 1935 version of Hannay's flat is totally modernist: streamlined, ruthlessly ordered and systematically pared-down in design (see pl. 10.1). Much of the furniture has a highly technologized finish, especially the mahogany and glass drinks cabinet (as opposed to Buchan's humble tray). There are built-in cupboards, black and white rectangular floor patterns, and walls that are all-over white and almost completely bare. Fixtures, fittings and furniture are given highly simplified structures. The ensemble is completely divested of individuating detail: there are no keepsakes, no objects that are in any way incongruous with the slightly futuristic scenario. But what is chiefly remarkable in this story about fifth columnists, about the infiltration of German agents into British everyday life, is that this flat has unmistakable elements of Bauhaus design, especially in the windows with their rows of horizontal separators. What Hitchcock's carefully contrived film-set implies is that it is precisely in the domestic interior, in the sphere of our everyday lives, where we perform the actions that 'time has worn smooth', that cultural identity is being negotiated, and even contested.

Hitchcock's slightly earlier film, *The Man Who Knew Too Much* (1934), had also been concerned with the presence of foreign agents on British soil. The action takes place mainly in Wapping, with widely varying settings that nonetheless mirror one another in covert fashion. A group of political assassins operates out of the headquarters of a religious sect known as the 'Tabernacle of the Sun'. The elements of this space are anticipated in a visit to a dentist's surgery, and echoed later by events at the Albert Hall, where the assassination is supposed to take place. Both surgery and temple are equipped with padded doors to muffle the cries of those being operated on one way or another. The singing of the congregation and playing of the organ in the Tabernacle perform a similar function, and are paralleled by the musical performance at the Albert Hall, where a crescendo is intended to cover the sound of the sniper's pistol-shot. These correlations between the very un-English seeming Tabernacle, the familiar dentist's office and the national monument of the Albert Hall, suggest the coexistence of the everyday and the exotic, the domestic and the alien. In the climactic shoot-out between the spies and the British authorities, the police commandeer the living rooms and bedrooms of a row of working-class terraced homes. This violent intrusion of international conflict into the domestic interior is accentuated by the remark of one police marksman, improvising a barricade with a mattress that he notes is 'still warm'.

After 1939, this culture of suspicion developed at times into a paranoid anxiety about the scope of fifth column activity on the home front. During the early war years in particular, much ink and celluloid was used up in the imagining of treachery at home. The most well-known representation of Nazi invasion of the domestic interior was a tableau in the American film *Mrs Miniver* (1942), shot almost entirely in the studio. A more revealing version of the same basic scenario, made in the same year, was the British *Went the Day Well* (1942) directed by Alberto Cavalcanti, who photographed the crucial scenes in an English village location. The fictional village is seen being infiltrated by an advance column of German invaders dressed as British soldiers. The turncoat they have been liaising with is regarded as the leading light in the village, and seems to be the most gentlemanly, although his treachery is emotional as well as political, since he has been cultivating a romantic attachment to the female protagonist, the vicar's daughter.

Quite early in the film, the camera pans over a wide range of domestic interiors, all of which demonstrate an adherence to principles of composure, order and, above all, symmetry. This depiction of a coherent and regulated lifestyle holds good for all classes, whether the household being observed is the working-class dwelling of the local policeman, the focus of whose ground floor is the 'Welsh dresser', a piece of furniture emblematic of 'simple', 'honest' lifestyles, or the vicarage with its numerous side-tables accommodating various symmetrical arrangements. The traitor's house is, of course, the most English – he is first seen sitting in one of a set of seventeenth-century style chairs with barley-sugar legs, hinting at the deep historical roots of this pervasive atmosphere of order and stability. But the order and symmetry also suggest, in fact require, a degree of doubling; they ensure the omnipresence of matching pairs, of mirror-images, of left

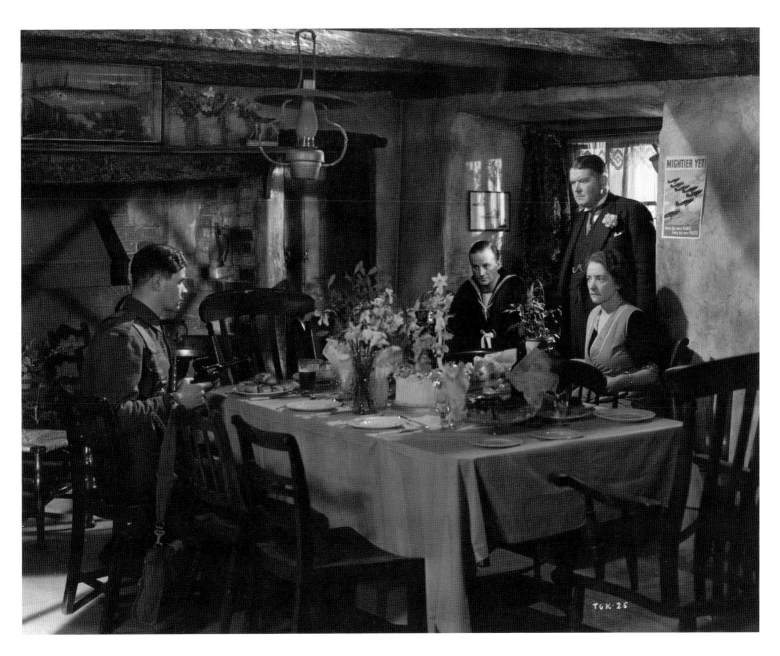

10.2

Alberto Cavalcanti, *Went the Day Well*. Ealing Studios. 1942

reflecting right. What this allows for is at least the possibility of a degree of opposition between the overt and the covert, between light and dark, between good and bad qualities in things that look the same. What it warns of is the possibility of a Nazi reality hiding within an English appearance.

Elizabeth Bowen's novel *The Heat of the Day* (1948) is another text that revolves around the dread of emotional and political betrayal during wartime. Set in the early years of the war, it features a high incidence of elaborate descriptions of different domestic interiors. These do not simply reflect the social positions and attitudes

of those who live in them, but seem to play a formative role in the construction of their identities. Holme Dene, the house in which the character suspected of treason has grown up, is organized along lines that make the tendency towards subterfuge seem inevitable:

The many twists of the passages had always made it impossible to see down them; some other member of the family, slightly hastening the step as one's own was heard, had always got round the next corner just in time. A pause just inside, to make sure that the coast was clear, had preceded the opening of any door, the emergence of anyone from a room. The unwillingness of the Kelways to embarrass themselves or each other by inadvertent meetings had always been marked. Their private hours, it could be taken, were spent in nerving themselves for inevitable family confrontations such as meal-times, and in working onto their faces the required expression of having nothing to hide.[9]

The necessity for concealment, the maintenance of barriers between different members of the household, is conceived of in terms of indirectness and obstruction. But the violent removal of screens, the loss of any sure means of keeping other people at a safe distance, is experienced as catastrophically unsettling; becoming more unnerving as the likelihood of bomb-damage increased during the Blitz:

> That autumn, she was living in lodgings in a house in a square: raising the sash of her bedroom window—which, glassless since two or three nights ago, ran up with a phantom absence of weight—she leaned out and called to the square's gardener, impassively at work just inside the railings with rake and barrow…. The non-existence of her window, the churchyard hush of the square, the grit which had drifted on to her dressing-table all became ominous for the first time. More than once she reached for the telephone which was out of order. Trying to dress in haste in the blinding sunshine, she threw away any time she had gained by standing still while something inside her head, never quite a thought, made felt a sort of imprisoned humming.[10]

The sense of entrapment does not issue from a literal confinement, since the various membranes separating the character from the outside world have all become permeable. Rather, the feeling of captivity derives from a sudden awareness of exposure, of vulnerability to interference. Domestic interiors during the Blitz became open to the passage of glass and grit, doors and windows became difficult and sometimes impossible to close. The war entered into the most private of enclaves.[11]

One of the most remarkable aspects of the domestic interiors in *Went the Day Well* is their ability to accommodate what comes into them from the outside: breezes rustling the curtains, typical country noises, huge quantities of cut flowers, all things that *invade*, pacifically of course, a variety of deep, and deeply English, interiors (see pl.10.2). The presence of flowers indoors is suggestive of the classic wartime scenario of the bombed house, where the interior is now exterior, and where the havens of domestic intimacy have been torn open and exposed, transformed into a seedbed for various wild flowers (most iconically, the rose bay willow-herb). Michael Powell and Emeric Pressburger's seminal film *The Life and Death of Colonel Blimp* (1945) finishes with a scene in which the protagonist, Clive Candy, is seen inspecting the ruins of a bombed house (his own), together with his young female adjutant and his German friend and adversary. Candy's house is now just a shell, and is being used as an official water-tank. Its interior has become a great reflecting pool, whose surface is broken by falling leaves. As the three figures bending over the pool are reflected on its surface, the soundtrack evokes Candy's memory of an earlier moment when his dead sweetheart had anticipated a future similar scenario. The fact that the dead sweetheart had been physically identical to the young adjutant (both played by Deborah Kerr) means that this reflection of different ages, classes and nationalities turns the domestic interior – or the loss of it – into a threshold between a past and a future whose relations need to be revised, reconfigured and projected anew. Candy, whose outdated chivalric ethos has been side-lined by the military authorities, becomes determined to regard his being superseded by the modernizing values of the next generation as part of a natural cycle (indicated by the presence in the tank of the autumn leaves) rather than a traumatic form of historical discontinuity.

Powell and Pressburger's film, already anticipating the end of the war and victory, can afford to negotiate the relations of past and future with some confidence. Earlier attempts to tackle a similar subject matter were much less sure-footed. William Sansom's stories of fire-fighting in the Blitz, for example, engage with the process of creating ruins before the survivors have had a chance to acclimatize to the aftermath of destruction. The extraordinary text 'Fireman Flower' employs imagery almost identical to that favoured by Powell and Pressburger, in the course of a destructive confrontation between the claims of the past and the future where the future remains almost entirely abstract and beyond conceptual reach: 'One wishes to envisage the future: one cannot: one casts around for a substitute: one substitutes the picture of the past, sufficiently alien from the present, a vision – yet one that can be controlled.'[12] In Sansom's text, the vision of the past takes the form of a dream-like domestic interior, magically intact at the centre of an immense warehouse fire. The reflective surface of Clive Candy's pool is paralleled by the apparition of a tall mirror that Flower encounters just before entering the mysterious room. This device locates him with reference to the time, as well as the space, he has just come from: 'In front the reflection of his past masqueraded as the darkling ghost of the future.'[13] In order to struggle free from the past and project a meaningful future, Flower needs to shatter this image. When he emerges from the room, the mirror has vanished, but the means by which this victory is achieved remain obscure, conveying the psychological uncertainty of the historical moment to which the story is tied.

The bombed houses of the Second World War provided British culture with some of its most disturbing images of the domestic interior. The longevity of many of the bombsites made it inevitable that a succession of different meanings would accrue to them: they were both elegies to interrupted lives and symbols of national defiance. But when the war ended

and the threat of further raids was removed, it was striking how quickly the denuded interior could become a back-drop for the acting out of alternative futures. Carol Reed's brooding *The Third Man* (1949) used the ruins of Vienna in the immediate post-war period to convey the instability of moral and political structures. But among films set in the debris of London, the bombed house became the focal point for a competition between widely varying social blueprints.

The very first Ealing comedy, Charles Crichton's *Hue and Cry* (1947), takes place in a devastated London, where a very high proportion of the scenes are set in the damaged interiors of ordinary working-class homes (see pl.10.3). The dilapidated version of the family home becomes the natural habitat for members of the juvenile gang at the centre of the action. *Hue and Cry* could almost be said to inaugurate a tradition in which the juvenile gang becomes a crucial presence in post-war British film culture. Changes in the character of the juvenile gang serve as indicators of broader social change (compare *Hue and Cry* with *Lord of the Flies* (1963) and *A Clockwork Orange* (1971), for example). Interestingly, the gang in Crichton's film is perceived as the source – indeed the only source – of moral renewal in a post-war world where nearly all the adults are corrupt. Policemen and traders are routinely complicit with the activities of the other gang in the film, the gang of thieves who are eventually outwitted by the youths. The children's occupation of the space of the ruined domestic interior involves a mimicry and distortion of adult housekeeping and various familiar chores. But this takes place within the context of building a collective identity, outside the family structure, in a society of equals where rivalries are good-natured and superficial, and where everyone is united by a common purpose. The destruction of the domestic interior symbolizes the possibility of replacing the values of the past with a more communitarian ethos.

There is a very different approach to the idea of community in *Passport to Pimlico* (1949), a comedy scripted two years later by the same

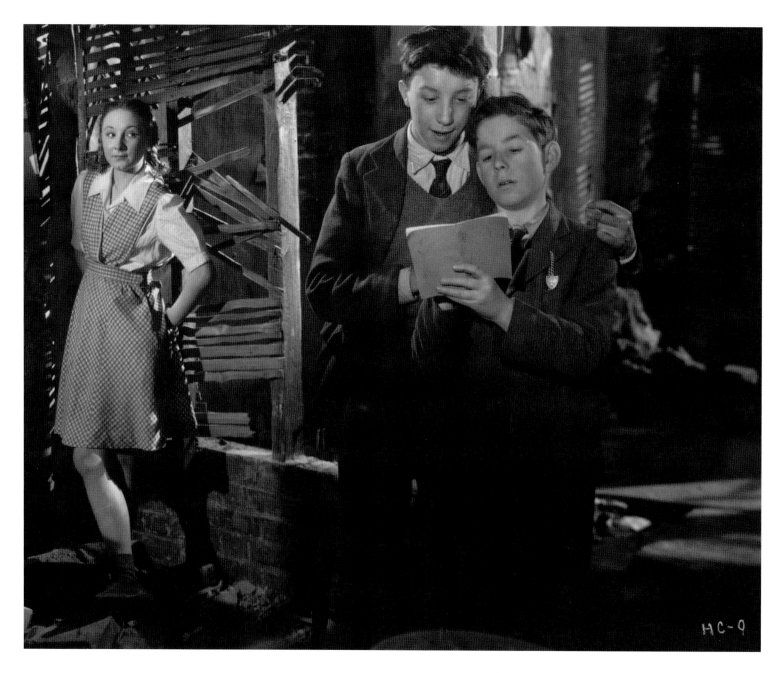

writer T.E.B. Clarke, but directed by Henry Cornelius. Certain subtle changes have taken place in the layout and the furnishings of the 'average' domestic interior. Sets have been dressed to show the near-universal separation of the dining room from the kitchen; there are writing desks in working-class parlours, and a solitary television set in the sitting room of the local spiv. Once again, however, the most significant interiors are partly destroyed. The action is set in a Pimlico neighbourhood, dominated by, and indeed centred on, a large, bomb-damaged square, in which the front wall

of nearly every house is missing. Right at the heart of this huge array of externalized domestic interiors is where another juvenile gang disturbs and sets off a large, unexploded bomb (see pl.10.4).

The new act of destruction results in the discovery of a fifteenth-century tomb under the foundations of one of the derelict houses. The whole premise of the film, and the stimulus for much of its comic business, depends on the retrieval of a manuscript from the site that proves that Pimlico is legally a part of Burgundy. The outcome of this revelation, in

10.3

Charles Crichton, *Hue and Cry*. Ealing Studios. 1947

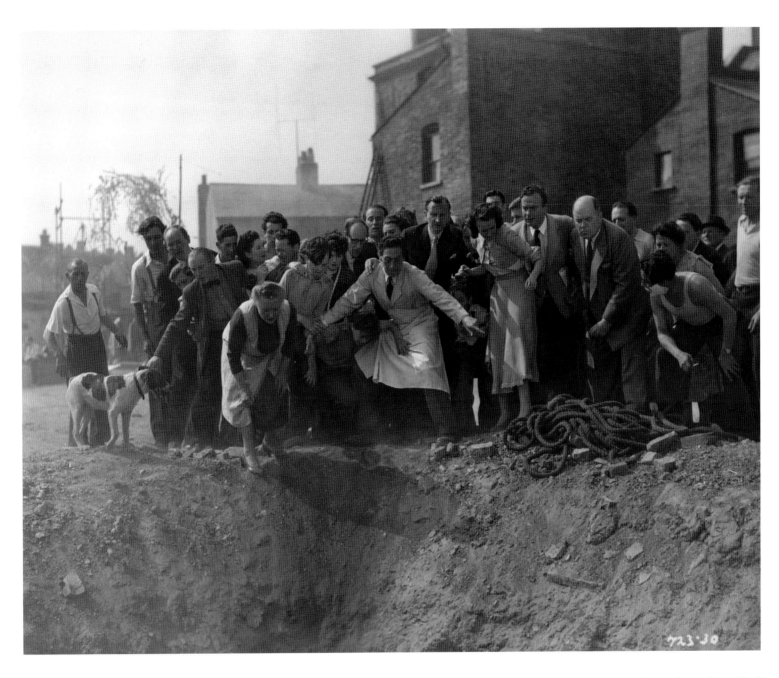

10.4
Henry Cornelius, *Passport to Pimlico*. Ealing Studios. 1949

an era of rationing and of the tight control of the movement of goods, is that the newly independent Pimlico becomes a haven for black market activity, which a hastily assembled ruling council decides to legitimize. This opportunism suggests that buried deep within the culture, as within the family home, is a national character wedded to both individualism and solidarity as well as to enterprise, free trade and nonconformism. The paradoxical nature of this *laissez-faire* solidarity is epitomized in the brilliant line: 'We're English. We've always been English. And it's precisely because we're

English that we claim the right to be called Burgundian!'

In *The Magnet* (1950), a comedy directed by Charles Frend, the insistence on individual autonomy is pursued much more impatiently and polemically. Although a crucial phase of the action involves a juvenile gang, the film starts by exploring the day to day relations of a mother, father and young son in a middle-class home in Birkenhead, Lancashire. The camera dwells on the evidence for middle-class taste, orderliness and symmetry. However, the film opens by making it clear that this rather

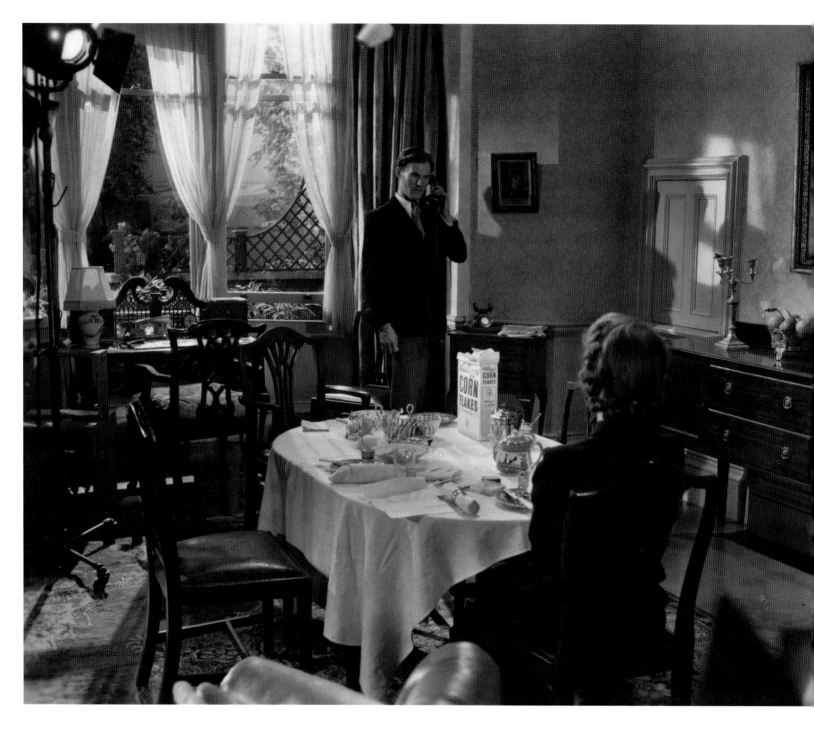

10.5
Charles Frend, *The Magnet*.
Ealing Studios. 1950

decorous environment is in the process of being customized by the young son, who is setting up Heath-Robinson-like contraptions around the house, cannibalizing bits and pieces of equipment in order to turn them to uses they were not originally intended for. The telephone bell, for example, has been converted into a means of announcing the moment the breakfast eggs have been boiled in the kitchen. This youthful improvisation gradually transforms the domestic interior into an environment where the adult characters are constantly surprised by finding things in all the wrong places. The middle-class home is identified as the locus for innovation of adaptability and displacement.

The resourceful youth is accepted into a juvenile gang, which, as in *Hue and Cry*, is constantly thrown back on itself in order to try to work out the principles of right and wrong in an ambiguous moral climate. The most insidious forms of demoralization seem to come from within the middle-class household itself. The father figure in *The Magnet* is a child psychologist whose psychoanalytic discourse is clearly intended to be distrusted. His psycho-babble is gauged against of a background debate over the advantages and disadvantages of the new National Health Service on the one hand, and of private health care on the other. A fundraising drive to purchase an iron lung – which plays a decisive role in the plot towards the end – is used to suggest that the standardizing effects of public health care, in respect of both physical and mental health, are to be resisted. Ultimately, the film promotes a model of citizenship in which the values of self-reliance, of independent resourcefulness and innovativeness, are paramount.

Bizarrely, the young protagonist's other main interest, apart from the rigging up of gadgets, is the secret language of tramps, suggesting that he is both future model citizen and potential outsider. If a main point about tramps is that they remain outside domesticity, displaced from society while taking what they need from it, it is curious how a parallel form of independent-mindedness and practical ingenuity is shown to start with –and be symbolized by – the customizing of the domestic interior.

Throughout the 1930s and 1940s, the domestic interior appears in film and fiction as a kind of stage for the acting out of certain ideas about society, addressing issues of standardization and individuality, of order and of threats to that order, of class and national character, and of cultural continuity. Fictional representations of the spaces that we actually live in accentuate the way in which we fill them up and arrange them in order to inhibit our fears and project our desires. Domestic interiors are performative spaces in every respect. The perception that a system of decoration proposes a system of fundamental social relations is given radical scope in the neglected fiction of Julia Strachey. In her *Cheerful Weather for the Wedding* (1932), it is precisely in the settings of home that the most alienating aspects of contemporary life are located. In *The Man on the Pier* (1951), the dissociation of sensibility is first realized in the estrangement of familiar surroundings:

Five minutes before he had been surrounded by props: tables, footstools, lamps and chairs – and the illusion had been complete. Now things were making themselves clearer, stepping up closer, as inexplicit as a nightmare and as convincing as the waking up. First he began to understand that he was surrounded by something merely gimcrack, something accepted as a temporally useful way of viewing things, and then afterwards he knew where he really was. This substance walling him, this adamant tomb, this dining-room, what was it but that formidable prison cell the present moment? That gaol where each finds himself locked without reprieve for evermore? In that moment, sitting on the window-seat, Ned knew himself to be looking from the cell of his gaol at its few accoutrements—at the straw pallet, bucket, and wash bowl—alternatively the lamp standards, fire-irons, and chairs.[14]

For Strachey, furnishings always mean more than just one thing: they organize our relation to time as well as to space, and they may either disable or enable our imagining of the right way to live. If the present moment is experienced as a form of imprisonment, its limitations are best appreciated in the context of settings found in other fictions and films, where the domestic interior is made the dynamic focus for working out the relations of past and future, and for questions about the scope and velocity of cultural change. But Strachey's 'man on the pier' is pitching these questions in a new way, using a vocabulary that marks a shift from concerns about cultural authenticity to anxieties about existential status. In this sense, her agenda is already looking forward to some of the key projects of the next two decades of British film and fiction.

The 'West Indian' Front Room: migrant aesthetics in the home

Michael McMillan

The 'West Indian' front room represents a moment when cultural-political shifts mediated by anti-colonialist struggles for independence, the Civil Rights and Black Power movements were emblematic of a decolonizing process. That moment for West Indian immigrants was also arriving with dignity and respectability packed deep in their 'grips' (suitcases), pressed and dressed in their Sunday best, in preparation for whatever was to happen next. Many found work as soon as they arrived. Finding somewhere to live was a different story. Signs in windows saying, 'No Irish, No Dogs, No Coloured', are a painful reminder of the one room cramped and squalid conditions many of my parent's generation experienced. When spouses and families arrived in post-war

Britain, there was a need for more space, and many used an informal localized saving scheme called the 'Pardner Hand' to raise the deposit for a house or flat. Once they moved in, a front room began to take shape.

Like those of other migrant communities, the West Indian front room expressed a yearning for social mobility and as an aspirational shrine was dressed by the mother of the home and was only used if there were guests or on special occasions. Regardless of wealth, she ensured that the front room always looked good, because it symbolized decency and a desire for status and respectability. Its maintenance and social function followed codes of *good grooming* and conduct that had their roots in the colonial fusion of

10.6
The 'West Indian' front room from the exhibition and installation. 2005–6. Geffrye Museum, London

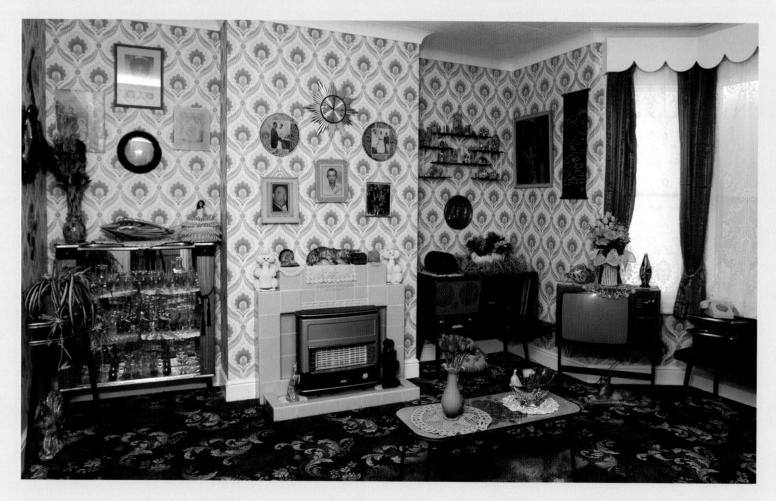

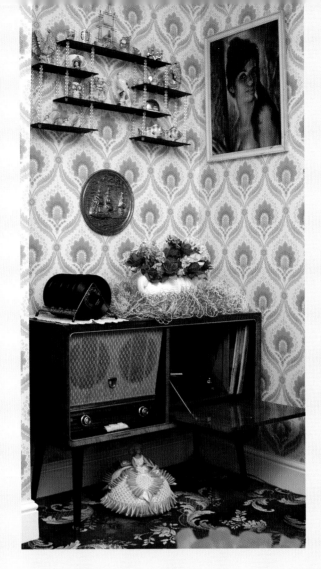

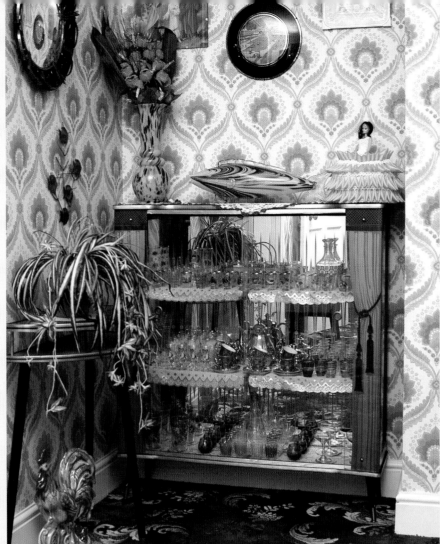

religion, hygiene and the Protestant Work Ethic embodied in proverbs such as: 'Cleanliness as next to godliness' and 'By the sweat of your brow, thou shall eat bread'. These ideals were presented in a highly personalized style and self-controlled expression of a specific aesthetic. One's heart was set on opulence in the front room, through a consumer fetish for particular types of furniture, ornaments and homemade soft furnishings.

'Classic' objects included plastic flowers in ornate vases on crocheted doilies placed on a drinks cabinet presenting rarely used glass and chinaware. There was a wooden cabinet housed radiogram or 'Blue Spot' and music was wide ranging, though Sundays were reserved for Country and Western crooners such as Jim Reeves. The carpet had heavily floral patterns with a maroon background. And juxtaposed on similarly patterned wallpaper would be framed family photographs, black velour scrolls with the map of a Caribbean island, religious homilies and prints of *The Last Supper* and J.H. Lynch's *Tina*. The three-piece leatherette or fabric upholstered suite might be difficult

to sit on, if it was covered in plastic, because it would often stick to the skin.

This aesthetic is not so much a valorization of white-bias ideals of beauty, but rather the performativity of status and the Creolization of popular culture. There was a desire for artificial things because they lasted longer and things were covered over because they were cherished for the future. As a phenomenon, the front room resonates across diaspora, but this is metaphorical, rather than a search for the pure and authentic homeland, it lives through and with a conception of identity as process: disruptive and continuous. Responding to displacement, exile and alienation, the front room for migrants is a public frontline on a private backyard. Its contradictory nature reveals how post-colonial identities have been contested through inter-generational identifications, disavowal and the negotiation of gendered practices in the domestic domain. It raises fundamental questions about modernity as a theatre of popular desires for material culture in the domestic interior.

10.7
'Blue Spot' Radiogram

10.8
The drinks cabinet

10.9
The paraffin heater

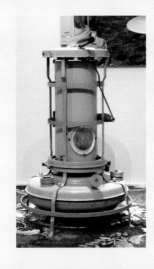

11

Dream Homes and DIY: television, new media and the domestic makeover

Viviana Narotzky

'There's not a house in Britain left untouched by the *Changing Rooms* attitude.'[1]

RUNNING FROM 1996 until its last season in 2005, the television reality show *Changing Rooms* has been a fundamental contributor to current representations of the home. The programme features two neighbouring couples, who exchange their homes for two days, redecorating each other's space under the guidance of an interior designer within a fixed, limited budget. By 1998, *Changing Rooms* was regularly attracting 12 million viewers to its prime-time slot on BBC1 and was soon to generate numerous international spin-offs.

While interior designer Laurence Llewelyn-Bowen's claim that it has left no house untouched might seem at first to be far-fetched, its profound impact on mainstream ideas of the home, domesticity and the design of interiors cannot be denied. Through programmes such as *Changing Rooms*, and other interior design series such as *Design Rules* or *Home Front*, reality TV domestic makeover shows have developed and established an overarching discourse of design in the home that seamlessly merges traditional perceptions of interior design with the latest lifestyle and cultural trends.

The long-standing Victorian premise of the home as a safe haven, a retreat from the cares and worries of public life that provides the stage for the most intimate expressions of individual identity through design and decoration, is given a post-modern twist in an attitude that refuses to engage with notions of good or bad taste. The New Age's design gurus no longer tell one what to like. Rather, they aim to help us find ourselves, announcing that 'there is no right way, no wrong way, but only your way.'[2]

But this domestic ideal of the home as a personal sanctuary, constructed by means of regulated aesthetic practices and individual expression, is a composite picture in more than just its relation to aesthetic form. If the medium is the message, as media and communications theorist Marshall MacLuhan proposed almost half a century ago, then this message is a very fragmented one. Following the economic logic of contemporary merchandizing and product tie-ins, programmes such as *Changing Rooms* and *Home Front* have spawned their own microcosm of multi-media incarnations, offering branded products across a diverse range of technological and media platforms, from books, to computer software, to the Internet. Each one of them elaborates its particular variation on this narrative of home, giving rise to a unique phenomenon in which these discourses are adapted to suit varying modes of representation and mediation.

The TV programmes favour dramatic tension, drawing the viewers into a private space where the ultimate success or failure of the makeover is above all an expression of the home as a site of emotional investment. At the same time, working with the flexibility inherent to new media, the BBC's *Changing Rooms* website presents the home as a blank canvas made of pre-defined colour-in areas, the discrete receptacles of a seemingly endless choice of possible dream-worlds. The books, on the other hand, engage comfortably with a long tradition of advice literature, providing know-how, inspiration and practical tips from the experts. But more importantly, they offer to position our relationship with domestic interior design as a natural outcome of our personal engagement with the *Zeitgeist*. They tell us, in other words, that 'home' is the ultimate expression of who we are right now: diverse, creative, expressive, changeable, unique and in control.

Essentially an evolution from DIY and design advice programmes, contemporary domestic makeover TV shows are part of a culturally and historically framed discourse on the home, design and interiors. Drawing on the mass appeal of reality TV and celebrity culture, they have popularized a vicarious, shifting and essentially 'spectacular' experience of the contemporary domestic interior.

The good home

There is an absence at the heart of domestic makeover shows, as has historically been the case with other attempts to help home-dwellers improve their domestic environment. Put bluntly, a perceived absence of taste. But it is the pre-supposed absence of a very particular kind of taste that drives design advice, the ever-elusive *good taste*, as well as the lack of a certain type of skill in the general public: the specialist know-how that underpins *good design*. Interior decorating has long been a 'middle-class ritual',[3] largely officiated by women (see pl.11.1). If the nineteenth-century saw women mostly as the sensitive agents that shaped the private sphere, by the turn of the century the emphasis of an emerging modernist discourse was on the interior as the manifestation of an artistic individuality, an outlet for women of a particular class to be creative.[4] In that sense, while remaining somewhat distant from the lofty realms of High Art, amateur home decorating was seen as a practice strongly linked both to aesthetic skills and to individual expression. Expert advice on such matters, therefore, can be seen as a constant endeavour not just to educate an

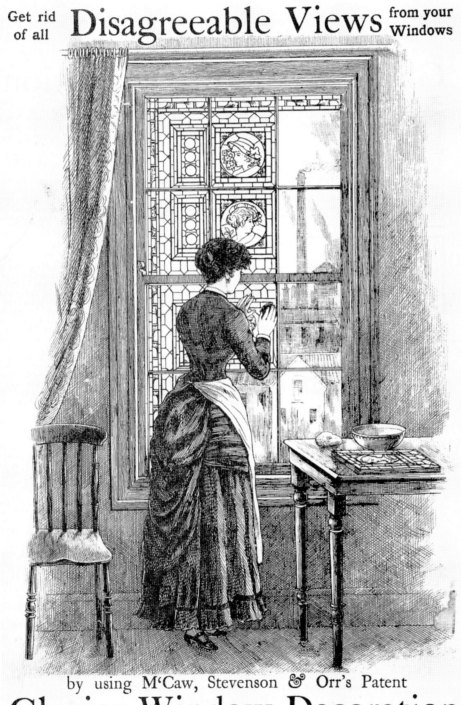

11.1
McCaw, Stevenson & Orr's
Window Decoration. 1890.
John Johnson Collection,
Bodleian Library, Oxford

Get rid of all **Disagreeable Views** from your Windows

by using M'Caw, Stevenson & Orr's Patent
Glacier Window Decoration

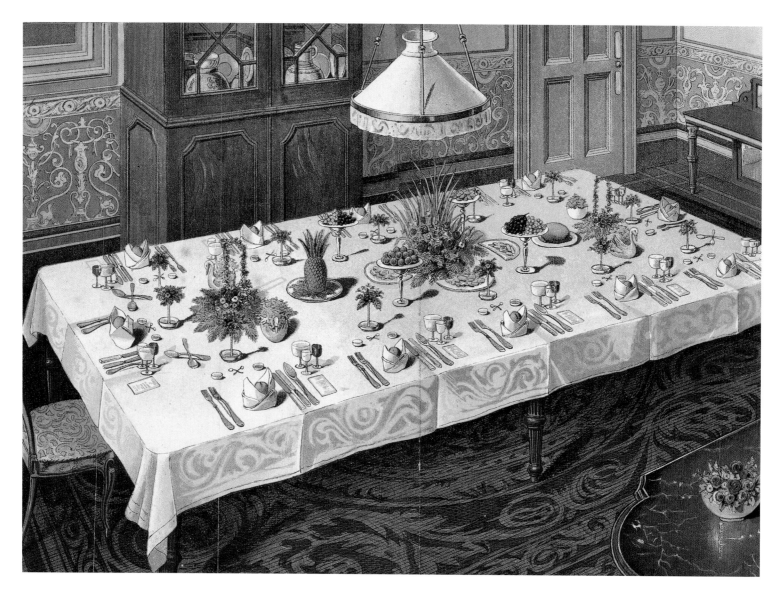

easily misled public, but also as an attempt to police the formal boundaries of this creative drive, circumscribing its expression to the limits set by the professionals.

Throughout the nineteenth and twentieth centuries, an ever-increasing abundance of books, specialist magazines, exhibitions, commercial fairs, trade manuals and museum displays offered encouragement and inspiration on how best to be an artist of the domestic sphere (see pl.11.2). Home makeover shows therefore participate in a now well-established historical lineage of multi-media design advice, mediating design ideas and representing an ideal dwelling space. Before the advent of television, and in this particular case reality television, trade shows and model homes were

among the main sites where prospective home-makers could come as close as possible to 'real' interior design solutions. The Ideal Home Shows, for instance, established in Britain in 1908 and now a biannual event, would have supported the quest for inspiration and advice, offering a commodified palette of fashionable trends, new materials, emerging domestic technologies and shifting cultural priorities.

In the USA, the Idea House project, which took place in 1941 and 1947 under the auspices of the Walker Art Center of Minneapolis, Minnesota, was a striking example of the merging of art and commerce in the construction of the domestic sphere.[5] Idea House was a Modernist exercise in design promotion, developed in the context of the Depression and American post-

11.2
'Dinner Table with Floral Decorations, Arranged for 12 Persons', frontispiece from *Mrs Beeton's Book on Household Management*.
Chromolithograph. 1888.
Private collection

war reconstruction (see pl.11.3). It offered fully-fitted, architect-designed display houses as a source of ideas for the visiting public to draw inspiration from. The two houses were constructed with the support of manufacturers who contributed materials, furnishings and fittings. While none of these were listed in the show houses themselves, information leaflets were made available to the public with full details of items, prices and suppliers. In the words of Daniel Defenbacher, the project's instigator, 'As a consumer, every man uses art…. His medium he obtains from stores, manufacturers and builders. His composition is his

environment'.[6] An unprecedented combination of cultural and commercial aims, Idea House offered the home artist a catalogue of tools. It has been suggested that 'the discourse around the modern house is fundamentally linked to the commercialisation of domestic life'.[7] While these various settings of ideal interiors were undoubtedly a direct manifestation of this trend, they nevertheless upheld the enduring rhetoric of the homeowners as artists, inspired creators of the everyday.

From the mid-1940s, television offered an even easier way of consuming the art of home-making and what seemed to be a perfect

11.3
William Friedman and Hilde Reiss, Living Room, *Idea House II*. 1947. Walker Art Center, Minneapolis

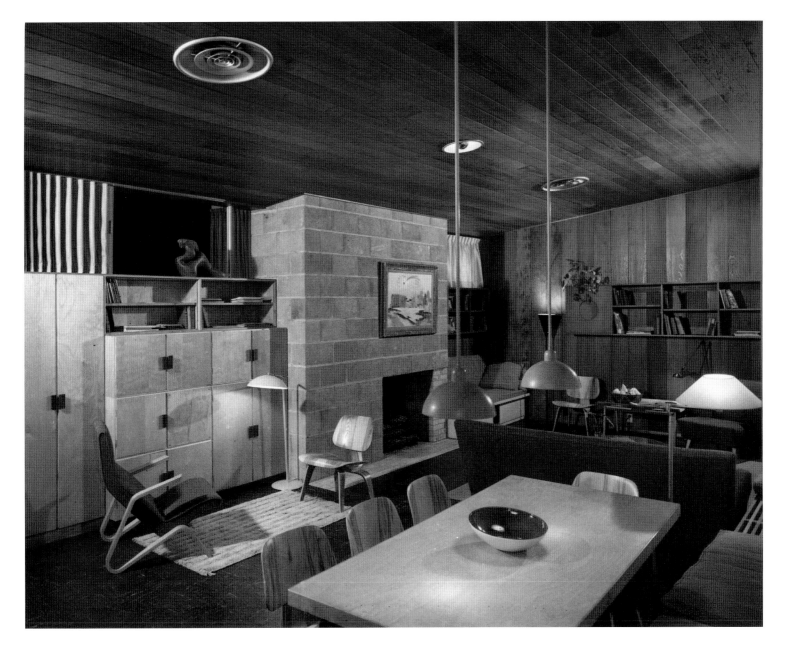

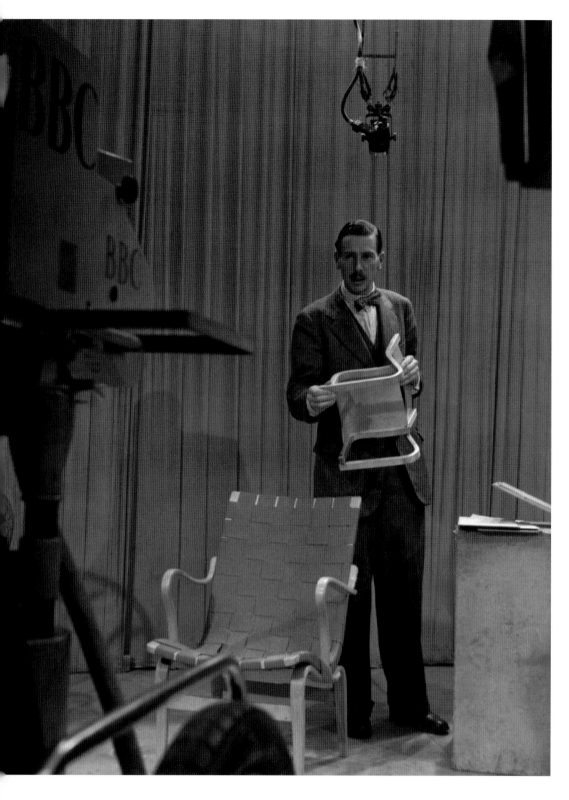

What's in a chair?, BBC
broadcast. 27 October 1947.
The Design Archive, Brighton

provided the perfect occasion for a joint effort between the two institutions to raise public awareness through programmes such as *What Is Good Design?*, *What's in a Chair?* and *The Designer Looks Ahead* (see pl.11.4). These extremely didactic offerings soon gave way to a slightly more consumer-oriented approach, in which the BBC left behind the CoID's concerns with reaching out to designers, retailers and manufacturers, shifting instead towards productions that tried to address the interests of the average homeowner and provide a modicum of televisual entertainment. Thus, in 1951, *Rooms to Let Unfurnished* followed a family of four in its upwardly-mobile relocation from a basement in Bermondsey to a larger, three-bedroom modern council flat in Streatham. With the help of a designer and a budget of £150, contemporary furnishings were carefully chosen to enhance their new environment, while considering how best to adapt the family's existing possessions to fit in with the modern style.[8]

Given the rather tenuous links between contemporary domestic makeover programmes such as *Changing Rooms* and the established canon of high design, however, it is tempting to place them more squarely in the DIY camp. The rise of self-built home improvement in 1930s and 1940s America coincided with the launch of government-sponsored loans aimed at creating better quality housing, by encouraging home ownership and facilitating projects such as electrification and the installation of new technologies and appliances in the home. It was therefore closely linked to the structural modernization of households, driven by a social agenda that sought to promote a better standard of living through the shared effort of federal funding and individual labour. DIY was presented as a patriotic activity, especially in the context of a make do and mend war-time ethos, and later as a practice that enabled returning war veterans to settle down into a well-deserved, comfortable suburban life. The remodelling of homes was also intensely pushed by manufacturers, who engaged both with the government's economic plans and with the domestic dreams

platform for the dissemination of notions of good design. In 1946, the newly established Council of Industrial Design joined the BBC (British Broadcasting Corporation) in an increasingly uneasy partnership. The *Britain Can Make It* exhibition held at the V&A in 1946

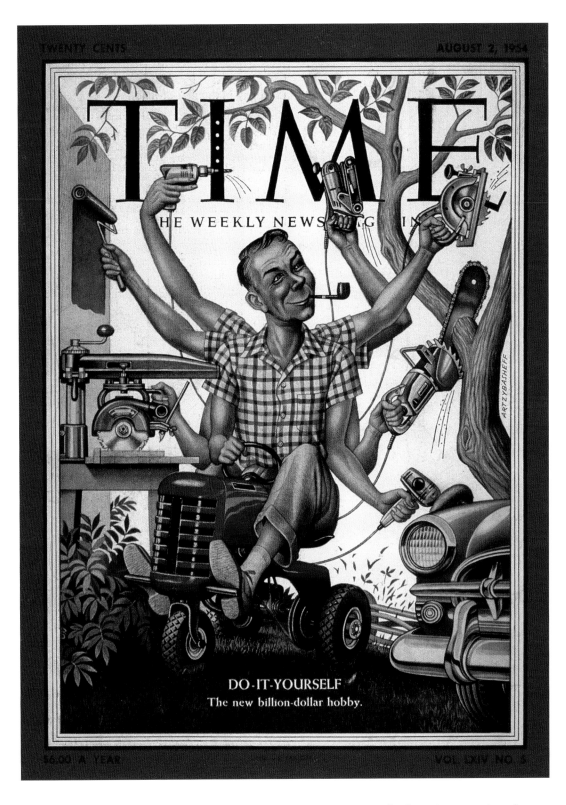

11.5
Boris Artzybasheff, 'Do-it-
yourself craze', cover of *Time*
magazine, 2nd August 1954.
Time Life Pictures

of a generation accessing home ownership for
the first time. By the 1950s, DIY had become a
huge industry and a mass culture phenomenon
(see pl.11.5). Ambiguously positioned between
work and leisure, it was associated with a cult of
suburban family life that presented the home not
just as an essentially feminine space, but also as a
space protected from the alienating drudgery of
corporate life, where men could engage in the
construction of domesticity through suitably
gendered practices (see pl.11.6).[9] DIY in the
USA, therefore, posited the home as a space of

empowering self-regulated male work, creative freedom and constructive leisure.

In Britain, the 1950s also saw the appearance of televised home improvement programmes, most famously Barry Bucknell's *Do-It-Yourself* BBC series, which attracted over seven million viewers, and what was possibly the first ever home makeover show, Bucknell's *1962 House* (see pl.11.7). Through the course of 39 weekly episodes, Bucknell transformed a derelict Victorian house in Ealing into a sleek and modern home. Gone were the quaint fireplaces, moulded doors, picture rails and other period features. Walls came down to make way for more up-to-date open-plan layouts, while modular functional furniture and the latest appliances

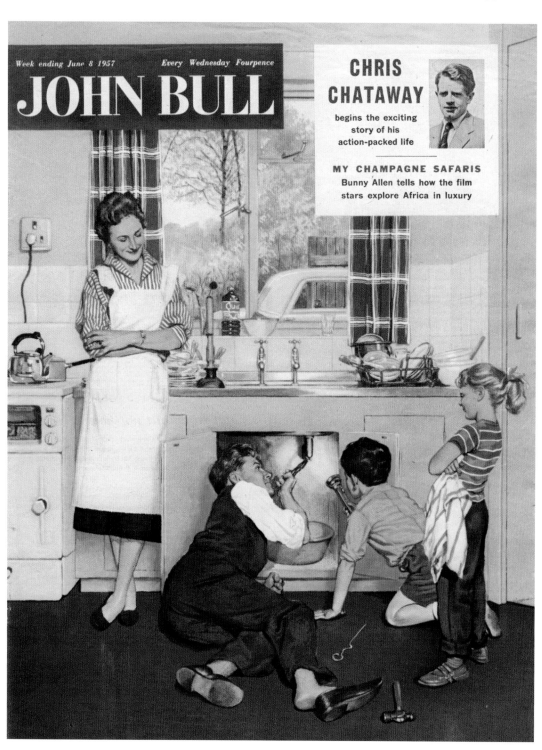

11.6
Cover of *John Bull* magazine, 8th June 1957. The Advertising Archives, London

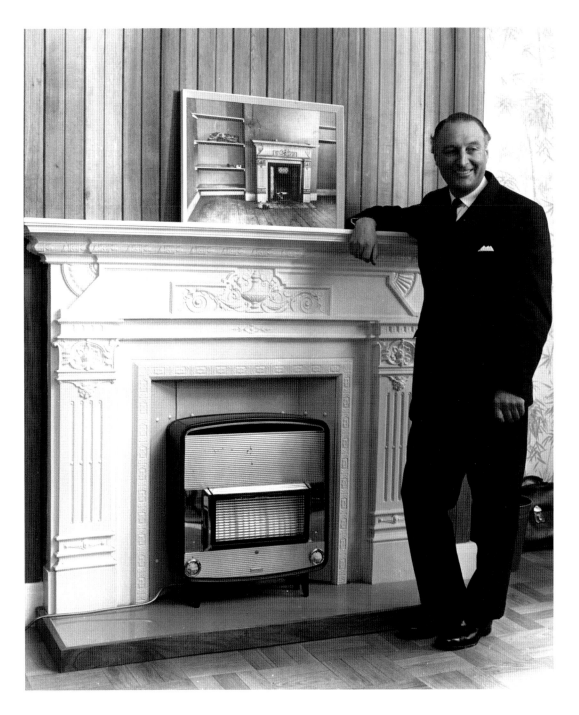

11.7
Barry Bucknell in the drawing
room of 'Bucknell's House',
BBC broadcast. 1963. BBC,
London

completed a breathtaking transformation, drag-
ging British interiors into the '60s' and leaving
behind a cloud of paint fumes and particle-board
sawdust. As had been the case in the USA, the
post-war government supported home improvements through the Housing Act of 1949, and the
Rent Act of 1954, which enabled Local Authorities to provide generous loans to that effect.[10] By
the late 1950s, ideas about how to transform the
home, and how best to do it oneself, had been
made accessible to the public in a staggering vari-

ety of venues. These included the *Britain Can
Make It* exhibition, the successive British Industries Fairs after the war, the Festival of Britain in
1951, the annual national Handicrafts and Do-
It-Yourself exhibitions in the Empire Hall at
Olympia from 1953, the 'Do-It-Yourself Theatre
at the Ideal Home Exhibitions from 1955, and
the DIY exhibitions at the Empress Hall, Earl's
Court, from 1958 (see pl.11.8). The first British
DIY magazine, *The Practical Householder*,
appeared in October 1955 and by March 1957

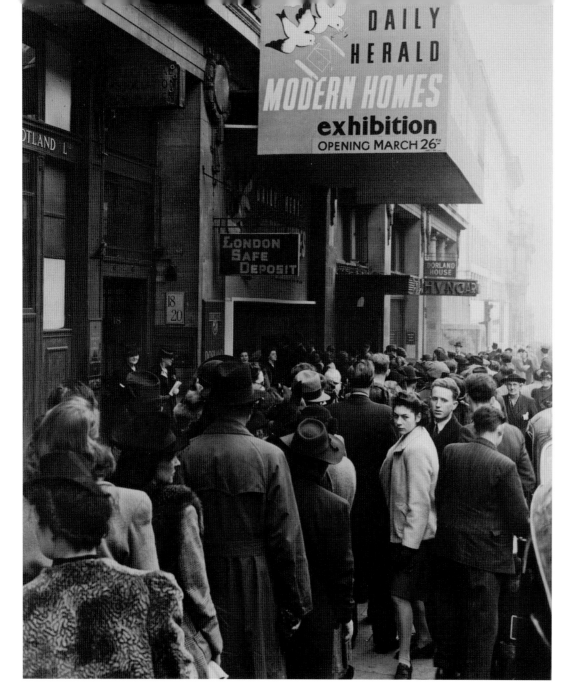

11.8
Crowds outside Dorland Hall,
Lower Regent Street, London,
Daily Herald Modern Homes
Exhibition. 27 March 1946.
Daily Herald Archive

it had become the biggest selling technical journal ever, with a circulation of one million.

As with other forms of making, DIY involved the development of specific skills and the expression of personal aesthetic judgement. It also celebrated thrift, being in part a result of economic necessity as the 1956 editorial pages of the magazine *The Practical Householder* indicated:

> From the large number of letters we receive from both men and women readers it is apparent that the Do-It-Yourself movement is here to stay and not, as some thought, a passing phase. It is also evident from those letters that

two reasons are responsible for it. The first is the enormous charges now being made for repairs and decorations ... and the second is the deterioration in the quality of the work, notwithstanding the heavy prices asked....[11]

For the average homeowner in 1950s Britain, DIY represented a manageable way of negotiating the rather daunting, if appealing, post-war modernity that Bucknell and the Design Council were so earnestly promoting through the BBC.[12] Self-built home improvements offered scope for the customization of the modern, both in terms of cost and of formal appearance, providing the know-how to construct a domesticated and affordable version of contemporary 'good design'.

The emphasis on design-led 'making' that is part and parcel of domestic makeover TV shows might lead one to locate them within a historical narrative that stretches back to the emergence of DIY and the popularization of 'good design', as a modernist project of self-constructed material progress. However, it is the ways in which makeover shows diverge from that story that define the particular nature of this popular contemporary mode of representing the home and our relationship to it.

Throughout the twentieth century, the idea of the home as a site of social reform, the 'good' home as Utopian project, has been contending with the idea of domestic space as an expression of middle-class taste and an emotional sanctuary. This tension can be easily mapped onto the contrasting narrative styles that structured the early DIY programmes, on the one hand, and home makeover shows on the other. While the former's educational vocation focused on the clear, step by step presentation of a process and on skill acquisition, makeovers prioritize narrative, appearance, outcome and drama. They lay bare a shift from function to representation in terms of the media's contribution to the self-made domestic interior.

These programmes are not about improving standards of living, or incorporating new domestic technologies in order to make positive structural changes to dwellings. They certainly do not have a background ideology linking them to a social agenda promoted by government institutions or public policies. If anything, they are one of many extremely successful manifestations of the priorities of contemporary consumer culture, a site for the mediation of versions of middle-class taste and their relation to lifestyle as a vague, and vaguely life-enhancing, thing. Crucially, however, the way in which they present the transformation of the home, or rather, the transformation of rooms within the home, subjects the conceptualization of the domestic interior to the overarching demands of the medium itself. As a consequence, televi-

sion is no longer only a channel through which pre-existing ideas about the home and its appearance can be conveyed, but the very process through which they are constructed.

Domestic intrusion

Through its constant and banal presence at the heart of the everyday experience of domesticity, television as a medium is by its very nature linked with the spaces of the home – and not just the home as a physical space, but as a space of the mind as well:

> Once one takes seriously the fact that television is a domestic medium (and is characterised by programme forms specifically designed for that purpose), it becomes clear that the domestic context of television viewing is not some secondary factor, which can be subsequently sketched in. Rather, the domestic context of TV viewing, it becomes clear, is constitutive of its meaning.'[13]

These meanings arise out of the sharing of televisual experiences, the interpersonal dynamics involved in what is watched when, how and by whom, or the transformation of TV programmes and topics into a common currency that can be exchanged in the cultural economy of everyday life.

Home makeover shows have been described as a hybrid between two separate television formats: talk shows and reality TV.[14] On the one hand, the hosts engage in conversation with the homeowners whose rooms are being redecorated, encouraging them to share their ideas and concerns about the process that they are participating in. On the other, these programmes transgress the boundaries of the home, intruding on the intimacy of the domestic environment by subjecting it to the gaze of millions of viewers, who watch them from the privacy of their own living rooms. This paradox of public intimacy underpins the voyeur's pleasure, which reality television has made safely available to all.

In breaching the boundaries between public and private, domestic makeover shows embody one of the main tenets of Modernist architecture's Utopian vision, the attempt to erase the visual distinction between the inside and the outside. Television itself was from its earliest inception presented as a technology that would erase physical distance and conquer space, as an open window through which 'the outside world [could] be brought into the home, and thus one of mankind's long-standing ambitions [could] be achieved'.[15] It is the home that is now being brought to the outside world. Whether we really want an open window into our bedrooms is debatable, but the phenomenal success of domestic makeover shows seems to suggest that we do.[16] It would appear that we have become comfortable with the notion that our homes might be subject to surveillance, that reality TV can do on the inside what CCTV cameras do on the outside, that Big Brother is not just a necessary evil, but actually good fun.

However, this suggestion of a relaxed domesticity, at ease with the idea of a foreign gaze accessing the intimate sphere of the home, is belied by the dynamics that are responsible for the fascination that programmes such as *Changing Rooms* exert on their audiences. The high narrative point of home makeover shows, the final moment of truth known as 'the reveal', is in fact the dramatic representation of domesticity under threat. As the veil is lifted on the changes made over the course of the programme, the audience holds its collective breath and watches the participants' reaction to their revamped Swahili-themed living-room – secretly hoping that they will hate it. Subjected to the often eccentric creative whims of the designers, themselves bound by the producer's need to generate a televisual spectacle out of watching paint dry, homeowners are caught between the contradictory demands of show-business, aesthetic judgement and an improved domestic environment. While design can help provide a more impressive dining room or a more sensual bedroom (see pl.11.9), it can also be threatening to a placid, simple and enjoyable domestic life. Style is one of the ways in which

the home can be put at risk: 'Maybe it's too arty for them' says a concerned neighbour about the scheme that is being suggested for her friends' bedroom. 'We could do it safe … but we won't' counters Laurence Llewelyn-Bowen, 'Come on, be brave. Trust me, I'm a designer'.[17]

The anxieties so often expressed by makeover show participants, about the emotional havoc that might be caused by an inappropriate assessment of the owners' taste – or by TV designers blatantly disregarding the owners' aesthetic preferences – speak of a deep-seated perception of the home as an emotionally vulnerable site. This very personal, carefully calibrated emotional balance, constructed in part through home possessions and visual form, can be easily threatened and destroyed by professionals. It is precisely this aspect that shows such as *Changing Rooms* or *Home Front* exploit to the full. In 2000, the *Changing Rooms* team gave an eighteenth-century vicarage an 'outlandish and funky' makeover. On returning to her home the following day, the owner was furious: 'I think it's absolute crap, I really do. I think it's a traditional house and you've put a modern design in. The sooner we get it out, the better. I mean, breeze blocks in a house of this age? It's appalling'.[18] Every lime green brushstroke, every MDF folly, is the potential harbinger of a breakdown in the owners' pre-established sense of what is, for them, an appropriate visual expression of domesticity, leading to live televised distress and a surge in ratings.

At the same time, the design of the makeovers recognizes the primacy of our emotional attachment to domestic objects in the configuration of a pleasurable experience of the home. Cherished possessions are frequently singled out as focal points for the reorganization of a room, or given pride of place in especially designed display features. Unfortunately, this does not necessarily diminish the risk involved in letting a designer manipulate those objects, as the owner of a valued collection of antique china teapots discovered when some hastily put together hanging shelves collapsed halfway through the makeover process.[19]

Although they pay their dues to the logic of commercial television in their quest for dramatic

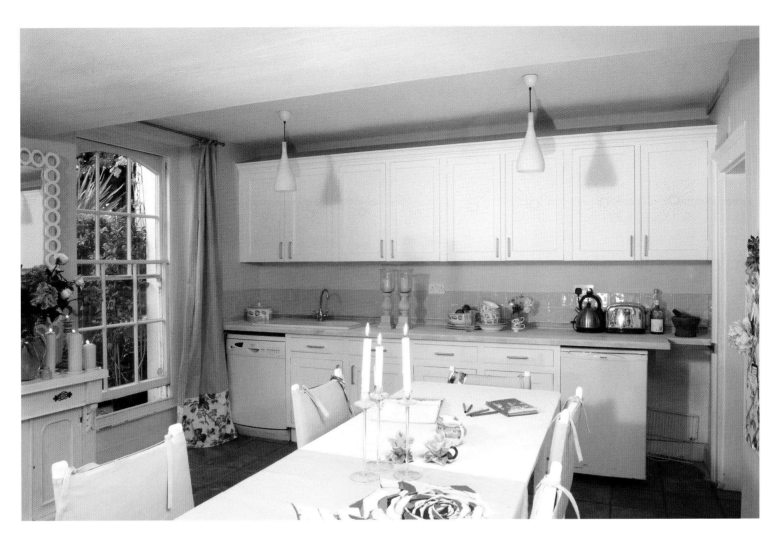

11.9
Laurence Llewelyn-Bowen's
kitchen redesigned by Linda
Barker. *Changing Rooms*, 100th
edition. September 2002. BBC,
London

confrontations, TV makeover shows are the popular expression of an evolving and tense relationship between high-cultural or design-led discourses about the aesthetics of domestic interiors and mainstream taste. It is a conflict that has been with us throughout the twentieth century, and which has seen the home as the main battleground between highbrow and lowbrow taste, experts and neophytes, professionals and amateurs. It is taken to its extreme in these reality shows where the conflict sometimes ends in tears, in front of the nation's eyes. But television had already provided a platform for equally intense, if more high-cultural, confrontations, such as Nicholas Barker and photographer Martin Parr's *Signs of the Times* documentary series, shown on BBC2 in 1991. Constructed as a series of interviews about the way in which people decorate their homes, *Signs of the Times* (with its apparently candid subtitle: 'A Portrait of the Nation's Tastes') extended Parr's interests in class and consumerism into the interior (see pl.11.10). It preceded the onslaught of reality TV makeover shows by just a few years, and in its producer's words, it set out, 'film narrative permitting, … to record as objectively as possible a wide range of contemporary tastes, and to present them so that viewers could judge them for themsleves.'[20] Nevertheless, the result was a subtle but damning critique of middle-class tastes in home decoration and the discourses of social aspirations and personal identity that surrounded them.

Multimedia

While the concept of the makeover, which is essentially about highly visible and spectacular transformation, has a natural affinity with the medium of television, domestic makeover shows have found their way (as have others) into a whole range of different media. The rise

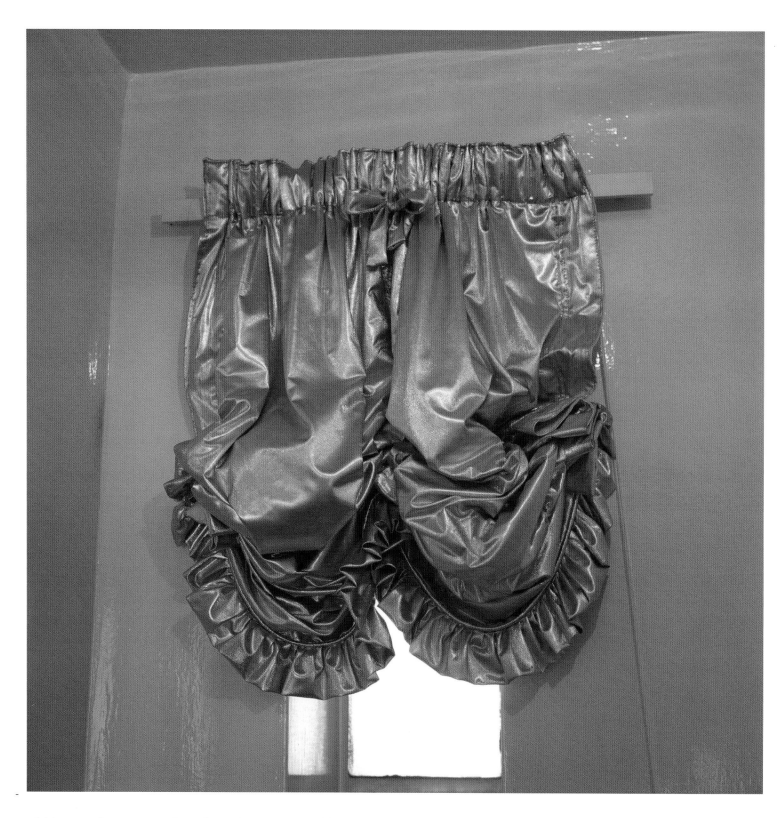

of this type of programme from the mid-1990s coincided with the consolidation and expansion of the World Wide Web and of Internet access as something that was no longer restricted to the workplace. As the numbers in PC ownership and personal Internet accounts grew, the domestication of new technologies established a more organic connection between watching home improvement programmes, using makeover software and browsing related Internet sites in a domestic context.

Essentially driven by commercial interests rather than by the intention to disseminate a particular idea through a variety of communi-

11.10
Martin Parr, *I get such pleasure from them every day when I sit in the bath.* 1991

cation channels, this cross-media expansion adapted the televisual model of interior design advice to a variety of platforms. As a result, the discourses about the home, interior design and visual form were often contradictory across the platforms, responding to the internal logic of the media without always presenting a cohesive approach.

This is particularly evident in relation to the role of both designers and owners in the process of home improvement. The TV programmes, by the nature of their format, emphasize the agency of the designers, while paying lip service to homeowners' requests or suggestions as to what they would like their interior to look and feel like (see pl.11.11). Ultimately, the owners' degree of control over the decisions taken and the final result is extremely limited. They are asked by the show's designers to perform certain tasks, ranging from painting walls to others that might involve a greater degree of personal contribution, such as making drawings. In most cases, however, not only have they not 'designed' what they are making, they also have little information as to how their work relates to the greater scheme under construction, and no choice as to where particular objects will be placed. TV domestic makeover shows are the celebrity designers' playground, an expression of their, not the owners', tastes. By being eccentric, demanding, stubborn or inspired, they reconfigure the home as a locus of dramatic narrative, presenting the practice of home improvement as a fun and exciting experience. The owners become a cast of secondary characters supporting the stars, in a script that involves celebrity design snobbery and populist entertainment.

In contrast, the spin-off books that accompany the series tend to reinforce more established notions of home improvement, that engage both with traditional approaches to design advice and contemporary discourses of individual control over the interior as an expression of personal identity. They hand over the baton of taste to the amateur designer, reassuringly stating that 'your design should be down to your own personal taste – the concept

of good and bad taste no longer has any credibility.'[21] Indeed, much of the advice and suggestions contained in these books – often proposing highly ornamental schemes, a mixture of period styles, and homecraft practices such as stencilling, textile dyeing or goldleaf application – would make any follower of 'good design' and 'good taste' shudder. But these are combined with more general information about colour, composition, the use of light and the effect and manipulation of materials. With the judicious application of all this, the amateur home improvers should be able, in contrast to their televised peers, to truly experience the home as a site of individual expression and creativity. 'Somewhere', as the books suggest, 'where you, and you alone, have total personal control'.[22] Here, the populism of the TV shows, built around crowd-pleasing drama and celebrity appeal, turns into a populism that seeks to pacify middle-class taste anxiety: 'change in design was led by the dictates of powerful taste gurus who pronounced … that rococo was out and neo-classical was in. Design [has] moved seamlessly overnight from an autocracy to a democracy and the bloodless revolution was effected by us, the people'.[23]

Yes, the books seem to imply, by your home you shall be judged. Our living rooms are us, our kitchens an expression of 'what [we] want to say about [ourselves]'.[24] But we have now, in a post-modern fashion, moved beyond taste. There are no more taste gurus, is the earnest message of the domestic makeover gurus themselves. We are all creative, taste is a democratic commodity, we can all do it ourselves, and we will always get it right (see pl.11.12).

The BBC's website presents yet another vision of domestic space. *Changing Rooms* nestles under 'Design', as part of a hierarchy that structures, tellingly, the 'Lifestyle' section of the site. There, the 'Home' subsite is an umbrella for areas such as 'DIY', 'Design', 'Property' and 'TV and Radio'. This is the place to find 'design inspiration' online, and that particular menu takes the browser to a page where the BBC's design celebrities offer expert solutions for transforming and redesigning interiors. The

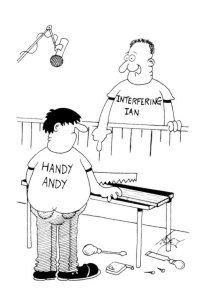

11.11
Adey Bryant, *Handy Andy/Interfering Ian*

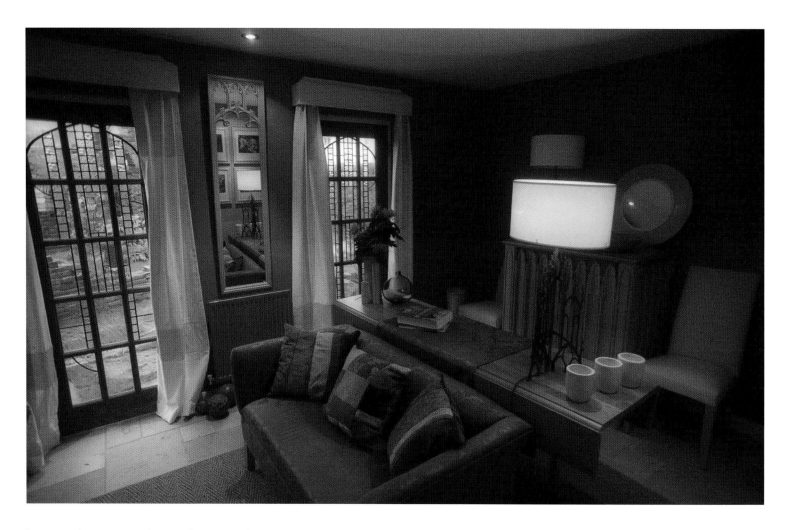

11.12
Laurence Llewelyn-Bowen, 'Gothic' living room. *Home Front*, 2001. BBC, London

home is shown as made up of a series of separate spaces: the bedroom, the kitchen, the dining room, the lounge, the attic, the playroom, the study. It is a traditional, essentially middle-class organization of domestic activities, and offers no radical re-configuration of space. While colour or a favourite designer can be selected as the guiding source of inspiration, it is style, or better still, styles, that are offered as the main building blocks of the self-designed interior, the alphabet of the domestic makeover (see pl.11.14). They come neatly packaged, in a hybrid DIY reinterpretation of period features, design movements and ethnic influences.

The website forcefully presents domestic space as a themed environment, an Aladdin's Cave of available styles to suit a variety of tastes. Or even, as the online test linking attitudes and individual behaviour patterns to styles ultimately suggests, to a range of personalities. And if style and taste reflect our personality, then who

could doubt that the alchemy of the domestic makeover will always be successful: as intimated by the gurus, it's not good or bad, it's 'me'.

Finally, the CD-ROM software, with three levels of 'design guidance', a range of layouts and styles, customisable inspiration boards, colour palettes, furniture selectors and photo-realistic mock-ups, is perhaps the ultimate tool for the DIY representation of the domestic interior (see pl.11.13). Coming full circle, it provides the instant means not so much to physically alter our home, but to endlessly indulge in constructing changing representations of what it could be.

In its dizzying and ever-accelerating journey through the television screen, the home has undergone some fundamental transformations. While some of these have been for the most part a mediated reflection of various pre-established perceptions, the medium itself has increasingly become the crucible in which

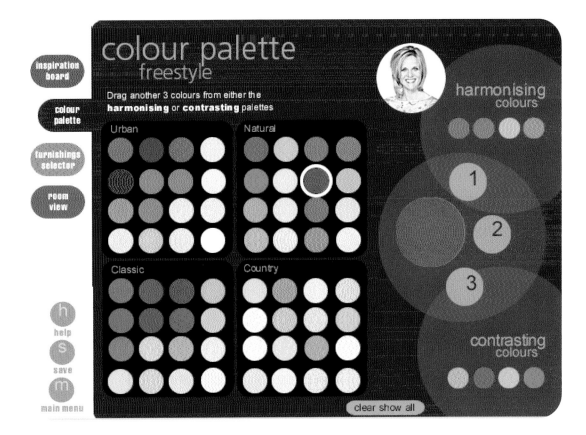

11.13

Colour palette from *Changing Rooms: Interior Designer* CD-ROM. 1999. BBC Worldwide

11.14

BBC *Homes Design Inspiration* webpage. 2006. BBC, London

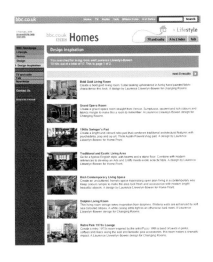

ideas of domesticity have been formed.

In their recent request for advice to the interior design magazine *LivingEtc.*, a couple explained their dilemma in the following words: 'We have been slowly converting each room of our house with a theme. Cocktail Kitchen and Two-Tone Living Room were the first couple, and now we're moving onto the bathroom. We want it to be rock inspired'.[25] Enhanced by the do-it-yourself capabilities of computer software and interactive websites, the 'themed' home seems to have struck the mainstream. Proactive homemakers experiment with styles as they would with colour or patterned wallpaper, cutting up their home into neat, discrete boxes and painting by numbers. Historically, the different rooms in a house have often had a particular visual character, generally derived from or related to their use. The Modernist home resisted such discrimination, insisting on a clear overarching discourse of interior space. What emerges here, however, is not just a return to interior 'decoration', but the notion of fragmented spaces separated from their entire domestic system. Defined through form at least as much as

through function, indifferent to 'good taste' as much as to 'good design', eclectic, playful and descriptive, they painstakingly construct a themed narrative of domesticity that courts spectacle, acknowledges ephemerality, and celebrates representation itself.

Over the course of more than half a century, television has shifted from representing the spaces of the modern home as the site of rational, progress-informed agency, to offering a vision of domesticity that foregrounds drama, vulnerability, emotional attachments and scenographic display. This move from making to feeling mirrors a wider cultural transfer from post-war civic priorities to the more spectacular, and often self-indulgent, dynamics of our post-industrial consumer culture, and from a moral dimension to a fundamentally visual one. Certainly, the home has not been the only site where these changes have taken place, or even where they might be traced most accurately. Nevertheless, it does offer an exquisite setting for doing so, and has proved to be particularly responsive to the impact of mass-media representations of the domestic space.

Ethnographic Representations of the Home

Inge Maria Daniels

The study of the home has always been key to classical ethnography. However, with increasing numbers of anthropologists studying their own communities and the continuing privatization of everyday life in the second half of the twentieth century, attention moved away from the domestic arena. It is only recently, with the rise of material culture studies within anthropology, that we see a renewed interest in the home as a major research topic. One pivotal study this body of research builds on is Pierre Bourdieu's 1970 analysis of the Kabyle House in Algeria. The French sociologist describes the house as an inverted microcosm organized according to series of homologous oppositions such as high:low, light:dark, day:night, east:west, male:female. Bourdieu's main contribution lies in the fact that he goes beyond structuralist dichotomies by stressing how these symbolic divisions are constantly negotiated through social practice. He mainly employs vivid textual descriptions to depict Berber home life, but the mechanisms at work are also clearly visualized in two floor plans (see pl.11.15).

Floor plans continue to be employed within ethnographic studies of the domestic but there seems to be a propensity for textual representations. These can take the form of detailed passages describing the researcher's personal observations as well as literal quotations based on transcribed interviews or conversations with the people studied (see pl.11.16). Photographs of the domestic interior also feature in ethnographic accounts of the home but they are few and tend to be used as illustrations that authenticate the experience discussed and give authority to the researcher concerned. An exception is David Halle's richly illustrated study of the consumption of art in Manhattan homes, which balances the use of text and image, ethnographic description and analysis.

The rise of visual anthropology together with a strong push for more informant participation in ethnographic research, however, has resulted in an increased use of visual representation. Plates 11.17 and 11.18 show two different types of representation

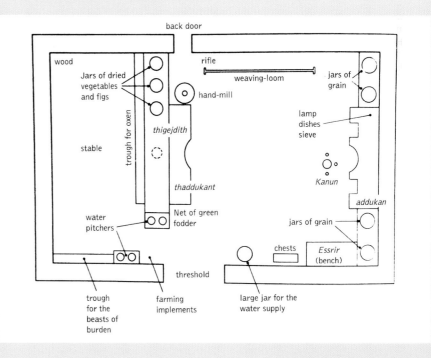

Kelly stands apart from other informants in the street due to the overwhelming enthusiasm she has expressed for formal principles of interior decoration. Her living room has a white fitted carpet, white walls, a white leather three-piece suite and a mirrored rear wall which, she says, is used to accentuate a 'monochrome feeling'. She made the rouched curtains herself, 'before everyone else had them', in shiny pale pink using exclusive cut-price fabric from a friend working in a prestigious fabric shop in the West End. Previously, the room had been decorated in an even more extreme monochromatic style with a black ceiling:

Yes it looks incredible [with a black ceiling] it's amazing it looks so different you wouldn't believe it's the same room and the carpet was a grey with it. It had black in it, it wasn't plain but it wasn't a pattern, anyway everything else was white. I had a white suite but the same kind of colours because most designers work with black and white [the effect] is really funny, strange.

11.15
Plan of the Kabyle House, from P. Bourdieu, 'The Kabyle House or the World Reversed', *The Logic of Practice* (1992).

11.16
Extract from an interview transcription, 'The Aesthetics of Social Aspirations' by A. Clarke. From D. Miller, *Home Possessions* (2001).

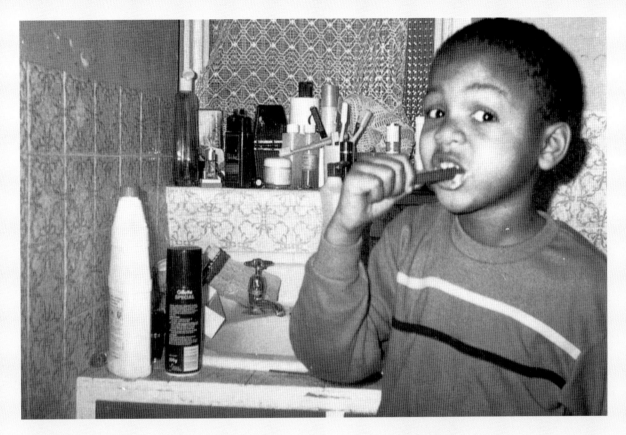

supplied by people who have actively contributed to
the research. Plate 11.17 shows a photograph taken
with a throw-away camera by a child who participated
in the Blackfriars Photographic Project (1990), which
used ethnographic techniques in order to gain an
understanding of how children from a variety of ethnic
backgrounds viewed their homes. Plate 11.18 depicts
a sketch drawn from memory by a woman in her late
sixties of her home in London during the 1950s.
Generally, photographs of the domestic interior used
within ethnographic research about the home focus
on the visible, easy accessible display areas in the
home. Visual as well as textual representations of the
hidden, often contested, home remain rare.

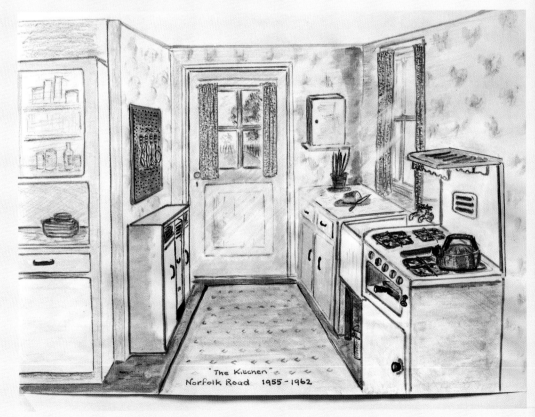

Modernism on Holiday

Olivier Richon and Alexandra McGlynn

In Claude Chabrol's *Les Biches* (1968) a young and ambitious architect, played by Jean-Louis Trintignant, builds a marina near Saint-Tropez. Like the village of Port Grimaud, built by François Spoerry from 1966 to 1981, Trintignant's marina resembles a Mediterranean fishing village, but the houses have a mooring for a yacht – adding luxury to the spontaneous vernacular sought by the holidaymakers. We see Trintignant seducing a young, destitute art student on the hill overlooking Saint-Tropez at dusk. In the background is Latitude 43, a hotel completed by Georges-Henri Pingusson in 1931 to house artists and intellectuals. Like many International Style projects, it recalls a vast ocean liner, with a chimney that inspired the rooftop of Le Corbusier's Unité d'Habitation in Marseilles.

The Provençal bungalow or the *belle époque* construction – rusticity or ostentation – these are the dominant dream images of the holiday dwelling on the Côte d'Azur. Yet three post-war architectural projects near Le Lavandou form a modernist triangle that stands in opposition to such nostalgia. In the late 1950s, the architect André Lefèvre built his house in a cliff overlooking the Mediterranean. Only the chimney, recalling the conning tower of a submarine, is visible from the road above the house. One enters Le Pin Blanc by a gangplank leading to stairs descending to the rooftop – stepping on the house before stepping inside the house. Upstairs, floor to ceiling windows provide continuity between the sea view and the interior view; the lower floor has portholes. Le Pin Blanc is not a picture. It does not reveal its image easily if by image we mean the frontal view of its façade, which can only be seen from the sea.

Between 1960 and 1970, Lefèvre and his collaborator Jean Aubert realized one of the most successful integrations of dwellings into the Mediterranean landscape. Commissioned to build the Village des Fourches in the Domaine du Gaou-Bénat, they chose an architectural vocabulary guided by the site rather than references to the Modern Movement.

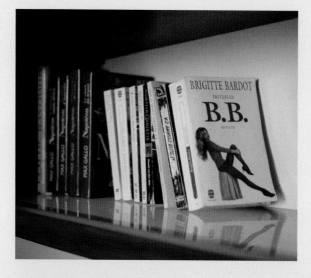

11.19
Sente des Langoustiers, Les Fourches. 2003. Photograph by Olivier Richon and Alexandra McGlynn

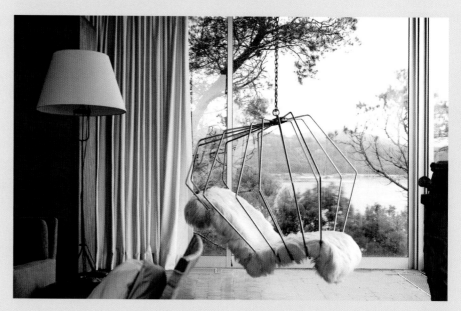

11.20
L'Esquillette, Cap Bénat. 2003. Photograph by Olivier Richon and Alexandra McGlynn

Yet references to Mies van der Rohe and Le Corbusier would not be out of place. The hillsides overlooking the sea are densely covered with pines and cork oak trees. The site called for a rhetoric of concealment, a troglodism of built volumes, with dwellings partially buried into the hillside and made of specific materials: local stone, varnished wood, concrete and cement.

In the early 1960s Philip Johnson designed L'Esquillette, a house in the Cap Bénat for the

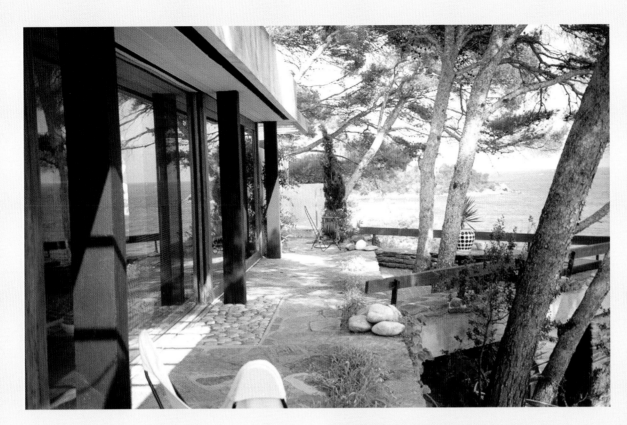

11.21
Terrace, Le Pin Blanc, Saint Clair. 2004. Photograph by Olivier Richon and Alexandra McGlynn

Boissonnas, clients renowned for their passion for Modernism. Johnson's design consists of five separated pavilions, not unlike a Miesian village, with a terrace protected by a wavy rooftop recalling Eero Saarinen and overlooking the spectacular Iles d'Hyères. Johnson met Lefèvre, visited his house and asked him to oversee the construction of L'Esquillette. Le Pin Blanc, Les Fourches and L'Esquillette each achieve a sensuous contingence between landscape, dwelling and materials. Modernism has often been linked to a puritan morality, cleanliness and physical effort. Yet it can equally be in the service of idleness and sensuousness. The Modernist dwelling shelters the Mediterranean siesta, where sleep or half sleep takes us away from the world of work, a torpor found in some moments of Françoise Sagan's *Bonjour Tristesse* (1954), an emblematic story of incestuous desire also located on the Côte d'Azur.

Modernism evoked a future, yet this future rarely happened. It is now a historical project, yet its future tense is still perceptible. Is it because what happened to Modernism is that it did not quite happen? A project now grounded in the past, it still has the evocative power to announce a future. Past and future tense collide, constructing the paradoxical reverie of the Modernist siesta: a nostalgia for the future.

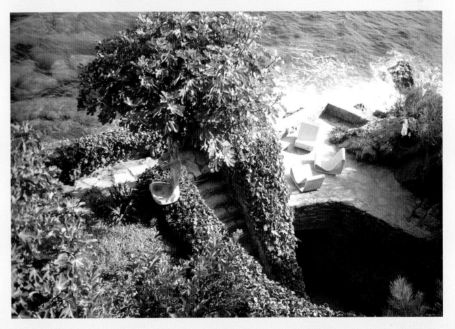

11.22
Garden, Le Pin Blanc, Saint Clair. 2004. Photograph by Olivier Richon and Alexandra McGlynn

Notes

Introduction, Chapter 1

1. The Domestic Interiors Database address is http://www.rca.ac.uk/csdi/didb/
2. Praz (1964)
3. Hugh Honour, 'From the House of Life', *The New York Review of Books* (3 March 1983) quoted in Thornton (1984), p.8
4. Ibid., p.8
5. Saumarez Smith (1993); Gere (1989); Calloway (1998); Thornton (1991). Prior to *Authentic Décor*, there had also been Thornton, *Seventeenth-Century Interior Decoration in England, France and Holland* (1983).
6. The project, funded by the Leverhulme Trust between 1991 and 1994, was published as Annette Carruthers (ed.), *The Scottish Home* (Edinburgh, 1996).
7. Dewing (2003)
8. Dewing (2003), p.9
9. For example, Grant (2005).
10. Tristram (1989)
11. Bryden and Floyd (1999); Marcus (1999)
12. Logan (2001)
13. Bender (1987); Varey (1990); Moretti (1999)
14. Wilk (2002); see also Keeble, Martin and Sparke (2006).
15. Auslander (1996)
16. Habermas (1989)
17. Davidoff and Hall (1987). For further commentary see Vickery (1993) and Eger, Grant, Ó Gallchoir and Warburton (2001), pp.3–9.
18. Said (1978); Mackenzie (1995); Jaffer and Jackson (2004)
19. Girouard (1978)
20. Mandler (1997)
21. Johnson (1999)
22. Rybczynski (1986)
23. Bryden and Floyd (1999)
24. This was posited as an idea by a delegate at the CSDI symposium, *Approaching the Domestic Interior 1400 to the Present*, V&A, London, 5 December 2001.
25. Douglas and Isherwood (1996)
26. Ibid., p.xv; Mauss (1970)
27. Miller (2001)
28. Newton and Putnam (1990). The ideas rehearsed in that project were subsequently extended, for example, in Attfield (2000). Since its formation in 2004, the journal *Home Cultures* (Oxford, 2004–) has provided an interdisciplinary forum for new approaches to the domestic, often informed by Anthropology and Material Culture Studies.
29. John Murdoch, in Newton and Putnam (1990), p.5.
30. In Britain, this tradition of historical research can be traced to the publication of Thompson ([1963] 1980). *History Workshop* (Oxford, 1976–) is also the forum for new research on gender and class in history and society.
31. Ariès (1962); Stone (1977)
32. Hayden (2000)
33. Sarti (2002)
34. Vickery (1998)
35. Attfield and Kirkham (1989)
36. Friedman (1998). For an extension of these debates, see Heynen and Baydar (2005).
37. Reed (1996). See also Reed (2004) and McKellar and Sparke (2004).
38. Light (2001)
39. For an extended consideration of the Renaissance interior, see Ajmar and Dennis (2006).
40. Woolf (1992), pp.146–7
41. Thornton (1984), p.9

Chapter 2

I would like to thank my colleagues at the AHRC Centre for the Study of the Domestic Interior and the members of the research team for the V&A exhibition *At Home in Renaissance Italy* for their insights and encouragement over the past four years. I am particularly grateful to Marta Ajmar-Wollheim, Hannah Greig, Mary Hollingsworth, Ann Matchette, Liz Miller, Michelle O'Malley, Alexander Masters, Luke Syson, Amanda Vickery and the editors of this book for their invaluable comments on drafts of this chapter.

1. Boccaccio (1905), pp.232–3, with amendments by the author.
2. Fra Giovanni Dominici, *Regola del governo di cura familiare* (c.1403), quoted in Ringbom (1984), p.33.
3. *Libro devoto e fruttuoso a ciascun fedel christiano chiamato giardino de orationi*, known as *Giardino de orationi* or *Garden of Prayer* (1454) and widely available in the 15th and 16th centuries, quoted and translated in Andrews (1995), p.29.
4. Goldthwaite (1987); Goldthwaite (1993)
5. On painting for the domestic sphere see Callmann (1974), Pope-Hennessy and Christiansen (1980), Lydecker (1987), Callmann (1988); on *spalliere* see Barriault (1994); on *cassone* see Schubring (1915), Hughes (1997) and Baskins (1998).
6. Musacchio (1999); Goldthwaite (1989); Wilson (1987)
7. 'cassette fatte à quadretti', quoted in Andrews (1995), p.71
8. Hartt (1997), p.67
9. Campbell (1990); Mann and Syson (1998)
10. Randolph (1998)
11. Pilliod (2001); Tazartes (2003)
12. Owen Hughes (1988)
13. Murphy (2003), pp.117–36
14. On printed images, see Landau and Parshall (1994); Bury (2001). On texts, see Richardson (1999).
15. Alexander (1994)
16. Landau and Parshall (1994); Bury (2001)
17. Hart and Hicks (1998)
18. Palladio (1997); Barbieri and Bettramini (2003)
19. Hollingsworth (1984). On Francesco di Giorgio Martini see Bellosi (1993) and Fiore and Tafuri (1993); on Alberti, see Grafton (2000). For their architectural treatises, see Alberti (1988); Filarete (1965), and Francesco di Giorgio Martini (c.1979–1994).
20. Alberti (1973), vol.III, p.46; see also Ceriana (2005).
21. Frigo (1985); Romano (1996), pp.3–42; Ajmar (2004)
22. Shepherd (forthcoming) and Welch (2002)
23. Giovanni Pontano, *De splendore*, quoted and translated in Welch (2002), p.223.
24. *Leggi e memorie venete sulla prostituzione fino alla caduta della republica*, no.105, 108–9: Archivio di Stato, Venice, Senato, Terra, Reg. 32, 1542–1543 (21 February 1542, m.v.), quoted and translated in Fortini Brown (2004), p.183. On sumptuary legislation, see Kovesi Killerby (1991).
25. '*Et quanto alle pitture de' Santi…è molto espediente haver nelle case proprie…et è bene collocarle secondo la grandezza della casa, non confusamente, ma in certi luoghi principali*', Antoniano (1584), fol.54v.
26. '…*il buon padre, il quale pretende di allevare christianamente i figliuoli suoi, si ha da guardare grandissimamente di non tener in casa simili vane, et dishoneste pitture, le quale possono esser fomento, & stimolo di grandissimi vitii*', ibid., fol.55v.
27. '…*de' fili, & delle tele per l'uso, & per l'ornamento della casa, nè delle politezza de' mobili, dell'essercitio dell'ago, della conocchia, dell'arcolaio, dell'allevare i cavalieri da seta, del visitar la cantina, il granaio, la dispensa, l'horto, il pollaio…del tener conto de' bucati, & di tutte le stoviglie, del cucinar le vivande ordinarie, & delle conserve per tutto l'anno…*', Guazzo (1586), fol.132v.
28. Archivio di Stato, Florence, Libri di Commercio e di Famiglia, 4402, Maria Ridolfi Strozzi, 1550–1554; see, for example, fols 3v, 21v, 26r.
29. Christiansen (1983), p.9
30. Fiaccadori and d'Arcano (1996), pp.90, 92
31. I am grateful to Marta Ajmar-Wollheim for bringing this engraving to my attention.
32. Christiansen (2005), pp.258–66
33. Brown and Marini (1992); Mason (1999)
34. Syson (2006)
35. Resmini (2001)
36. Archivio di Stato di Firenze, Carte strozziane, ser.5, no.1750 (accounts and *ricordanze* of Bartolomeo di Tommaso Sassetti), 1455–71, fol.181 left, in Goldthwaite (1972), p.983.
37. Vasari (1878–1906), vol.I, pp.501–3
38. See the *ricordi* of Bernardo Machiavelli, in Branca (1999), pp.143–9 (I am grateful to Ann Matchette for this reference); Cohen and Cohen (1993)
39. Cohen (1992); Cohen and Cohen

(2001–2002)

40. Ruggiero (1993), pp.112–15 and p.167

41. Ruda (1993), pp.240–44; Holmes (1999), pp.141–5

42. Johnson (1997) and Musacchio (2000)

43. Musacchio (1999); Watson (2001), pp.201–2

44. Anton Francesco Doni, Letter to Girolamo Fava, 1 March 1550, quoted and translated in Pullen and Chambers (1992), pp.181–2.

45. '…Suave compagnia, dolce concerto / L'oca la gatta, e tutti / La vecchia, e'l porco, e i putti / La galina, e'l mio amor sotto un coverto / Ma in cento parte discoverto / Dove la Luna, e'l Sol / Fa tanto più la casa allegra, e chiara…', Anon. (1607), fol.2v.

46. Boschloo (1974); Bayer (2004)

47. Franzoni (1990)

48. 'famosissime statue; equestri; pedestri; erette; sedenti; prostrate… di variate petre, feree… argentee; auree', Achillini (1510), fol.4r.

49. '…e tutte le tele aragne / che se trova per casa / cum massarie e vasa / de diverse sorte / tre fusa e due sporte / un Nasporela Rocca / Un Boccal senza Bocca… / Un pugno de stecchi / e tre solfanelli / cum doi pestelli / e megia scudella / item una pianella / cum tre scarpe rotte…', Anon. ([16th century]), fol.6v.

50. 'La casa dove posa il mio thesoro / E piu d'ogni altra gratiosa & bella / Le mura d'alabastro il tetto d'oro / De Zephir la fenestra ove sta quella / D'avorio l'uscio de si bel lavoro', Olimpo degli Alessandri (1532), fol.9r.

51. 'Felice sedie e casse / Dove spesso se pone /… Per riposarse', ibid., fol.59v.

52. 'O leticel dove costei si posa / Lenzoletti sottil chel corpo amanta / O guancia…O coverta gentil & pretiosa… / O molle pime dove lei si volta / Parlate voi per me, si non m'ascolta', Olimpo degli Alessandri ([1580]), fol.8v.

53. Cocchiara (1980), pp.159–87; Pleij (2001)

54. 'In letti di bombace è il tuo dormire / Con lenzuola di renso, e di cortina / Coperte, e paviglion, che fan stupire / Tutti i traponti alla damaschina', Anon. (1588), fol.4r.

55. 'Le case belle vi vi voglio contare / di cacio pecorino son le mura / e di ricotta le fanno imbiancare', Anon. ([c.1540?]), fols 2r–2v.

56. 'E tutto il matonato / Vò che sia di malitie di Villani / La Loggia, di Bugie di Ceretani, / Le Sale, & i Mezani / Sian di sospir d'Amanti appassionati / E doglie di meschini Infranciosati / Di furia di Soldati / Saran le porte, gli usci, & i balconi / Tutti di sfacciatagin di Buffoni', Croce (1607), p.5.

57. 'La sala di pomata, e la Cucina / Di sapon nero… Tutto il resto è di lana / Succida, pettinata a poco a poco / Da un Babuin di cera appresso il foco', ibid., pp.14–15.

58. 'Once you have put everything in its place, whenever you wish to recall something, start again at the entrance and move through the house, where you will find all the images linked one to another as in a chain or a chorus.' Ad Herennium, quoted in Kent (2002), p.122.

59. Ibid., pp.124–32

Chapter 3

1. For details of audiences see Gurr (2004).

2. For more on the amplification function see Foakes (2002), pp.19–21

3. Hatchuel (2004), p.4

4. Rutter (1999); Foakes (2002). The original inventories of properties belonging to the Admiral's Men have been lost since they were recorded by Edward Malone in 1790.

5. For a full analysis of the inventories see Lena Orlin, 'Things with little social life' in Korda and Harris (2002).

6. All quotations are from Wells and Taylor (1986).

7. Dessen (1984), p.61

8. See Michael Dobson, 'Improving on the Original: actresses and adaptations' in Jackson and Bate (2001), p.46

9. Quoted in Finkel (1996), p.10

10. Peter Holland, 'The Age of Garrick', in Jackson and Bate (2001), p.77–8. See also Benedetti (2001).

11. 1570, A2v.

12. Gouge (1622), p.18

13. Cleaver (1598), p.177

14. For the texts of these domestic plays see Wiggins (2007); for a more detailed analysis of domestic representation in these plays, see Richardson (2006).

Chapter 4

1. The Canadian architectural theorist Withold Rybczynski, in his book on the history of the home, devoted a chapter entitled 'Domesticity' to the 17th-century Dutch house. His account, however, is largely based on an uncritical interpretation of contemporary traveller reports and paintings of the domestic interior. Rybczynski (1986), pp.51–75.

2. Two economic historians have independently arrived at this approximate level of production for 17th-century Dutch painters using different methods of estimation. See Montias (1990) and Van der Woude (1991).

3. There have been a considerable number of recent publications that address the 17th-century Dutch interior and its depiction in art, as well as issues of domesticity. See De Jong et al. (2000); Loughman and Montias (2000); Westermann (2001); Fock (2001); Fock et al. (2001); Muizelaar and Phillips (2003).

4. An engaging recent survey of 17th-century Dutch genre painting is Franits (2004).

5. For European marriage and family trends, see Barbagli and Kertzer (2001), pp.ix–xxxii.

6. De Vries and Van der Woude (1997), pp.163–4

7. Watt (2001). Van der Heijden (1996) explores the supervision of marriage by the secular and Reformed church authorities in 17th-century Rotterdam.

8. The most important discussion on domestic conduct books and their relevance for the art of the period is Franits (1993).

9. On the economic role of women, see De Vries and Van der Woude (1997), pp.596–606.

10. De Vries (1993)

11. Dibbits (1996) discusses the changing appearance and cultural significance of linen cupboards.

12. These carpets were actually manufactured in Anatolia, but have received their modern name through their prominent survival in Transylvanian Protestant churches. Ydema (1991), p.48.

13. Grijzenhout and Van Veen (1999) is a useful collection of essays dealing with the history of scholarship and approaches to 17th-century Dutch painting.

14. Franits (2004), pp.17–64

15. Potterton (1986), pp.32–3, summarizes the interpretative possibilities of this painting.

16. For this painting, see Franits (2004), pp.206–8.

17. Sutton (1998), pp.68–75, analyzes the artistic and cultural context of De Hooch's domestic imagery.

18. On the market for Ter Borch's paintings, see Kettering (1997), p.106.

19. Carlson (1994)

20. For these various rooms and a discussion of their etymology, see Van der Veen (1997) and Van der Veen (2000).

21. For this painting, see Fock et al. (2001), p.153.

22. Van der Veen (2000)

23. For a discussion of civility and Dutch books of manners, see Spierenburg (1981) and Roodenburg (1991).

24. Goeree (1681), pp.135–6. For Goffman's analogies between human behaviour and stage performance, see Goffman (1956).

25. Gaba-van Dongen (2004)

26. Lighting conditions in Dutch houses has been recently treated by Muizelaar and Phillips (2003), pp.56–61.

27. Franits (1993), pp.95–100

28. Laurence (1994), pp.130 notes that most travellers' accounts, irrespective of their country of origin or destination, include comments on cleanliness. Even Dutch visitors to England were impressed by the sanitary conditions. For the Dutch 'obsession' with cleanliness, see Schama (1987), pp.375–97.

29. Van Strien (1993), pp.43, 212
30. On Metsu's painting, see Westermann (2001), pp.64–5, 182, and Franits (2004), pp.183–5.
31. Other painters such as Pieter de Hooch also incorporated architectural features from Amsterdam's most famous building into their scenes of domestic life. See Sutton (1997).
32. Fock (2001), pp.91–5
33. Fock (2001), pp.85–91
34. Ydema (1991)
35. Wijsenbeek-Olthuis (1996), p.153
36. Ydema (1991), p.145
37. Wijsenbeek-Olthuis (1996), p.154
38. Fock (2001), p.95
39. Franits (1993)
40. Wijsenbeek-Olthuis (1996), p.153
41. This is the conclusion of Fock (2001). Franits (2004), p.187, has qualified some of Fock's conclusions.
42. Westermann has also drawn analogies between present-day advertising photographs and 17th-century representations of the interior. Westermann (2004), pp.17–24.

Chapter 5

I am indebted to the Director and the staff of the Yale Centre for British Art for providing me with a guest fellowship, extensive access to their collections and particularly generous assistance with my research. Invaluable comments and suggestions were also offered by Quintin Colville, Flora Dennis, Liz Miller, Kate Retford, Giorgio Riello and Amanda Vickery, for which I am extremely grateful.

1. Porter (1990), pp.37–9, 191–3
2. Robinson (1953)
3. Cranfield (1978)
4. Brewer (1997), pp.131–3; Porter (1990), pp.234–5
5. Barker (2000), pp.29–30; Porter (1990), p.234; Cranfield (1978), p.57
6. Brewer (1997), pp.451–5. For details on the print culture of the period see particularly Donald (1996); Hallett (1999).
7. Depictions of certain interior elements (particularly basic furniture such as beds, tables and chairs) can be found in early modern woodcuts and illustrated broadsheets. These tend to be partial views of aspects of the interior, rather than full portrayals of interior scenes, but are useful for tracing early precedents of themes discussed here.
8. Saumarez Smith (2000), p.10; J. Cornforth (1978), p.15
9. Saumarez Smith (2000), pp.1, 33–7, 59–64, 139–48
10. Oct 19 [1737] 'Finish'd my 4th seat of a chair viz;- that from the 3rd Print in the Harlott's Proggress; Aug 16–19 [1740] Finish'd my 5th Seat of a chair – that taken from an old Ballad. Began my 6th taken from 'The Jews Lodging' in The Harlott's Progress'. Savile (1997), pp.241, 234.
11. Paulson (1965) vol.1, pp.41–3; Hallett (1999), pp.93–132; Uglow (1997), p.212
12. The pristine condition of this seat cover raises significant questions as to whether or not it was ever used.
13. Praz (1971), for definition of the conversation piece see pp.33–4; Pointon (1993), pp.177–89.
14. Kennedy, 'Taking Tea,' in Snodin and Styles (2001), pp.252–4
15. Leppert (1988), pp.182, 197
16. Saumarez Smith (2000), p.102
17. Praz (1971), pp.45–58
18. Borsay (1991); Summerson (2003)
19. Brewer and Porter (1993), especially introduction pp.1–19 and chapter by Lorna Weatherhill.
20. Weatherhill (1998), pp.24–38, table 2.1
21. Klein (1984) and Klein (1994). The term 'sociability' was coined in the early 1700s to describe a 'society' that was distinct from the state and to describe the social requirements of politeness. Detailed studies of the culture and functions of 18th-century sociability are only just beginning to emerge. For a discussion of the use of the term and patterns of sociability in London see Whyman (1999), pp.87–90. For studies of sociability in 18th-century France and America see Goodman (1994) and Shields (1997). These works draw on longer debates about the social aspects of public life, which use Jürgen Habermas's theory of the public sphere as a departure point. See Habermas (1989); Vickery (1998), pp.225–7.
22. Lady Hertford to Lady Pomfret, 26 March 1741 in Hughes (1940), p.174
23. Mrs. Boscawen to Admiral Boscawen, 1 January 1748, in Aspinall-Oglander (1940), p.68.
24. British Library, Althorp Mss. 75927, Lavinia Countess Spencer to Earl Spencer (23 March 1786).
25. Styles and Vickery (2006)
26. *The Woman of Taste in a Second Epistle from Clelia in Town to Sappho in the Country*, printed for J. Bately (London, 1733)
27. Mrs Boscawen to Admiral Boscawen, 11 December 1747, in Aspinall-Oglander (1940), p.66.
28. British Library, Add.Mss.22226, f.135, Countess of Strafford to the Earl (8 April 1712).
29. Kugler (2002), p.133
30. Saumarez Smith (2000), pp.99–102
31. *The Duet* (pl.5.11) is therefore unusual in this regard as it suggests a far broader spatial scheme than other paintings by Devis [see pl.5.16 and pl.5.1].
32. Vickery (1998), pp.172–4
33. British Library, Althorp Mss. 75770 f.199, 'Rates, taxes, repairs and furniture for Spencer House St James's and St James's Place, 1772–1775'.

Chapter 6

I would like to thank my colleagues at the AHRC Centre for the Study of the Domestic Interior and the participants in the *Literature and the Domestic Interior* conference (V&A, 2004) and *interior/interiority* symposium (Queen Mary, University of London, 2005) for providing a stimulating environment for this work. I am particularly grateful to Michèle Barrett, Elizabeth Eger, Markman Ellis, Geoffrey Gilbert, Corinna Russell, Morag Shiach and Barry Smith for their comments and suggestions.

1. James (1995), pp.222–3
2. James (1995), p.8
3. Cather (1936), p.47
4. Reeve (1785), pp.111
5. Lukacs (1970), p.623
6. Ibid.
7. Rybczinski (1986)
8. Cather (1936), p.52
9. Cather (1936), p.55
10. Watt (1957), p.26
11. Defoe (1968), p.137
12. Watt (1957), p.26
13. Defoe (1996), p.212
14. Defoe (1996), p.210
15. Defoe (1996), p.223
16. Defoe (1996), p.221
17. Clery (2004), p.136; Wall (2004), pp.118–20; Lipsedge (2006)
18. Richardson (1742), pp.474–5.
19. Ballaster (1992)
20. Eaves and Kimple (1971); Eagleton (1982); Keymer (1992)
21. Hayley was described as 'the work-basket poet of that day. His verses were upon every Girl's Sopha,' in Alexander (1993), p.26.
22. Brewer (1996) and Tadmor (1996). For a survey of recent criticism see also Brewer (1997), pp.192–7.
23. Chalker (1969)
24. Lewis (1754)
25. Lonsdale (1989), p.xxvi
26. Collier (1739), lines 75–86
27. Ibid., lines 150–5
28. Austen (1980), p.179
29. Anne Brontë's *Agnes Grey* (1847) and Charlotte Brontë's *Jane Eyre* (1847) are the best known examples of a genre of governess novels. See Wadsö-Lecaros (2001).
30. Austen (1980), pp.173–4
31. Eliot (1965), p.99
32. James (1995), p.287
33. Austen (1996), pp.201–5
34. Eliot (1965), p.100
35. Ibid., p.358
36. Ibid., p.25
37. Ibid., p.56
38. Wall (2004), p.120
39. Ibid.
40. Finn (2002)
41. Dickens (1977), pp.86–7
42. Dickens (1850), chapter III, p.22
43. Grant (1984), p.87
44. Grant (1984), p.88
45. Small (1996)
46. Grant (1984), p.40
47. Dickens (1998), p.49
48. Dickens (1998), pp.167–8

49. Austen (1980), p.174
50. Woolf (1992), p.38

Chapter 7

1. Benjamin (1999), p.9
2. Ibid.
3. Ibid.
4. Originally published in 1934 as a limited series of five volumes under the title of *Une semaine de bonté*.
5. Foster (1993), pp.174–82
6. For the development of more 'sophisticated' means of representing the domestic interior in magazines, for example, see Aynsley and Berry (2005).
7. Sidlauskas (2000), pp.20–60
8. Ibid., pp.11–18, 36–46
9. Marcus (1999), pp.19–32
10. At the same time sentimental representations of rural households executed under the aesthetic idiom of Realism, such as Pierre Edouard Frère's *The Little Cook* (pl.7.5), garnered approval when exhibited at the annual Paris Salon.
11. Brisset (1853), p.250: 'Next to the dining room there is a narrow and sombre room. A skylight placed very high allows into this obscure den a little air and light, and even this air and this light often only come from a stairwell or a small courtyard surrounded by high walls. It is by this insufficient opening that asphyxiating coal fumes and the smell of the dishes being prepared can escape; for this sad and unhealthy cubbyhole is the kitchen found in small Parisian apartments. It's just as well, since it is with the aid of this important nook that the reception rooms are able to maintain their honourable purpose!' Unless otherwise stated all translations are mine.
12. Ibid., p.250: 'The stew cooking in the bedroom belongs essentially to the working-class household. Whether real or only apparent, it is the most sharply defined boundary between the harsh necessity of the worker and bourgeois comfort. Now that dress is the same for all social classes, now that widespread education gives to all practically the same speech, there are just two major

demarcations that separate them: at the top the carriage and at the bottom the location of the stew.'
13. For the liminal class position of the *portière*, the new apartment building's female equivalent to the concierge, see Marcus (1999), pp.42–80.
14. Brisset (1853), p.250: 'The broom, the feather duster in her hand, she tidies, sorts, cleans; she lovingly dusts and shines each piece of furniture in which she is reflected; she cares for them with a sense of gratitude, for they all form a part of her happiness.' For further discussion of Brisset's representation of domestic labour see Berry (1998), pp.68–70.
15. De Circourt (1853), p.38: 'Today the suite of parading rooms (*appartements de parade*) are at the same time those for habitation; the bedroom of the mistress of the house, this sanctuary for the English, is not even always kept private.'
16. Adler (1989); Hellerstein (1976); Hellerstein, Parker Hume and Offen (1981); Higonnet (1987); McMillan (1981); Perrot (1990); Pollock (1988); Smith (1981); Struminger (1979); Vickery (1993); Wolff (1985)
17. Marcus (1999), pp.135–65. Marcus argues that the conceptualization of the domestic interior as a space distinct from urban space declined in the 1880s. I would suggest the opposite: the concept of interiority intensified in the *fin-de-siècle*, whilst the interior itself became more publicly exposed in representation, thus betraying any claims to privacy.
18. 'The domestic interior is an inviolable sanctuary that no impure wind can soil. The street belongs to men, the domestic interior to woman.' Larousse (1866–1890), p.690.
19. P. Janet (1857), pp.68–9: 'The tired, troubled man returns to his dwelling in search of relaxation. It must be for him not only a well-run interior, not only an ornate interior, but also it must be an ornate spirit. The woman must not forget that she is the joy, the charm, the recreation of the family: the major principle of domestic politics is to ensure for the husband

that his interior is more agreeable than that of others.' For more on the orderly household see Hellerstein (1976).
20. Daly (1864–77), p.15: 'In effect, this existence divides into two very distinct parts: one is entirely dedicated to intimacy, to the duties and affections of the family, and they claim architectural arrangements that guarantee the liberty and the secrecy of private life; the other is mingled with the exterior world by our acquaintances, whether they are business or pleasure, and this second, one might say public, side of our existence, consists more of luxurious gold brilliance than the first. This double aspect … naturally indicates a primary division in the dwelling place. For public life … one needs the largest and richest rooms of the residence. For family life, one needs the interior apartment, with its character of intimacy and comfort. Finally, domestic service, which unites itself with these two sides of life, requires a judiciously chosen place in order to satisfy promptly and conveniently the requirements of the one and the other.'
21. In the first chapter the building's new tenant Octave Mouret is shown into an apartment's kitchen and immediately made aware of the building's transgressive fluidity: 'Despite the cold, the window was wide open. Leaning over the rail, the dark maidservant and a fat old cook were looking down into the narrow well of the inner courtyard, which let some light into the kitchens that faced each other on every floor. Bending forward, they were both yelling, while from the bowels of the courtyard rose the sound of crude laughter, mingled with curses. It was as if a sewer had brimmed over. All the domestics in the house were there, letting off steam. Octave thought of the bourgeois majesty of the grand staircase.' Zola (1999), p.9
22. After approving the initial image the imperial household imposed no reproduction rights or restrictions on the production and sale of what

amounted to hundreds of thousands of *carte-de-visite* portraits of Napoleon III and his family. McCauley (1994), p.305
23. Lucie-Smith (1977), p.17
24. The official decorating manual of the Third Republic described the dining table as 'the altar where on a daily basis one is sacrificed to the pure joys of the family and of friendship.' Havard (1884), p.366
25. Fried (2002), p.94
26. Fried borrows the term 'lived perspective' from a key 20th-century theorist of embodied viewing, Maurice Merleau-Ponty. Ibid., p.92
27. A reference to Caillebotte's *The Luncheon* may be included in the following extract: 'And, as we are solidly embracing nature, we will no longer separate the figure from the background of an apartment or the street. In actuality, a person never appears against neutral or vague backgrounds. Instead, surrounding him and behind him are the furniture, fireplaces, curtains and walls that indicate his financial position, class and profession. The individual … will be having lunch with his family or sitting in his armchair near his worktable, absorbed in thought.' Duranty (1986), p.44
28. Ibid., p.45
29. Sidlauskas (2000), p.12
30. Groom (1995), p.181; Garb (1998), p.31
31. In relation to Caillebotte's *The Luncheon* Michael Fried has written that although the viewer is strongly implicated in the painting, the absorbed figures 'evoke a mood of inwardness or "cloistering"…'. According to Fried, Duranty was key in developing the theory of the cloister 'into a theory of the apartment'. Fried (2002), pp.91–4
32. Havard (1884), pp.243–44: 'Were one to permit us a trivial image, we would say that the habitation can be compared to the toilette. Externally we are obliged to take account of fashion, to not individualize ourselves too much, to don on certain days, or at certain hours, the black suit and

the shirt front; but of what one can call the interior toilette, neither the public, nor our friends have anything to see, and we are free, if we feel like it, to wear flannel, or not.'

33. See Fried (2002), p.75 for analysis of the painting in terms of the absorptive qualities of each figure and the reader's embodied identification with the figure seen from behind.

34. Pollock (1988), pp.81–7; Adler (1989), pp.10–11

35. Groom (1995), p.206

36. Uzanne (1892), p.259. For the development of more personal attitudes to interior decoration see Auslander (1996), pp.261–305. For the gendering of subjective interior decoration see Tiersten (1996), Tiersten (2001), pp.150–84 and Berry (2005).

37. Larroumet (1896), p.100: 'Above all, living at home more than us, they arrange the most comfortable, the most agreeable and the most flattering setting, so that it is most suitable to their beauty, so that it directs towards them and concentrates on them the gaze and attention.'

38. The author of a 1900 article sought to explain recent developments within the discipline of psychology by reference to 'unwelcome visitors' in the 'mental chamber'. He recommended the following steps as a means of maintaining mental health: '1. Retire each day to a quiet apartment and remain alone in silence. 2. Take up the most restful position possible, in a comfortable armchair, for example…. 3. Shut the door of your thoughts to the outside world…'. Bois (1900), pp.29–30. See Silverman (1989), pp.75–106 for a full analysis of the new psychological meanings attached to the interior.

39. Foveau de Courmelles (1896), p.11

40. Jourdain (1902) pp.37–8: 'His dream would be to live in a house where the doors would silently open, the carpets would muffle the sound of footsteps and thick curtains would prevent all external sounds. The service would be carried out by mute blonde women dressed in pink

gowns….The whole of life passed as such in restful silence, in a radiant light, voluptuously enveloped by the calm warmths of the home, far from the din, from the street which one forgets, which one ignores…'.

41. Molly Nesbit has shown that despite Atget's commitment to categorizing the professional status of each interior he photographed, a number of the interiors in the *Parisian Interiors* album produced in 1910 had fictional owners. Certainly there was no hat-maker registered as living in the Place St.André des Arts. Nesbit (1992), p.122

42. In an article in the British architectural magazine *The Architectural Record*, the French author Paul Frantz Marcou described the Parisian's desire for isolation: 'It is there that at the present time we meet with the real type of Parisian residence, combining every modern comfort and convenience, all the numerous arrangements to charm the sight and make life pleasant, to isolate each tenant from contact with those above and beneath, to separate him also from the family living alongside him on the same landing, to make him forget that in one of these horizontal slices of house superposed like a chest of drawers, he is not entirely *chez lui*, and, in a word, to produce as far as possible the illusion of being in his own house, while sparing him the burdens and cares incumbent upon a house-owner.' Marcou (1893), p.325

43. For further analysis of the relationship between figure and setting in Vuillard's interiors see Sidlauskas (2000), pp.91–123

44. Proust (1913)

Chapter 8

1. Adolf Loos, 'Regarding Economy,' in Colomina (1994), p.64

2. For a consideration of television and interiors see Viviana Narotzky in this volume. For film and interiors, see Albrecht (1987).

3. The number of visitors to the Great Exhibition is given in Richards (1990), p.35.

4. Benjamin (1983), pp.162–6

5. Richards (1990), p.29

6. The majority of 22 were from France, 8 from England, and other examples from Belgium, Prussia, Austria, Württemberg, Switzerland, Sweden, Italy, Egypt and China, the last two were typical, modest country houses. See Ducuing (1867) and Bömches (1868).

7. *The British Section at the Vienna Universal Exhibition, 1873, Official Catalogue, with plans and illustrations*, published by J. M. Johnson and sons for the British Royal Commission, 1873.

8. Richards (1990), p.31

9. Muthesius ([1904–5] 1979), p.10

10. John Gloag, introduction, in Eastlake (1969), p.ix

11. Eastlake (1864)

12. For the context of artistic prescription for the home, see Gere and Hoskins (2000). Emma Ferry explores the particular circumstances of the Art in the Home series, Ferry (2004). See also Ferry (2003).

13. For conventions of historical museum display, see Conn (1998), Noordergraaf (2004), and Joachimides (1995). Specifically on period rooms, see Aynsley in Keeble, Martin and Sparke (2006).

14. Peck (1996)

15. Nilsson (1911); Edenheim and Arnö-Berg (1995)

16. Kirshenblatt-Gimblett, in Karp and Levine (1991), pp.401–43

17. Aynsley (2005), pp.43–60

18. Colson (1904), vol.15, no.4

19. Beetham (1996); Gruber Garvey (1996)

20. Grossmith and Grossmith ([1945] 1985), pp.19–20

21. Mackintosh (1902)

22. Snodin and Stavenow-Hidemark (1997)

23. Bogart (1995)

24. For the equivalent in architectural books, see Bresciani (2003)

25. Swenarton (1981)

26. The literature on Modernist design is substantial. For a recent contribution see Wilk (2006).

27. Aynsley (2000)

28. For a commentary on the rational

kitchen see Sparke (1995) and Henderson in Coleman, Danze and Henderson (1996).

29. Meyer ([1926] 1975). Shortly afterwards, Meyer would become Director of the Bauhaus, before emigrating to the Soviet Union in 1933.

30. Otto and Pommer (1991)

31. Hitchcock and Johnson (1966) and commentary on this exhibition, Riley (1992).

32. Kerner (2003)

33. For the full context of this exhibition, see Overy (2004) and Brunhammer and Tise (1990), pp.157–183.

34. The concept of conservative modernity was developed in relation to literature in Light (1991).

35. Ryan (1997)

36. Robach (2002)

37. Guenther (1984)

38. Evans (1992) and Pahnicke, Honnef et al. (1991)

39. On Hine, see Posever and Mallach (1984); also Riis *Battle with the Slum* (1902), *How the Other Half Lives* ([1901] 1971) and *A Ten Year's War: an account of the battle with the slum in New York* (n.d.).

40. Brooks (1948)

41. Brandt (1948), p.12

42. Ibid., p.19

43. For Abram Games see Games, Moriarty and Rose (2003).

44. *Picture Post* (1941), vol.10, no.1.

Chapter 9

1. Benjamin (1969). Walter Benjamin's text has spawned a huge literature since the publication of the collection of essays *Illuminations*, without his central argument being seriously challenged.

2. Safran and Wang (1985), p.106. Cited in an excerpted and de-contextualised form in Colomina (1994), p.31. Colomina's project is to demonstrate that Loos's architecture operates as a mask, to disguise identity while apparently exposing the (female) inhabitant in a ritualized form of theatre. For Colomina, 'modern architecture only becomes modern with its engagement with

the media' (p.14), a thesis she demonstrates by interpreting the pronouncements of Loos and Le Corbusier in a way the authors did not intend. While Loos and Le Corbusier are both at pains to assert the unique and specific characteristics of three-dimensional architectural form and space, and the need to move through actual buildings, Colomina reduces their buildings to the spectacle of two-dimensional imagery. Loos was so insistent that people visit his houses in the flesh that he published a leaflet offering a guided tour for 20 crowns – with the strict admonition to wipe your feet! Adolf Loos, *Wohnungs Wanderungen* (1907), in Kurrent and Spalt (1970), p.30.

3. Kurrent and Spalt (1970), p.29. The photographer is identified as Atelier Gerlach.

4. Loos, 'Architecture', in Safran and Wang (1985), pp.105–6. This kind of argument, which in the writings of Roger Fry, Clive Bell and Clement Greenberg came to identify the dominant strand of theory about Modernism, was shared by many modern architects.

5. Greenberg (1961), in Frascina and Harris (1992), p.309.

6. The best known statements are in Le Corbusier (1964), p.60 (the Maison La Roche as a 'promenade architecturale') and Le Corbusier and Jeanneret (1935), p.24: 'Arab architecture offers us a precious insight. It is on foot and in movement that the organisation of architecture can be appreciated. This is the opposite principle to that of Baroque architecture which is conceived on paper around a fixed viewpoint. I prefer the lesson of Arab architecture'. For Colomina, this insistence on the actual experience of buildings is turned into 'a space that is not made of walls but of images. Images as walls.' Colomina (1994), p.6

7. Benjamin (1996), p.235

8. Colomina (1988), p.9, cited in Niedenthal (1993), p.101

9. For example, no 20th-century illustrations have spawned as many imitators as the plates in the architectural treatises of Sebastiano Serlio, Andrea Palladio or Fischer von Erlach.

10. Ward (2001), pp.1–2. Ward distinguishes the 'dazzling' effects of 1920s Modernism from the notions of 'simulacrum' and 'spectacle' formulated by post-Modern writers such as Jean Baudrillard and Guy Debord.

11. Ibid., p.2

12. I use the anachronistic term Modernism, derived from post-war art criticism, to refer to the theory and practice of what Anglo-Saxon writers referred to in the interwar period as 'the modern movement'. For a more considered explanation and history of Modernism in architecture see Benton (2006). An accessible and comprehensive recent account is Colquhoun (2002).

13. There is a long history of dissatisfied clients in the history of Modernism, see, for example, Benton (1987) and Friedman (1996). Rybczynski (1987) generalizes this to include Modernism as a theory and praxis, as does Reed (1996).

14. We know from the visitors' books in Le Corbusier's houses that they were regularly visited from the outset, as were many Modernist houses in Europe and America.

15. When we filmed the Moller house in Vienna in 1973 it was still little visited (Open University A305 TV 10). As the Israeli residence in Vienna, it was relatively inaccessible and the Muller house was in Prague, which was at that time still behind the Iron Curtain. The Tristan Tzara house in Paris has always been difficult to visit, as have most of the private houses and apartments in Vienna. Colour illustrations of Loos' houses only began to appear in the 1980s and 1990s. Colomina confirms Benjamin's lack of understanding of Loos' architecture – Colomina (1994), p.353, n.101.

16. See, for example, Josep Quetglas's analysis of the photographs of Mies's pavilion and the significance of the line of classical columns excluded from these images – Quetglas (2000).

17. Deutscher Werkbund (1927); Graeff (1928)

18. Johnson, Hitchcock et al. (1969), p.12. Henry-Russell Hitchcock, one of the organizers of the International Architecture Exhibition, was an inveterate visitor of buildings and knew most of the buildings illustrated in the exhibition at first hand.

19. International exhibitions in Europe, such as those in Paris (1925, 1937), London (1924), Barcelona (1929) and Stockholm (1930), also played a significant role in allowing people to walk through full-size domestic environments, although, with the exception of the Stockholm exhibition, the interiors were highly eclectic in style and dominated by traditional or Art Deco styles rather than Modernism.

20. Ryan (1997), pp.55–6. The 'House of the Future' was designed by S. Rowland Pierce and R.A. Duncan with a steel frame, flat roof and steel windows. An exception was a house for the model train manufacturer Bassett-Lowke, which was designed by a German architect, Peter Behrens. In 1930 and 1931 the Ideal Home exhibition ran competitions for non-architects to design houses, which were subsequently built: the 'House that Jill built' (by Mrs Phyllis Lee) in 1930 and the 'House that Jack built' (by Thomas Dalgliesh McLean) in 1931. Ryan (1997), pp.64–7.

21. 'The house interior as an object of positivist study will undergo Taylorist dissection, the breaking down of all movement into basic units, studied and timed in order to reorganize each and every task into perfectly coordinated diagrams lacking in interference', Abalos (2001), p.73. She is referring here to Taylor's *Principles of Scientific Management* and the use of time and motion study principles in the design of kitchens, in the works of Christine Frederick in America and various architects and designers in Europe. According to Abbalos, Modernism in architecture was determined and limited by the positivism of Auguste Comte 'the stratum, in short, that those who have the authority to do so agree is the only one that is undoubtedly exhausted, whose validity has ended'. Abalos (2001), p.8

22. See for example Sears Roebuck catalogue, *c.*1910 (*Homes in a Box*, Schiffer Design, Atglen, PA, n.d.).

23. Le Corbusier exhibited house models every year from 1922 to 1924: the Citrohan II house (1922) and the Maison Ribot (1923) as well as built or unbuilt projects for private houses: Villa Besnus (1922), the Nestlé Villa (Rambouillet) (1923), Maison La Roche (1923). It is clear from the correspondence with Raoul La Roche and Daniel Nestlé that exhibiting these models was of capital importance for Le Corbusier, in terms of publicity. The wooden model for the Maison La Roche was made (October 1923) during a transitional stage in the design process, on the basis of imprecise plans, when the interior had not been designed at all, Benton (1998), pp.238 and 243 n.55. The Salon d'Automne opened on 1 November 1923.

24. Le Corbusier (1964), p.45

25. Bois and Reichlin (1985)

26. Well-illustrated histories of Modernist architecture followed shortly, for example Platz (1927), Behrendt (1927), Taut (1929) and Platz (1933). Domestic interiors were well represented in the photographic plates in these works.

27. Aubrey Beardsley was one of the first to insist on the photo-mechanical reproduction of his drawings, and his example encouraged architects such as Mackintosh and Baillie-Scott to produce coloured renderings of their interiors which could provide attractive reproductions in the journals.

28. Baillie Scott absolves himself from 'expert knowledge in the arts of literature or illustration', claiming that his book *Houses and Gardens* 'has been done in leisure moments snatched from the time which must

be devoted to the labours of the architect'. Baillie Scott (1995), p.34; Kurrent and Spalt (1970), p.29.

29. An example in *Houses and Gardens* was Bexton Croft, already published in the *Studio* in January 1895 in the form of engravings and watercolours under the heading of 'An ideal suburban house', see Benton, Benton and Sharp (1975), pp.7–9. One exterior photograph, four interior photos and two plans are included in *Houses and Gardens*.

30. By 'wide angle' (a photographer's term) I mean the angle of view. The human eye normally grasps a field of view of around 60º (although peripheral vision is much wider). Anything wider than 75º would be considered 'wide angle'. A lens covering more than 90º will tend to distort objects in the foreground and even produce a spherical image. A skilful artist can represent a field of view of 90º or more without observable distortion.

31. Spielman and Layard (1905), pp.56, 64–5. This book was engraved and printed by Edmund Evans on wood blocks with up to eight colour blocks. The authors compare the effects of Evans's coloured woodblocks with the modern 'Three Colour Process'.

32. This drawing (FLC 28618, March 1934) is by Junzo Sakakura, one of the best draughtsmen in Le Corbusier's atelier. For my analysis of the Arts and Crafts and anarchist imagery in Pierre Jeanneret's sketches for the 'petite maison de weekend' at La Celle-St Cloud (1935) see Benton (2002).

33. Larsson (1922). The Blaue Bücher edition included illustrations from the five folio editions published in Sweden by Albert Bonnier in Stockholm, including *Ett hem* (A Home, 1899) between 1899 and 1913, as well as sketches published in the book *In Memoriam Carl Larsson*, 1919. Larsson's home and studio Lilla Hyttnas in the village of Sundborn (one of several artist's cottages in this picturesque village in Dalarna) is regularly visited by Swedish and

foreign admirers. For the background in Scandinavian National Romanticism and the Open Air Museum movement, see Lane (2000).

34. Bachelard (1969), p.30. For Gaston Bachelard, of course, the phenomenology of 'home' descends deeper into primitive dream images: 'For instance, in the house itself, in the family sitting-room, a dreamer of refuges dreams of a hut, of a nest, or of nooks and corners in which he would like to hide away, like an animal in its hole.'

35. Facos (1996), pp.81–91

36. See Facos (1996), p.82 for the sources of this reforming zeal in William Morris and the publications in Sweden of Ellen Kay and Edmond Grosse.

37. See Benton (1987), pp.144–5

38. For example, Le Corbusier praised women for the reform of their costume, cutting their hair and simplifying their clothing in order to lead an active life. Le Corbusier (1991), pp.106–7

39. Perriand was addicted to sport and published a project for a 'salle de sport et de travail' entitled 'Travail et Sport' (*Repertoire du goût moderne*, edition Albert Levy, vol. 2, fin 1928, planches 18–22) and also published as 'Salle de culture physique' in *L'Art international d'aujourd'hui*, Intérieurs VI, Editions d'art Charles Moreau, 1929, planche 25; see Barsac (2005).

40. The history of the kitchen and its determination by Taylorist notions of time and motion studies has been well covered in the literature. The American Christine Frederick first translated Taylorist principles into guidelines for the design of kitchens – Frederick (1913) – and her work was quickly translated and circulated in Europe, leading to influential books such as Meyer (1925) and Bernège (1928a) and Bernege (1928b). For a more cultural history, see Clarisse (2004), with bibliography.

41. The use of strips of film, complete with sprocket holes, as illustrations to books about the home is

characteristic of the period. For example, Gropius (1965).

42. *Architectural Review*, C85 (March 1939), pp.121–132

43. Ibid., pp.129–31

44. Wright (2003). For a wider perspective on comfort in the American home and the role of women, see Wright (1977).

45. Colour photography reached the mass journals and popular books at the end of the 1930s. The genre of the populated colour interior was particularly well developed in America.

46. Dione Neutra recounts how she would help out during photographic shoots of Richard Neutra's houses : 'And I remember … how when houses were photographed … we would bring furniture along and photograph the house as long as it was empty and not defiled by old furniture.' Neutra, D. (n.d.), p.271

47. Benjamin (1977) cited in Reed (1996a), p.10. See Naylor (1999) for a discussion of this issue.

48. Ibid.

49. For a moving and accurate account of the importance of familiar objects and clutter and a sense of well-being, see Rybczynski (1987), pp.15–20.

50. Lancaster (1939), p.76

51. Le Corbusier and Ernö Goldfinger are two notable examples; see the enlightening and well-observed article by Naylor (1999), which engages with Benjamin's 'Erfahrung und Armut'.

52. For example in *Maison et jardin*, 'La premiere residence crée par Le Corbusier depuis 1935', no.34, Feb. 1956, pp.34–7. See Maniaque (2005).

53. Patmore (1933). *House and Garden* and similar magazines quickly introduced colour printing when it became available.

54. Bois (1982)

55. See Van Doesburg's 'analyse de l'architecture (contre construction)' at the Paris exhibition, Bois and Reichlin (1985), p.151. The Swiss-Italian architect Alberto Sartoris made a trademark sign of his axonometric renderings, slickly presented in de Stijl primary colours.

56. The supposed antagonism of Modernist architects with respect to the connected themes of domesticity and comfort have been the subject of a growing literature. See Reed (1996b) and Rybczynski (1987). For example, citing Adolf Behne, Rybczynski notes: 'Extreme measures were required to 'prevent us from falling prey to dullness, to habit, to *comfort*'. Rybczynski (1987), p.200. The mistake of Modernists such as Le Corbusier, he claimed, was that they were concerned with appearance (a modern style) rather than the reality of comfort. Ibid., p.193. Later, he explains the rejection of Modernism in the American eclectic interior: 'Domestic well-being is a fundamental human need that is deeply rooted in us, and that must be satisfied. If this need is not met in the present, it is not unnatural to look for comfort in the traditional.' Ibid., p.217.

57. For example, Bruno Taut, in his *die neue Wohnung* ('dedicated to woman as creator') included several comparison photographs showing the old-fashioned interior compared to a cleaned-up version, Taut (1924), p.36. For Benjamin's views on simplification as a purifying and necessary form of destruction, see Heynen (1999), pp.110–11. {Taut, 1924 #4275}{Taut, 1924 #4275}{Taut, 1924 #4275}

58. Muthesius (1979), p.164

59. Becket (1980), pp.90–124

60. Velasquez (2002) and Da Silva (2001). The drawings analyzed are FLC 31525 (October 1925) and FC 31514 (April 1926) from the last project for the Villa Meyer. See Benton (1987), pp.143–53.

61. FLC 19583; for my analysis of the drawings for this house, see Benton (1982). My analysis has been challenged recently, see Quetglas (2004), pp.65–79.

62. Hermann Lange had an important collection of modern art, and his house had to double as an art gallery, which explains certain aspects of Mies's design. What is missing, of course, are the clients and their guests

and the presence of music, emanating from the organ discreetly placed behind the curtain in the centre of the rear wall.

63. The photograph was first published in Walter Cohen, 'Haus Lange in Krefeld', *Museum der Gegenwart*, 1 (1930–1), with the accent firmly on the collection – see Maruhin (2001), p.320, fig. 2 and note 29. Jan Maruhin claims that Mies retained control of every publication of an image of his work and presumably ensured that these houses were not reviewed or illustrated in the contemporary architectural journals with the above exception.

64. The challenge is to avoid the tunnel effect produced by short focal length lenses, typically by one of two means. In one standard type, a twin point perspective is used, so that the orthogonal lines, instead of receding like a funnel to a vanishing point in the middle of the image, project forwards and recede to vanishing points to left and right of the photograph. Alternatively, the space can be photographed into the corner, creating a strong 'V' of the join of wall and ceiling. The other standard device is the frontal view with the facing wall lined up with the picture plane and a sharply receding wall on one side (usually the right).

65. Mies van der Rohe, 'Office building', *G*, no.1 (July 1923), cited in Neumeyer (1991), p.241.

66. Among the relevant sources are Adolf von Hildebrand's *Das Problem der Form in der bildenden Kunst* (1893), August Schmarsow's lecture 'Das Wesen der architektonischen Schöpfung' (1893) and Theodor Lipps's 'Raumästhetik und Geometrisch-Optische Täuschugen' (1893), cited in Forty (2000), pp.260–61. See also Schwarzer (1991).

67. The Resors, prominent members of the New York modern art scene (Mrs Resor was a trustee of MoMA) met Mies in Paris in 1937 and invited him to America, offering him the chance to complete a half-executed project (by Philip Goodwin) to build a house astride the Snake river in Jackson Hole, Wyoming.

68. MoMA 716.63

69. Sylvia Lavin provides an interesting analysis of the design of this house, which won an AIA First Honor award. Lavin (2004), pp.103–13

70. Neutra used terms such as 'view-commanding balcony', 'unobstructed views', 'sweeping views' and 'agreeable outlook' as captions of Shulman's photographs in their book of photographs. Neutra (1951)

71. Undated letter from Orline Moore (Neutra Archive) cited in Lavin (2004), p.110.

72. In an unpublished essay Neutra admitted that openness to the landscape could promote both fear and pleasure – Lavin (2004), p.112. Lavin concludes that 'The libidinal charge of the Moore house corner stimulates the survival reflex: the desire for unimpeded visual access to assault lines brings with it the need for protection from enemies that attack from the rear.' Lavin (2004), p.112

73. Cited from Neutra (1969), in Isenstadt (2000), p.102.

74. Anastasia Clother, 'Anastasia Just Not Ready for Super Modern Home', *Marion Indiana Chronical-Tribune*, February 7, 1954, cited in Lavin (2004), p.101. See also Friedman (1996) for an account of the concerns of Edith Farnsworth with respect to the house Mies designed for her.

75. Neutra (1951)

76. Isenstadt comments on Neutra's rather simplistic view of psychology and empathy, which Talbot Hamlin noted in his review of Neutra' book *Survival through Design*, and his selective reading of the scientific literature. Isenstadt (2000), pp.111–14

77. Neutra (1969), p.219. Isenstadt supports this by noting the work of perceptual psychologist J.J. Gibson.

78. Neutra (1969), p.92, in Isenstadt (2000), p.106

79. Neutra (1969), p.68 and Neutra (1951), p.60, in Isenstadt (2000), p.107

80. Niedenthal cites Neutra's biographer Thomas Hines as describing this as 'one of modern architecture's most brilliant and famous photographs', illustrated in architectural publications all over the world. Niedenthal (1993)

81. Niedenthal (1993), p.101

82. Niedenthal recounts the detailed history of the publication of the photograph. Niedenthal (1993). The house was first published in *Los Angeles Times Home Magazine* on June 15, 1947, using Shulman's photographs, but not this one.

83. Niedenthal (1993), p.104

84. The editors of *Life* accentuated this reading by cropping the lower part of the photograph to accentuate the association between Mrs Kaufman's body and the white daybed, while also enlarging the house interior.

85. Niedenthal (1993), p.106, citing a letter to *Fortune magazine* in June 1947.

86. Neutra, D. (n.d.), p.260

87. Neutra (1962)

88. Ibid.

Chapter 10

1. Greenwood (1933), pp.13–14
2. *New Statesman and Nation*, 30 January 1937, p.155
3. Glancy, in Richards (2000), pp.57–72
4. Grierson (1946), p.80
5. Hampson (1931), p.23
6. Green (1939), pp.133–4
7. Ibid., p.134
8. Buchan (2004), p.8
9. Bowen (1962), p.256
10. Ibid., pp.93–4
11. Mengham (2001), pp.124–133
12. Sansom (1944), p.150
13. Ibid., p.146
14. Strachey (1951), p.49

Chapter 11

1. Laurence Llewelyn-Bowen, *Changing Rooms* designer, *Daily Mirror*, 7 August 2004.
2. Llewelyn-Bowen and Gavin (2002), p.25
3. Tiersten (1996), p.20
4. Tiersten (1996), p.28
5. Griffith Winton (2004), pp.377–96
6. Ibid., p.380
7. Beatriz Colomina in Griffith Winton (2004), p.379
8. Jones (2003), pp.307–18
9. Goldstein (1998)
10. See Bucknell (1964)
11. Jackson (1965), pp.97–107
12. Camm (1956), p.671
13. Oram (2004), pp.174–90
14. Morley (1995), p.321
15. Everett (2004), pp.157–81
16. Hutchinson, in Spigel (2002), pp.325–38
17. See Brunsdon (2003), pp.5–23 and Methuen (2004)
18. *Changing Rooms. Trust Me, I'm A Designer.* DVD, BBC 2002
19. Ibid.
20. Ibid.
21. Barker (1992), n/p
22. Llewelyn-Bowen and Gavin (2002), p.9
23. Ibid., p.17
24. Ibid., p.16
25. Ibid., p.25
26. T&S. *Livingetc* (2005), p.121

Bibliography

The bibliography is arranged in parts following the organisation of the book

Introduction

Ajmar-Wollheim, Marta, and Flora Dennis (eds), *At Home in Renaissance Italy* (London, 2006)

Ariès, Philippe, *Centuries of Childhood* (Harmondsworth, 1962)

Attfield, Judith, *Wild Things: the material culture of everyday life* (Oxford, 2000)

Attfield, Judith, and Pat Kirkham, *A View from the Interior: feminism, women and design history* (London, 1989)

Auslander, Leora, *Taste and Power: furnishing modern France* (Berkeley and Los Angeles, 1996)

Bender, John, *Imagining the Penitentiary: fiction and architecture of mind in eighteenth-century England* (Chicago and London, 1987)

Bryden, Inga, and Janet Floyd, *Domestic Space: reading the nineteenth-century interior* (Manchester and New York, 1999)

Buchli, Victor, Alison Clarke and Dell Upton (eds), *Home Cultures* (Oxford, 2004)

Calloway, Stephen, *Twentieth-Century Decoration: the domestic interior from 1900 to the present* (London, 1998)

Carruthers, Annette (ed.), *The Scottish Home* (Edinburgh, 1996)

Davidoff, Leonora, and Catherine Hall, *Family Fortunes: men and women of the English middle class, 1780–1850* (London, 1987)

Dewing, David (ed.), *Home and Garden: paintings and drawings of English, middle-class, urban domestic spaces, 1675–1914* (Geffrye Museum, London, exhib. cat., 2003)

Douglas, Mary, and Baron Isherwood, *The World of Goods: towards an anthropology of consumption, with a new introduction* (London and New York, [1979] 1996)

Eger, Elizabeth, Charlotte Grant, Clíona Ó Gallchoir and Penny Warburton (eds), *Women, Writing and the Public Sphere 1700–1830* (Cambridge, 2001)

Friedman, Alice T., *Women and the Making of the Modern House: a social and architectural history* (New York, 1998)

Gere, Charlotte, *Nineteenth-Century Decoration: design and the domestic interior in England* (London, 1989)

Girouard, Mark, *Life in the English Country House* (London and New Haven, 1978)

Grant, Charlotte (ed.), 'The Domestic Interior in British Literature', *Home Cultures* (November 2005), vol.2, issue 3

Hayden, Dolores, *The Grand Domestic Revolution: a history of feminist designs for American homes, neighborhoods, and cities* (Cambridge, Mass., [1982] 2000)

Heynen, Hilde, and Gülsüm Baydar, *Negotiating Domesticity: spatial productions of gender in modern architecture* (London and New York, 2005)

Jaffer, Amin and Anna Jackson (eds), *Encounters: the meeting of Asia and Europe 1500–1800* (London, 2004)

Johnson, Matthew, *Archaeological Theory: an introduction* (Oxford, 1999)

Keeble, Trevor, Brenda Martin and Penny Sparke (eds), *The Modern Period Room* (London, 2006)

Light, Alison, 'Literature and the Domestic Interior', unpublished paper from the CSDI symposium *Approaching the Domestic Interior 1400 to the Present*, V&A, London, December 2001

Logan, Thad, *The Victorian Parlour: a cultural study* (Cambridge, 2001)

Mackenzie, John, *Orientalism: history, theory and the arts* (Manchester, 1995)

Mandler, Peter, *The Fall and Rise of the Stately Home* (London and New Haven, 1997)

Marcus, Sharon, *Apartment Stories: city and home in nineteenth-century Paris and London* (Berkeley and Los Angeles, 1999)

Mauss, Marcel, *The Gift* (London, 1970)

McKellar, Susie and Penny Sparke, *Interior Design and Identity* (Manchester, 2004)

Miller, Danny (ed.), *Home Possessions: material culture behind closed doors* (Oxford and New York, 2001)

Moretti, Franco, *Atlas of the European Novel, 1800–1900* (London, 1999)

Newton, Charles, and Tim Putnam (eds), *Household Choices* (Middlesex University, 1990)

Praz, Mario, *An Illustrated History of Interior Decoration, from Pompeii to Art Nouveau* (London, 1964)

Reed, Christopher, *Not at Home: the suppression of domesticity in modern art and architecture* (London and New York, 1996)

Reed, Christopher, *Bloomsbury Rooms: modernism, subculture and domesticity* (London and New York, 2004)

Rybczynski, Witold, *Home: a short history of an idea* (Harmondsworth, 1986)

Said, Edward, *Orientalism* (London, 1978)

Sarti, Raffaella, *Europe at Home: family and material culture, 1500–1800* (London and New Haven, 2002)

Saumarez Smith, Charles, *Eighteenth-Century Decoration: design and the domestic interior in England* (London, 1993)

Stone, Lawrence, *The Family, Sex and Marriage in England 1500–1800* (Oxford, 1977)

Thompson, E.P., *The Making of the English Working Class* (Harmondsworth, [1963] 1980)

Thornton, Peter, *Seventeenth-Century Interior Decoration in England, France and Holland* (New Haven and London, 1983)

Thornton, Peter, *Authentic Décor: the domestic interior 1620–1920* (London, 1984)

Thornton, Peter, *The Italian Renaissance Interior 1400–1600* (London, 1991)

Tristram, Philippa, *Living Space in Fact and Fiction* (London, 1989)

Varey, Simon, *Space and the Eighteenth-Century Novel* (Cambridge, 1990)

Vickery, Amanda, 'Golden Ages to Separate Spheres? A Review of the Categories and Chronology of English Women's History', *Historical Journal* (1993), 36.2

Vickery, Amanda, *The Gentleman's Daughter: women's lives in Georgian England* (London and New Haven, 1998)

Wilk, Christopher, 'The Period Room', unpublished paper from the CDSI symposium *Representing the Domestic Interior 1400 to the Present*, V&A, London, May 2002

Woolf, Virginia, *Orlando* (London, [1928] 1992)

Part One

Achillini, Giovanni Filoteo, *Epistole… al magnificentissimo Missere Antonio Rudolpho Germani* (Bologna, c.1510)

Ajmar, Marta, *Women as Exemplars of Domestic Virtue in the Literary and Material Culture of the Italian Renaissance* (unpublished doctoral thesis, The Warburg Institute, University of London, 2004)

Alberti, Leon Battista, *Opere volgari*, 3 vols (ed.) Cecil Grayson (Bari, 1960–1973)

Alberti, Leon Battista, *De re aedificatori, On the Art of Building in Ten Books* (trans.) Joseph Rykwert, Neil Leach and Robert Tavernor (Cambridge, Mass., 1988)

Alexander, Jonathan J.G. (ed.), *The Painted Page: Italian Renaissance book illumination*

1450–1550 (Munich and New York, 1994)

Allerston, Patricia, 'Le marché d'occasion à Venise aux XVIe e XVIIe siècles', *Echanges et cultures textiles dans l'Europe pre-industrielle*, special issue of *Revue du Nord, Collection Histoire* (1993), 12, pp.1–15

Allerston, Patricia, 'The Market in Secondhand Clothes and Furnishings in Venice circa 1500–1650' (unpublished doctoral thesis, European University, Florence, 1996)

Andrews, Lew, *Story and Space in Renaissance Art: the rebirth of continuous narrative* (Cambridge, 1995)

Anon., *Homilie Agaynst Disobedience and Wylful Rebellion* (London, 1570)

Anon., *Opera nova sopra la strazzosa* (Vicenza, 1607)

Anon., *Testamento novamente fatto per Messer Faustin Terdotio* (n.d., [16th century])

Anon., *Il piacevole viaggio di Cuccagna* (Cesena, 1588)

Anon., *Capitolo di Cuccagna* (Siena, [c.1540])

Antoniano, Silvio, *Tre libri dell'educatione christiana dei figliuoli* (Verona, 1584)

Archivio di Stato, Florence, Libri di Commercio e di Famiglia, 4402, Maria Ridolfi Strozzi, 1550–1554

Barbieri, Franco and Guido Bettramini, *Vincenzo Scamozzi, 1548–1616* (Venice, 2003)

Barriault, Anne B., *Spalliera Paintings of Renaissance Tuscany: fables of poets for patrician homes* (University Park, Penn., 1994)

Bartrum, Giulia Albrecht, *Dürer and His Legacy* (London, 2002)

Baskins, Cristelle L., *Cassone Painting, Humanism and Gender in Early Modern Italy* (Cambridge and New York, 1998)

Bayer, Andrea (ed.), *Painters of Reality: the legacy of Leonardo and Caravaggio in Lombardy* (New Haven and London, 2004)

Bedaux, Jan Baptist, 'The Reality of Symbols: The Question of Disguised Symbolism in Jan van Eyck's *Arnolfini Portrait*', *Simiolus* (1986), 16, pp.5–28

Bellosi, Luciano (ed.), *Francesco di Giorgio e il Rinascimento a Siena, 1450–1500* (Milan, 1993)

Benedetti, Jean, *David Garrick and the Birth of Modern Theatre* (London, 2001)

Boccaccio, Giovanni, *The Decameron*, Eighth day, novella VIII (trans.) J.M. Rigg (London, 1905)

Boschloo, Anton W.A., *Annibale Carracci in Bologna: visible reality in art after the Council of Trent* (s'Gravenhage, 1974)

Branca, Vittore (ed.) and Murtha Baca (trans.), *Merchant Writers of the Italian Renaissance* (New York, 1999)

Brown, Beverly and Paola Marini (eds), *Jacopo Bassano c.1510–1592* (Bologna, 1992)

Bury, Michael, *The Print in Italy, 1550–1620* (London, 2001)

Callmann, Ellen, *Apollonio di Giovanni* (Oxford, 1974)

Callmann, Ellen, 'Apollonio di Giovanni and Painting for the Early Renaissance Room', *Antichità viva* (1988), XXVII, pp.5–18

Campbell, Lorne, *Renaissance Portraits: European portrait painting in the 14th, 15th and 16th centuries* (New Haven and London, 1990)

Campbell, Lorne, *National Gallery Catalogues: the fifteenth century Netherlandish schools* (London, 1998)

Carlson, Marybeth, 'A Trojan horse of worldliness? Maidservants in the burgher household in Rotterdam at the end of the seventeenth century', in Els Kloek et al. (eds), *Women of the Golden Age: an international debate on women in seventeenth-century Holland, England and Italy* (Hilversum, 1994), pp.127–36

Carroll, Margaret, 'In the name of God and Profit: Jan van Eyck's Arnolfini Portrait', *Representations* (1993), 44, pp.96–132

Ceriana, Matteo, 'Fra Carnevale and the Practice of Architecture', in Keith Christiansen (ed.), *From Filippo Lippi to Piero della Francesca: Fra Carnevale and the making of a Renaissance master* (New York, Milan and New Haven, 2005), pp.97–135

Christiansen, Keith, 'Early Renaissance Narrative Painting in Italy', *Metropolitan Museum of Art Bulletin* (Fall, 1983)

Christiansen, Keith (ed.), *From Filippo Lippi to Piero della Francesca: Fra Carnevale and the making of a Renaissance master* (New York, Milan and New Haven, 2005)

Cleaver, Robert, *A godlie forme of hovseholde government* (London, 1598)

Cocchiara, Giuseppe, *Il paese di Cuccagna e altri studi di folklore* (Turin, 1980)

Cohen, Elizabeth S., 'Honor and Gender in the Streets of Early Modern Rome', *Journal of Interdisciplinary History* (1992), XXII, 597–625

Cohen, Elizabeth S. and Thomas V. Cohen, *Words and Deeds in Renaissance Rome: trials before the Papal magistrates* (Toronto, 1993)

Cohen, Elizabeth S. and Thomas V. Cohen, 'Open and Shut: the social meanings of the Renaissance Italian house', *Studies in the Decorative Arts* (2001–2002), IX, pp.61–84

Croce, Giulio Cesare, *Palazzo fantasico et bizzarro* (Bologna, 1607)

Dessen, Alan, *Elizabethan Stage Conventions and Modern Interpreters* (Cambridge, 1984)

Dibbits, Hester C., 'Between Society and Family Values: the linen cupboard in early-modern households', in Anton Schuurman and Pieter Spierenburg, *Private Domain, Public Inquiry: families and life-styles in the Netherlands and Europe, 1550 to the present* (Hilversum, 1996), pp.125–45

Dubbe, B., 'Het huisraad in het Oostnederlanse burgerwoonhuis in de late middeleeuwen' in *Thuis in de late middeleeuwen. Het Nederlands burgerinterieur, 1400–1535* (Provinciaal Overijssels Museum, Zwolle, catalogue, 1980), pp.21–86

Fiaccadori, Gianfranco and Maruizio Grattoni d'Arcano (eds), *In domo habitationis. L'arredo in Friuli nel tardo Medioevo* (Venice, 1996)

Filarete [Antonio di Piero Averlino], *Treatise on Architecture*, 2 vols (trans.) John R. Spencer (New Haven, 1965)

Finkel, Alicia, *Romantic Stages: set and costume design in Victorian England* (London, 1996)

Fiore, Francesco Paolo, and Manfredo Tafuri (eds), *Francesco di Giorgio: architetto* (Milan, 1993)

Foakes, Reginald A., *Henslowe's Diary* (Cambridge, [1961] 2002)

Fock, C. Willemijn, 'Semblance or Reality? The Domestic Interior in Seventeenth-Century Dutch Genre Painting', in Mariët Westermann (ed.), *Art and Home: Dutch interiors in the age of Rembrandt* (Denver Art Museum, Denver, catalogue, and The Newark Museum, Newark, catalogue, 2001), pp.83–101

Fock, C. Willemijn et al., *Het Nederlandse interieur in beeld 1600–1900* (Zwolle, 2001)

Fortini Brown, Patricia, *Private Lives in Renaissance Venice* (New Haven and London, 2004)

Franits, Wayne, *Dutch Seventeenth-Century Genre Painting: its stylistic and thematic evolution* (New Haven and London, 2004)

Franits, Wayne, *Paragons of Virtue: women and domesticity in seventeenth-century Dutch art* (Cambridge, 1993)

Franzoni, Claudio, 'Le raccolte del *Theatro* di Ombrone e il viaggio in oriente del pittore: Le *Epistole* di Giovanni Filoteo Achillini', in *Rivista di letteratura italiana* (1990), VIII, pp.287–335

Frigo, Daniela, *Il padre di famiglia. Governo della casa e governo civile nella tradizione dell' "economica" tra Cinque e Seicento* (Rome, 1985)

Gaba-Van Dongen, Alexandra, 'Between Fantasy and Reality: utensils in seventeenth-century

Dutch art', in *Senses and Sins: Dutch painters of daily life in the seventeenth century* (Museum Boijmans van Beuningen, Rotterdam, catalogue, and Städelsches Kunstinstitut, Frankfurt, catalogue, 2004), pp.32–8

Goeree, William, *D'Algemeene Bouwkunde volgens d'Antyke en Hedengaagse Manier* (Amsterdam, 1681)

Goffman, Erving, *The Presentation of Self in Everyday Life* (London, [1956] 1990)

Goldthwaite, Richard A., 'The Florentine Palace as Domestic Architecture', *American Historical Review* (1972), LXXVII, pp.977–1012

Goldthwaite, Richard A., 'The Empire of Things: consumer demand in Renaissance Italy', in Francis W. Kent and Patricia Simons (eds) *Patronage, Art and Society in Renaissance Italy* (Oxford, 1987), pp.153–75

Goldthwaite, Richard A., 'The Economic and Social World of Italian Renaissance Maiolica', *Renaissance Quarterly* (1989), XLII, pp.1–32

Goldthwaite, Richard A., *Wealth and the Demand for Art in Italy 1300–1600* (Baltimore, 1993)

Gouge, William, *Of Domestical Duties* (London, 1622)

Grafton, Anthony, *Leon Battista Alberti: master builder of the Italian Renaissance* (New York, 2000)

Grijzenhout, Frans and Henk van Veen (eds), *The Golden Age of Dutch Painting in Historical Perspective* (Cambridge, 1999)

Guazzo, Stefano, *Dell'onor delle donne* (Venice, 1586)

Guidetti, Armando, *San Carlo Borromeo: la vita nell'iconografia e nei documenti* (Milan, 1984)

Gurr, Andrew, *Playgoing in Shakespeare's London* (Cambridge, [1987] 2004)

Harbison, Craig, 'Visions and Meditations in Early Flemish Painting', *Simiolus* (1985), 15, pp.87–118

Harbison, Craig, 'Sexuality and Social Standing in Jan van Eyck's Arnolfini Double Portrait', *Renaissance Quarterly* (1990), 43, pp.249–91

Harbison, Craig, *Jan van Eyck: the play of realism* (London, 1991)

Harbison, Craig, 'Fact, Symbol, Ideal: roles for realism in early Netherlandish painting', in Maryan W. Ainsworth (ed.), *Petrus Christus in Renaissance Bruges: an interdisciplinary approach* (New York and Turnhout, 1995), pp.21–34

Hart, Vaughan, and Peter Hicks (eds), *Paper Palaces: the rise of the Renaissance architectural treatise* (New Haven and London, 1998)

Hartt, Frederick, *The Metropolitan Museum of Art. The Renaissance in Italy and Spain* (New York, 1997)

Hatchuel, Sarah, *Shakespeare, from Stage to Screen* (Cambridge, 2004)

Held, Julius Samuel, 'Artis pictoriae amator: an Antwerp art patron and his collection', *Gazette des Beaux-Arts* (1957), 6th ser, 50, pp.53–84

Hinton, Jack, 'By Sale, By Gift: Aspects of the Resale and Bequest of Goods in Late-Sixteenth-Century Venice', *Journal of Design History* (2002), vol. 15, no. 4, pp.245–62

Hollingsworth, Mary, 'The Architect in Fifteenth-Century Florence', *Art History* (1984), XII, pp.385–410

Holmes, Megan, *Fra Filippo Lippi: the Carmelite painter* (New Haven and London, 1999)

Hughes, Graham, *Renaissance Cassoni. Masterpieces of Early Italian Art: painted marriage chests, 1400–1550* (Alfriston, 1997)

Ivins, William, *Prints and Visual Communication* (London, 1953)

Jackson, Russell, and Jonathon Bate (eds), *The Illustrated History of Shakespeare on Stage* (Oxford, 2001)

Johnson, Geraldine, 'Art or Artefact? Madonna and Child Reliefs in the Early Renaissance', in Stuart Currie and Peta Motture (eds), *The Sculpted Object 1400–1700* (Aldershot, 1997), pp.1–17

Jong, Jan de et al. (eds), *Wooncultuur in de Nederlanden / The Art of the Home in the Netherlands 1500–1800* (Zwolle, 2000), *Nederlands Kunsthistorisch Jaarboek* 51 (2000)

Kent, Dale, 'Michele del Giogante's House of Memory', in William J. Connell (ed.), *Society and Individual in Renaissance Florence* (Berkeley and London, 2002), pp.110–36

Kertzer, David, and Marzio Barbagli (eds), *The History of the European Family. Volume One: Family Life in Early Modern Times 1500–1789* (New Haven and London, 2001)

Kettering, Alison McNeil, 'Ter Borch's Ladies in Satin', in Wayne Franits, *Looking at Seventeenth-Century Dutch Art. Realism Reconsidered* (Cambridge, 1997), pp.98–115

Koster, Margaret L., 'The Arnolfini double portrait: a simple solution', *Apollo* (September, 2003), 158, pp.3–14

Korda, Natasha, and Gil Harris (eds), *Staged Properties* (Cambridge, 2002)

Kovesi Killerby, C.M., *Italian Sumptuary Legislation, 1200–1500* (Oxford, 1991)

Lambert, Susan, *Prints: art and techniques* (London, 2001)

Landau, David, and Peter Parshall, *The Renaissance Print, 1470–1550* (New Haven and London, 1994)

Laurence, Anne, 'How free were English women in the seventeenth century?', in Els Kloek et al. (eds) *Women of the Golden Age: an international debate on women in seventeenth-century Holland, England and Italy* (Hilversum, 1994), pp.127–36

Loughman, John, and John Michaels Montias, *Public and Private Spaces: works of art in seventeenth-century Dutch Houses* (Zwolle, 2000)

Lydecker, John Kent, *The Domestic Setting of the Arts in Renaissance Florence* (unpublished doctoral dissertation, The Johns Hopkins University, 1987)

Mann, Nicholas, and Luke Syson, *The Image of the Individual: portraits in the Renaissance* (London, 1998)

Martini, Francesco di Giorgio, *Trattati di architettura*, 3 vols (ed.) Pietro C. Marani (Florence, c.1979–1994)

Mason, Stefania, 'Low Life and Landscape: *minor pictura* in late sixteenth-century Venice', in Bernard Aikema and Beverly Louise Brown (eds), *Renaissance Venice and the North: crosscurrents in the time of Bellini, Dürer, and Titian* (Milan, 1999), pp.558–67

Matchette, Ann, 'Unbound Possessions: the circulation of used goods in Florence, c.1450–1600' (unpublished doctoral thesis, University of Sussex, 2005)

Matthews Grieco, Sara, 'Persuasive Pictures: didactic prints and the construction of the social identity of women in sixteenth-century Italy', in Letizia Panizza (ed.), *Women in Italian Renaissance Culture and Society* (Oxford, 2000), pp.285–314

Miller, Elizabeth, *16th-Century Italian Ornament Prints in the Victoria and Albert Museum* (London, 1999)

Montias, John Michael, 'Estimates of the Number of Dutch Master Painters, their Earnings and their Output in 1650', *Leidschrift* (1990), 6, pp.59–74

Montias, John Michael, *Art at Auction in 17th-century Amsterdam* (Amsterdam, 2002)

Muizelaar, Klaske, and Derek Phillips, *Picturing Men and Women in the Dutch Golden Age: paintings and people in historical perspective* (New Haven and London, 2003)

Musacchio, Jacqueline Marie, *The Art and Ritual of Childbirth in Renaissance Italy* (London and New Haven, 1999)

Musacchio, Jacqueline Marie, 'The Madonna and Child, a Host of Saints and Domestic Devotion in Renaissance Florence', in Gabriele Neher and Rupert Shepherd (eds),

Revaluing Renaissance Art (Aldershot, 2000), pp.147–59

Musacchio, Jacqueline Marie, 'The Medici Sale of 1495 and the Second-Hand Market for Domestic Goods in Late Fifteenth-Century Florence', in Marcello Fantoni, Louisa C. Matthew and Sara F. Matthews-Grieco (eds), *The Art Market in Italy, 15th–17th Centuries* (Modena, 2003), pp.313–23

Murphy, Caroline P., *Lavinia Fontana: a painter and her patrons in sixteenth-century Bologna* (New Haven and London, 2003)

Neilsen Blum, Shirley, 'Hans Memling's *Annunciation* with Angelic Attendants', *Metropolitan Museum Journal* (1992), 27, pp.43–58

Olimpo degli Alessandri, Caio Baldessare, *Camilla* (Venice, 1532)

Olimpo degli Alessandri, Caio Baldessare, *Gloria d'Amore* (Venice, [1580])

Owen Hughes, Diane, 'Representing the Family: portraits and purposes in Early Modern Italy', in Theodore K. Rabb and Jonathan Brown (eds), *Art and History: images and their meaning* (Cambridge, 1988), pp.7–15

Palladio, Andrea, *The Four Books on Architecture* (trans.) Robert Tavernor and Richard Schofield (Cambridge, Mass., 1997)

Panofsky, Erwin, *Early Netherlandish Painting: its origins and character* (Cambridge, MA, 1953)

Pilliod, Elizabeth, *Pontormo, Bronzino, Allori: a genealogy of Florentine art* (New Haven and London, 2001)

Pleij, Herman, *Dreaming of Cockaigne: medieval fantasies of the perfect life* (New York, 2001)

Pope-Hennessy, John, and Keith Christiansen, 'Secular Painting in 15th-Century Tuscany: birth trays, cassone panels and portraits', *Metropolitan Museum of Art Bulletin* (Summer, 1980)

Potterton, Homan, *Dutch Seventeenth and Eighteenth Century Paintings in the National Gallery of Ireland: a complete catalogue* (Dublin, 1986)

Pullen, Brian, and David Chambers (eds), *Venice: a documentary history, 1450–1630* (Oxford, 1992)

Randolph, Adrian, 'Performing the Bridal Body in Fifteenth-Century Florence', *Art History* (1998), XXI, pp.182–300

Resmini, Monica, 'Estimi e rilievi del primo cinquecento bergamasco: la casa di Paolo Girardelli e Leonardo Comenduno in via Porta Dipinta', in Aurora Scotti Tosini (ed.), *Aspetti dell'abitare in Italia tra 15. e 16 secolo:*

distribuzione, funzioni, impianti (Milan, 2001), pp.168–71

Reynolds, Catherine, 'Reality and Image: interpreting three paintings of the *Virgin and Child in an Interior* associated with Campin', in Susan Foister and Susie Nash (eds), *Robert Campin: new directions in scholarship* (Turnhout, 1996), pp.183–95

Richardson, Brian, *Printing, Writers and Readers in Renaissance Italy* (Cambridge, 1999)

Richardson, Catherine, *Domestic Life and Domestic Tragedy* (Manchester, 2006)

Ringbom, Sixten, *Icon to Narrative: the rise of the dramatic close-up in fifteenth-century devotional painting* ([1965] rev. 2nd ed., Doornspijk, 1984)

Romano, Dennis, *Housecraft and Statecraft: domestic service in Renaissance Venice, 1400–1600* (Baltimore and London, 1996)

Roodenburg, Herman, 'The "hand of friendship": shaking hands and other gestures in the Dutch Republic', in Jan Bremmer and Herman Roodenburg, *A Cultural History of Gesture from Antiquity till the Present Day* (Cambridge, 1991) pp.152–89

Ruda, Jeffrey, *Fra Filippo Lippi, Life and Work* (London, 1993)

Ruggiero, Guido, *Binding Passions: tales of magic, marriage and power at the end of the Renaissance* (Oxford, 1993)

Rutter, Carol, *Documents of the Rose Playhouse* (Manchester, 1999)

Rybczynski, Withold, *Home: a short history of an idea* (London, 1986)

Schama, Simon, *The Embarrassment of Riches. An Interpretation of Dutch Culture in the Golden Age* (London, 1987)

Schubring, Paul, *Cassoni, Truhen und Truhenbilder der italienischen Frührenaissance*, 2 vols and supplement (Leipzig, 1915)

Scott, Margaret, *The History of Dress Series: late Gothic Europe, 1400–1500* (London, Sydney and Toronto, 1980)

Shepherd, Rupert, 'Republican Anxiety and Courtly Confidence: the politics of magnificence and fifteenth-century Italian architecture', in Michelle O'Malley and Evelyn Welch (eds), *The Material Renaissance: costs and consumption in Italy, c.1400–1650* (Manchester, 2007)

Spierenburg, Pieter, *Elites and Etiquette: mentality and social structure in the early modern Northern Netherlands* (Rotterdam, 1981)

Sutton, Peter C., 'Images of the Interior', in Jan Peeters et al., *The Royal Palace of Amsterdam in Paintings of the Golden Age* (Zwolle and

Amsterdam, 1997) pp.18–29

Sutton, Peter C., *Pieter de Hooch, 1629–84* (Wadsworth Atheneum, Hartford, catalogue, and Dulwich Picture Gallery, London, catalogue, 1998)

Syson, Luke, 'Representing Domestic Interiors', in Marta Ajmar and Flora Dennis (eds), *At Home in Renaissance Italy* (London, 2006), pp.86–101

Tazartes, Maurizia, *Bronzino* (Milan, 2003)

Van der Heijden, Manon, 'Secular and Ecclesiastical Marriage Control: Rotterdam, 1550–1700', in Anton Schuurman and Pieter Spierenburg, *Private Domain, Public Inquiry: families and life-styles in the Netherlands and Europe, 1550 to the present* (Hilversum, 1996), pp.39–60

Van der Veen, Jaap, 'De verzamelaar in zijn kamer. Zeventiende-eeuwse privé-collecties in de Rupubliek', in Huub de Jonge (ed.), *Ons Soort Mensen. Levensstijlen in Nederland* (Nijmegen, 1997), pp.128–58

Van der Veen, Jaap, 'Eenvoudig en stil. Studeerkamers in zeventiende-eeuwse woningen, voornamelijk te Amsterdam, Deventer en Leiden', in *Nederlands Kunsthistorisch Jaarboek* 5 (2000), pp.137–72

Van der Woude, Ad, 'The Volume and Value of Paintings in Holland at the time of the Dutch Republic', in David Freedberg and Jan de Vries (eds), *Art in History/History in Art* (Santa Monica, 1991), pp.284–329

Van Strien, C.D., *British Travellers in Holland During the Stuart Period. Edward Browne and John Locke as Tourists in the United Provinces* (Leiden, 1993)

Vasari, Giorgio, *Le vite de' più eccellenti pittori, scultori e architettori*, 9 vols (ed.) G. Milanesi (Florence, 1878–1906)

Vries, Jan de, 'Between purchasing power and the world of goods; understanding the household economy in early modern Europe', in John Brewer and Roy Porter (eds), *Consumption and the World of Goods* (London, 1993), pp.85–132

Vries, Jan de, and Ad van der Woude, *The First Modern Economy: success, failure, and perseverance of the Dutch economy, 1500–1815* (Cambridge, 1997)

Watson, Wendy M., *Italian Renaissance Ceramics from the Howard I. and Janet H. Stein Collection and the Philadelphia Museum of Art* (Philadelphia, 2001)

Watt, Jeffrey R., 'The Impact of the Reformation and Counter-Reformation', in David I. Kertzer and Marzio Barbagli (eds),

The History of the European Family. Volume One: Family Life in Early Modern Times 1500–1789 (New Haven and London, 2001), pp.125–56

Welch, Evelyn, 'Public Magnificence and Private Display: Pontano's *De splendore*', *Journal of Design History* (2002), XV, pp.211–27

Welch, Evelyn, 'From Retail to Resale: artistic value and the second-hand market in Italy, 1400–1550', in Marcello Fantoni, Louisa C. Matthew and Sara F. Matthews-Grieco (eds), *The Art Market in Italy, 15th–17th Centuries* (Modena, 2003), pp.283–300

Welch, Evelyn, *Shopping in the Renaissance: consumer cultures in Italy, 1400–1600* (New Haven and London, 2005)

Wells, Stanley, and Gary Taylor (eds), *The Oxford Shakespeare* (Oxford, 1986)

Westermann, Mariët (ed.), *Art and Home: Dutch interiors in the age of Rembrandt* (Denver Art Museum, Denver, catalogue, and The Newark Museum, Newark, catalogue, 2001)

Wiggins, Martin (ed.), *A Woman Killed With Kindness and Other Plays* (Oxford, 2007)

Wijsenbeek-Olthuis, Thera, 'Het Hollandse interieur in beeld en geschrift', *Theoretische Geschiedenis* (1996), 23, pp.145–61

Wilson, Timothy, *Ceramic Art of the Italian Renaissance* (London, 1987)

Ydema, Onno, *Carpets and their Datings in Netherlandish Paintings 1540–1700* (Woodbridge, 1991)

Part Two

Adler, Kathleen, 'The Suburban, the Modern and "Une Dame de Passy"', *The Oxford Art Journal* (1989) vol.12, no.1, pp.3–13

Alexander, David, *Affecting Moments: prints of English literature made in the age of romantic sensibility 1775–1800* (York, 1993)

Arkell, Tom, Nesta Evans and Nigel Goose (eds), *When Death Do Us Part: understanding and interpreting the probate records of early modern England* (Oxford, 2000)

Aspinall-Oglander, Cecil Faber, *Admiral's Wife: being the life and letters of the Hon. Mrs Edward Boscawen from 1719–1761* (London, 1940)

Auslander, Leora, *Taste and Power: furnishing modern France* (Berkeley and Los Angeles, 1996)

Austen, Jane, *Mansfield Park* (Harmondsworth, [1814] 1980)

Austen, Jane, *Pride and Prejudice* (Harmondsworth, [1813] 1996)

Austen, Jane, *Emma* (Harmondsworth, [1816] 1980)

Aynsley, Jeremy, and Francesca Berry (eds), 'Publishing the Modern Home: magazines and the domestic interior 1870–1965', *The Journal of Design History* (April 2005), vol.18, no.1

Balfour, Clara Lucas, *The Two Homes* (London, 1860)

Ballaster, Ros, *Seductive Forms: women's amatory fiction from 1684–1740* (Oxford and New York, 1992)

Barker, Hannah, *Newspapers: politics and English society 1695–1855* (London, 2000)

Barrell, John, *The Dark Side of the Landscape: the rural poor in English painting, 1730–1840* (Cambridge, 1980)

Barthes, Roland, *The Rustle of Language* (trans.) Richard Howard (Berkley and Los Angeles, 1989)

Becherer, Richard, *Between Science and Sentiment: César Daly and the formulation of modern architectural theory* (Cornell University, 1982)

Beggs, Thomas, and William Logan, *The Moral Statistics of Glasgow* (Glasgow, 1840)

Benjamin, Walter, *The Arcades Project* (Cambridge, Mass., 1999)

Bermingham, Ann, 'The Simple Life: cottages and Gainsborough's cottage doors', in Peter de Bolla, Nigel Leask and David Simpson (eds), *Land, Nation and Culture, 1740–1840: thinking the republic of taste* (Basingstoke, 2005), pp.37–62

Berry, Francesca, 'Designing the Reader's Interior: subjectivity and the woman's magazine in early twentieth-century France', *Journal of Design History* (April 2005), vol.18, no.1, pp.61–79

Berry, Francesca, 'Working Mothers: the representation of domestic and professional labour in Edouard Vuillard's interiors', *Object* (1998), 1, pp.62–83

Bois, Jules, 'Les guérisons par la pensée', *La Revue* (October 1990), vol.35, pp.16–33

Borsay, Peter, *The English Urban Renaissance: culture and society in the provincial town 1660–1770* (Oxford, 1991)

Brewer, John, *The Pleasures of the Imagination: English culture in the eighteenth century* (London, 1997)

Brewer, John and Roy Porter (eds), *Consumption and the World of Goods* (London, 1993)

Brewer, John, 'Reconstructing the Reader: prescriptions, texts and strategies in Anna Larpent's reading' in James Raven, Helen Small and Naomi Tadmor (eds), *The Practice and Representation of Reading in England* (Cambridge, 1996), pp.226–45

Brisset, Jules, 'La ménagère parisienne', *Les Français peints par eux-mêmes*, vol.2 (Paris, [1840–42] 1853), pp.249–53

Cardon, Emile, *L'Art au foyer domestique* (Paris, 1884)

Cather, Willa, 'The Novel Démeublé', in Willa Cather, *Not Under Forty* (London, Toronto, Melbourne and Sydney, 1936), pp.47–56

Chalker, John, *The English Georgic* (London, 1969)

Clark, Timothy J., *The Image of the People: Gustave Courbet and the 1848 Revolution* (London, 1973)

Clery, Emma, 'Out of the Closet: Richardson and the cult of literary women', in Emma Clery, *The Feminization Debate in Eighteenth-Century England: literature, commerce and luxury* (Houndsmill, Basingstoke, 2004), pp.132–8

Cohn, Albert M., *George Cruikshank: a catalogue raisonné* (London, 1924)

Collier, Mary, 'The Woman's Labour' in David Fairer and Christine Gerrard (eds), *Eighteenth-Century Poetry* (Oxford, 2004)

Cornforth, John, *English Interiors 1790–1848: the quest for comfort* (London, 1978)

Cranfield, Geoffrey Alan, *The Press and Society from Caxton to Northcliffe* (London, 1978)

Crowley, John, 'From Luxury to Comfort and Back Again: landscape architecture and the cottage in Britain and America', in Maxine Berg and Elizabeth Eger (eds), *Luxury in the Eighteenth Century: debates, desires and delectable goods* (Basingstoke, 2003), pp.135–50

Cruikshank, George, *The Bottle* (London, 1847)

Daly, César, *Architecture privée au dix-neuvième siècle sous Napoléon III: nouvelles maisons des Paris et ses environs*, 9 vols (Paris, 1864–77)

Dennis, Victoria Solt, *Discovering Friendly and Fraternal Societies* (Princes Risborough, Buckinghamshire, 2005)

De Circourt, comte Albert, 'La maîtresse de maison', *Les Français peints par eux-mêmes*, vol. 3 (Paris, [1840–42] 1853), pp.34–8

De Reyniès, Nicole, *Le Mobilier domestique*, 2 vols (Paris, 1987)

Defoe, Daniel, 'A True Relation of the Apparition of One Mrs Veal', in James Sutherland (ed.), *Robinson Crusoe and other Writings* (Boston, [1706] 1968), pp.134–41

Defoe, Daniel, *Roxana* (Oxford, [1724] 1996)

Dickens, Charles, *David Copperfield* (London 1850)

Dickens, Charles, *Great Expectations* (Harmondsworth, [1861] 1977)

Dickens, Charles, *Little Dorrit* (London, [1861] 1998)

Donald, Diana, *The Age of Caricature: satirical prints in the age of George III* (London, 1996)

Dumur, Louis, 'De l'instinct sexuel et du mariage', *Le Mercure de France* (March 1890), vol.1, no.2, pp.65–71

Dumur, Louis, 'De la vénalité de l'amour chez la femme', *Le Mercure de France* (January 1891), vol.2, no.13, pp.39–43

Duncan, Carol, 'Happy Mothers and Other New Ideas in Eighteenth-Century France', in Norma Broude and Mary Garrard (eds), *Feminism and Art History* (London, 1982), pp.201–19

Dunlop, John, *Artificial Drinking Usages of North Britain* (Greenock, 1836)

Duranty, Louis Edmond, 'La nouvelle peinture', in Charles S. Moffett, *The New Painting: Impressionism, 1874–1886* (San Francisco, catalogue, [1876] 1986), pp.37–49

Eagleton, Terry, *The Rape of Clarissa: writing, sexuality and class struggle in Samuel Richardson* (Minneapolis, 1982)

Eaves, T.C. Duncan, and Ben Kimple, *Samuel Richardson, a Biography* (Oxford, 1971)

Eleb, Monique, and Anne Debarre, *L'Invention de l'habitation moderne, Paris 1880–1914. Architectures de la vie privée* (Paris, 1995)

Eliot, George, *Middlemarch: a story of provincial life* (Harmondsworth, [1871–2] 1965)

Ernst, Max, *Une semaine de bonté* (New York, [1934] 1976)

Finn, Margot, 'The Novel and the Romantic Domestic Interior: negotiating national identity in England and the Celtic fringe', paper presented at the CSDI symposium *Representing the Domestic Interior, 1400 to the Present*, V&A, 24–5 May 2002

Flaubert, Gustave, *Madame Bovary* (Harmondsworth, [1857] 1992)

Foster, Hal, *Compulsive Beauty* (Cambridge, Mass., 1993)

Foveau de Courmelles, Dr François V., 'Névroses féminines', *La Grande Dame* (April 1896), supplement, vol.4, p.11

Fried, Michael, 'Caillebotte's Impressionism', in Norma Broude (ed.), *Gustave Caillebotte and the Fashioning of Identity in Impressionist Paris* (New Brunswick and London, 2002), pp.66–116

Fried, Michael, *Manet's Modernism: or, the face of painting in the 1860s* (Chicago and London, 1996)

Garb, Tamar, *Bodies of Modernity: figure and flesh in fin-de-siècle France* (London, 1998)

Goodman, Dena, *The Republic of Letters* (New York, 1994)

Girouard, Mark, *Life in the French Country House* (London, 2000)

Grant, Allan, *A Preface to Dickens* (London and New York, 1984)

Greene, Vivien, and Margaret Towner, *The Vivien Greene Dolls' House Collection* (London, 1995)

Groom, Gloria, 'Interiors and Portraits', in K. Varnedoe (ed.), *Gustave Caillebotte: Urban Impressionist* (Art Institute of Chicago, Chicago, catalogue, 1995), pp.178–229

Habermas, Jürgen, *The Structural Transformation of the Public Sphere: an inquiry into a category of bourgeois society*, trans. Thomas Burger (Cambridge, 1989), originally published in German in 1962

Hallett, Mark, *The Spectacle of Difference: graphic satire in the age of Hogarth* (London, 1999)

Harvey, Karen, 'Gender, Space and Modernity in Eighteenth-Century England: a place called sex', *History Workshop Journal* (2001), 51, pp.158–79

Harvey, Karen, 'Spaces of Erotic Delight', in Miles Ogborn and Charles Withers (eds) *Georgian Geographies: essays on space, place and landscape in the eighteenth century* (Manchester, 2004), pp.130–50

Havard, Henry, *L'Art dans la maison, grammaire de l'ameublement* (Paris, 1884)

Havard, Henry, *Dictionnaire de l'ameublement* (Paris, 1887–90)

Hellerstein, Ellen, 'French Women and the Orderly Household, 1830–1870', *Proceedings of the Third Annual Meeting of the Western Society for French History* (1976), pp.378–89

Hellerstein, Ellen, Leslie Parker Hume and Karen M. Offen (eds), *Victorian Women: a documentary account of women's lives in nineteenth-century England, France and the United States* (Brighton, 1981)

Hellman, Mimi, 'Furniture, Sociablity and the Work of Leisure in Eighteenth-Century France', in *Eighteenth-Century Studies* (1999), vol.32, no.4, pp.415–45

Higonnet, Anne, 'Secluded Vision: Images of Feminine Experience in Nineteenth-Century Europe', *Radical History Review* (1987), vol.38, pp.16–36

Hughes, Helen Sard, *The Gentle Hertford: her life and letters* (New York, 1940)

Huysmans, Joris-Karl, *Against Nature* (London, [1884] 1959)

James, Henry, *The Portrait of a Lady* (Oxford, [1881] 1995)

Janet, Paul, *La Famille: leçons de philosophie morale* (Paris, [1856] 1857)

Jourdain, Frantz, *De Choses et d'autre* (Paris, 1902)

Keymer, Tom, *Richardson's Clarissa and the Eighteenth-Century Reader* (Cambridge, 1992)

King, Constance Eileen, *The Collectors' History of Dolls' Houses, House Dolls and Miniatures* (London, 1983)

King, Elspeth, *Scotland Sober and Free: the temperance movement* (Glasgow, 1979)

King, Peter, 'Pauper Inventories and the Material Lives of the Poor in the Eighteenth and Early Nineteenth Centuries', in Tim Hitchcock, Peter King and Pamela Sharpe (eds), *Chronicling Poverty: the voices and strategies of the English poor, 1640–1840* (Basingstoke, 1997), pp.155–91

Klein, Lawrence E., 'The Third Earl of Shaftesbury and the Progress of Politeness', *Eighteenth-Century Studies* (1984), vol.18, no.2, pp.186–214

Klein, Lawrence E., *Shaftesbury and the Culture of Politeness: moral discourse and cultural politics in early eighteenth-century England* (Cambridge, 1994)

Kugler, Anne, *Errant Plagiary: the life and writing of Lady Sarah Cowper, 1644–1720* (Stanford, Cal. and London, 2002)

Larousse, Pierre, *Dictionnaire du dix-neuvième siècle*, 17 vols (Paris, 1866–1890)

Larroumet, Gustave, 'L'Art décoratif et les femmes', *Revue des Arts décoratifs* (April 1896), vol.16, pp.100–105

Leppert, Richard, *Music and Image: domesticity, ideology and socio-cultural formation in eighteenth-century England* (Cambridge, 1988)

Lewis, Esther, 'A Mirror for Detractors. Addressed to a Friend' (written 1748, published 1754)

Lipsedge, Karen, 'Enter into thy closet', in John Styles and Amanda Vickery (eds), *Gender, Taste and Material Culture in Britain and North America in the Long Eighteenth Century* (New Haven and London, 2006)

Lonsdale, Roger, *Eighteenth-Century Women Poets* (Oxford, 1989)

Lucie-Smith, Edward, *Fantin-Latour* (Oxford, 1977)

Lukacs, John, 'The Bourgeois Interior', *American Scholar* 39 (1970), no.4, pp.616–30

Marcou, Paul F., 'The Modern House in Paris', *The Architectural Record* (1893), vol.2, pp.324–31

Marcus, Sharon, *Apartment Stories: city and home in nineteenth-century Paris and London* (Berkeley, Los Angeles and London, 1999)

McBride, Teresa, *The Domestic Revolution: the modernisation of household service in England and France, 1820–1920* (New York, 1976)

McCauley, Elizabeth, *A.A.E. Disdéri and the Carte de Visite Portrait Photograph* (New Haven, 1985)

McCauley, Elizabeth, *Industrial Madness: commercial photography in Paris 1848–1871* (New Haven, 1994)

McMillan, James F., *Housewife or Harlot: the place of women in French society, 1870–1940* (Brighton, 1981)

McWilliam, Neil, and Christopher Parsons, 'Le Paysan de Paris: Alfred Sensier and the Myth of Rural France', *Oxford Art Journal* (1983), vol.6, no.2, pp.38–58

Nesbit, Molly, *Atget's Seven Albums* (New Haven, 1992)

Nochlin, Linda, 'A House Is Not a Home: Degas and the subversion of the family', Richard Kendall and Griselda Pollock (eds), *Dealing with Degas: representations of women and the politics of vision* (London, 1992), pp.43–65

Orlin, Lena Cowen, 'Fictions of the early modern English probate inventory', in Henry S. Turner (ed.), *The Culture of Capital: property, cities, and knowledge in early modern England* (New York and London, 2002), pp.51–83

Overton, Mark, Jane Whittle, Darron Dean and Andrew Hann, *Production and Consumption in English Households, 1600–1750* (London and New York, 2004)

Palmari, Demetra, 'The shark who swallowed his epoch: family, nature and society in the novels of Emile Zola', in Virginia Tufte and Barbara Myerhoff (eds), *Changing Images of the Family* (New Haven and London, 1979), pp.155–72

Pardhailhé-Galabrun, Annik, *The Birth of Intimacy: privacy and domestic life in early modern Paris* (trans.) Jocelyn Phelps (Cambridge, [1988] 1991)

Pasierbska, Halina, 'It's a Child's Life in the Dolls' House', *Country Life* (11 January 1991), vol.195, no.2

Paulson, Ronald, *Hogarth's Graphic Works,* 2 vols (London, 1965)

Payne, Christiana, *Rustic Simplicity: scenes of cottage life in nineteenth-century British art* (Gloucester, 1998)

Perrot, Michelle (ed.), *A History of Private Life*, vol.4 (trans.) A. Goldhammer (Cambridge, Mass., and London, 1990)

Pointon, Marcia, *Hanging the Head: portraiture and social formation in eighteenth-century England* (London, 1993)

Pollock, Griselda, 'Modernity and the Spaces of Femininity', in Griselda Pollock, *Vision and Difference: femininity, feminism and the histories of art* (London, 1988), pp.50–90

Porter, Roy, *English Society in the Eighteenth Century* (London, 1990)

Poster, Mark, *Critical Theory of the Family* (London, 1978)

Praz, Mario, *Conversation Pieces: a survey of the informal group portrait in Europe and America* (London, 1971)

Proust, Marcel, *In Search of Lost Time*, vol. 1 (trans.) Charles K. Scott-Moncrieff and Terence Kilmartin (London, [1913] 1996)

Rand, Richard, *Intimate Encounters: love and domesticity in eighteenth-century France* (Hood Museum of Art, Princeton, catalogue, 1997)

Raven, James, Helen Small and Naomi Tadmor (eds), *The Practice and Representation of Reading in England* (Cambridge, 1996)

Reed, Christopher (ed.), *Not at Home: the suppression of domesticity in modern art and architecture* (London, 1996)

Reeve, Clara, *The Progress of Romance*, 2 vols, vol.1 (London, 1785)

Retford, Kate, *The Art of Domestic Life: family portraiture in eighteenth-century England* (London, 2006)

Robinson, Howard, *Britain's Post Office: a history of development from the beginnings to the present day* (London, 1953)

Rybcznski, Witold, *Home: a short history of an idea* (New York, 1986)

Saisselin, Remy, *Bricabracomania: the bourgeois and the bibelot* (London, [1984] 1985)

Sargentson, Carolyn, *Merchants and Luxury Markets: the marchands merciers of eighteenth-century Paris* (London and Malibu, 1996)

Sargentson, Carolyn, 'Looking at Furniture Inside Out', in Dena Goodman and Kathryn Norberg (eds), *Furnishing the Century: what furniture can tell us about the European and American past* (New York, 2006)

Saumarez Smith, Charles, *The Rise of Design: design and the domestic interior in eighteenth-century England* (London, 2000)

Savile, Gertrude, *Secret Comment: the diaries of Gertrude Savile 1721–1757*, ed. Alan Savile with Marjorie Penn (Kingsbridge, 1997)

Shields, David, *Civil Tongues and Polite Letters in British America* (Chapel Hill, N.C. and London, 1997)

Sidlauskas, Susan, 'Psyche and Sympathy: staging interiority in the early modern home', in Christopher Reed (ed.), *Not at Home: the suppression of domesticity in modern art and architecture* (London, 1996), pp.65–80

Sidlauskas, Susan, *Body, Place and Self in Nineteenth-Century Painting* (Cambridge, 2000)

Silverman, Debora, *Art Nouveau in Fin-de-Siècle France: politics, psychology and style* (Berkeley and Los Angeles, 1989)

Small, Helen, 'A Pulse of 124: Charles Dickens and a pathology of the mid-Victorian reading public' in James Raven, Helen Small and Naomi Tadmor (eds), *The Practice and Representation of Reading in England* (Cambridge, 1996), pp.263–90

Smith, Bonnie G., *Ladies of the Leisure Class: the bourgeoises of Northern France in the nineteenth century* (Princeton, 1981)

Solkin, David, 'Crowds and Connoisseurs: looking at genre painting at Somerset House', in David H. Solkin (ed.), *Art on the Line: the Royal Academy exhibitions at Somerset House, 1780–1836* (London, 2001), pp.157–71

Solkin, David, 'The Other Half of the Landscape: Thomas Heaphy's watercolour nasties', in Peter de Bolla, Nigel Leask and David Simpson (eds), *Land, Nation and Culture, 1740–1840: thinking the republic of taste* (Basingstoke, 2005), pp.63–96

Snodin, Michael, and John Styles, *Design and the Decorative Arts: Britain 1500–1900* (London, 2001)

Spacks, Patricia Meyer, *Privacy: concealing the eighteenth-century self* (London, 2003)

Stafford, Barbara, and Margaret Terpak, *Devices of Wonder* (Los Angeles, 2001)

Strumingher, Laura S., '*L'Ange de la maison*: mothers and daughters in nineteenth-century France', *International Journal of Women's Studies* (January–February 1979), vol.2, no.1, pp.51–61

Styles, John, 'Custom or Consumption? Plebeian fashion in eighteenth-century England', in Maxine Berg and Elizabeth Eger (eds), *Luxury in the Eighteenth Century: debates, desires and delectable goods* (Basingstoke, 2003), pp.103–15

Styles, John, and Amanda Vickery (eds), *Gender, Taste and Material Culture in Britain and North America in the Long Eighteenth Century* (New Haven and London, 2006)

Summerson, John, *Georgian London* (London, 2003)

Swift, Jonathon, *The Lady's Dressing Room* (London, 1732)

Tadmor, Naomi, '"In the even, my wife read to me": women, reading and household life in the eighteenth century', in James Raven, Helen Small and Naomi Tadmor (eds), *The*

Practice and Representation of Reading in England (Cambridge, 1996), pp.162–74

Tiersten, Lisa, *Marianne in the Market: envisioning consumer society in fin-de-siècle France* (Berkeley, 2001)

Tiersten, Lisa, 'The Chic Interior and the Feminine Modern: home decorating as high art in turn-of-the-century Paris', in Christopher Reed (ed.), *Not at Home: the suppression of domesticity in modern art and architecture* (London, 1996), pp.18–32

Toulalan, Sarah, '"Private Rooms and Back Doors in Abundance": the illusion of privacy in pornography in seventeenth-century England', *Women's History Review* (2001), 10, 4, pp.701–19

Uglow, Jennifer, *Hogarth: a life and a world* (London, 1997)

Uzanne, Octave, 'Notes sur le goût intime et la décoration personelle de l'habitation moderne', *L'Art et l'idée* (1892), pp.257–76

Van der Woude, Ad, and Anton Schuurman (eds), *Probate Inventories: a new source for the historical study of wealth, material culture, and agricultural development*, papers presented at the Leeuwenborch Conference (Wageningen, 5–7 May 1980)

Varnedoe, Kirk (ed.), *Gustave Caillebotte: urban Impressionist* (Art Institute of Chicago, Chicago, catalogue, 1995)

Vickery, Amanda, *The Gentleman's Daughter: women's lives in Georgian England* (London, 1998)

Vogler, Richard, *Graphic Works of George Cruikshank* (Dover and New York, 1979)

Von Wickens, Leonie, *Mansions in Miniature* (London, 1980)

Wadsö-Lecaros, Cecilia, *The Victorian Governess Novel* (Lund, 2001)

Wall, Cynthia, 'Gendering Rooms: domestic architecture and literary acts', *Eighteenth-Century Fiction* (July 1993), 5, 4, pp.349–72

Wall, Cynthia, 'A Geography of Georgian Narrative Space', in Miles Ogborn and Charles W.J. Withers (eds), *Georgian Geographies: essays on space, place and landscape in the eighteenth century* (Manchester and New York, 2004), pp.114–29

Walton, Whitney, *France at the Crystal Palace: bourgeois taste and artisan manufacture in the nineteenth century* (Berkeley, Los Angeles and Oxford, 1992)

Watt, Ian, *The Rise of The Novel* (London, 1957)

Weatherhill, Lorna, *Consumer Behaviour and Material Culture in Britain 1660–1760* (London, 1998)

Weisberg, Gabriel P., *The Realist Tradition: French painting and drawing 1830–1900* (Cleveland Museum of Art, Cleveland, catalogue, 1980)

Whitehead, John, *The French Interior* (London, 1992)

Whyman, Susan, *Sociability and Poser in Late-Stuart England: the cultural worlds of the Verneys, 1660–1720* (Oxford, 1999)

Wolff, Janet, 'The Invisible Flâneuse: women and the literature of modernity', *Theory, Culture and Society* (1985), vol.2, no.3, pp.37–46

Woolf, Virginia, *To The Lighthouse* (Oxford, [1927] 1992)

Zeldin, Theodor, *France 1848–1945*, vol.1 (Oxford, 1973)

Zola, Emile, *Pot-Bouille* (Oxford, [1884] 1999)

Part Three

Abalos, Inaki, *The Good Life: a guided visit to the houses of modernity* (Barcelona, 2001)

Albrecht, Donald, *Designing Dreams: modern architecture in the movies* (London, 1987)

Anon., *The British Section at the Vienna Universal Exhibition, 1873, Official Catalogue, with plans and illustrations* (London, 1873)

Aynsley, Jeremy, *Graphic Design in Germany, 1900–1945* (London, 2000)

Aynsley, Jeremy, 'The Modern Period Room – a contradiction in terms?', in Trevor Keeble, Brenda Martin and Penny Sparke (eds), *The Modern Period Room* (London, 2006), pp.9–30

Aynsley, Jeremy, and Francesca Berry, *Journal of Design History*, special issue 'Publishing the Modern Home, magazines and the domestic interior 1870–1965' (2005), vol.18, no.1

Avril, Jean Louis, 'Aubert et Lefèvre au Cap Bénat', *AMC Le Moniteur architecture* (1996), no.70, pp.44–8

Bachelard, Gaston, *The Poetics of Space* (New York, [1958] 1969)

Baillie Scott, Mackay H., *Houses and Gardens Arts and Crafts Interiors* (Aberdeen, [1906] 1995)

Barker, Nicholas, *Signs of the Times: a portrait of the nation's tastes* (Manchester, 1992)

Barnes, Martin, 'Photography in Britain and America', in Karen Livingstone and Linda Parry (eds), *International Arts and Crafts* (London, 2005), pp.132–43

Barsac, Jacques, *Charlotte Perriand: un art d'habiter* (Paris, 2005)

Barsacq, Leon, *Caligari's Cabinet and Other Grand Illusions* (ed.) Elliot Stein (New York, 1978)

Becket, Jane, 'The Abstract Interior', in Michael Compton (ed.), *Towards a New Art: essays on*

the background to abstract art (London, 1980), pp.90–124

Beetham, Margaret, *A Magazine of her Own: domesticity and desire in the woman's magazine 1800–1914* (London, 1996)

Behrendt, Walter Curt, *The Victory of the New Building Style* ([1927] Santa Monica, 2000)

Benjamin, Walter, 'Erfahrung und Armut', in Rolf Tiedemann and Hermann Schweppenhauser (eds), *Gesammelte Schriften*, vol.2, part 1 (Frankfurt am Main, 1977), pp.217–18

Benjamin, Walter, 'The medium through which works of art continue to influence later ages (fragment)', in Michael Jennings (ed.), *Walter Benjamin Selected Writings*, vol.1 (Cambridge, [1929] 1996), p.235

Benjamin, Walter, 'The work of art in the age of mechanical reproduction', in Hannah Arendt (ed.), *Illuminations* (New York, [1936] 1969), pp.219–54

Benjamin, Walter, 'Grandville or the World Exhibitions', in Walter Benjamin, *Charles Baudelaire, a Lyric Poet in the Era of High Capitalism* (London, 1983), pp.162–6

Benton, Charlotte, Tim Benton and Dennis Sharp (eds), *Form and Function: a source book for the history of architecture and design 1890–1939* (London, 1975)

Benton, Tim, 'Building Utopia', in Christopher Wilk (ed.), *Modernism: designing a new world 1914–1939* (London, 2006)

Benton, Tim, 'The little "maison de week-end" and the Parisian suburbs', *Massilia* (2002), vol.2, pp.112–19

Benton, Tim, *The Villas of Le Corbusier, 1920–1930* (London, 1987)

Benton, Tim, '"Villa La Rocca" Die Planungs- und Baugeschichte der Villa La Roche', in Katharina Schmidt and Hartwig Fischer (ed.), *Ein Haus für den Kubismus: Die Sammlung Raoul La Roche* (Basel, 1998), pp.227–43

Benton, Tim, 'Villa Savoye and the Architect's Practice', in Allen Brooks (ed.), *The Le Corbusier Archive*, vol.VII (New York, 1982), pp.ix–xxii

Bernège, Paulette, *De la méthode ménagère* (Paris, 1928a)

Bernège, Paulette, *Si les femmes faisaient les maisons* (Orléans, 1928b)

Bogart, Michelle H., *Artists, advertising and the borders of art* (Chicago, 1995)

Bois, Yve-Alain, '"Avatars de l'axonométrie"; à Bruno Reichlin', *Archithèse* (Sulgen, 1982), vol.2, no.82

Bois, Yve-Alain, and Bruno Reichlin, *De Stijl et*

l'architecture en France (Brussels, 1985)

Bömches, Friedrich, Die Arbeiterhäuser auf der Pariser Weltausstellung von 1867 (Vienna, 1868)

Bourdieu, Pierre, 'The Kabyle house or the world reversed', in Pierre Bourdieu, The Logic of Practice (Cambridge, [1970] 1990), appendix

Bowen, Elizabeth, The Heat of the Day (London, 1962)

Brandt, Bill, Camera in London (London, 1948)

Bresciani, Elisabetta, Modern: Architecktur aus der Sammlung Marzona (Vienna, 2003)

Brooks, Collin, Devil's Decade: portraits of the nineteen-thirties (London, 1948)

Brunhammer, Yvonne, and Suzanne Tise, French Decorative Art, the Société des Artistes Décorateurs, 1900–1942 (Paris, 1990)

Brunsdon, Charlotte, 'Lifestyling Britain', International Journal of Cultural Studies (2003), vol.6, no.1, pp.5–23

Buchan, John, The Thirty-Nine Steps (London, [1915] 2004)

Buchli, Victor, An Archeology of Socialism (Oxford, 1999)

Bucknell, Barry, Bucknell's House (Edinburgh, 1964)

Camm, F.J., The Practical Householder (August 1956), vol.1, no.9, p.671

Carringer, Robert L., The Making of Citizen Kane (London, 1985)

Chevalier, Sophie, 'From Woollen Carpet to Grass Carpet: bridging house and garden in an English suburb', in Daniel Miller (ed.), Material Cultures (London, 1998), pp.47–71

Chevalier, Sophie, 'Destins de cadeaux' in Ethnologie Française (1999), vol.28, no.4, pp.506–14

Chossegros, Pascal, and Nicolas Borel, Mediterranean Houses (Barcelona, 1991)

Clarisse, Catherine, Cuisine, recettes d'architecture (Besançon, 2004)

Cohn, David L. et al., The good old days: a history of American manners and morals as seen through the Sears Roebuck catalogues (New York, 1976)

Colomina, Beatriz, Architectureproduction (New York, 1988)

Colomina, Beatriz, Privacy and Publicity: modern architecture and mass media (Cambridge, Mass., 1994)

Colquhoun, Alan, Modern Architecture (Oxford, 2002)

Colson, Ethel M., 'A Yellow Dining Room', House Beautiful (March 1904), vol.15, no.4, pp.208–10

Commichau, Felix, Das Haus eines Kunst-Freundes: ein Entwurf in zwölf Tafeln (Darmstadt, 1902)

Conn, Steven, Museums and American Intellectual Life, 1876–1926 (Chicago and London, 1998)

Crawford, Elizabeth, Enterprising Women: the Garretts and their circle (London, 2002)

Daniels, Inge, 'Scooping, Raking, Beckoning Luck: luck, agency and the interdependence of people and things in Japan', The Journal of the Royal Anthropological Institute (2003), vol.9, pp.619–38

Da Silva, Fabio Atta, 'Os desenhos de Le Corbusier para a Villa Meyer', Massilia (2001), vol.1, pp.40–70

Darton, Frederick J. Harvey, Children's Books in England: five centuries of social life, 3rd ed., revised by Brian Alderson (London, [1932] 1999)

Deutscher Werkbund, Bau und Wohnung; die Bauten der Weissenhofsiedlung in Stuttgart errichtet 1927 nach Vorschlägen des Deutschen Werkbundes im Auftrag der Stadt Stuttgart und im Rahmen der Werkbundausstellung 'Die Wohnung' (Stuttgart, 1927)

Ducuing, M. Fr. (ed.), L'Exposition Universelle de 1867 Illustrée, Administration Publication Internationale Autorisée par la Commission Impériale (Paris, 1867)

Eastlake, Charles L., 'The Fashion of Furniture', Cornhill Magazine (London, March 1864), pp.337–49

Eastlake, Charles L., Hints on Household Taste in Furniture, Upholstery and Other Details (New York, [1878] 1969)

Eastlake, Lady Elizabeth, 'Photography', Quarterly Review (April 1857), reprinted in Beaumont Newell (ed.), Photography: essays and images (London, 1980)

Edenheim, Ralph, and Inga Arnö-Berg Skansen: traditional Swedish style (London, 1995)

Egoff, Sheila E., Children's Periodicals of the Nineteenth Century: a survey and bibliography (London, 1951)

Evans, David, John Heartfield, AIZ: Arbeiter-Illustrierte Zeitung, Volks Illustrierte, 1930–1938 (Kent and New York, 1992)

Everett, Anna, 'Trading Private and Public Spaces @ HGTV and TLC: on new genre formations in transformation TV', Journal of Visual Culture (2004), vol.3, no.2, pp.157–81

Facos, Michelle, 'The Ideal Swedish Home: Carl Larsson's Lilla Hyttnäs', in Christopher Reed (ed.), Not at Home (London, 1996), pp.81–91

Ferry, Emma, 'Gilding the Cage?': interior design and the professional 'lady' expert, 1875–1885 (unpublished doctoral thesis, Kingston University, 2004)

Ferry, Emma, 'Decorators may be compared to doctors': an analysis of Rhoda and Agnes Garrett's Suggestions for House Decoration in Painting, Woodwork and Furniture (1876)' Journal of Design History (Oxford, 2003), vol.16, no.1, pp.15–34

Forty, Adrian, Words and Buildings: a vocabulary of modern architecture (London, 2000)

Francis, Errol, 'From Generation to Generation: "The Installation" Obaala Arts Collective', Ten 8 (1986), no.22, p.41

Frascina, Francis, and Jonathan Harris (eds), Art in Modern Culture: an anthology of critical texts (London, 1992)

Frayling, Christopher, Ken Adam: the art of production design (London, 2005)

Frederick, Christopher, The New Housekeeping: efficiency studies in home management (New York, 1913)

Friedman, Alice T., 'Domestic Differences: Edith Farnsworth, Mies van der Rohe, and the Gendered Body', in Christopher Reed (ed.), Not at Home: the suppression of domesticity in modern art and architecture (London, 1996), pp.179–92

Frizot, Michel (ed.), A New History of Photography (Köln, 1998)

Games, Naomi, Catherine Moriarty and June Rose, Abram Games, Graphic Designer: maximum meaning, minimum means (Aldershot, 2003)

Gere, Charlotte, and Lesley Hoskins, The House Beautiful (London, 2000)

Glancy, H. Mark, 'Hollywood and Britain: MGM and the British "Quota" legislation', in Jeffrey Richards, The Unknown 1930s (London, 2000), pp.57–72

Goldstein, Carolyn, Do It Yourself: home improvement in 20th-century America (Princeton, N.J., 1998)

Gooden, Susanna, At the Sign of the Four Poster: a history of Heals (London, 1984)

Graeff, Werner, Innenräume (Stuttgart, 1928)

Green, Henry, Party Going (London, 1939)

Greenberg, Clement, 'Modernist Painting', Arts Yearbook (1961), vol.4, pp.101–8

Greenwood, Walter, Love on the Dole (London, 1933)

Grierson, John, Grierson on Documentary (ed.) Forsyth Hardy (London, 1946)

Griffith Winton, Alexandra, '"A Man's House is his Art": the Walker Art Center's Idea House Project and the marketing of domestic design 1941–1947', Journal of Design History (2004), vol.17, no.4, pp.377–96

Gropius, Walter, The New Architecture and the Bauhaus (London, [1930] 1965)

Grossmith, George, and Weedon Grossmith, The

Diary of a Nobody (Harmondsworth, [1892] 1985)

Gruber Garvey, Ellen, *The Adman in the Parlor: magazines and the gendering of consumer culture, 1880s to 1910s* (Oxford, 1996)

Guenther, Sonja, *Das Deutsche Heim: Luxusinterieurs und Arbeitermöbel von der Gründerzeit bis zum 'Dritten Reich'* (Berlin, 1984)

Hall, Stuart, 'Aspiration and Attitude: reflections on Black Britain in the nineties', in *New Formations: Frontlines/Backyards* (London, Spring 1998), no.33, pp.38–46

Halle, David, *Inside Culture: art and class in the American home* (Chicago, 1993)

Hambley, John, and Patrick Downing *The Art of Hollywood* (London, 1979)

Hampson, John, *Saturday Nigh at the Greyhound* (London, 1931)

Hebdige, Dick, *Cut 'N' Mix: culture, identity and Caribbean music* (London, 1987)

Hecht, Anat, 'Home Sweet Home', in Daniel Miller (ed.), *Home Possessions: material culture behind closed doors* (Oxford, 2001), pp.123–45

Heisner, Beverly, *Hollywood Art – art direction in the days of the great studios* (North Carolina, 1990)

Henderson, Susan R., 'A Revolution in the Woman's Sphere: Grete Lihotzky and the Frankfurt Kitchen', in Debra Coleman, Elizabeth Danze and Carol Henderson, *Architecture and Feminism* (New York, 1996)

Heynen, Hilde, *Architecture and Modernity* (Cambridge, Mass., 1999)

Hitchcock, Henry-Russell, and Philip Johnson, *The International Style* (New York, 1966)

Hollander, Anne, *Moving Pictures* (Harvard, 1991)

Hunt, Peter (ed.), *Children's Literature: an illustrated history* (Oxford, 1995)

Isenstadt, Sandy, 'Richard Neutra and the Psychology of architectural consumption', in Sarah W. Goldhagen (ed.), *Anxious Modernisms* (Cambridge MA, 2000), pp.97–117

Jackson, Anthony, 'The Politics of Architecture: English architecture 1929–1951', *The Journal of the Society of Architectural Historians* (March 1965), vol.24, no.1, pp.97–107

Joachimides, Alexis, *Museumsinszenierungen: zur Geschichte der Institution des Kunstmuseums: die Berliner Museumslandschaft 1830–1990* (Dresden, 1995)

Johnson, Philip, Henry-Russell Hitchcock et al., *Modern Architecture International Exhibition* (New York, [1932] 1969)

Jones, Michelle, 'Design and the Domestic Persuader: television and the BBC's

promotion of post-war "Good Design"' *Journal of Design History* (2003), vol.16 no.4, pp.307–18

Kerner, Wolfgang, *Willi Baumeister und die Werkbund – Ausstellung 'Die Wohnung' 1927* (Stuttgart, 2003)

Kirshenblatt-Gimblett, Barbara, 'Objects of Ethnography', in Ivan Karp and Steven D. Levine, *Exhibiting Cultures: the poetics and politics of museum display* (Washington and London, 1991), pp.401–43)

Kinchin, Juliet, 'Interiors: nineteenth-century essays on the 'masculine' and the 'feminine' room', in Pat Kirkham (ed.), *The Gendered Object* (Manchester, 1996), pp.18–20

Kurrent, Friedrich and Johannes Spalt, 'Unbekanntes von Adolf Loos', *Bauforum* (1970), vol.3, no.21, pp.29–48

Lancaster, Osbert, *Homes Sweet Homes* (London, 1939)

Lane, Barbara M., *National Romanticism and Modern Architecture* (Cambridge, 2000)

Larsson, Carl, *Das Haus in der Sonne* (Konigstein im Taunus and Leipzig [originally published in 5 folio parts by Albert Bonnier in Stockholm: Ettheim (1899), Larssons (1902), Spadarfvet (1906), Åt Solsiden (1910), Andras Barn (1913), reissued as *In Memoriam Carl Larsson*, Karl Robert Langewiesche], 1922)

Lavin, Sylvia, *Form follows Libido* (Cambridge, Mass., 2004)

Le Corbusier, *Le Corbusier et Pierre Jeanneret; oeuvre complète de 1910–1929* (Zurich, [1929] 1964)

Le Corbusier, *Précisions sur un état présent de l'architecture et de l'urbanisme avec un prologue américain un corollaire Brésilien suivi d'une température Parisienne et d'une atmosphère Muscovite* (Paris, [1930] 1960)

Le Corbusier, *Precisions on the present state of architecture and city planning: with an American prologue, a Brazilian corollary followed by The temperature of Paris and The atmosphere of Moscow* (Cambridge, Mass., [1930] 1991)

Le Corbusier and Pierre Jeanneret, *Oeuvre Complète de 1929–1934*, vol.2 (Paris, 1935)

Light, Alison, *Forever England: femininity, literature and conservatism between the wars* (London, 1991)

Llewelyn-Bowen, Laurence, and Diarmuid Gavin, *Home Front Inside Out* (London, 2002)

Mackintosh, Charles Rennie, *Haus eines Kunstfreundes* (Darmstadt, 1902)

Maffei, Grace Lees, 'Studying Advice: historiography, methodology, commentary, bibliography', *Journal of Design History* (2003), vol.16, no.1, pp.1–14

Mandler, Peter, *The Fall and Rise of the Stately Home* (New Haven and London, 1997)

Maniaque, Caroline, *Le Corbusier: Les Maisons Jaoul projets et fabrique* (Paris, 2005)

Maruhin, Jan, 'Building for Art: Mies van der Rohe as the architect for art collectors', in Terence Riley et al., *Mies in Berlin* (New York, 2001), pp.318–23

Mengham, Rod, 'Broken Glass', in Rod Mengham, *The Fiction of the 1940s: stories of survival* (Basingstoke, 2001) pp.124–133

Mercer, Kobena, 'Black Hair/Style Politics', in Kobena Mercer, *Welcome to the Jungle: New Positions in Black Cultural Studies* (London, 1994), pp.97–128

Methuen, Nicola, 'Curtains for *Changing Rooms*', *Daily Mirror* (27 August 2004)

Meyer, Erna, *Der neue Haushalt, ein Wegweiser zur Wissenschaftlichen Hausfeuerung* (Stuttgart, 1925)

Meyer, Hannes, 'Die Neue Welt' (trans.) Charlotte Benton, Tim Benton and Dennis Sharp (eds), *Form and Function: a source book for the history of architecture and design, 1890–1939* (St Albans, 1975), p.106

Miller, Daniel, 'Fashion and Ontology in Trinidad', in *Culture and History* (1999), issue 7, pp.49–77

Miller, Daniel (ed.), *Home Possessions: material culture behind closed doors* (Oxford, 2001)

Morley, David, 'Theories of Consumption in Media Studies', in Daniel Miller (ed.), *Acknowledging Consumption* (London, 1995), pp.296–328

Morris, Charles H., *The Illustration of Children's Books* (London, 1957)

Morris, Edward, 'Advertising and the Acquisition of Contemporary Art', *Journal of the History of Collections* (1992), vol.4, pp.195–200

Morris, Edward, *Victorian and Edwardian Paintings in the Lady Lever Art Gallery* (National Museums and Galleries on Merseyside, 1994)

Muthesius, Hermann, *The English House* (trans.) Janet Seligman (London, [1904–5] 1979)

Naylor, Gillian, 'Modernism and Memory: leaving traces', in Marius Kwint, Christopher Breward and Jeremy Aynsley (eds), *Material Memories* (Oxford, 1999), pp.91–106

Neumann, Dietrich (ed.), *Film Architecture – set design from Metropolis to Blade Runner* (New York, 1996)

Neumeyer, Fritz, *The Artless Word: Mies van der Rohe on the building art* (Cambridge, Mass., 1991)

Neutra, Dione, *To Tell the Truth* (Los Angeles, UCLA oral history project, n.d.)

Neutra, Richard, *Mystery and Realities of the Site* (Scarsdale, 1951)

Neutra, Richard, 'The Photographer and the Architect', in Julius Shulman (ed.), *Photographing Architecture and Interiors* (New York, 1962), p.vi

Neutra, Richard, *Survival through Design* (Oxford, [1954] 1969)

Niedenthal, Simon, '"Glamourized Houses": Neutra, photography, and the Kaufmann house', *Journal of Architectural Education* (Nov 1993), vol.47, no.2, pp.101–12

Nilsson, Axel, *Guide to Skansen: the historical and ethnographic department of Skansen* (Stockholm, 1911)

Noordergraaf, Julia, *Strategies of Display: museum presentation in nineteenth and twentieth century visual culture* (Rotterdam, 2004)

Oram, Scott, '"Constructing Contemporary": common-sense approaches to "going modern" in the 1950s', in Susie McKellar and Penny Sparke (eds), *Interior Design and Identity* (Manchester, 2004), pp.174–90

Otto, Christian F., and Richard Pommer, *Weissenhof 1927 and the Modern Movement in Architecture* (Chicago and London, 1991)

Overy, Paul, 'Visions of the Future and the Immediate Past: the Werkbund Exhibition, Paris 1930', *Journal of Design History* (December 2004), vol.17, pp.337–57

Pahnicke, Peter, Klaus Honnef et al., *John Heartfield, 1891–1968* (Cologne, 1991)

Patmore, Derek, *Colour Schemes for the Modern Home* (London, 1933)

Peck, Amelia et al., *Period Rooms in the Metropolitan Museum of Art* (New York, 1996)

Phillips, Barty, *Conran and the Habitat Story* (London, 1984)

Picture Post, Hulton's National Weekly (London, 4 January 1941), vol.10, no.1

Platz, Gustav, *Die Baukunst der neuesten Zeit* (Berlin, 1927)

Platz, Gustav, *Innenräume der Gegenwart* (Berlin, 1933)

Posever, Verna, and Stanley Mallach, *Photography and Reform: Lewis Hine and the National Child Labor Committee* (Milwaukee, 1984)

Quetglas, Josep, *Fear of Glass: Mies van der Rohe's Pavilion in Barcelona* (Barcelona, 2000)

Quetglas, Josep, *Villa Savoye 'Les heures claires' 1928–1962* (Madrid, 2004)

Reed, Christopher (ed.), *Not at Home* (London, 1996)

Rich, Rachel, 'Designing the Dinner Party:

advice on dining in London and Paris', *Journal of Design History* (2003), vol.16, no.1, pp.49–61

Richards, Thomas, *The Commodity Culture of Victorian England: advertising and spectacle, 1851–1914* (Stanford and London, 1990)

Riley, Terence, *The International Style: exhibition 15 and the Museum of Modern Art* (New York, 1992)

Riis, Jacob, *Battle with the Slum* (New York and London, 1902)

Riis, Jacob, *How the Other Half Lives* (New York, [1901] 1971)

Riis, Jacob, *A Ten Year's War: an account of the battle with the slum in New York* (New York, n.d.)

Robach, Cilla, 'Design for Modern People', in Cecilia Widenheim (ed.), *Utopia and Reality – Modernity in Sweden 1900–1960* (New York, 2002)

Rose, Gillian, *Visual Methodologies: an introduction to the interpretation of visual materials* (London, 2001)

Ryan, Deborah Sugg, *The Ideal Home through the 20th Century* (London, 1997)

Rybczynski, Witold, *Home: a short history of an idea* (London, [1986] 1987)

Safran, Yehuda, and Wilfried Wang, *The Architecture of Adolf Loos: an Arts Council exhibition* (London, 1985)

Sansom, William, *Fireman Flower and Other Stories* (London, 1944)

Schulze, Franz, *Philip Johnson, Life and Work* (Chicago, 1994)

Schwarzer, Mitchell, 'The Emergence of Architectural Space: August Schmarsow's theory of Raumgestaltung', *Assemblage* (New York, 1991), no.15, pp.50–61

Silver, Kenneth E., *Making Paradise: art, modernity and the myth of the French Riviera* (Massachusetts, 2001)

Slade, Thomas M., '"The Crystal House" of 1934', *Journal of the Society of Architectural Historians* (Dec 1970), vol.29, no.4, pp.350–53

Snodin, Michael, and Elisabet Stavenow-Hidemark (eds), *Carl and Karin Larsson: creators of the Swedish style* (London, 1997)

Sparke, Penny, *As Long as it's Pink: the sexual politics of taste* (London, 1995)

Spigel, Lynn, 'Installing the Television Set', in Ben Highmore (ed.), *The Everyday Life Reader* (London, 2002), pp.325–38

Spielman, Marion Harry, and George Somes Layard, *Kate Greenaway* (London, 1905)

Strachey, Julia, *The Man on the Pier* (London, 1951)

Swenarton, Mark, *Homes fit for Heroes: the politics*

and architecture of early state housing in Britain (London, 1981)

Tacchi, Jo, 'Radio Textures: between self and others', in Daniel Miller (ed.), *Material Cultures: why some things matter* (Chicago, 1997), pp.25–45

Talbot, William Henry Fox, *The Pencil of Nature* (London, 1844–6)

T&S, *Livingetc* (March 2005)

Taut, Bruno, *Die neue Wohnung; Die Frau als Schöpferin* (Berlin, 1924)

Taut, Bruno, *Modern Architecture* (London, 1929)

Tiersten, Lisa, 'The Chic Interior and the Feminine Modern: home decorating as high art in turn-of-the-century Paris', in Christopher Reed (ed.), *Not at Home: the suppression of domesticity in modern art and architecture* (London, 1996), pp.18–32

Velasquez, Victor Hugo, 'Un dibujo de la Villa Meyer', *Massilia* (2002), vol.1, pp.71–83

Walton, Kamina, 'Home Lives', in Tim Putnam and Charles Newton (eds), *Household Choices* (London, 1990), pp.66–73

Ward, Janet, *Weimar Surfaces: urban visual culture in 1920s Germany* (Berkley, Los Angeles and London, 2001)

Wells, Liz (ed.), *Photography: a critical introduction* (London, 1997)

Whalley, Joyce Irene, and Tessa Rose Chester, *A History of Children's Book Illustration* (London, 1988)

White, Gleeson, 'Children's Books and their Illustrators', *Studio* (1898, Special Winter number)

Wilk, Christopher (ed.), *Modernism: designing a new world 1914–1939* (London, 2006)

Wright, Mary, and Russel Wright, *Guide to Easier Living* (Salt Lake City, [1950] 2003)

Wright, Gwendolyn, 'The Model Domestic Environment: icon or option?', in Susana Torre (ed.), *Women in American Architecture: a historic and contemporary perspective* (New York, 1977), pp.18–31

Index

Picture credits